Turbo Pascal®

Reference Guide

Version 5.0

Copyright© 1987, 1988
All rights reserved

Borland International
1800 Green Hills Road
P.O. Box 660001
Scotts Valley, CA 95066-0001

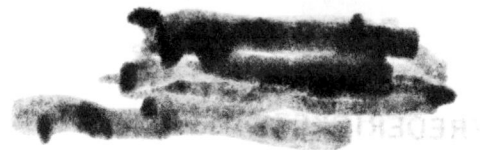

This manual was produced with
Sprint® The Professional Word Processor

All Borland products are trademarks or registered trademarks of
Borland International, Inc. Other brand and product names are trademarks
or registered trademarks of their respective holders.
Copyright© 1988 Borland International.

Printed in the U.S.A.

10 9 8 7 6 5 4 3 2

Table of Contents

Introduction   1
What's On Your Disks 1
   Installing Turbo Pascal On Your System 4
About This Manual 4
Typography 5
How to Contact Borland 5

Part 1 Programmer's Reference

Chapter 1 Tokens and Constants   9
Special Symbols and Reserved Words 9
Identifiers 11
Labels 12
Numbers 13
Character Strings 14
Constant Declarations 15
Comments 16
Program Lines 16

Chapter 2 Blocks, Locality, and Scope   17
Syntax 17
Rules of Scope 19
Scope of Interface and Standard Identifiers 19

Chapter 3 Types   21
Simple Types 22
   Ordinal Types 22
      Integer Types 23
      Boolean Type 24
      Char Type 24
      Enumerated Types 24
      Subrange Types 25
   Real Types 26
      Software Floating Point 26
      8087 Floating Point 27
String Types 27
Structured Types 28
   Array Types 28
   Record Types 29
   Set Types 31
   File Types 31

Pointer Types 32
Procedural Types 33
Identical and Compatible Types 33
    Type Identity 33
    Type Compatibility 34
    Assignment Compatibility 34
The Type Declaration Part 35

Chapter 4 Variables   37

Variable Declarations 37
    The Data Segment 38
    The Stack Segment 38
    Absolute Variables 39
Variable References 39
Qualifiers 40
    Arrays, Strings, and Indexes 41
    Records and Field Designators 41
    Pointers and Dynamic Variables 42
Variable Typecasts 42

Chapter 5 Typed Constants   45

Simple-Type Constants 46
String-Type Constants 46
Structured-Type Constants 46
    Array-Type Constants 47
    Record-Type Constants 48
    Set-Type Constants 48
Pointer-Type Constants 49

Chapter 6 Expressions   51

Expression Syntax 52
Operators 54
    Arithmetic Operators 54
    Logical Operators 56
    Boolean Operators 56
    String Operator 57
    Set Operators 58
    Relational Operators 58
        Comparing Simple Types 59
        Comparing Strings 59
        Comparing Packed Strings 60
        Comparing Pointers 60
        Comparing Sets 60
        Testing Set Membership 60
    The @ Operator 61
        @ with a Variable 61

@ with a Value Parameter	61
@ with a Variable Parameter	62
@ with a Procedure or Function	62
Function Calls	62
Set Constructors	63
Value Typecasts	64

Chapter 7 Statements 65
Simple Statements	65
Assignment Statements	66
Procedure Statements	66
Goto Statements	67
Structured Statements	67
Compound Statements	67
Conditional Statements	68
If Statements	68
Case Statements	69
Repetitive Statements	70
Repeat Statements	70
While Statements	71
For Statements	72
With Statements	74

Chapter 8 Procedures and Functions 77
Procedure Declarations	77
Forward Declarations	78
External Declarations	79
Inline Declarations	80
Function Declarations	80
Parameters	82
Value Parameters	82
Variable Parameters	83
Untyped Variable Parameters	83
Procedural Types	84
Procedural Type Declarations	84
Procedural Variables	85
Procedural Type Parameters	87
Procedural Types in Expressions	89

Chapter 9 Programs and Units 93
Program Syntax	93
The Program Heading	93
The Uses Clause	93
Unit Syntax	94
The Unit Heading	95
The Interface Part	95

    The Implementation Part 95
    The Initialization Part 96
    Indirect Unit References 96
    Circular Unit References 97
        Sharing Other Declarations 99

Chapter 10 Input and Output   101

An Introduction to I/O 101
Standard Procedures and Functions for All Files 102
    Procedures 102
    Functions 103
Standard Procedures and Functions for Text Files 103
    Procedures 104
    Functions 104
Standard Procedures and Functions for Untyped Files 105
The FileMode Variable 105
Devices in Turbo Pascal 106
    DOS Devices 106
        The CON Device 107
        The LPT1, LPT2, and LPT3 Devices 107
        The COM1 and COM2 Devices 107
        The NUL Device 107
    Text File Devices 108

Chapter 11 Standard Procedures and Functions   109

Flow Control Procedures 109
Dynamic Allocation Procedures and Functions 109
    Procedures 110
    Functions 110
Transfer Functions 110
Arithmetic Functions 110
Ordinal Procedures and Functions 111
    Procedures 111
    Functions 111
String Procedures and Functions 112
    Procedures 112
    Functions 112
Pointer and Address Functions 112
Miscellaneous Procedures and Functions 112
    Procedures 112
    Functions 113

Chapter 12 Standard Units   115

Standard Unit Dependencies 116
The System Unit 116
The Printer Unit 119

The Dos Unit 119
   Constants, Types, and Variables 120
     Flags Constants 120
     File Mode Constants 120
     File Record Types 120
     File Attribute Constants 121
     The Registers Type 122
     The DateTime Type 122
     The SearchRec Type 122
     The File-Handling String Types 123
     The DosError Variable 123
   Interrupt Support Procedures 123
   Date and Time Procedures 124
   Disk Status Functions 124
   File-Handling Procedures and Functions 124
     Procedures 124
     Functions 125
   Process-Handling Procedures and Functions 125
     Procedures 125
     Functions 125
   Environment-Handling Functions 125
   Miscellaneous Procedures and Function 125
     Procedures 125
     Function 126
The Crt Unit 126
   The Input and Output Files 126
   Windows 126
     Special Characters 127
     Line Input 127
   Constants, Types, and Variables 128
     Crt Mode Constants 128
     Text Color Constants 128
     Crt Variables 129
       CheckBreak 129
       CheckEOF 130
       CheckSnow 130
       DirectVideo 130
       LastMode 131
       TextAttr 131
       WindMin and WindMax 131
     Procedures 132
     Functions 132
The Graph Unit 133
   Drivers 133
     IBM 8514 Support 134

v

Coordinate System	135
Current Pointer	135
Text	136
Figures and Styles	136
Viewports and Bit Images	137
Paging and Colors	137
Error-Handling	137
Getting Started	138
User-Written Heap Management Routines	140
Graph Unit Constants, Types and Variables	142
Constants	142
Types	146
Variables	148
Procedures	148
Functions	151
The Turbo3 Unit	152
Interface Section	152
Kbd	153
CBreak	154
Procedures	154
Functions	154
The Graph3 Unit	155
Procedures	155

Chapter 13 Overlays   159

The Overlay Unit	160
Constants and Variables	161
The OvrResult Variable	161
Result Codes	161
Procedures and Functions	162
OvrInit	162
OvrInitEMS	162
OvrSetBuf	163
OvrGetBuf	163
OvrClearBuf	163
Designing Overlaid Programs	164
Overlay Code Generation	164
The FAR Call Requirement	164
Initializing the Overlay Manager	165
Initialization Sections in Overlaid Units	167
What Not to Overlay	168
Debugging Overlays	169
External Routines in Overlays	169

Chapter 14 Using the 8087   171

The 8087 Data Types	172

Extended Range Arithmetic 173
Comparing Reals 174
The 8087 Evaluation Stack 175
Writing Reals with the 8087 176
Units Using the 8087 176
    Detecting the 8087 176
    Using 8087 Emulation in Assembly Language 178

Chapter 15 Inside Turbo Pascal   179
The Heap Manager 181
    Disposal Methods 182
    The Free List 185
    The Heap Error Function 187
Internal Data Formats 188
    Integer Types 188
    Char Types 189
    Boolean Types 189
    Enumerated Types 189
    Floating-Point Types 189
        The Real Type 189
        The Single Type 190
        The Double Type 190
        The Extended Type 191
        The Comp Type 191
    Pointer Types 192
    String Types 192
    Set Types 192
    Array Types 193
    Record Types 193
    File Types 193
    Procedural Types 194
Calling Conventions 195
    Variable Parameters 195
    Value Parameters 195
    Function Results 196
    NEAR and FAR Calls 197
    Nested Procedures and Functions 197
    Entry and Exit Code 198
    Register-Saving Conventions 199
Linking with Assembly Language 199
    Turbo Assembler and Turbo Pascal 200
    Examples of Assembly Language Routines 201
        Turbo Assembler Example 204
Inline Machine Code 205
    Inline Statements 205
    Inline Directives 207

Direct Memory and Port Access 208
    The Mem, MemW, and MemL Arrays 208
    The Port and PortW Arrays 208
Interrupt Handling 209
    Writing Interrupt Procedures 209
Text File Device Drivers 210
    The Open Function 211
    The InOut Function 212
    The Flush Function 212
    The Close Function 212
    Examples of Text File Device Drivers 212
Exit Procedures 216
Automatic Optimizations 217
    Constant Folding 218
    Constant Merging 218
    Short-Circuit Evaluation 218
    Order of Evaluation 219
    Range-Checking 219
    Shift Instead of Multiply 219
    Automatic Word Alignment 219
    Dead Code Removal 220
    Smart Linking 220

Chapter 16 Turbo Pascal Reference Lookup   223
Sample procedure 223
Abs function 224
Addr function 224
Append procedure 225
Arc procedure 226
ArcTan function 226
Assign procedure 227
AssignCrt procedure 228
Bar procedure 229
Bar3D procedure 229
BlockRead procedure 230
BlockWrite procedure 232
ChDir procedure 233
Chr function 233
Circle procedure 234
ClearDevice procedure 234
ClearViewPort procedure 235
Close procedure 236
CloseGraph procedure 236
ClrEol procedure 237
ClrScr procedure 237
Concat function 238

Copy function	239
Cos function	239
CSeg function	240
Dec procedure	240
Delay procedure	240
Delete procedure	241
DelLine procedure	241
DetectGraph procedure	242
DiskFree function	243
DiskSize function	243
Dispose procedure	244
DosExitCode function	245
DosVersion function	245
DrawPoly procedure	246
DSeg function	247
Ellipse procedure	247
EnvCount function	248
EnvStr function	248
Eof function (text files)	249
Eof function (typed, untyped files)	249
Eoln function	250
Erase procedure	250
Exec procedure	251
Exit procedure	253
Exp function	253
FExpand function	254
FilePos function	254
FileSize function	255
FillChar procedure	255
FillEllipse procedure	256
FillPoly procedure	257
FindFirst procedure	258
FindNext procedure	259
FloodFill procedure	259
Flush procedure	261
Frac function	261
FreeMem procedure	261
FSearch function	262
FSplit procedure	263
GetArcCoords procedure	264
GetAspectRatio procedure	265
GetBkColor function	266
GetCBreak procedure	267
GetColor function	267
GetDate procedure	268

GetDefaultPalette function	268
GetDir procedure	269
GetDriverName function	270
GetEnv function	270
GetFAttr procedure	271
GetFillPattern procedure	272
GetFillSettings procedure	273
GetFTime procedure	274
GetGraphMode function	274
GetImage procedure	276
GetIntVec procedure	277
GetLineSettings procedure	277
GetMaxColor function	278
GetMaxMode function	279
GetMaxX function	280
GetMaxY function	281
GetMem procedure	281
GetModeName function	282
GetModeRange procedure	283
GetPalette procedure	283
GetPaletteSize function	284
GetPixel function	285
GetTextSettings procedure	285
GetTime procedure	287
GetVerify procedure	287
GetViewSettings procedure	287
GetX function	288
GetY function	289
GotoXY procedure	290
GraphDefaults procedure	291
GraphErrorMsg function	291
GraphResult function	292
Halt procedure	294
Hi function	295
HighVideo procedure	295
ImageSize function	296
Inc procedure	297
InitGraph procedure	297
Insert procedure	300
InsLine procedure	300
InstallUserDriver function	301
InstallUserFont function	304
Int function	305
Intr procedure	305
IOResult function	306

Keep procedure	307
KeyPressed function	307
Length function	308
Line procedure	308
LineRel procedure	309
LineTo procedure	310
Ln function	311
Lo function	312
LowVideo procedure	312
Mark procedure	313
MaxAvail function	313
MemAvail function	314
MkDir procedure	314
Move procedure	315
MoveRel procedure	316
MoveTo procedure	317
MsDos procedure	318
New procedure	318
NormVideo procedure	319
NoSound procedure	319
Odd function	319
Ofs function	320
Ord function	320
OutText procedure	320
OutTextXY procedure	322
OvrClearBuf procedure	323
OvrGetBuf function	324
OvrInit procedure	325
OvrInitEMS procedure	325
OvrSetBuf procedure	327
PackTime procedure	328
ParamCount function	328
ParamStr function	328
Pi function	329
PieSlice procedure	329
Pos function	330
Pred function	331
Ptr function	331
PutImage procedure	331
PutPixel procedure	334
Random function	334
Randomize procedure	335
Read procedure (text files)	335
Read procedure (typed files)	337
ReadKey function	337

Readln procedure	338
Rectangle procedure	339
RegisterBGIdriver function	340
RegisterBGIfont function	342
Release procedure	344
Rename procedure	345
Reset procedure	345
RestoreCrtMode procedure	346
Rewrite procedure	347
RmDir procedure	348
Round function	349
RunError procedure	349
Sector procedure	350
Seek procedure	351
SeekEof function	351
SeekEoln function	352
Seg function	352
SetActivePage procedure	353
SetAllPalette procedure	354
SetAspectRatio procedure	355
SetBkColor procedure	356
SetCBreak procedure	357
SetColor procedure	358
SetDate procedure	358
SetFAttr procedure	359
SetFillPattern procedure	359
SetFillStyle procedure	361
SetFTime procedure	362
SetGraphBufSize procedure	362
SetGraphMode procedure	363
SetIntVec procedure	365
SetLineStyle procedure	366
SetPalette procedure	367
SetRGBPalette procedure	369
SetTextBuf procedure	370
SetTextJustify procedure	372
SetTextStyle procedure	373
SetTime procedure	374
SetUserCharSize procedure	375
SetVerify procedure	376
SetViewPort procedure	376
SetVisualPage procedure	378
SetWriteMode procedure	379
Sin function	380
SizeOf function	381

Sound procedure	381
SPtr function	382
Sqr function	382
Sqrt function	382
SSeg function	382
Str procedure	383
Succ function	383
Swap function	384
SwapVectors procedure	384
TextBackground procedure	385
TextColor procedure	385
TextHeight function	386
TextMode procedure	387
TextWidth function	389
Trunc function	390
Truncate procedure	391
UnpackTime procedure	391
UpCase function	391
Val procedure	392
WhereX function	393
WhereY function	393
Window procedure	394
Write procedure (text files)	395
Write procedure (typed files)	397
Writeln procedure	397

Part 2 Appendices

Appendix A Comparing Turbo Pascal 5.0 with ANSI Pascal 401

Exceptions to ANSI Pascal Requirements	401
Extensions to ANSI Pascal	403
Implementation-Dependent Features	405
Treatment of Errors	406

Appendix B Compiler Directives 407

Switch Directives	408
Align Data	408
Boolean Evaluation	409
Debug Information	410
Emulation	410
Force FAR Calls	411
Input/Output-Checking	411
Local Symbol Information	412
Numeric Processing	412
Overlay Code Generation	413
Range-Checking	413

Stack-Overflow Checking	414
Var-String Checking	414
Parameter Directives	415
Include File	415
Link Object File	415
Memory Allocation Sizes	416
Overlay Unit Name	416
Conditional Compilation	416
Conditional Symbols	417
The DEFINE Directive	419
The UNDEF Directive	419
The IFDEF Directive	419
The IFNDEF Directive	419
The IFOPT Directive	420
The ELSE Directive	420
The ENDIF Directive	420
Appendix C Reference Materials	421
ASCII Codes	421
Extended Key Codes	424
Keyboard Scan Codes	425
Appendix D Error Messages and Codes	427
Compiler Error Messages	427
Run-time Errors	443
DOS Errors	443
I/O Errors	445
Critical Errors	446
Fatal Errors	447
Index	449

List of Figures

Figure 15.1: Turbo Pascal Memory Map 180
Figure 15.2: Disposal Method Using Mark and Release 182
Figure 15.3: Heap Layout with Release(P) Executed 183
Figure 15.4: Creating a "Hole" in the Heap 184
Figure 15.5: Enlarging the Free Block 184
Figure 15.6: Releasing the Free Block 185

List of Tables

Table 3.1: Predefined Integer Types 23
Table 3.2: Real Data Types 26
Table 6.1: Precedence of Operators 51
Table 6.2: Binary Arithmetic Operations 55
Table 6.3: Unary Arithmetic Operations 55
Table 6.4: Logical Operations 56
Table 6.5: Boolean Operations 56
Table 6.6: String Operation 57
Table 6.7: Set Operations 58
Table 6.8: Relational Operations 59
Table 6.9: Pointer Operation 61
Table 12.1: Standard Units 116
Table 16.1: Components of the Output String 396
Table 16.2: Components of the Fixed-Point String 396
Table C.1: ASCII Table 422
Table C.2: Extended Key Codes 424
Table C.3: Keyboard Scan Codes 426

INTRODUCTION

Welcome to the second book in the Turbo Pascal 5.0 set. The first book, *Turbo Pascal User's Guide,* provided you with many basics (and more) for getting started with programming in Turbo Pascal, plus guided you through using the integrated environment. Now you're ready to delve into the details of the Turbo Pascal language.

What's On Your Disks

The distribution disks that come with this manual include two different versions of the Pascal compiler: an integrated environment version and a stand-alone, command-line version.

You might not need all the files that come on your distribution disks. Use the INSTALL program and then delete the files you don't need from your working disks. (See the "Turbo Pascal Utilities" Appendix in the *User's Guide* for information on INSTALL.) The README file contains a complete file list. For your reference, here's a summary of most of the files on disks and how to determine which ones to retain:

README To see any last-minute notes and corrections, type README at the system prompt. (If you have a printer, you can print it out.) Once you review this material, keep it around for future reference.

HELPME!.DOC Contains answers to many common questions about Turbo Pascal 5.0.

TURBO.EXE This is the integrated (menu-driven) environment version of Turbo Pascal. It lets you edit, compile, run, and debug your program. See Chapter 7 in the *User's Guide,* "All About the Integrated Environment," for more information.

TURBO.TPL This contains the units (program libraries) that come with Turbo Pascal, including *System, Crt, Dos, Overlay,* and *Printer*—this is a must! See Chapter 12, "Standard Units," for more information on these units.

TURBO.HLP   This contains the online, context-sensitive help text used by the integrated environment and the THELP utility. See the section "Online Help" in Chapter 2 of the *User's Guide* for details on the help feature, and Appendix C of the *User's Guide*, "Turbo Pascal Utilities, for information on THELP.

THELP.COM   This is the memory-resident that provides access to Turbo Pascal's context-sensitive help system from any program. See Appendix C in the *User's Guide*, "Turbo Pascal Utilities."

TPC.EXE   This is the command-line version of Turbo Pascal. If you use a separate editor, make heavy use of batch files, and so on, you'll probably want to use this. Refer to Chapter 8, "Command-Line Reference," in the *User's Guide* for information on how to use the command-line compiler.

GRAPH.TPU   This contains the *Graph* unit (the Borland Graphics Interface unit). See the section "The Graph Unit" in Chapter 12 of this manual for more information.

*.ARC files   Packed files that contain documentation files, example programs, graphics drivers fonts, interface section listings for Turbo Pascal's units, and more. Chapter 1 of the *User's Guide* walks you through the dearchiving of these files with the INSTALL program.

*.BGI files   BGI graphics device drivers.

*.CHR files   BGI graphics stroked character fonts.

*.DOC files   These include the interface section listings for all the standard units.

*.PAS files   These include an overlay example and the MicroCalc source files, as well as other sample programs.

INSTALL.EXE   This new utility sets up Turbo Pascal on your system. Refer to Chapter 1 of the *User's Guide* for information on INSTALL.

TPUMOVER.EXE   This utility allows you to move units to or remove units from the TURBO.TPL file. Appendix C in the *User's Guide*, "Turbo Pascal Utilities," contains information on TPUMOVER.

TINST.EXE	This utility allows you to customize certain features of TURBO.EXE. See Appendix D in the *User's Guide*, "Customizing Turbo Pascal," for more information.
TINSTXFR.EXE	This utility transfers the customized settings you created with TINST in 4.0 to 5.0. See Appendix D in the *User's Guide*, "Customizing Turbo Pascal."
MAKE.EXE	This is an intelligent project manager that allows you to keep your programs up-to-date and is especially useful when mixing assembler and Pascal and using the command-line compiler (TPC.EXE). See Appendix C in the *User's Guide*, "Turbo Pascal Utilities," for more informaztion on using MAKE.
GREP.COM	This is a fast, powerful text search utility. See Appendix C in the *User's Guide*, "Turbo Pascal Utilities," for more information on using GREP.
TOUCH.COM	This utility changes the date and time of one or more files to the current date and time, making it "newer" than the files that depend on it. It's generally used in conjunction with MAKE.EXE.
BINOBJ.EXE	Use this utility to convert a binary data file to an .OBJ file.
TPCONFIG.EXE	This utility takes your integrated environment configuration file and converts it to work with the command-line compiler (as TPC.CFG). It's helpful if you want to use the integrated environment to set all your options, but want to compile with the command-line version. This utility will also convert a TPC.CFG file to a .TP file.
UPGRADE.DTA UPGRADE.EXE	This utility does a quick upgrade of Turbo Pascal version 3.0 source files, modifying them for compatibility with Turbo Pascal version 5.0. See the section on UPGRADE in Appendix A of the *User's Guide* for more information.
GRAPH3.TPU TURBO3.TPU	These are version 3.0 compatibility units. Refer to Appendix A in the *User's Guide*, "Differences Between Turbo Pascal 3.0, 4.0, and 5.0.")
README.COM	This is the program to display the README file. Once you've read the README, you can delete this.

Installing Turbo Pascal On Your System

Your Turbo Pascal package includes all the files and programs necessary to run both the integrated environment and command-line versions of the compiler. A new program, INSTALL.EXE, sets up Turbo Pascal on your system. INSTALL works on both floppy-based and hard disk systems. Refer to Chapter 1 in the *User's Guide* for information about INSTALL.

About This Manual

This book is split into two parts: a programmer's reference and appendices. The first part of this manual, "Programmer's Reference," offers technical information on the following features of the language:

- Chapter 1: Tokens and Constants
- Chapter 2: Blocks, Locality, and Scope
- Chapter 3: Types
- Chapter 4: Variables
- Chapter 5: Typed Constants
- Chapter 6: Expressions
- Chapter 7: Statements
- Chapter 8: Procedures and Functions
- Chapter 9: Programs and Units
- Chapter 10: Input and Output
- Chapter 11: Standard Procedures and Functions
- Chapter 12: Standard Units
- Chapter 13: Overlays
- Chapter 14: Using the 8087
- Chapter 15: Inside Turbo Pascal
- Chapter 16: Turbo Pascal Reference Lookup

Part two, "Appendices," discusses 5.0 and ANSI Pascal, covers the compiler directives provided, provides some reference materials (an ASCII chart, extended key codes, and keyboard scan codes), and lists all the compiler and run-time error messages generated by Turbo Pascal.

- Appendix A: Comparing Turbo Pascal 5.0 with ANSI Pascal
- Appendix B: Compiler Directives
- Appendix C: Reference Materials
- Appendix D: Error Messages and Codes

Typography

This manual was produced by Borland's Sprint: The Professional Word Processor on a PostScript printer. The different typefaces displayed are used for the following purposes:

Italics In text, this typeface represents constant identifiers, field identifiers, and formal parameter identifiers, as well as unit names, labels, variables, procedures, and functions.

Boldface Turbo Pascal's reserved words are set in this typeface.

Monospace This type represents text that appears on your screen.

Keycaps This typeface indicates a key on your keyboard. It is often used when describing a key you have to press to perform a particular function; for example, "Press *Esc* to exit from a menu."

How to Contact Borland

If, after reading this manual and using Turbo Pascal, you would like to contact Borland with comments or suggestions, we suggest the following procedures:

- The best way is to log on to Borland's forum on CompuServe: Type GO BPROGA at the main CompuServe menu and follow the menus to section 2. Leave your questions or comments here for the support staff to process.
- If you prefer, write a letter detailing your problem and send it to

> Technical Support Department
> Borland International
> P.O. Box 660001
> 1800 Green Hills Road
> Scotts Valley, CA 95066-0001

Please note: If you include a program example in your message, it must be limited to 100 lines or less. We request that you submit it on disk, include all the necessary support files on that disk, and provide step-by-step instructions on how to reproduce the problem. Before you decide to get technical support, try to replicate the problem with the code contained on a floppy disk, just to be sure we can duplicate the problem using the disk you provide us.

- You can also telephone our Technical Support department at (408) 438-5300. To help us handle your problem as quickly as possible, have these items handy before you call:
  - product name and version number
  - product serial number
  - computer make and model number
  - operating system and version number

If you're not familiar with Borland's No-Nonsense License statement, now's the time to read the agreement at the front of this manual and mail in your completed product registration card.

PART 1

Programmer's Reference

C H A P T E R

1

Tokens and Constants

Tokens are the smallest meaningful units of text in a Pascal program, and they are categorized as special symbols, identifiers, labels, numbers, and string constants.

A Pascal program is made up of tokens and separators, where a separator is either a blank or a comment. Two adjacent tokens must be separated by one or more separators if each token is a reserved word, an identifer, a label, or a number.

Separators cannot be part of tokens except in string constants.

Special Symbols and Reserved Words

Turbo Pascal uses the following subsets of the ASCII character set:

- **Letters**—the English alphabet, *A* through *Z* and *a* through *z*.
- **Digits**—the Arabic numerals 0 through 9.
- **Hex digits**—the Arabic numerals 0 through 9, the letters *A* through *F*, and the letters *a* through *f*.
- **Blanks**—the space character (ASCII 32) and all ASCII control characters (ASCII 0 to 31), including the end-of-line or return character (ASCII 13).

What follows are *syntax diagrams* for letter, digit, and hex digit. To read a syntax diagram, follow the arrows. Alternative paths are often possible; paths that begin at the left and end with an arrow on the right are valid. A path traverses boxes that hold the names of elements used to construct that portion of the syntax.

The names in rectangular boxes stand for actual constructions. Those in circular boxes—reserved words, operators, and punctuation—are the actual terms to be used in the program.

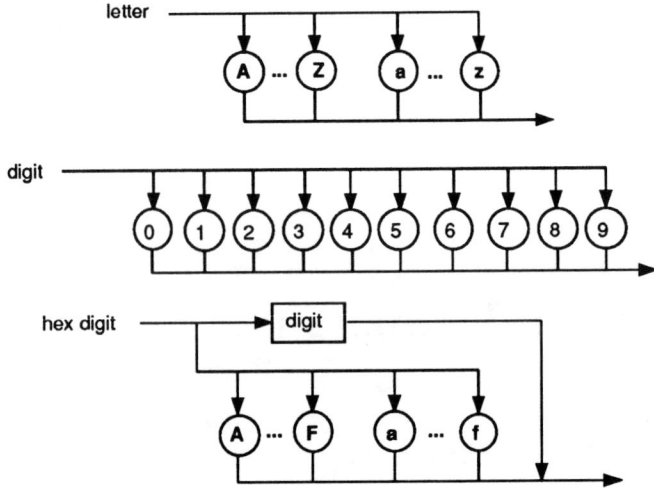

Special symbols and reserved words are characters that have one or more fixed meanings. These single characters are special symbols:

+ − * / = < > [ ] . , ( ) : ; ^ @ { } $ #

These character pairs are also special symbols:

<= >= := .. (* *) (. .)

Some special symbols are also operators. A left bracket ([) is equivalent to the character pair of left parentheses and a period ((.). Similarly, a right bracket (]) is equivalent to the character pair of a period and a right parentheses (.)).

Following are Turbo Pascal's reserved words:

absolute	end	inline	procedure	type
and	external	interface	program	unit
array	file	interrupt	record	until
begin	for	label	repeat	uses
case	forward	mod	set	var
const	function	nil	shl	while
div	goto	not	shr	with
do	if	of	string	xor
downto	implementation	or	then	
else	in	packed	to	

Reserved words appear in lowercase **boldface** throughout this manual. Turbo Pascal isn't case sensitive, however, so you can use either uppercase or lowercase letters in your programs.

Identifiers

Identifiers denote constants, types, variables, procedures, functions, units, programs, and fields in records. An identifier can be of any length, but only the first 63 characters are significant.

An identifier must begin with a letter or an underscore character and cannot contain spaces. Letters, digits, and underscore characters (ASCII $5F) are allowed after the first character. Like reserved words, identifiers are not case sensitive.

When several instances of the same identifier exist, you may need to qualify the identifier by a unit identifier in order to select a specific instance (units are described in Chapter 4 of the *User's Guide* and 12 of this manual). For example, to qualify the identifier *Ident* by the unit identifier *UnitName*, you would write *UnitName.Ident*. The combined identifier is called a *qualified identifier*.

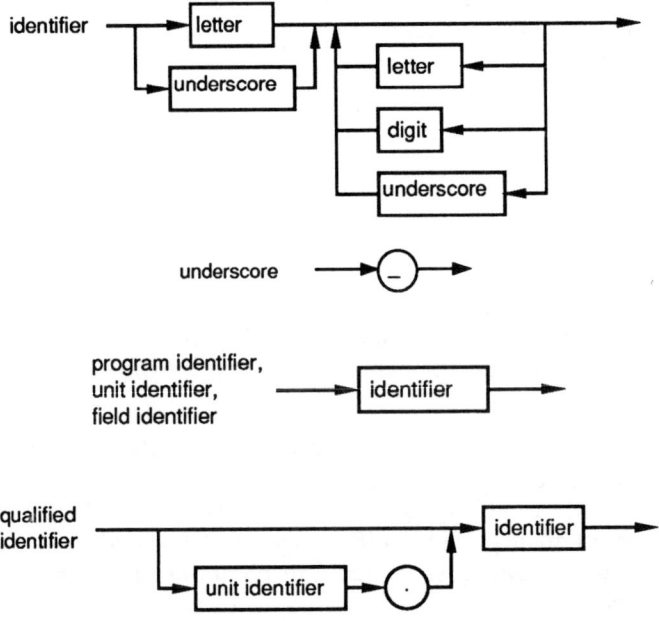

Here are some examples of identifiers:

```
Writeln
Exit
Real2String
System.MemAvail
Dos.Exec
Crt.Window
```

In this manual, standard and user-defined identifiers are *italicized* when they are referred to in text.

Labels

A *label* is a digit sequence in the range 0 to 9999. Leading zeros are not significant. Labels are used with **goto** statements.

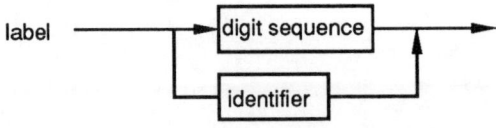

As an extension to standard Pascal, Turbo Pascal also allows identifiers to function as labels.

Numbers

Ordinary decimal notation is used for numbers that are constants of type integer and real. A hexadecimal integer constant uses a dollar sign ($) as a prefix. Engineering notation (*E* or *e*, followed by an exponent) is read as "times ten to the power of" in real types. For example, 7E-2 means 7×10^{-2}; 12.25e+6 or 12.25e6 both mean $12.25 \times 10^{+6}$. Syntax diagrams for writing numbers follow.

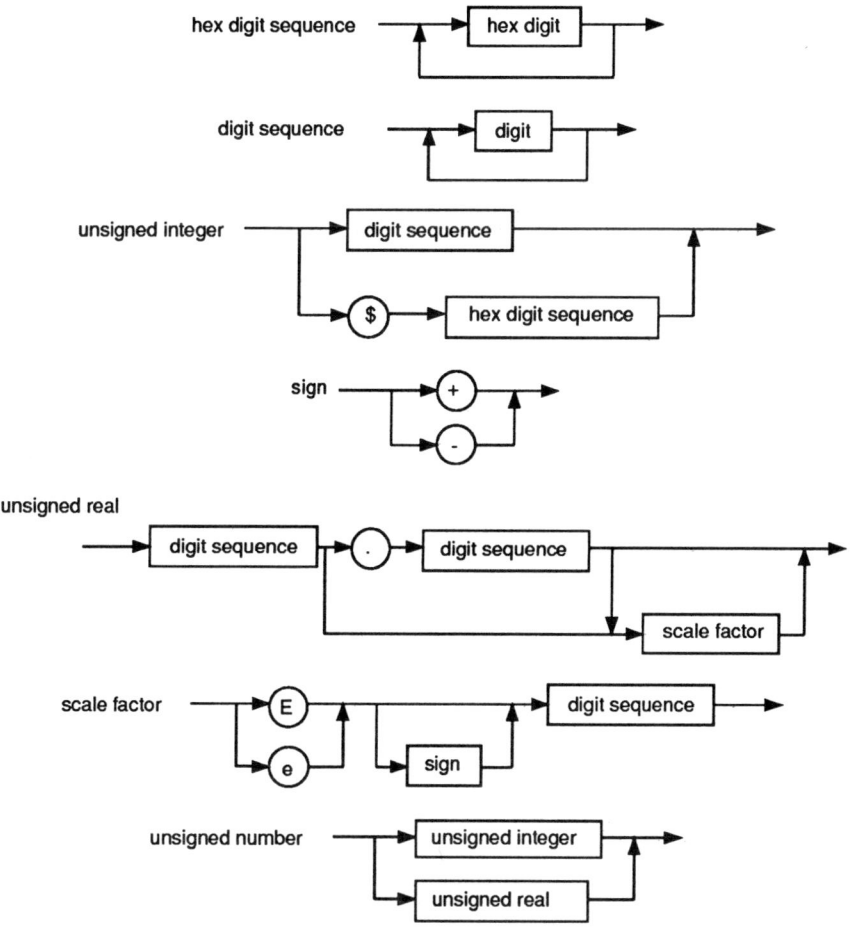

Chapter 1, Tokens and Constants

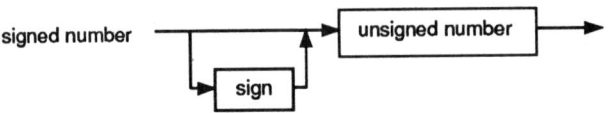

Numbers with decimals or exponents denote real-type constants. Other decimal numbers denote integer-type constants; they must be within the range –2147483648 to 2147483647.

Hexadecimal numbers denote integer-type constants; they must be within the range $00000000 to $FFFFFFFF. The resulting value's sign is implied by the hexademical notation.

Character Strings

A character string is a sequence of zero or more characters from the extended ASCII character set (Appendix C), written on one line in the program and enclosed by apostrophes. A character string with nothing between the apostrophes is a *null string*. Two sequential apostrophes in a character string denote a single character, an apostrophe. The length attribute of a character string is the actual number of characters within the apostrophes.

As an extension to standard Pascal, Turbo Pascal allows control characters to be embedded in character strings. The # character followed by an unsigned integer constant in the range 0 to 255 denotes a character of the corresponding ASCII value. There must be no separators between the # character and the integer constant. Likewise, if several control characters are part of a character string, there must be no separators between them.

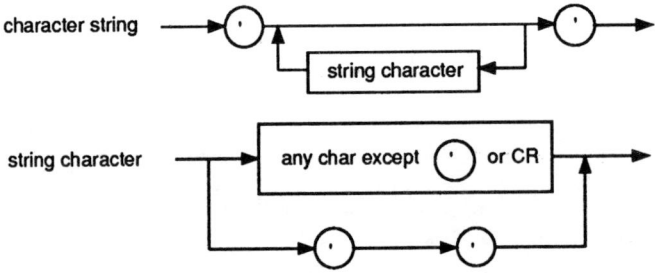

A character string of length zero (the null string) is compatible only with string types. A character string of length one is compatible with any char and string type. A character string of length *n*, where *n* is greater than or equal to 2, is compatible with any string type and with packed arrays of *n* characters.

Here are some examples of character strings:

```
'TURBO'      'You''ll see'       ''''        ';'         ' '
#13#10       'Line 1'#13'Line2'              #7#7'Wake up!'#7#7
```

Constant Declarations

A constant declaration declares an identifier that marks a constant within the block containing the declaration. A constant identifier cannot be included in its own declaration.

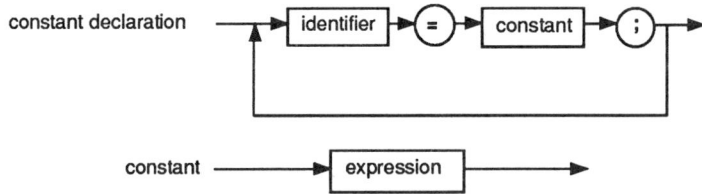

As an extension to standard Pascal, Turbo Pascal allows use of constant expressions. A *constant expression* is an expression that can be evaluated by the compiler without actually executing the program. Examples of constant expressions follow:

```
100
'A'
256 - 1
(2.5 + 1) / (2.5 - 1)
'Turbo' + ' ' + 'Pascal'
Chr(32)
Ord('Z') - Ord('A') + 1
```

The simplest case of a constant expression is a simple constant, such as 100 or 'A'; wherever standard Pascal allows only a simple constant, Turbo Pascal allows a constant expression.

Since the compiler has to be able to completely evaluate a constant expression at compile time, the following constructs are *not* allowed in constant expressions:

- references to variables and typed constants
- function calls (except those noted in the following text)
- the address operator (@)

Chapter 1, Tokens and Constants　　　　　　　　　　　　　　　　　　　　15

Except for these restrictions, constant expressions follow the exact syntactical rules as ordinary expressions (described in Chapter 6, "Expressions").

The following standard functions are allowed in constant expressions:

Abs	Chr	Hi	Length	Lo	Odd	Ord
Pred	Ptr	Round	SizeOf	Succ	Swap	Trunc

Here are some examples of the use of constant expressions in constant declarations:

```
const
  Min      = 0;
  Max      = 100;
  Center   = (Max - Min) div 2;
  Beta     = Chr(225);
  NumChars = Ord('Z') - Ord('A') + 1;
  Message  = 'Out of memory';
  ErrStr   = ' Error: ' + Message + '. ';
  ErrPos   = 80 - Length(ErrorStr) div 2;
  Ln10     = 2.302585092994045684;
  Ln10R    = 1 / Ln10;
  Numeric  = ['0'..'9'];
  Alpha    = ['A'..'Z','a'..'z'];
  AlphaNum = Alpha + Numeric;
```

Comments

The following constructs are comments and are ignored by the compiler:

```
{ Any text not containing right brace }
(* Any text not containing star/right parenthesis *)
```

A comment that contains a dollar sign ($) immediately after the opening { or (* is a compiler directive. A mnemonic of the compiler command follows the $ character. The compiler directives are summarized in Appendix B.

Program Lines

Turbo Pascal program lines have a maximum length of 126 characters.

CHAPTER 2

Blocks, Locality, and Scope

A block is made up of declarations, which are written and combined in any order, and statements. Each block is part of a procedure declaration, a function declaration, or a program or unit. All identifiers and labels declared in the declaration part are local to the block.

Syntax

The overall syntax of any block follows this format:

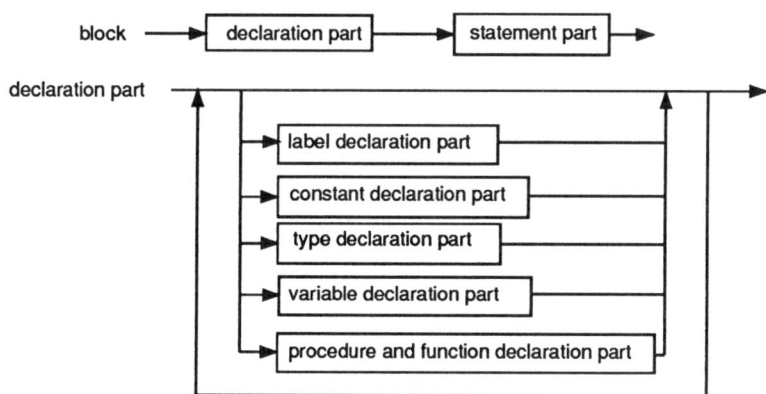

The *label declaration part* is where labels that mark statements in the corresponding statement part are declared. Each label must mark only one statement.

Chapter 2, Blocks, Locality, and Scope 17

The digit sequence used for a label must be in the range 0 to 9999.

The *constant declaration part* consists of constant declarations local to the block.

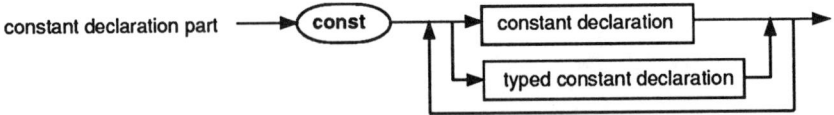

The *type declaration part* includes all type declarations local to the block.

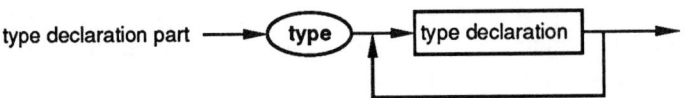

The *variable declaration part* is composed of variable declarations local to the block.

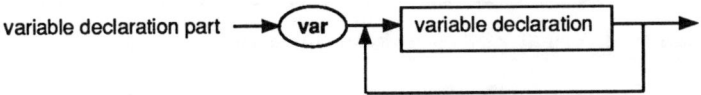

The *procedure and function declaration part* comprises procedure and function declarations local to the block.

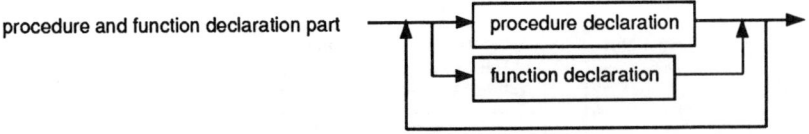

The *statement part* defines the statements or algorithmic actions to be executed by the block.

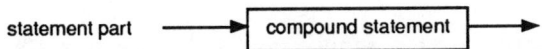

Rules of Scope

The presence of an identifier or label in a declaration defines the identifier or label. Each time the identifier or label occurs again, it must be within the *scope* of this declaration. The scope of an identifier or label encompasses its declaration to the end of the current block, including all blocks enclosed by the current block; some exceptions follow.

- **Redeclaration in an enclosed block:** Suppose that *Exterior* is a block that encloses another block, *Interior*. If *Exterior* and *Interior* both have an identifier with the same name, for example, *j*, then *Interior* can only access the *j* it declared, and similarly *Exterior* can only access the *j* it declared.

- **Position of declaration within its block:** Identifiers and labels cannot be used until after they are declared. An identifier or label's declaration must come before any occurrence of that identifier or label in the program text, with one exception.

  The base type of a pointer type can be an identifier that has not yet been declared. However, the identifier must eventually be declared in the same type declaration part that the pointer type occurs in.

- **Redeclaration within a block:** An identifier or label can only be declared *once* in the outer level of a given block. The only exception to this is when it is declared within a contained block or is in a record's field list.

  A record field identifier is declared within a record type and is significant only in combination with a reference to a variable of that record type. So, you can redeclare a field identifier (with the same spelling) within the same block but not at the same level within the same record type. However, an identifier that has been declared can be redeclared as a field identifier in the same block.

Scope of Interface and Standard Identifiers

Programs or units containing **uses** clauses have access to the identifiers belonging to the interface parts of the units in those **uses** clauses.

Each unit in a **uses** clause imposes a new scope that encloses the remaining units used and the entire program. The first unit in a **uses** clause represents the outermost scope, and the last unit represents the innermost scope. This implies that if two or more units declare the same identifier, an unqualified reference to the identifier will select the instance declared by the last unit in the **uses** clause. However, by writing a qualified identifier, every instance of the identifier can be selected.

The identifiers of Turbo Pascal's predefined constants, types, variables, procedures, and functions act as if they were declared in a block enclosing all used units and the entire program. In fact, these standard objects are defined in a unit called *System*, which is used by any program or unit before the units named in the **uses** clause. This suggests that any unit or program can redeclare the standard identifiers, but a specific reference can still be made through a qualified identifier, for example, *System.Integer* or *System.Writeln*.

CHAPTER

3

Types

When you declare a variable, you must state its type. A variable's *type* circumscribes the set of values it can have and the operations that can be performed on it. A *type declaration* specifies the identifier that denotes a type.

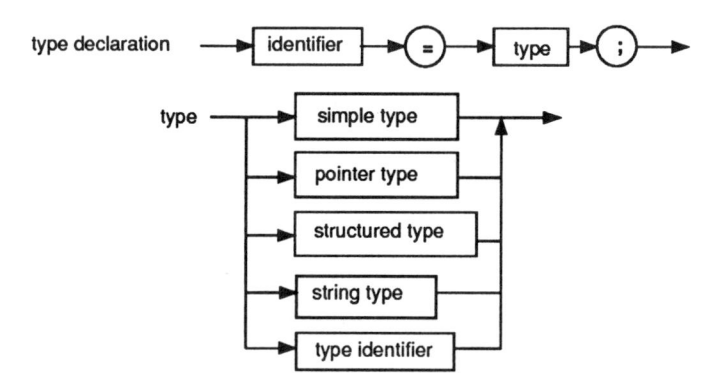

```
type declaration ──▶[ identifier ]──▶(=)──▶[ type ]──▶(;)──▶

type ──┬──▶[ simple type ]──┐
       ├──▶[ pointer type ]─┤
       ├──▶[ structured type ]─┤
       ├──▶[ string type ]──┤
       └──▶[ type identifier ]─┘
```

When an identifier occurs on the left side of a type declaration, it is declared as a type identifier for the block in which the type declaration occurs. A type identifier's scope does not include itself except for pointer types.

There are five major classes of types:

- simple types
- string types
- structured types
- pointer types
- procedural types

Each of these classes are described in the following sections.

Simple Types

Simple types define ordered sets of values.

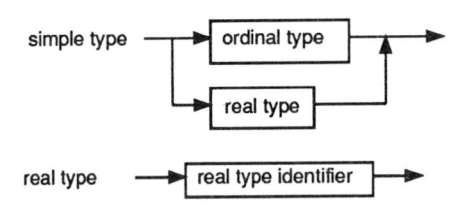

```
simple type  ──→┌─→ ordinal type ──┐──→
                │                  │
                └─→ real type ─────┘

real type  ──→ real type identifier ──→
```

A type real identifier is one of the standard identifiers: real, single, double, extended, or comp. Refer to the sections entitled "Numbers" and "String Constants" in Chapter 1 to find out how to denote constant type integer and real values.

Ordinal Types

Ordinal types are a subset of simple types. All simple types other than real types are ordinal types, which are set off by four characteristics:

- All possible values of a given ordinal type are an ordered set, and each possible value is associated with an *ordinality*, which is an integral value. Except for type integer values, the first value of every ordinal type has ordinality 0, the next has ordinality 1, and so on for each value in that ordinal type. A type integer value's ordinality is the value itself. In any ordinal type, each value other than the first has a predecessor, and each value other than the last has a successor based on the ordering of the type.
- The standard function *Ord* can be applied to any ordinal-type value to return the ordinality of the value.
- The standard function *Pred* can be applied to any ordinal-type value to return the predecessor of the value. If applied to the first value in the ordinal type, *Pred* produces an error.
- The standard function *Succ* can be applied to any ordinal-type value to return the successor of the value. If applied to the last value in the ordinal type, *Succ* produces an error.

The syntax of an ordinal type follows.

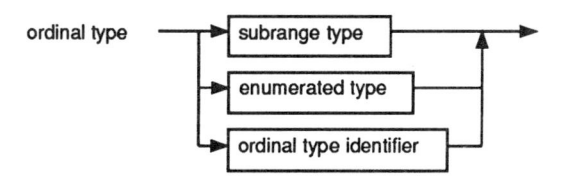

Turbo Pascal has seven predefined ordinal types: integer, shortint, longint, byte, word, boolean, and char. In addition, there are two other classes of user-defined ordinal types: enumerated types and subrange types.

Integer Types

There are five predefined integer types: shortint, integer, longint, byte, and word. Each type denotes a specific subset of the whole numbers, according to the following table:

Table 3.1: Predefined Integer Types

Type	Range	Format
shortint	–128 .. 127	Signed 8-bit
integer	–32768 .. 32767	Signed 16-bit
longint	–2147483648 .. 2147483647	Signed 32-bit
byte	0 .. 255	Unsigned 8-bit
word	0 .. 65535	Unsigned 16-bit

Arithmetic operations with type integer operands use 8-bit, 16-bit, or 32-bit precision, according to the following rules:

- The type of an integer constant is the predefined integer type with the smallest range that includes the value of the integer constant.
- For a binary operator (an operator that takes two operands), both operands are converted to their common type before the operation. The *common type* is the predefined integer type with the smallest range that includes all possible values of both types. For instance, the common type of integer and byte is integer, and the common type of integer and word is longint. The operation is performed using the precision of the common type, and the result type is the common type.
- The expression on the right of an assignment statement is evaluated independently from the size or type of the variable on the left.
- Any byte-sized operand is converted to an intermediate word-sized operand that is compatible with both integer and word before any arithmetic operation is performed.

An integer type value can be explicitly converted to another integer type through typecasting. (Typecasting is described in Chapters 4 and 6.)

Boolean Type

Type boolean values are denoted by the predefined constant identifiers *false* and *true*. Because boolean is an enumerated type, these relationships hold:

- *false < true*
- *Ord(false)* = 0
- *Ord(true)* = 1
- *Succ(false) = true*
- *Pred(true) = false*

Char Type

This type's set of values are characters, ordered according to the extended ASCII character set (Appendix C). The function call *Ord(Ch)*, where *Ch* is a char value, returns *Ch*'s ordinality.

A string constant of length 1 can denote a constant character value. Any character value can be generated with the standard function *Chr*.

Enumerated Types

Enumerated types define ordered sets of values by enumerating the identifiers that denote these values. Their ordering follows the sequence in which the identifiers are enumerated.

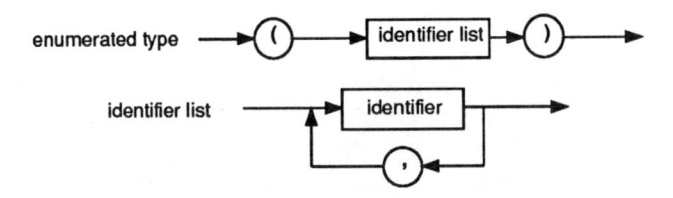

enumerated type ⟶ (⟶ identifier list ⟶) ⟶

identifier list ⟶ identifier ⟶
              ↑_____,_____↓

When an identifier occurs within the identifier list of an enumerated type, it is declared as a constant for the block in which the enumerated type is declared. This constant's type is the enumerated type being declared.

An enumerated constant's ordinality is determined by its position in the identifier list in which it is declared. The enumerated type in which it is declared becomes the constant's type. The first enumerated constant in a list has an ordinality of zero.

An example of an enumerated type follows:

```
type
  suit = (club,diamond,heart,spade);
```

Given these declarations, *diamond* is a constant of type *suit*.

When the *Ord* function is applied to an enumerated type's value, *Ord* returns an integer that shows where the value falls with respect to the other values of the enumerated type. Given the preceding declarations, *Ord(club)* returns zero, *Ord(diamond)* returns 1, and so on.

Subrange Types

A subrange type is a range of values from an ordinal type called the *host type*. The definition of a subrange type specifies the least and the largest value in the subrange; its syntax follows:

subrange type ⟶ constant ⟶ .. ⟶ constant ⟶

Both constants must be of the same ordinal type. Subrange types of the form *a..b* require that *a* is less than or equal to *b*.

Examples of subrange types:

```
0..99
-128..127
club..heart
```

A variable of a subrange type has all the properties of variables of the host type, but its run-time value must be in the specified interval.

One syntactic ambiguity arises from allowing constant expressions where Standard Pascal only allows simple constants. Consider the following declarations:

```
const
  x = 50;
  y = 10;
type
  color = (red,green,blue);
  scale = (x-y)*2..(x+y)*2;
```

Standard Pascal syntax dictates that, if a type definition starts with a parenthesis, it is an enumerated type, such as the *color* type described previously. However, the intent of the declaration of *scale* is to define a subrange type. The solution is to either reorganize the first subrange expression so that it does not start with a parenthesis, or to set another constant equal to the value of the expression, and then use that constant in the type definition:

type
    scale = 2*(x-y)..(x+y)*2;

Real Types

A real type has a set of values that is a subset of real numbers, which can be represented in floating-point notation with a fixed number of digits. A value's floating-point notation normally comprises three values—*m*, *b*, and *e*—such that $m \times b^e = n$, where *b* is always 2, and both *m* and *e* are integral values within the real type's range. These *m* and *e* values further prescribe the real type's range and precision.

There are five kinds of real types: real, single, double, extended, and comp.

The real types differ in the range and precision of values they hold (see Table 3.2).

Table 3.2: Real Data Types

Type	Range	Significant Digits	Size in Bytes
real	$2.9 \times 10^{-39} .. 1.7 \times 10^{38}$	11-12	6
single	$1.5 \times 10^{-45} .. 3.4 \times 10^{38}$	7-8	4
double	$5.0 \times 10^{-324} .. 1.7 \times 10^{308}$	15-16	8
extended	$3.4 \times 10^{-4932} .. 1.1 \times 10^{4932}$	19-20	10
comp	$-2^{63}+1 .. 2^{63}-1$	19-20	8

Note: The comp type holds only integral values within the range $-2^{63}+1$ to $2^{63}-1$, which is approximately -9.2×10^{18} to 9.2×10^{18}.

Turbo Pascal supports two models of code generation for performing real-type operations: *software* floating point and *8087* floating point. The appropriate model is selected through the $N compiler directive. If no 8087 is present, enabling the {$E} compiler directive will provide full 8087 emulation in software.

Software Floating Point

In the {$N-} state, which is selected by default, the code generated performs all real type calculations in software by calling run-time library routines. For reasons of speed and code size, only operations on variables of type real are allowed in this state. Any attempt to compile statements that operate on the single, double, extended, and comp types generates an error.

8087 Floating Point

In the {$N+} state, the code generated performs all real type calculations using 8087 instructions. This state permits the use of all five real types.

Turbo Pascal includes a run-time library that will automatically *emulate* an 8087 in software if one is not present; the $E compiler directive is used to determine whether or not the 8087 emulator should be included in a program.

For further details on 8087 floating-point code generation and software emulation, refer to Chapter 14, "Using the 8087."

String Types

A type string value is a sequence of characters with a dynamic length attribute (depending on the actual character count during program execution) and a constant size attribute from 1 to 255. A string type declared without a size attribute is given the default size attribute 255. The length attribute's current value is returned by the standard function *Length*.

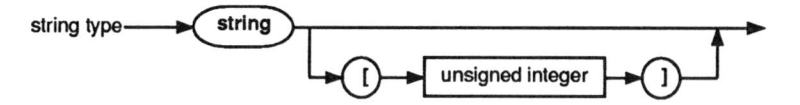

The ordering between any two string values is set by the ordering relationship of the character values in corresponding positions. In two strings of unequal length, each character in the longer string without a corresponding character in the shorter string takes on a higher or greater-than value; for example, 'Xs' is greater than 'X'. Null strings can only be equal to other null strings, and they hold the least string values.

Characters in a string can be accessed as components of an array, as described in "Arrays, Strings, and Indexes" in Chapter 4. Type string operators are described in "String Operator" and "Relational Operators" in Chapter 6, "Expressions." Type string standard procedures and functions are described in "String Procedures and Functions" on page 112.

Structured Types

A structured type, characterized by its structuring method and by its component type(s), holds more than one value. If a component type is structured, the resulting structured type has more than one level of structuring. A structured type can have unlimited levels of structuring.

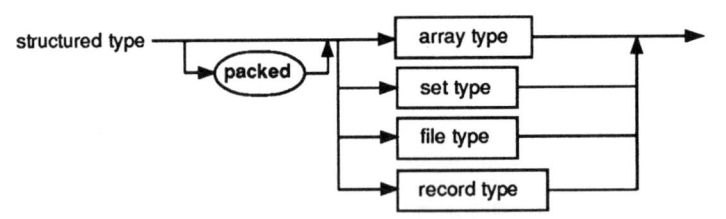

```
structured type ──┬──────────────┬──▶ array type ──┬──▶
                  └─▶ packed ────┤                 │
                                 ├──▶ set type ────┤
                                 ├──▶ file type ───┤
                                 └──▶ record type ─┘
```

The word **packed** in a structured type's declaration tells the compiler to compress data storage, even at the cost of diminished access to a component of a variable of this type. The word **packed** has no effect in Turbo Pascal; instead packing occurs automatically whenever possible.

Note: The maximum permitted size of any structured type in Turbo Pascal is 65520 bytes.

Array Types

Arrays have a fixed number of components of one type—the component type. In the following syntax diagram, the component type follows the word **of**.

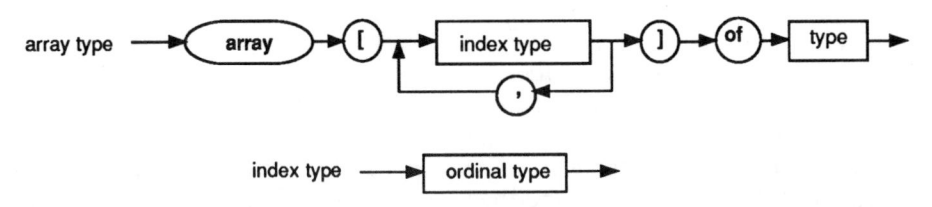

```
array type ──▶ array ──▶ [ ──┬──▶ index type ──┬──▶ ] ──▶ of ──▶ type ──▶
                             └──────── , ──────┘

index type ──▶ ordinal type ──▶
```

The index types, one for each dimension of the array, specify the number of elements. Valid index types are all ordinal types except longint and subranges of longint. The array can be indexed in each dimension by all values of the corresponding index type; the number of elements is therefore the number of values in each index type. The number of dimensions is unlimited.

The following is an example of an array type:

    array[1..100] **of** real

If an array type's component type is also an array, you can treat the result as an array of arrays or as a single multidimensional array. For instance,

    array[boolean] **of array**[1..10] **of array**[Size] **of** real

is interpreted the same way by the compiler as

    array[boolean,1..10,Size] **of** real

You can also express

    packed array[1..10] **of packed array**[1..8] **of** boolean

as

    packed array[1..10,1..8] **of** boolean

You access an array's components by supplying the array's identifier with one or more indexes in brackets (see "Arrays, Strings, and Indexes" in Chapter 4).

An array type of the form

    packed array[m..n] **of** char

where *m* is less than *n* is called a packed string type (the word **packed** may be omitted, because it has no effect in Turbo Pascal). A packed string type has certain properties not shared by other array types (see "Identical and Compatible Types" later in this chapter).

Record Types

A record type comprises a set number of components, or fields, that can be of different types. The record type declaration specifies the type of each field and the identifier that names the field.

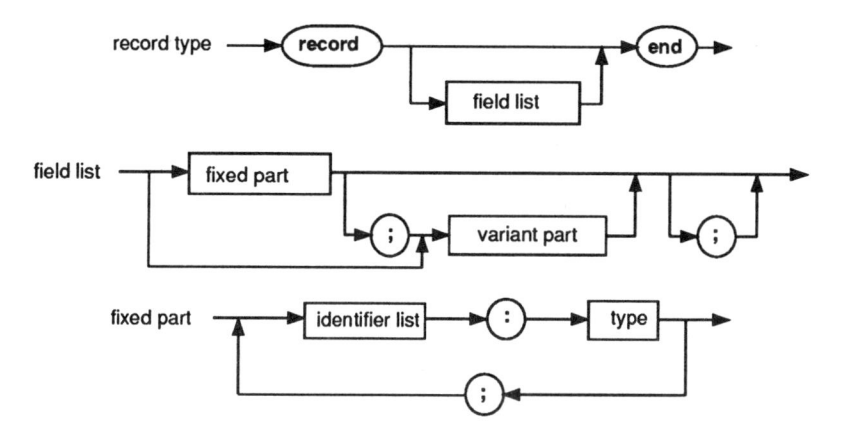

The fixed part of a record type sets out the list of fixed fields, giving an identifier and a type for each. Each field contains information that is always retrieved in the same way.

The following is an example of a record type:

```
record
   year:  integer;
   month: 1..12;
   day:   1..31;
end
```

The variant part shown in the syntax diagram of a record type declaration distributes memory space for more than one list of fields, so the information can be accessed in more ways than one. Each list of fields is a *variant*. The variants overlay the same space in memory, and all fields of all variants can be accessed at all times.

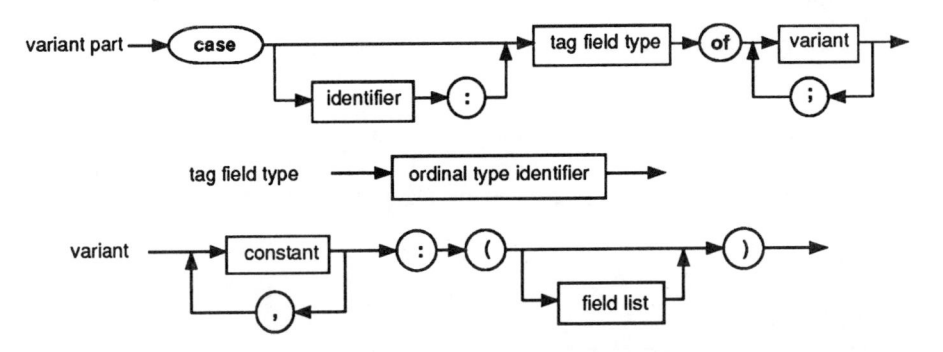

You can see from the diagram that each variant is identified by at least one constant. All constants must be distinct and of an ordinal type compatible with the tag field type. Variant and fixed fields are accessed the same way.

An optional identifier, the tag field identifier, can be placed in the variant part. If a tag field identifier is present, it becomes the identifier of an additional fixed field—the tag field—of the record. The program can use the tag field's value to show which variant is active at a given time. Without a tag field, the program selects a variant by another criterion.

Some record types with variants follow.

```
record
   firstName,lastName : string[40];
   birthDate : Date;
```

```
    case citizen : boolean of
      true  : (birthPlace: string[40]);
      false : (country   : string[20];
               entryPort : string[20];
               entryDate : Date;
               exitDate  : Date);
end

record
  x,y : real;
  case kind : Figure of
    rectangle : (height,width: real);
    triangle  : (side1,side2,angle: real);
    circle    : (radius: real);
end
```

Set Types

A set type's range of values is the power set of a particular ordinal type (the base type). Each possible value of a set type is a subset of the possible values of the base type.

A variable of a set type can hold from none to all values of the set.

set type ⟶ (set) ⟶ (of) ⟶ [ordinal type] ⟶

The base type must not have more than 256 possible values, and the ordinal values of the upper and lower bounds of the base type must be within the range 0 to 255. For these reasons, the base type of a set cannot be shortint, integer, longint, or word.

Set-type operators are described in the section entitled "Set Operators" in Chapter 6. "Set Constructors" in the same chapter shows how to construct set values.

Every set type can hold the value [ ], which is called the *empty set*.

File Types

A file type consists of a linear sequence of components of the component type, which can be of any type except a file type or any structured type with a file-type component. The number of components is not set by the file-type declaration.

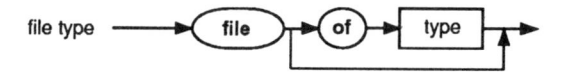

file type ⟶ (file) ⟶ (of) ⟶ [type] ⟶

Chapter 3, Types   31

If the word **of** and the component type are omitted, the type denotes an untyped file. Untyped files are low-level I/O channels primarily used for direct access to any disk file regardless of its internal format.

The standard file type *text* signifies a file containing characters organized into lines. Text files use special input/output procedures, which are discussed in Chapter 10, "Input and Output."

Pointer Types

A pointer type defines a set of values that point to dynamic variables of a specified type called the *base* type. A type pointer variable contains the memory address of a dynamic variable.

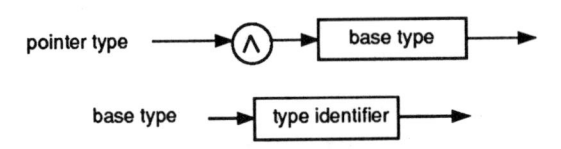

```
pointer type ─────▶(^)─▶ base type ─────▶

base type ─────▶ type identifier ─────▶
```

If the base type is an undeclared identifier, it must be declared in the same type declaration part as the pointer type.

You can assign a value to a pointer variable with the *New* procedure, the @ operator, or the *Ptr* function. The *New* procedure allocates a new memory area in the application heap for a dynamic variable and stores the address of that area in the pointer variable. The @ operator directs the pointer variable to the memory area containing any existing variable, including variables that already have identifiers. The *Ptr* function points the pointer variable to a specific memory address.

The reserved word **nil** denotes a pointer-valued constant that does not point to anything.

The predefined type pointer denotes an untyped pointer, that is, a pointer that does not point to any specific type. Variables of type pointer cannot be dereferenced; writing the pointer symbol ^ after such a variable is an error. Like the value denoted by the word **nil**, values of type pointer are compatible with all other pointer types.

See Chapter 4's section entitled "Pointers and Dynamic Variables" for the syntax of referencing the dynamic variable pointed to by a pointer variable.

Procedural Types

Standard Pascal regards procedures and functions strictly as program parts that can be executed through procedure or function calls. Turbo Pascal has a much broader view of procedures and functions: It allows procedures and functions to be treated as objects that can be assigned to variables and passed as parameters. Such actions are made possible through *procedural types*.

For a complete discussion of procedural types, please refer to the "Procedural Types" section on page 84.

Identical and Compatible Types

Two types may be the same, and this sameness (identity) is mandatory in some contexts. At other times, the two types need only be compatible or merely assignment-compatible. They are identical when they are declared with, or their definitions stem from, the same type identifier.

Type Identity

Type identity is required only between actual and formal variable parameters in procedure and function calls.

Two types—say, *T1* and *T2*—are identical if one of the following is True: *T1* and *T2* are the same type identifier; *T1* is declared to be equivalent to a type identical to *T2*.

The second condition connotes that *T1* does not have to be declared directly to be equivalent to *T2*. The type declarations

```
T1 = integer;
T2 = T1;
T3 = integer;
T4 = T2;
```

result in *T1, T2, T3, T4,* and *integer* as identical types. The type declarations

```
T5 = set of integer;
T6 = set of integer;
```

don't make *T5* and *T6* identical, since **set of** *integer* is not a type identifier. Two variables declared in the same declaration, for example:

```
V1, V2: set of integer;
```

are of identical types—unless the declarations are separate. The declarations

```
V1: set of integer;
V2: set of integer;
V3: integer;
V4: integer;
```

mean *V3* and *V4* are of identical type, but not *V1* and *V2*.

Type Compatibility

Compatibility between two types is sometimes required, such as in expressions or in relational operations. Type compatibility is important, however, as a precondition of assignment compatibility.

Type compatibility exists when at least one of the following conditions is True:

- Both types are the same.
- Both types are real types.
- Both types are integer types.
- One type is a subrange of the other.
- Both types are subranges of the same host type.
- Both types are set types with compatible base types.
- Both types are packed string types with an identical number of components.
- One type is a string type and the other is a string type, packed string type, or char type.
- One type is pointer and the other is any pointer type.
- Both types are procedural types with identical result types, an identical number of parameters, and a one-to-one identity between parameter types.

Assignment Compatibility

Assignment compatibility is necessary when a value is assigned to something, such as in an assignment statement or in passing value parameters.

A value of type T_2 is assignment-compatible with a type T_1 (that is, $T_1 := T_2$ is allowed) if any of the following are True:

- T_1 and T_2 are identical types and neither is a file type or a structured type that contains a file-type component at any level of structuring.

- T_1 and T_2 are compatible ordinal types, and the values of type T_2 falls within the range of possible values of T_1.
- T_1 and T_2 are real types, and the value of type T_2 falls within the range of possible values of T_1.
- T_1 is a real type, and T_2 is an integer type.
- T_1 and T_2 are string types.
- T_1 is a string type, and T_2 is a char type.
- T_1 is a string type, and T_2 is a packed string type.
- T_1 and T_2 are compatible, packed string types.
- T_1 and T_2 are compatible set types, and all the members of the value of type T_2 fall within the range of possible values of T_1.
- T_1 and T_2 are compatible pointer types.
- T_1 and T_2 are compatible procedural types.
- T_1 is a procedural type, and T_2 is a procedure or function with an identical result type, an identical number of parameters, and a one-to-one identity between parameter types.

A compile or run-time error occurs when assignment compatibility is necessary and none of the items in the preceding list are True.

The Type Declaration Part

Programs, procedures, and functions that declare types have a type declaration part. An example of this follows:

```
type
  Range       = integer;
  Number      = integer;
  Color       = (red,green,blue);
  CharVal     = Ord('A')..Ord('Z');
  TestIndex   = 1..100;
  TestValue   = -99..99;
  TestList    = array[TestIndex] of TestValue;
  TestListPtr = ^TestList;
  Date        = record
                  year: integer;
                  month: 1..12;
                  day: 1..31;
                end;
  MeasureData = record
                  when: Date;
                  count: TestIndex;
                  data: TestListPtr;
                end;
```

```
MeasureList = array[1..50] of MeasureData;
Name        = string[80];
Sex         = (male,female);
Person      = ^PersonData;
PersonData  = record
                name,firstName: Name;
                age:            integer;
                married:        boolean;
                father,child,sibling: Person;
                case s: Sex of
                male:   (bearded: boolean);
                female: (pregnant: boolean);
              end;
PersonBuf   = array[0..SizeOf(PersonData)-1] of Byte;
People      = file of PersonData;
```

In the example, *Range*, *Number*, and *integer* are identical types. *TestIndex* is compatible and assignment-compatible with, but not identical to, the types *Number*, *Range*, and *integer*. Notice the use of constant expressions in the declarations of *CharVal* and *PersonBuf*.

CHAPTER 4

Variables

Variable Declarations

A variable declaration embodies a list of identifiers that designate new variables and their type.

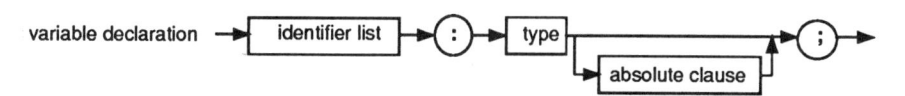

```
variable declaration → identifier list → : → type → ; →
                                              ↳ absolute clause ↲
```

The type given for the variable(s) can be a type identifier previously declared in a **type** declaration part in the same block, in an enclosing block, or in a unit; it can also be a new type definition.

When an identifier is specified within the identifier list of a variable declaration, that identifier is a variable identifier for the block in which the declaration occurs. The variable can then be referred to throughout the block, unless the identifier is redeclared in an enclosed block. Redeclaration causes a new variable using the same identifier, without affecting the value of the original variable.

An example of a variable declaration part follows:

```
var
  X,Y,Z: real;
  I,J,K: integer;
  Digit: 0..9;
  C: Color;
  Done,Error: boolean;
  Operator: (plus, minus, times);
  Hue1,Hue2: set of Color;
```

```
    Today: Date;
    Results: MeasureList;
    P1,P2: Person;
    Matrix: array[1..10,1..10] of real;
```

Variables declared outside procedures and functions are called *global variables*, and reside in the *data segment*. Variables declared within procedures and functions are called *local variables*, and reside in the *stack segment*.

The Data Segment

The maximum size of the data segment is 65520 bytes. When a program is linked (this happens automatically at the end of the compilation of a program), the global variables of all units used by the program, as well as the program's own global variables, are placed in the data segment.

If you need more than 65520 bytes of global data, you should allocate the larger structures as dynamic variables. For further details on this subject, see "Pointers and Dynamic Variables" on page 42.

The Stack Segment

The size of the stack segment is set through a $M compiler directive—it can be anywhere from 1024 to 65520 bytes. The default stack segment size is 16384 bytes.

Each time a procedure or function is activated (called), it allocates a set of local variables on the stack. On exit, the local variables are disposed. At any time during the execution of a program, the total size of the local variables allocated by the active procedures and functions cannot exceed the size of the stack segment.

The $S compiler directive is used to include stack overflow checks in the code. In the default {$S+} state, code is generated to check for stack overflow at the beginning of each procedure and function. In the {$S-} state, no such checks are performed. A stack overflow may very well cause a system crash, so don't turn off stack checks unless you are absolutely sure that an overflow will never occur.

Absolute Variables

Variables can be declared to reside at specific memory addresses, and are then called *absolute variables*. The declaration of such variables must include an **absolute** clause following the type:

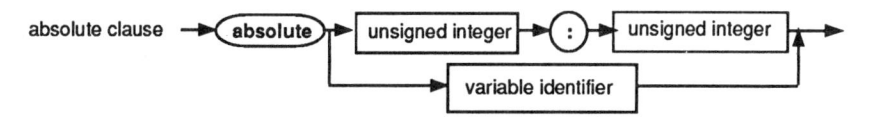

```
absolute clause → ( absolute ) → [ unsigned integer ] → ( : ) → [ unsigned integer ] →
                                 → [ variable identifier ] →
```

Note that the variable declaration's identifier list can only specify one identifier when an **absolute** clause is present.

The first form of the **absolute** clause specifies the segment and offset at which the variable is to reside:

```
CrtMode : byte absolute $0040:$0049;
```

The first constant specifies the segment base, and the second specifies the offset within that segment. Both constants must be within the range $0000 to $FFFF (0 to 65535).

The second form of the **absolute** clause is used to declare a variable "on top" of another variable, meaning it declares a variable that resides at the same memory address as another variable.

```
var
  Str: string[32];
  StrLen: byte absolute Str;
```

This declaration specifies that the variable *StrLen* should start at the same address as the variable *Str*, and because the first byte of a string variable contains the dynamic length of the string, *StrLen* will contain the length of *Str*.

Variable References

A variable reference signifies one of the following:

- a variable
- a component of a structured- or string-type variable
- a dynamic variable pointed to by a pointer-type variable

The syntax for a variable reference is

```
variable reference ──┬─▶ variable identifier ──┬────────────────▶
                     ├─▶ variable typecast ────┤   ┌─qualifier─┐
                     └─▶ function call ─▶(^)───┴───┴───────────┘
```

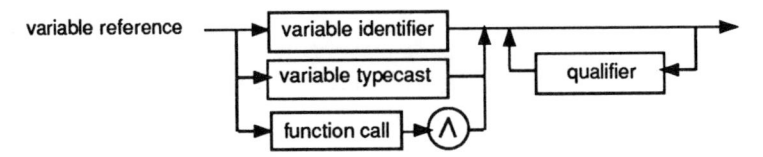

Note that the syntax for a variable reference allows a function call to a pointer function. The resulting pointer is then dereferenced to denote a dynamic variable.

Qualifiers

A variable reference is a variable identifier with zero or more qualifiers that modify the meaning of the variable reference.

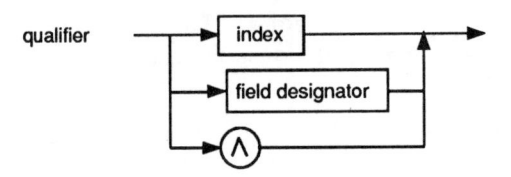

```
qualifier ──┬─▶ index ───────────┬──▶
            ├─▶ field designator ┤
            └─▶ (^) ─────────────┘
```

An array identifier with no qualifier, for example, references the entire array:

    Results

An array identifier followed by an index denotes a specific component of the array—in this case a structured variable:

    Results[Current+1]

With a component that is a record, the index can be followed by a field designator; here the variable access signifies a specific field within a specific array component.

    Results[Current+1].data

The field designator in a pointer field can be followed by the pointer symbol (a ^) to differentiate between the pointer field and the dynamic variable it points to.

    Results[Current+1].data^

If the variable being pointed to is an array, indexes can be added to denote components of this array.

    Results[Current+1].data^[J]

Arrays, Strings, and Indexes

A specific component of an array variable is denoted by a variable reference that refers to the array variable, followed by an index that specifies the component.

A specific character within a string variable is denoted by a variable reference that refers to the string variable, followed by an index that specifies the character position.

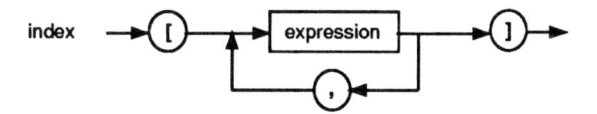

```
index ──▶[──┬─▶ expression ─┬─▶]──▶
            └──────,─────────┘
```

The index expressions select components in each corresponding dimension of the array. The number of expressions can't exceed the number of index types in the array declaration. Furthermore, each expression's type must be assignment-compatible with the corresponding index type.

When indexing a multidimensional array, multiple indexes or multiple expressions within an index can be used interchangeably. For example:

    Matrix[I][J]

is the same as

    Matrix[I,J]

You can index a string variable with a single index expression, whose value must be in the range 0..n, where n is the declared size of the string. This accesses one character of the string value, with the type char given to that character value.

The first character of a string variable (at index 0) contains the dynamic length of the string; that is, *Length(S)* is the same as *Ord(S[0])*. If a value is assigned to the length attribute, the compiler does not check whether this value is less than the declared size of the string. It is possible to index a string beyond its current dynamic length. The characters thus read are random, and assignments beyond the current length will not affect the actual value of the string variable.

Records and Field Designators

A specific field of a record variable is denoted by a variable reference that refers to the record variable, followed by a field designator specifying the field.

```
field designator ──▶( . )──▶[ field identifier ]──▶
```

Some examples of a field designator include:

```
Today.year
Results[1].count
Results[1].when.month
```

In a statement within a **with** statement, a field designator doesn't have to be preceded by a variable reference to its containing record.

Pointers and Dynamic Variables

The value of a pointer variable is either **nil** or the address of a value that points to a dynamic variable.

The dynamic variable pointed to by a pointer variable is referenced by writing the pointer symbol (^) after the pointer variable.

You create dynamic variables and their pointer values with the standard procedures *New* and *GetMem*. You can use the @ (address-of) operator and the standard function *Ptr* to create pointer values that are treated as pointers to dynamic variables.

nil does not point to any variable. The results are undefined if you access a dynamic variable when the pointer's value is **nil** or undefined.

Some examples of references to dynamic variables:

```
P1^
P1^.sibling^
Results[1].data^
```

Variable Typecasts

A variable reference of one type can be changed into a variable reference of another type through a *variable typecast*.

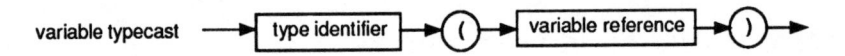

```
variable typecast ──▶[ type identifier ]──▶( ( )──▶[ variable reference ]──▶( ) )──▶
```

When a variable typecast is applied to a variable reference, the variable reference is treated as an instance of the type specified by the type identifier. The size of the variable (the number of bytes occupied by the variable) must be the same as the size of the type denoted by the type identifier. A variable typecast can be followed by one or more qualifiers, as allowed by the specified type.

Some examples of variable typecasts follow:

```
type
  ByteRec = record
              lo,hi: byte;
            end;
  WordRec = record
              low,high: word;
            end;
  PtrRec  = record
              ofs,seg: word;
            end;
  BytePtr = ^Byte;
var
  B: byte;
  W: word;
  L: longint;
  P: pointer;
begin
  W := $1234;
  B := ByteRec(W).lo;
  ByteRec(W).hi := 0;
  L := $01234567;
  W := WordRec(L).lo;
  B := ByteRec(WordRec(L).lo).hi;
  B := BytePtr(L)^;
  P := Ptr($40,$49);
  W := PtrRec(P).seg;
  Inc(PtrRec(P).ofs, 4);
end.
```

Notice the use of the *ByteRec* type to access the low- and high-order bytes of a word; this corresponds to the built-in functions *Lo* and *Hi*, except that a variable typecast can also be used on the left hand side of an assignment. Also, observe the use of the *WordRec* and *PtrRec* types to access the low- and high-order words of a long integer, and the offset and segment parts of a pointer.

CHAPTER

5

Typed Constants

Typed constants can be compared to initialized variables—variables whose values are defined on entry to their block. Unlike an untyped constant (see the section entitled "Constant Declarations" in Chapter 1), the declaration of a typed constant specifies both the type and the value of the constant.

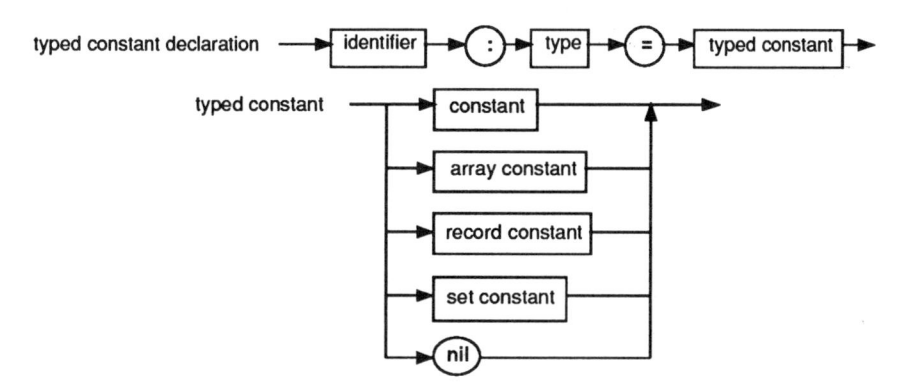

typed constant declaration → identifier → : → type → = → typed constant →

typed constant →
- constant
- array constant
- record constant
- set constant
- nil

Typed constants can be used exactly like variables of the same type, and can appear on the left-hand side in an assignment statement. Note that typed constants are initialized *only once*—at the beginning of a program. Thus, for each entry to a procedure or function, the locally declared typed constants are not reinitialized.

Chapter 5, Typed Constants 45

Simple-Type Constants

Declaring a typed constant as a simple type simply specifies the value of the constant:

```
const
  Maximum  : integer = 9999;
  Factor   : real = -0.1;
  Breakchar : char = #3;
```

Because a typed constant is actually a variable with a constant value, it cannot be interchanged with ordinary constants. For instance, it cannot be used in the declaration of other constants or types.

```
const
  Min : integer = 0;
  Max : integer = 99;
type
  Vector = array[Min..Max] of integer;
```

The *Vector* declaration is invalid, because *Min* and *Max* are typed constants.

String-Type Constants

The declaration of a typed constant of a string type specifies the maximum length of the string and its initial value:

```
const
  Heading  : string[7] = 'Section';
  NewLine  : string[2] = #13#10;
  TrueStr  : string[5] = 'Yes';
  FalseStr : string[5] = 'No';
```

Structured-Type Constants

The declaration of a structured-type constant specifies the value of each of the structure's components. Turbo Pascal supports the declaration of type array, record, set, and pointer constants; type file constants, and constants of array and record types that contain type file components are not allowed.

Array-Type Constants

The declaration of an array-type constant specifies, enclosed in parentheses and separated by commas, the values of the components.

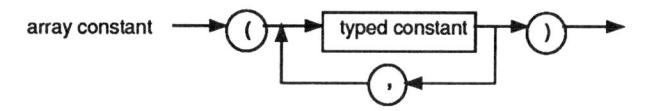

An example of an array-type constant follows:

```
type
  Status = (Active,Passive,Waiting);
  StatusMap = array[Status] of string[7];
const
  StatStr: StatusMap = ('Active','Passive','Waiting');
```

This example defines the array constant *StatStr*, which can be used to convert values of type *Status* into their corresponding string representations. The components of *StatStr* are

```
StatStr[Active]  = 'Active'
StatStr[Passive] = 'Passive'
StatStr[Waiting] = 'Waiting'
```

The component type of an array constant can be any type except a file type. Packed string-type constants (character arrays) can be specified both as single characters and as strings. The definition

```
const
  Digits: array[0..9] of char = ('0','1','2','3','4','5','6','7','8','9');
```

can be expressed more conveniently as

```
const
  Digits: array[0..9] of char = '0123456789';
```

Multidimensional array constants are defined by enclosing the constants of each dimension in separate sets of parentheses, separated by commas. The innermost constants correspond to the rightmost dimensions. The declaration

```
type
  Cube = array[0..1,0..1,0..1] of integer;
const
  Maze: Cube = (((0,1),(2,3)),((4,5),(6,7)));
```

provides an initialized array *Maze* with the following values:

```
Maze[0,0,0] = 0
Maze[0,0,1] = 1
Maze[0,1,0] = 2
Maze[0,1,1] = 3
Maze[1,0,0] = 4
Maze[1,0,1] = 5
Maze[1,1,0] = 6
Maze[1,1,1] = 7
```

Record-Type Constants

The declaration of a record-type constant specifies the identifier and value of each field, enclosed in parentheses and separated by semicolons.

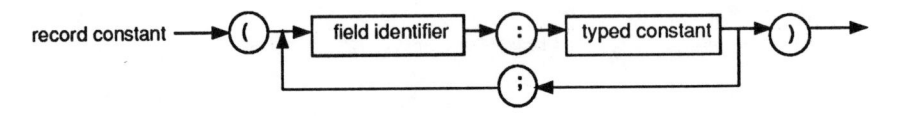

record constant ──▶(──▶ field identifier ──▶ : ──▶ typed constant ──▶)──▶
                         ▲   │
                         └──────────────── ; ◀──────────────────────┘

Some examples of record constants follow:

```
type
  Point  = record
             x,y: real;
           end;
  Vector = array[0..1] of Point;
  Month  = (Jan,Feb,Mar,Apr,May,Jun,Jly,Aug,Sep,Oct,Nov,Dec);
  Date   = record
             d: 1..31; m: Month; y: 1900..1999;
           end;
const
  Origin  : Point  = (x: 0.0; y: 0.0);
  Line    : Vector = ((x: -3.1; y: 1.5),(x: 5.8; y: 3.0));
  SomeDay : Date   = (d: 2; m: Dec; y: 1960);
```

The fields must be specified in the same order as they appear in the definition of the record type. If a record contains fields of file types, the constants of that record type cannot be declared. If a record contains a variant, only fields of the selected variant can be specified. If the variant contains a tag field, then its value must be specified.

Set-Type Constants

The declaration of a set-type constant specifies zero or more member constants, enclosed in square brackets and separated by commas. A member constant is a constant, or a range consisting of two constants, separated by two periods.

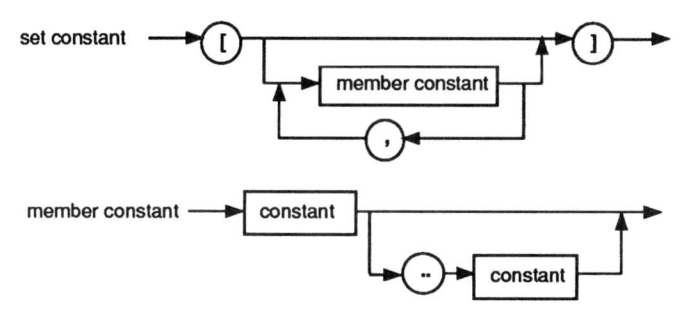

```
set constant ──▶[──┬─▶ member constant ─┬─▶]──▶
                   └─────── , ──────────┘

member constant ──▶ constant ─┬──────────────▶
                              └─▶ .. ─▶ constant ─┘
```

Some examples of set constants follow:

```
type
  Digits  = set of 0..9;
  Letters = set of 'A'..'Z';
const
  EvenDigits: Digits = [0,2,4,6,8];
  Vowels    : Letters = ['A','E','I','O','U','Y'];
  HexDigits : set of '0'..'z' = ['0'..'9','A'..'F','a'...'f'];
```

Pointer-Type Constants

The declaration of a pointer-type constant can only specify the value nil. Some examples include

```
type
  NamePtr = ^NameRec;
  NameRec = record
              Next: NamePtr;
              Name: string[31];
            end;
const
  NameList: NamePtr = nil;
  NoName: NameRec = (Next: nil; Name: '');
```

Chapter 5, Typed Constants   49

CHAPTER 6

Expressions

Expressions are made up of *operators* and *operands*. Most Pascal operators are *binary*, that is, they take two operands; the rest are *unary* and take only one operand. Binary operators use the usual algebraic form, for example, $a + b$. A unary operator always precedes its operand, for example, $-b$.

In more complex expressions, rules of precedence clarify the order in which operations are performed (see Table 6.1).

Table 6.1: Precedence of Operators

Operators	Precedence	Categories
@, not	first (high)	unary operators
*, /, div, mod, and, shl, shr	second	multiplying operators
+,-, or, xor	third	adding operators
=, <>, <, >, <=, >=, in	fourth (low)	relational operators

There are three basic rules of precedence:

1. First, an operand between two operators of different precedence is bound to the operator with higher precedence.
2. Second, an operand between two equal operators is bound to the one on its left.
3. Third, expressions within parentheses are evaluated prior to being treated as a single operand.

Operations with equal precedence are normally performed from left to right, although the compiler may at times rearrange the operands to generate optimum code.

Chapter 6, Expressions 51

Expression Syntax

The precedence rules follow from the syntax of expressions, which are built from factors, terms, and simple expressions.

A factor's syntax follows:

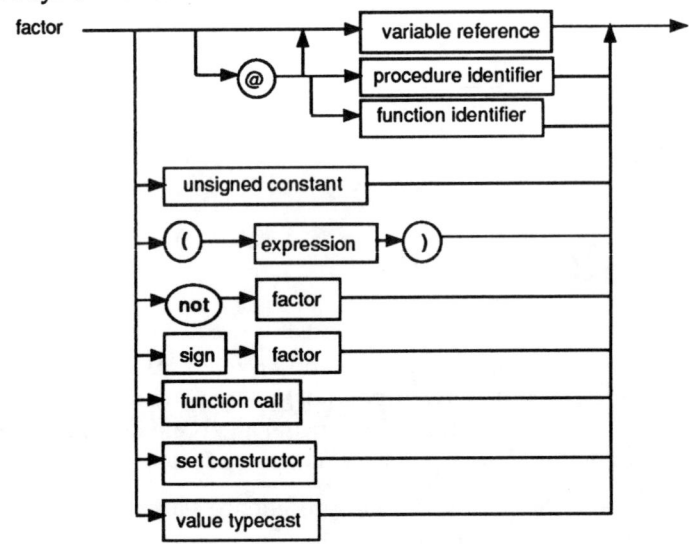

```
factor ──┬─────────────────┬──┬─► variable reference ──┬──►
         └─► @ ─────────────┘  ├─► procedure identifier ┤
                               └─► function identifier ─┘
         ├─► unsigned constant ─────────────────────────┤
         ├─► ( ─► expression ─► ) ──────────────────────┤
         ├─► not ─► factor ────────────────────────────┤
         ├─► sign ─► factor ───────────────────────────┤
         ├─► function call ────────────────────────────┤
         ├─► set constructor ──────────────────────────┤
         └─► value typecast ───────────────────────────┘
```

A function call activates a function and denotes the value returned by the function (see "Function Calls" on page 62). A set constructor denotes a value of a set type (see the "Set Constructors" section on page 63). A value typecast changes the type of a value (see "Value Typecasts" on page 64). An unsigned constant has the following syntax:

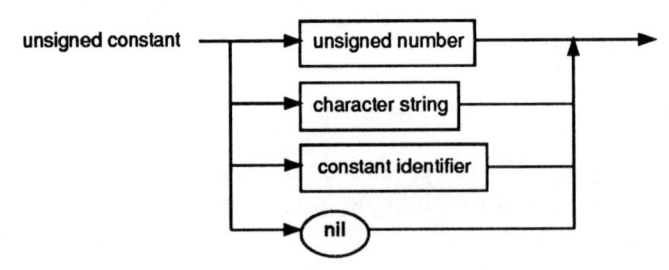

```
unsigned constant ──┬─► unsigned number ────┬──►
                    ├─► character string ───┤
                    ├─► constant identifier ┤
                    └─► nil ────────────────┘
```

Some examples of factors include

```
X                         { Variable reference }
@X                        { Pointer to a variable }
15                        { Unsigned constant }
(X+Y+Z)                   { Subexpression }
Sin(X/2)                  { Function call }
['0..'9','A'..'Z']        { Set constructor }
not Done                  { Negation of a boolean }
char(Digit+48)            { Value typecast }
```

Terms apply the multiplying operators to factors:

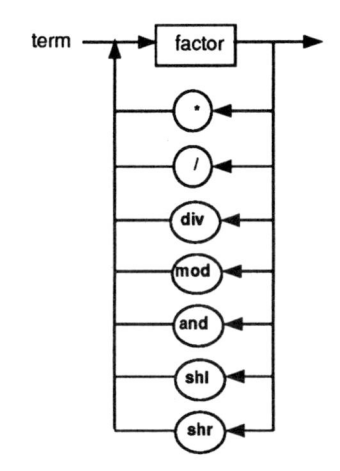

```
term ──►┬─►[ factor ]─┬─►
        ◄──( * )◄─────┤
        ◄──( / )◄─────┤
        ◄──( div )◄───┤
        ◄──( mod )◄───┤
        ◄──( and )◄───┤
        ◄──( shl )◄───┤
        ◄──( shr )◄───┘
```

Here are some examples of terms:

```
X*Y
Z/(1-Z)
Done or Error
(X <= Y) and (Y < Z)
```

Simple expressions apply adding operators and signs to terms:

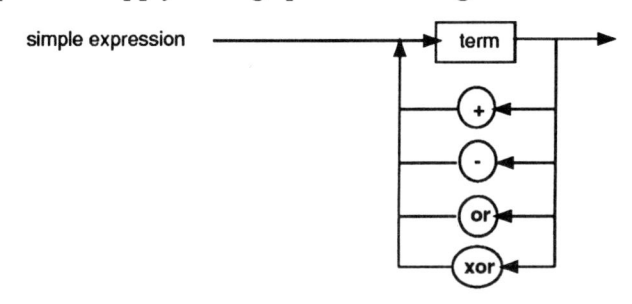

```
simple expression ──►┬─►[ term ]─┬─►
                    ◄──( + )◄────┤
                    ◄──( - )◄────┤
                    ◄──( or )◄───┤
                    ◄──( xor )◄──┘
```

Chapter 6, Expressions   53

Here are some examples of simple expressions:

```
X+Y
-X
Hue1 + Hue2
I*J + 1
```

An expression applies the relational operators to simple expressions:

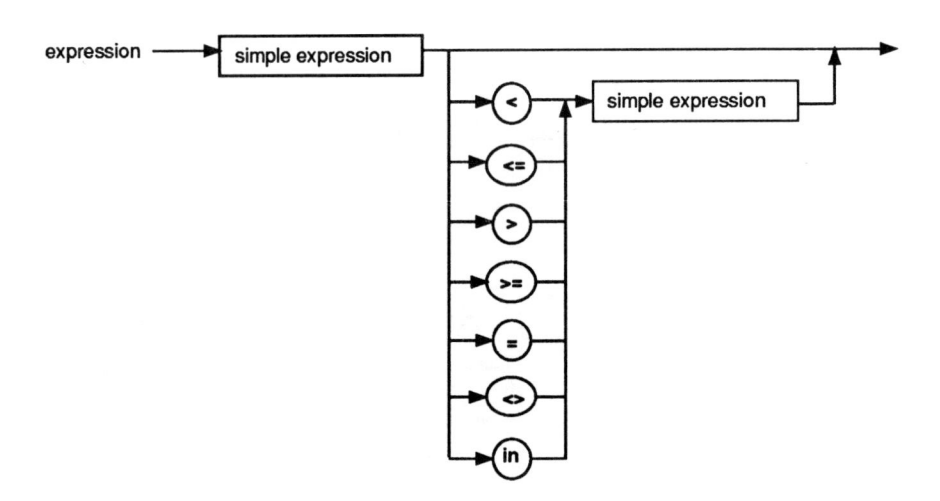

Here are some examples of expressions:

```
X = 1.5
Done <> Error
(I < J) = (J < K)
C in Hue1
```

Operators

The operators are classified as arithmetic operators, logical operators, string operators, set operators, relational operators, and the @ operator.

Arithmetic Operators

The following tables show the types of operands and results for binary and unary arithmetic operations.

Table 6.2: Binary Arithmetic Operations

Operator	Operation	Operand Types	Result Type
+	addition	integer type real type	integer type real type
−	subtraction	integer type real type	integer type real type
*	multiplication	integer type real type	integer type real type
/	division	integer type real type	real type real type
div	integer division	integer type	integer type
mod	remainder	integer type	integer type

Note: The + operator is also used as a string or set operator, and the +, −, and * operators are also used as set operators.

Table 6.3: Unary Arithmetic Operations

Operator	Operation	Operand Types	Result Type
+	sign identity	integer type real type	integer type real type
−	sign negation	integer type real type	integer type real type

Any operand whose type is a subrange of an ordinal type is treated as if it were of the ordinal type.

If both operands of a +, −, *, **div**, or **mod** operator are of an integer type, the result type is of the common type of the two operands. (See the section "Integer Types" in Chapter 3 for a definition of common types.)

If one or both operands of a +, −, or * operator are of a real type, the type of the result is real in the {$N-} state or extended in the {$N+} state.

If the operand of the sign identity or sign negation operator is of an integer type, the result is of the same integer type. If the operator is of a real type, the type of the result is real or extended.

The value of x/y is always of type real or extended regardless of the operand types. An error occurs if y is zero.

The value of i **div** j is the mathematical quotient of i/j, rounded in the direction of zero to an integer-type value. An error occurs if j is zero.

The **mod** operator returns the remainder obtained by dividing its two operands, that is,

```
i mod j = i - (i div j) * j
```

Chapter 6, Expressions

The sign of the result of **mod** is the same as the sign of *i*. An error occurs if *j* is zero.

Logical Operators

The types of operands and results for logical operations are shown in Table 6.4.

Table 6.4: Logical Operations

Operator	Operation	Operand Types	Result Type
not	Bitwise negation	integer type	integer type
and	Bitwise and	integer type	integer type
or	Bitwise or	integer type	integer type
xor	Bitwise xor	integer type	integer type
shl	Shift left	integer type	integer type
shr	Shift right	integer type	integer type

Note: The **not** operator is a unary operator.

If the operand of the **not** operator is of an integer type, the result is of the same integer type.

If both operands of an **and**, **or**, or **xor** operator are of an integer type, the result type is the common type of the two operands.

The operations *i* **shl** *j* and *i* **shr** *j* shift the value of *i* to the left or to the right by *j* bits. The type of the result is the same as the type of *i*.

Boolean Operators

The types of operands and results for Boolean operations are shown in Table 6.5.

Table 6.5: Boolean Operations

Operator	Operation	Operand Types	Result Type
not	negation	Boolean	Boolean
and	logical and	Boolean	Boolean
or	logical or	Boolean	Boolean
xor	logical xor	Boolean	Boolean

Note: The **not** operator is a unary operator.

Normal Boolean logic governs the results of these operations. For instance, *a* **and** *b* is True only if both *a* and *b* are True.

Turbo Pascal supports two different models of code generation for the **and** and **or** operators: complete evaluation and short-circuit (partial) evaluation.

Complete evaluation means that every operand of a Boolean expression, built from the **and** and **or** operators, is guaranteed to be evaluated, even when the result of the entire expression is already known. This model is convenient when one or more operands of an expression are functions with side effects that alter the meaning of the program.

Short-circuit evaluation guarantees strict left-to-right evaluation and that evaluation stops as soon as the result of the entire expression becomes evident. This model is convenient in most cases, since it guarantees minimum execution time, and usually minimum code size. Short-circuit evaluation also makes possible the evaluation of constructs that would not otherwise be legal; for instance:

```
while (I<=Length(S)) and (S[I]<>' ') do Inc(I);
while (P<>nil) and (P^.Value<>5) do P:=P^.Next;
```

In both cases, the second test is not evaluated if the first test is False.

The evaluation model is controlled through the $B compiler directive. The default state is {$B-} (unless changed using the Options/Compiler menu), and in this state short-circuit evaluation code is generated. In the {$B+} state, complete evaluation code is generated.

Since standard Pascal does not specify which model should be used for Boolean expression evaluation, programs depending on either model being in effect are not truly portable. However, sacrificing portability is often worth gaining the execution speed and simplicity provided by the short-circuit model.

String Operator

The types of operands and results for string operation are shown in Table 6.6.

Table 6.6: String Operation

Operator	Operation	Operand Types	Result Type
+	concatenation	string type, char type, or packed string type	string type

Turbo Pascal allows the + operator to be used to concatenate two string operands. The result of the operation *s* + *t*, where *s* and *t* are of a string type, a char type, or a packed string type, is the concatenation of *s* and *t*. The result is compatible with any string type (but not with char types and packed string types). If the resulting string is longer than 255 characters, it is truncated after character 255.

Set Operators

The types of operands for set operations are shown in Table 6.7.

Table 6.7: Set Operations

Operator	Operation	Operand Types
+	union	compatible set types
–	difference	compatible set types
*	intersection	compatible set types

The results of set operations conform to the rules of set logic:

- An ordinal value *c* is in *a* + *b* only if *c* is in *a* or *b*.
- An ordinal value *c* is in *a* – *b* only if *c* is in *a* and not in *b*.
- An ordinal value *c* is in *a* * *b* only if *c* is in both *a* and *b*.

If the smallest ordinal value that is a member of the result of a set operation is *a* and the largest is *b*, then the type of the result is **set of** *a..b*.

Relational Operators

The types of operands and results for relational operations are shown in Table 6.8.

Table 6.8: Relational Operations

Operator Type	Operation	Operand Types	Result Type
=	equal	compatible simple, pointer, set, string, or packed string types	Boolean
<>	not equal	compatible simple, pointer, set, string, or packed string types	Boolean
<	less than	compatible simple, string, or packed string types	Boolean
>	greater than	compatible simple, string, or packed string types	Boolean
<=	less or equal	compatible simple, string, or packed string types	Boolean
>=	greater or equal	compatible simple, string, or packed string types	Boolean
<=	subset of	compatible set types	Boolean
>=	superset of	compatible set types	Boolean
in	member of	left operand: any ordinal type *t*; right operand: set whose base is compatible with *t*.	Boolean

Comparing Simple Types

When the operands of =, <>, <, >, >=, or <= are of simple types, they must be compatible types; however, if one operand is of a real type, the other can be of an integer type.

Comparing Strings

The relational operators =, <>, <, >, >=, and <= compare strings according to the ordering of the extended ASCII character set. Any two string values can be compared, because all string values are compatible.

A character-type value is compatible with a string-type value, and when the two are compared, the character-type value is treated as a string-type value with length 1. When a packed string-type value with *n* components is compared with a string-type value, it is treated as a string-type value with length *n*.

Comparing Packed Strings

The relational operators =, <>, <, >, >=, and <= can also be used to compare two packed string-type values if both have the same number of components. If the number of components is *n*, then the operation corresponds to comparing two strings, each of length *n*.

Comparing Pointers

The operators = and <> can be used on compatible pointer-type operands. Two pointers are equal only if they point to the same object.

Note: When comparing pointers, Turbo Pascal simply compares the segment and offset parts. Because of the segment mapping scheme of the 80×86 processors, two logically different pointers can in fact point to the same physical memory location. For instance, *Ptr*($0040,$0049) and *Ptr*($0000,$0449) are two pointers to the same physical address. Pointers returned by the standard procedures *New* and *GetMem* are always normalized (offset part in the range $0000 to $000F), and will therefore always compare correctly. When creating pointers with the *Ptr* standard function, special care must be taken if such pointers are to be compared.

Comparing Sets

If *a* and *b* are set operands, their comparisons produce these results:

- *a* = *b* is True only if *a* and *b* contain exactly the same members; otherwise, *a* <> *b*.
- *a* <= *b* is True only if every member of *a* is also a member of *b*.
- *a* >= *b* is True only if every member of *b* is also a member of *a*.

Testing Set Membership

The **in** operator returns *true* when the value of the ordinal-type operand is a member of the set-type operand; otherwise, it returns *false*.

The @ Operator

A pointer to a variable can be created with the @ operator. Table 6.9 shows the operand and result types.

Table 6.9: Pointer Operation

Operator	Operation	Operand Types	Result Type
@	Pointer formation	Variable reference or procedure or function identifier	Pointer (same as **nil**)

@ is a unary operator that takes a variable reference or a procedure or function identifier as its operand, and returns a pointer to the operand. The type of the value is the same as the type of **nil**, therefore it can be assigned to any pointer variable.

Note: Special rules apply to use of the @ operator with a procedural variable. For further details, refer to the "Procedural Types" section on page 84.

@ with a Variable

The use of @ with an ordinary variable (not a parameter) is uncomplicated. Given the declarations

```
type
  TwoChar = array[0..1] of char;
var
  Int: integer;
  TwoCharPtr: ^TwoChar;
```

then the statement

```
TwoCharPtr := @Int;
```

causes *TwoCharPtr* to point to *Int*. *TwoCharPtr^* becomes a re-interpretation of the value of *Int*, as though it were an `array[0..1] of char`.

@ with a Value Parameter

Applying @ to a formal value parameter results in a pointer to the stack location containing the actual value. Suppose *Foo* is a formal value parameter in a procedure and *FooPtr* is a pointer variable. If the procedure executes the statement

Chapter 6, Expressions

```
FooPtr := @Foo;
```

then *FooPtr^* references *Foo*'s value. However, *FooPtr^* does not reference *Foo* itself, rather it references the value that was taken from *Foo* and stored on the stack.

@ with a Variable Parameter

Applying @ to a formal variable parameter results in a pointer to the actual parameter (the pointer is taken from the stack). Suppose *One* is a formal variable parameter of a procedure, *Two* is a variable passed to the procedure as *One*'s actual parameter, and *OnePtr* is a pointer variable. If the procedure executes the statement

```
OnePtr := @One;
```

then *OnePtr* is a pointer to *Two*, and *OnePtr^* is a reference to *Two* itself.

@ with a Procedure or Function

You can apply @ to a procedure or a function to produce a pointer to its entry point. Turbo Pascal does not give you a mechanism for using such a pointer. The only use for a procedure pointer is to pass it to an assembly language routine or to use it in an **inline** statement. See "Turbo Assembler and Turbo Pascal" on page 200 for information on interfacing Turbo Assembler and Turbo Pascal.

Function Calls

A function call activates the function specified by the function identifier. Any identifier declared to denote a function is a function identifier.

The function call must have a list of actual parameters if the corresponding function declaration contains a list of formal parameters. Each parameter takes the place of the corresponding formal parameter according to parameter rules set forth in Chapter 10, "Input and Output."

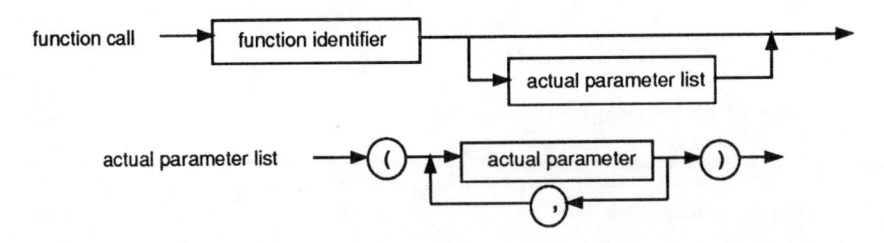

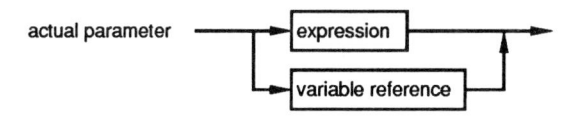

```
                 actual parameter ─────┬──▶┤ expression      ├──┬──▶
                                       │                        │
                                       └──▶┤ variable reference ├─┘
```

Some examples of function calls follow:

```
Sum(A,63)
Maximum(147,J)
Sin(X+Y)
Eof(F)
Volume(Radius,Height)
```

Note: A function can also be invoked via a procedural variable. For further details, refer to the "Procedural Types" section on page 84.

Set Constructors

A set constructor denotes a set-type value, and is formed by writing expressions within brackets ([]). Each expression denotes a value of the set.

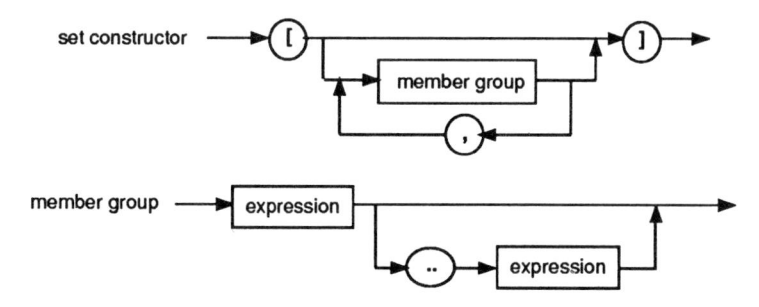

```
set constructor ──▶[──┬──────────────────────┬──▶]──▶
                      │   ┌──────────────┐   ▲
                      └──▶│ member group │───┤
                          └──────────────┘   │
                                  ▲          │
                                  └────,─────┘

member group ──▶┤ expression ├──┬────────────────────────▶
                                │                    ▲
                                └──▶ .. ──▶┤ expression ├─┘
```

The notation [ ] denotes the empty set, which is assignment-compatible with every set type. Any member group *x..y* denotes as set members all values in the range *x..y*. If *x* is greater than *y*, then *x..y* does not denote any members and [*x..y*] denotes the empty set.

All expression values in member groups in a particular set constructor must be of the same ordinal type.

Some examples of set constructors follow:

```
[red, C, green]
[1, 5, 10..K mod 12, 23]
['A'..'Z', 'a'..'z', Chr(Digit+48)]
```

Chapter 6, Expressions

Value Typecasts

The type of an expression can be changed to another type through a value typecast.

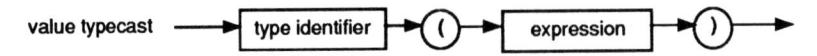

```
value typecast ─────▶ type identifier ─▶( ─▶ expression ─▶) ─▶
```

The expression type and the specified type must both be either ordinal types or pointer types. For ordinal types, the resulting value is obtained by converting the expression. The conversion may involve truncation or extension of the original value if the size of the specified type is different from that of the expression. In cases where the value is extended, the sign of the value is always preserved; that is, the value is sign-extended.

The syntax of a value typecast is almost identical to that of a variable typecast (see "Variable Typecasts" on page 42). However, value typecasts operate on values, not on variables, and can therefore not participate in variable references; that is, a value typecast may not be followed by qualifiers. In particular, value typecasts cannot appear on the left-hand side of an assignment statement.

Some examples of value typecasts include

```
integer('A')
char(48)
boolean(0)
Color(2)
Longint(@Buffer)
BytePtr(Ptr($40,$49))
```

CHAPTER

7

Statements

Statements describe algorithmic actions that can be executed. Labels can prefix statements, and these labels can be referenced by **goto** statements.

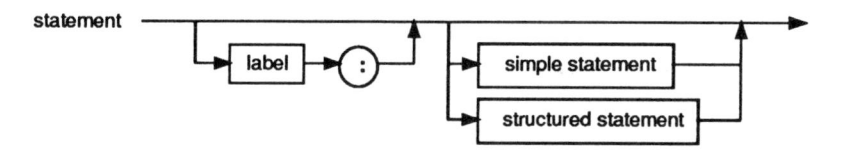

```
statement ──┬──────────────────────────────────────────┬──►
            │  ┌───────┐     ┌───┐  ┌──────────────────┐│
            └─►│ label │─►──(:)──┬►│ simple statement │┴►┤
               └───────┘         │ └──────────────────┘  │
                                 │ ┌──────────────────┐  │
                                 └►│structured statement│►┘
                                   └──────────────────┘
```

As you saw in Chapter 1, a label is either a digit sequence in the range 0 to 9999 or an identifier.

There are two main types of statements: simple statements and structured statements.

Simple Statements

A *simple* statement is a statement that doesn't contain any other statements.

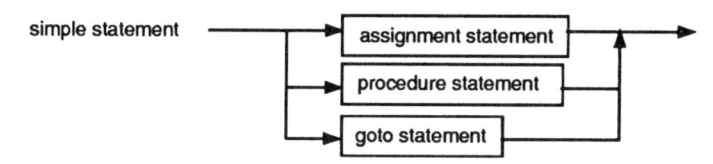

```
simple statement ──┬──►┌──────────────────────┐──┬──►
                   ├──►│ assignment statement │──┤
                   │   └──────────────────────┘  │
                   │   ┌──────────────────────┐  │
                   ├──►│ procedure statement  │──┤
                   │   └──────────────────────┘  │
                   │   ┌──────────────────────┐  │
                   └──►│   goto statement     │──┘
                       └──────────────────────┘
```

Assignment Statements

Assignment statements either replace the current value of a variable with a new value specified by an expression or specify an expression whose value is to be returned by a function.

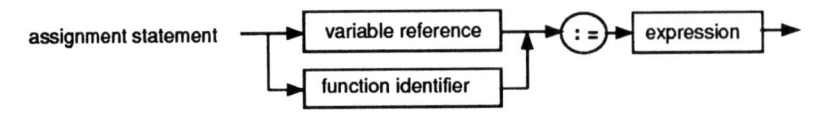

```
assignment statement ──▶─┬─▶ variable reference ──┬─▶( := )─▶ expression ─▶
                         └─▶ function identifier ─┘
```

The expression must be assignment-compatible with the type of the variable or the result type of the function (see the section "Type Compatibility" on page 34).

Some examples of assignment statements follow:

```
X    := Y+Z;
Done := (I>=1) and (I<100);
Hue1 := [blue,Succ(C)];
I    := Sqr(J) - I*K;
```

Procedure Statements

A **procedure** statement specifies the activation of the procedure denoted by the procedure identifier. If the corresponding procedure declaration contains a list of formal parameters, then the procedure statement must have a matching list of actual parameters (parameters listed in definitions are *formal* parameters; in the calling statement, they are *actual* parameters). The actual parameters are passed to the formal parameters as part of the call.

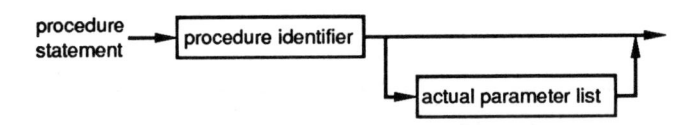

```
procedure
statement ──▶ procedure identifier ──┬──────────────────────▶
                                     └─▶ actual parameter list ─┘
```

Some examples of procedure statements follow:

```
PrintHeading;
Transpose(A,N,M);
Find(Name,Address);
```

Note: A procedure can also be invoked via a procedural variable. For further details, refer to the "Procedural Types" section on page 84.

Goto Statements

A **goto** statement transfers program execution to the statement prefixed by the label referenced in the **goto** statement. The syntax diagram of a **goto** statement follows:

The following rules should be observed when using **goto** statements:

- The label referenced by a **goto** statement must be in the same block as the **goto** statement. In other words, it is not possible to jump into or out of a procedure or function.
- Jumping into a structured statement from outside that structured statement (that is, jumping to a "deeper" level of nesting) can have undefined effects, although the compiler will not indicate an error.

Structured Statements

Structured statements are constructs composed of other statements that are to be executed in sequence (compound and **with** statements), conditionally (conditional statements), or repeatedly (repetitive statements).

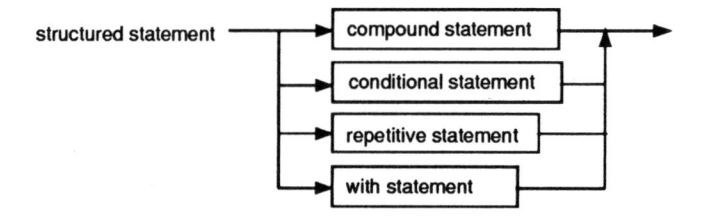

Compound Statements

The compound statement specifies that its component statements are to be executed in the same sequence as they are written. The component statements are treated as one statement, crucial in contexts where the Pascal syntax only allows one statement. **begin** and **end** bracket the statements, which are separated by semicolons.

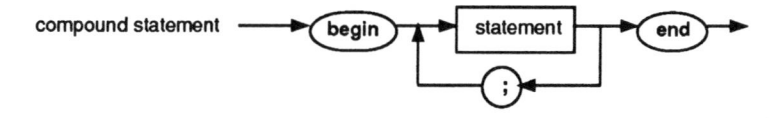

Chapter 7, Statements

Here's an example of a compound statement:

```
begin
  Z := X;
  X := Y;
  Y := Z;
end;
```

Conditional Statements

A conditional statement selects for execution a single one (or none) of its component statements.

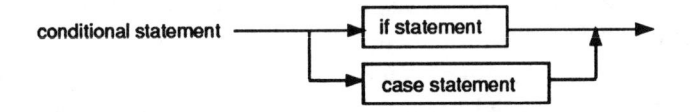

```
conditional statement ──┬─→ if statement ───┬─→
                        └─→ case statement ─┘
```

If Statements

The syntax for an **if** statement reads like this:

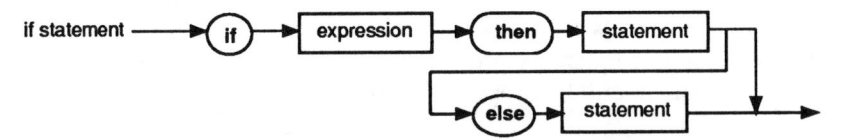

```
if statement ──→(if)──→[expression]──→(then)──→[statement]──┬──→
                                   └──→(else)──→[statement]─┘
```

The expression must yield a result of the standard type boolean. If the expression produces the value *true*, then the statement following **then** is executed.

If the expression produces *false* and the **else** part is present, the statement following **else** is executed; if the **else** part is not present, nothing is executed.

The syntactic ambiguity arising from the construct

```
if e1 then if e2 then s1 else s2
```

is resolved by interpreting the construct as follows:

```
if e1 then
begin
  if e2 then
    s1
  else
    s2
end
```

68   Turbo Pascal Reference Guide

In general, an **else** is associated with the closest **if** not already associated with an **else**.

Two examples of **if** statements follow:

```
if X < 1.5 then
    Z := X+Y
else
    Z := 1.5;

if P1 <> nil then
    P1 := P1^.father;
```

Case Statements

The **case** statement consists of an expression (the selector) and a list of statements, each prefixed with one or more constants (called case constants) or with the word **else**. The selector must be of an ordinal type, and the ordinal values of the upper and lower bounds of that type must be within the range –32768 to 32767. Thus, string types and the integer types longint and word are invalid selector types. All **case** constants must be unique and of an ordinal type compatible with the selector type.

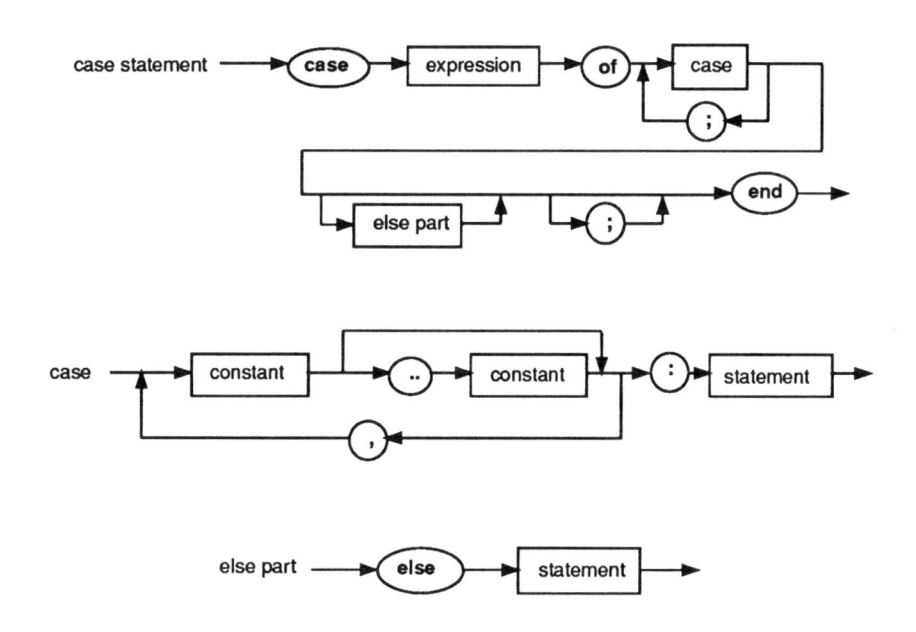

The **case** statement executes the statement prefixed by a **case** constant equal to the value of the selector or a **case** range containing the value of the selector. If no such **case** constant of the **case** range exists and an **else** part is

Chapter 7, Statements

present, the statement following **else** is executed. If there is no **else** part, nothing is executed.

Examples of **case** statements follow:

```
case Operator of
  plus:   X := X+Y;
  minus:  X := X-Y;
  times:  X := X*Y;
end;

case I of
  0,2,4,6,8: Writeln('Even digit');
  1,3,5,7,9: Writeln('Odd digit');
  10..100:   Writeln('Between 10 and 100');
else
  Writeln('Negative or greater than 100');
end;
```

Repetitive Statements

Repetitive statements specify certain statements to be executed repeatedly.

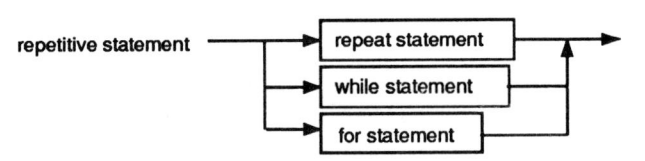

If the number of repetitions is known beforehand, the **for** statement is the appropriate construct. Otherwise, the **while** or **repeat** statement should be used.

Repeat Statements

A **repeat** statement contains an expression that controls the repeated execution of a statement sequence within that **repeat** statement.

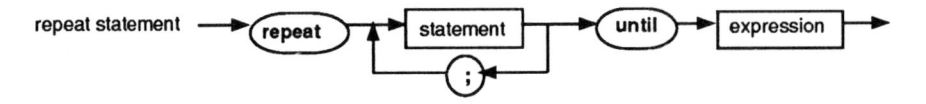

The expression must produce a result of type boolean. The statements between the symbols **repeat** and **until** are executed in sequence until, at the end of a sequence, the expression yields *true*. The sequence is executed at least once, because the expression is evaluated *after* the execution of each sequence.

Examples of **repeat** statements follow:

```
repeat
  K := I mod J;
  I := J;
  J := K;
until J = 0;

repeat
  Write('Enter value (0..9): ');
  Readln(I);
until (I >= 0) and (I <= 9);
```

While Statements

A **while** statement contains an expression that controls the repeated execution of a statement (which can be a compound statement).

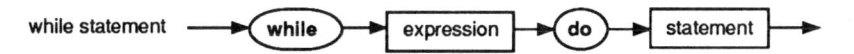

while statement ⟶ (while) ⟶ [expression] ⟶ (do) ⟶ [statement] ⟶

The expression controlling the repetition must be of type *boolean*. It is evaluated *before* the contained statement is executed. The contained statement is executed repeatedly as long as the expression is *true*. If the expression is *false* at the beginning, the statement is not executed at all.

Examples of **while** statements include:

```
while Data[I] <> X do I := I + 1;

while I > 0 do
begin
  if Odd(I) then Z := Z * X;
  I := I div 2;
  X := Sqr(X);
end;

while not Eof(InFile) do
begin
  Readln(InFile,Line);
  Process(Line);
end;
```

Chapter 7, Statements

For Statements

The **for** statement causes a statement (which can be a compound statement) to be repeatedly executed while a progression of values is assigned to a control variable.

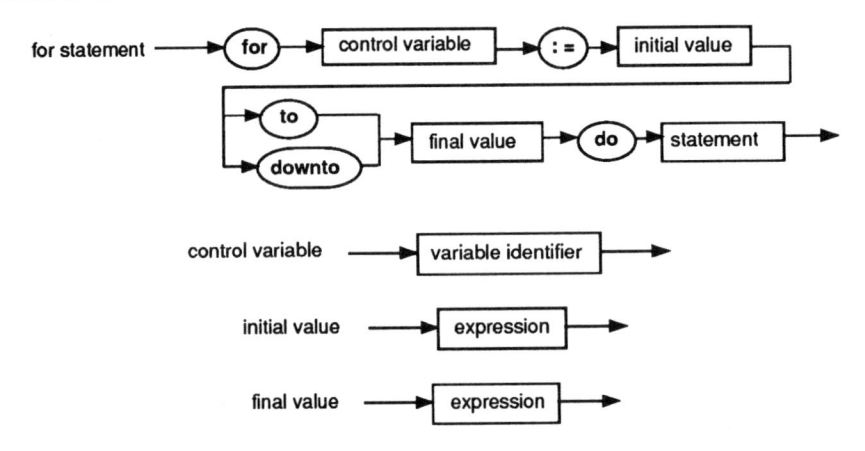

```
for statement ──▶( for )──▶[ control variable ]──▶( := )──▶[ initial value ]──┐
                                                                               │
        ┌──────────────────────────────────────────────────────────────────────┘
        │    ┌──( to )────┐
        └───▶┤            ├──▶[ final value ]──▶( do )──▶[ statement ]──▶
             └──(downto)──┘

control variable  ──▶[ variable identifier ]──▶

initial value     ──▶[ expression ]──▶

final value       ──▶[ expression ]──▶
```

The control variable must be a variable identifier (without any qualifier) that signifies a variable declared to be local to the block containing the **for** statement. The control variable must be of an ordinal type. The initial and final values must be of a type assignment-compatible with the ordinal type.

When a **for** statement is entered, the initial and final values are determined once for the remainder of the execution of the **for** statement.

The statement contained by the **for** statement is executed once for every value in the range *initial value* to *final value*. The control variable always starts off at *initial value*. When a **for** statement uses **to**, the value of the control variable is incremented by one for each repetition. If *initial value* is greater than *final value*, the contained statement is not executed. When a **for** statement uses **downto**, the value of the control variable is decremented by one for each repetition. If *initial value* value is less than *final value*, the contained statement is not executed.

It's an error if the contained statement alters the value of the control variable. After a **for** statement is executed, the value of the control variable value is undefined, unless execution of the **for** statement was interrupted by a **goto** from the **for** statement.

With these restrictions in mind, the **for** statement

    for V := Expr1 **to** Expr2 **do** Body;

is equivalent to

    begin

```
      Temp1 := Expr1;
      Temp2 := Expr2;
      if Temp1 <= Temp2 then
      begin
        V := Temp1;
        Body;
        while V <> Temp2 do
        begin
          V := Succ(V);
          Body;
        end;
      end;
    end;
```

and the **for** statement

```
    for V := Expr1 downto Expr2 do Body;
```

is equivalent to

```
    begin
      Temp1 := Expr1;
      Temp2 := Expr2;
      if Temp1 >= Temp2 then
      begin
        V := Temp1;
        Body;
        while V <> Temp2 do
        begin
          V := Pred(V);
          Body;
        end;
      end;
    end;
```

where *Temp1* and *Temp2* are auxiliary variables of the host type of the variable *V* and don't occur elsewhere in the program.

Examples of **for** statements follow:

```
    for I := 2 to 63 do
      if Data[I] > Max then Max := Data[I]
    for I := 1 to 10 do
      for J := 1 to 10 do
      begin
        X := 0;
        for K := 1 to 10 do
          X := X + Mat1[I,K] * Mat2[K,J];
        Mat[I,J] := X;
      end;

    for C := red to blue do Check(C);
```

With Statements

The **with** statement is shorthand for referencing the fields of a record. Within a **with** statement, the fields of one or more specific record variables can be referenced using their field identifiers only. The syntax of a **with** statement follows:

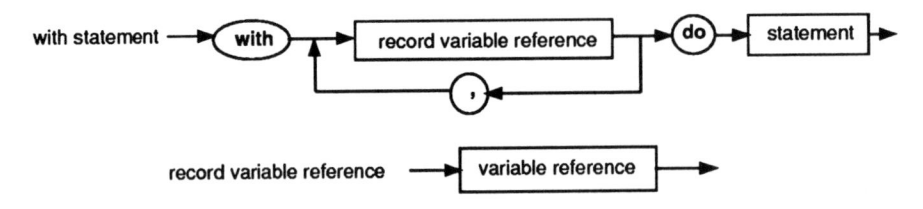

```
with statement ──▶( with )──▶┬─▶[ record variable reference ]─┬─▶( do )──▶[ statement ]──▶
                              ◀──────────( , )◀───────────────┘

record variable reference ──▶[ variable reference ]──▶
```

Following is an example of a **with** statement:

```
with Date do
  if month = 12 then
  begin
    month := 1;
    year  := year + 1
  end
  else
    month := month + 1;
```

This is equivalent to

```
if Date.month = 12 then
begin
  Date.month := 1;
  Date.year  := Date.year + 1
end
else
  Date.month := Date.month + 1;
```

Within a **with** statement, each variable reference is first checked to see if it can be interpreted as a field of the record. If so, it is always interpreted as such, even if a variable with the same name is also accessible. Suppose the following declarations have been made:

```
type
  Point = record
            x,y: integer;
          end;
var
  x: Point;
  y: integer;
```

74 Turbo Pascal Reference Guide

In this case, both *x* and *y* can refer to a variable or to a field of the record. In the statement

```
with x do
begin
  x := 10;
  y := 25;
end;
```

the *x* between **with** and **do** refers to the variable of type *Point,* but in the compound statement, *x* and *y* refer to *x.x* and *x.y*.

The statement

```
with V1,V2, ... Vn do s;
```

is equivalent to

```
with V1 do
  with V2 do
    ....
      with Vn do
        S;
```

In both cases, if *Vn* is a field of both *V1* and *V2*, it is interpreted as *V2.Vn*, not *V1.Vn*.

If the selection of a record variable involves indexing an array or dereferencing a pointer, these actions are executed once before the component statement is executed.

CHAPTER 8

Procedures and Functions

Procedures and functions allow you to nest additional blocks in the main program block. Each procedure or function declaration has a heading followed by a block. A procedure is activated by a procedure statement; a function is activated by the evaluation of an expression that contains its call and returns a value to that expression.

This chapter discusses the different types of procedure and function declarations and their parameters.

Procedure Declarations

A procedure declaration associates an identifier with a block as a procedure; that procedure can then be activated by a procedure statement.

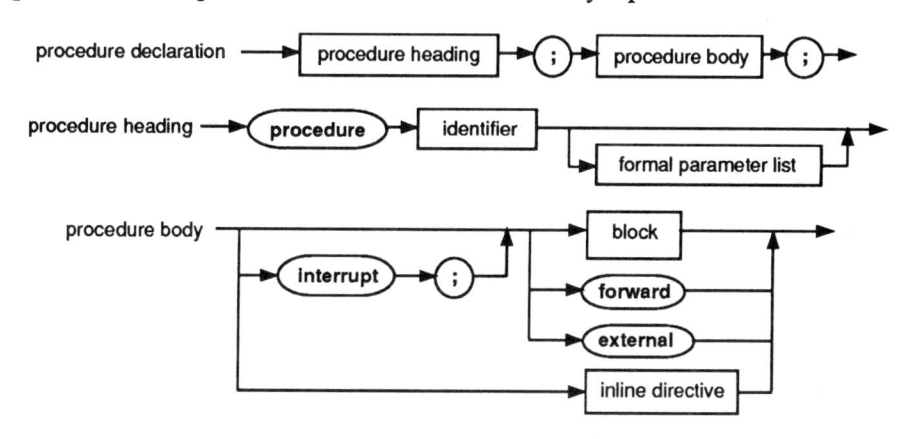

procedure declaration → procedure heading → ; → procedure body → ;

procedure heading → procedure → identifier → formal parameter list

procedure body → interrupt → ; → block / forward / external / inline directive

The procedure heading names the procedure's identifier and specifies the formal parameters (if any). The syntax for a formal parameter list is shown in the section "Parameters" on page 82.

A procedure is activated by a procedure statement, which states the procedure's identifier and any actual parameters required. The statements to be executed on activation are noted in the statement part of the procedure's block. If the procedure's identifier is used in a procedure statement within the procedure's block, the procedure is executed recursively (it calls itself while executing).

Here's an example of a procedure declaration:

```
procedure NumString(N: integer; var S: string);
var
  V: integer;
begin
  V := Abs(N);
  S := '';
  repeat
    S := Chr(N mod 10 + Ord('0')) + S;
    N := N div 10;
  until N = 0;
  if N < 0 then S := '-' + S;
end;
```

A procedure declaration can optionally specify an **interrupt** directive before the block, and the procedure is then considered an interrupt procedure. Interrupt procedures are described in full in Chapter 15, "Inside Turbo Pascal." For now, note that interrupt procedures cannot be called from procedure statements, and that every interrupt procedure must specify a parameter list exactly like the following:

```
procedure MyInt(Flags,CS,IP,AX,BX,CX,DX,SI,DI,DS,ES,BP: word);
interrupt;
```

Instead of the block in a procedure or function declaration, you can write a **forward**, **external**, or **inline** declaration.

Forward Declarations

A procedure declaration that specifies the directive **forward** instead of a block is a **forward** declaration. Somewhere after this declaration, the procedure must be defined by a *defining* declaration—a procedure declaration that uses the same procedure identifier but omits the formal parameter list and includes a block. The **forward** declaration and the defining declaration must appear in the same procedure and function declaration part. Other procedures and functions can be declared between them, and they can call the forward-declared procedure. Mutual recursion is thus possible.

The **forward** declaration and the defining declaration constitute a complete procedure declaration. The procedure is considered declared at the **forward** declaration.

An example of a **forward** declaration follows:

```
procedure Walter(m,n : integer); forward;
procedure Clara(x,y : real);
begin
  :
  Walter(4,5);
  :
end;
procedure Walter;
begin
  :
  Clara(8.3,2.4);
  :
end;
```

A procedure's defining declaration can be an **external** declaration; however, it cannot be an **inline** declaration or another **forward** declaration. Likewise, the defining declaration cannot specify an **interrupt** directive.

Forward declarations are not allowed in the interface part of a unit.

External Declarations

External declarations allow you to interface with separately compiled procedures and functions written in assembly language. The **external** code must be linked with the Pascal program or unit through {$L *filename*} directives. For further details on linking with assembly language, refer to Chapter 15.

Examples of **external** procedure declarations follow:

```
procedure MoveWord(var source,dest; count: word); external;
procedure MoveLong(var source,dest; count: word); external;

procedure FillWord(var dest; data: integer; count: word); external;
procedure FillLong(var dest; data: longint; count: word); external;
{$L BLOCK.OBJ}
```

You should use **external** procedures when you need to incorporate substantial amounts of assembly code. If you only require small amounts of code, use **inline** procedures instead.

Inline Declarations

The **inline** directive permits you to write machine code instructions instead of the block. When a normal procedure is called, the compiler generates code that pushes the procedure's parameters onto the stack, and then generates a CALL instruction to call the procedure. When you "call" an **inline** procedure, the compiler generates code from the inline directive instead of the CALL. Thus, an **inline** procedure is "expanded" every time you refer to it, just like a macro in assembly language. Here's a short example of two **inline** procedures:

```
procedure DisableInterrupts; inline($FA);   { CLI }
procedure EnableInterrupts; inline($FB);    { STI }
```

Inline procedures are described in full in Chapter 15, "Inside Turbo Pascal."

Function Declarations

A **function** declaration defines a part of the program that computes and returns a value.

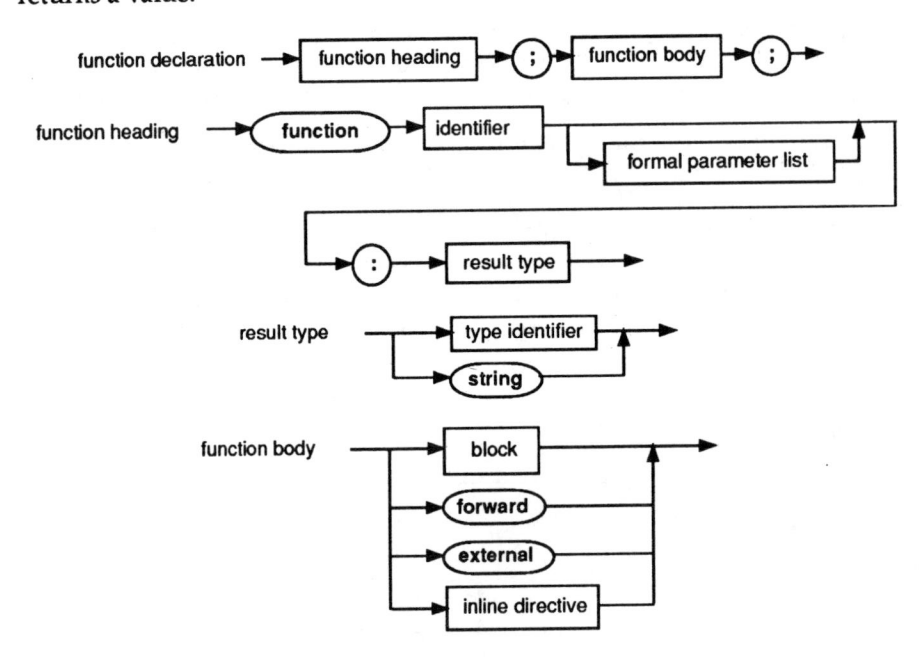

```
function declaration → function heading → ; → function body → ;

function heading → function → identifier → formal parameter list
                                        → : → result type →

result type → type identifier
           → string

function body → block
             → forward
             → external
             → inline directive
```

The **function** heading specifies the identifier for the function, the formal parameters (if any), and the function result type.

A function is activated by the evaluation of a **function** call. The **function** call gives the function's identifier and any actual parameters required by the function. A **function** call appears as an operand in an expression. When the expression is evaluated, the function is executed, and the value of the operand becomes the value returned by the function.

The statement part of the function's block specifies the statements to be executed upon activation of the function. The block should contain at least one assignment statement that assigns a value to the function identifier. The result of the function is the last value assigned. If no such assignment statement exists or if it is not executed, the value returned by the function is unspecified.

If the function's identifier is used in a function call within the function's block, the function is executed recursively.

Following are examples of **function** declarations:

```
function Max(a: Vector; n: integer): extended;
var
  x: extended;
  i: integer;
begin
  x := a[1];
  for i := 2 to n do
    if x < a[i] then x := a[i];
  Max := x;
end;

function Power(x: extended; y: integer): extended;
var
  z: extended;
  i: integer;
begin
  z := 1.0; i := y;
  while i > 0 do
  begin
    if Odd(i) then z := z * x;
    i := i div 2;
    x := Sqr(x);
  end;
  Power := z;
end;
```

Like procedures, functions can be declared as **forward**, **external**, or **inline**; however, **interrupt** functions are not allowed.

Chapter 8, Procedures and Functions

Parameters

The declaration of a procedure or function specifies a formal parameter list. Each parameter declared in a formal parameter list is local to the procedure or function being declared, and can be referred to by its identifier in the block associated with the procedure or function.

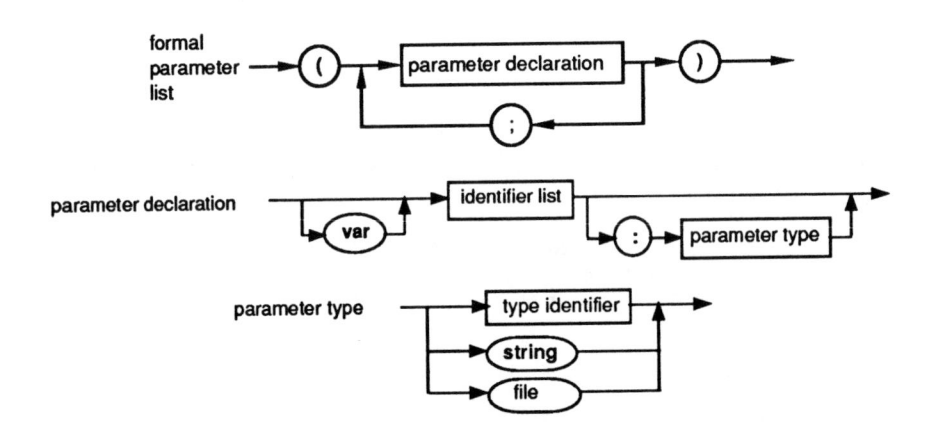

```
formal
parameter  ─→( ─┬─→ parameter declaration ─┬─→ ) ─→
list             │                          │
                 └──────────  ;  ←──────────┘

parameter declaration ──┬─────────┬──→ identifier list ──→ : ──→ parameter type ──→
                        └→ var ──→┘

parameter type ──┬──→ type identifier ──┬──→
                 ├──→ string ───────────┤
                 └──→ file ─────────────┘
```

There are three kinds of parameters: *value*, *variable*, and *untyped variable*. They are characterized as follows:

- A parameter group without a preceding **var** and followed by a type is a list of value parameters.
- A parameter group preceded by **var** and followed by a type is a list of variable parameters.
- A parameter group preceded by **var** and not followed by a type is a list of untyped variable parameters.

Value Parameters

A formal value parameter acts like a variable local to the procedure or function, except that it gets its initial value from the corresponding actual parameter upon activation of the procedure or function. Changes made to a formal value parameter do not affect the value of the actual parameter.

A value parameter's corresponding actual parameter in a procedure statement or function call must be an expression, and its value must not be of file type or of any structured type that contains a file type.

The actual parameter must be assignment-compatible with the type of the formal value parameter. If the parameter type is **string**, then the formal parameter is given a size attribute of 255.

Variable Parameters

A variable parameter is employed when a value must be passed from a procedure or function to the caller. The corresponding actual parameter in a procedure statement or function call must be a variable reference. The formal variable parameter represents the actual variable during the activation of the procedure or function, so any changes to the value of the formal variable parameter are reflected in the actual parameter.

Within the procedure or function, any reference to the formal variable parameter accesses the actual parameter itself. The type of the actual parameter must be identical to the type of the formal variable parameter (you can bypass this restriction through untyped variable parameters). If the formal parameter type is **string**, it is given the length attribute 255, and the actual variable parameter must be a string type with a length attribute of 255.

File types can only be passed as variable parameters.

If referencing an actual variable parameter involves indexing an array or finding the object of a pointer, these actions are executed before the activation of the procedure or function.

Untyped Variable Parameters

When a formal parameter is an untyped variable parameter, the corresponding actual parameter may be any variable reference, regardless of its type.

Within the procedure or function, the untyped variable parameter is typeless; that is, it is incompatible with variables of all other types, unless it is given a specific type through a variable typecast.

An example of untyped variable parameters follows:

```
function Equal(var source,dest; size: word): boolean;
type
  Bytes = array[0..MaxInt] of byte;
var
  N: integer;
begin
  N := 0;
  while (N<size) and (Bytes(dest)[N] <> Bytes(source)[N]) do Inc(N);
```

```
    Equal := N = size;
end;
```

This function can be used to compare any two variables of any size. For instance, given the declarations

```
type
  Vector = array[1..10] of integer;
  Point  = record
             x,y: integer;
           end;
var
  Vec1,Vec2: Vector;
  N: integer;
  P: Point;
```

then the function calls

```
Equal(Vec1,Vec2,SizeOf(Vector))
Equal(Vec1,Vec2,SizeOf(integer)*N)
Equal(Vec[1],Vec1[6],SizeOf(integer)*5)
Equal(Vec1[1],P,4)
```

compare *Vec1* to *Vec2*, compare the first *N* components of *Vec1* to the first *N* components of *Vec2*, compare the first five components of *Vec1* to the last five components of *Vec1*, and compare *Vec1[1]* to *P.x* and *Vec1[2]* to *P.y*.

Procedural Types

As an extension to Standard Pascal, Turbo Pascal allows procedures and functions to be treated as objects that can be assigned to variables and passed as parameters; *procedural types* make this possible.

Procedural Type Declarations

A procedural type declaration specifies the parameters and, for a function, the result type.

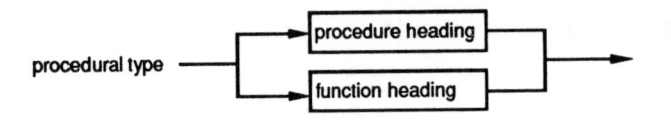

```
procedural type ──┬── procedure heading ──┬──►
                  └── function heading  ──┘
```

In essence, the syntax for writing a procedural type declaration is exactly the same as for writing a procedure or function header, except that the identifier after the **procedure** or **function** keyword is omitted. Some examples of procedural type declarations follow:

```
type
  Proc       = procedure;
  SwapProc   = procedure(var X,Y: integer);
  StrProc    = procedure(S: string);
  MathFunc   = function(X: real): real;
  DeviceFunc = function(var F: text): integer;
  MaxFunc    = function(A,B: real; F: MathFunc): real;
```

The parameter names in a procedural type declaration are purely decorative—they have no effect on the meaning of the declaration.

Note: Turbo Pascal does not allow you to declare functions that return procedural type values; a function result value must be a string, real, integer, char, boolean, pointer, or a user-defined enumeration.

Procedural Variables

Once a procedural type has been defined, it becomes possible to declare variables of that type. Such variables are called *procedural variables*. For example, given the preceding type declarations, the following variables can be declared:

```
var
  P: SwapProc;
  F: MathFunc;
```

Like an integer variable that can be assigned an integer value, a procedural variable can be assigned a *procedural value*. Such a value can of course be another procedural variable, but it can also be a procedure or a function identifier. In this context, a procedure or function declaration can be viewed as a special kind of constant declaration, the value of the constant being the procedure or function. For example, given the following procedure and function declarations,

```
{$F+}
procedure Swap(var A,B: integer);
var
  Temp: integer;
begin
  Temp := A; A := B; B := Temp;
end;

function Tan(Angle: real): real;
begin
  Tan := Sin(Angle) / Cos(Angle);
end;

{$F-}
```

Chapter 8, Procedures and Functions

The variables *P* and *F* declared previously can now be assigned values:

```
P := Swap;
F := Tan;
```

Following these assignments, the call `P(I,J)` is equivalent to `Swap(I,J)`, and `F(X)` is equivalent to `Tan(X)`.

As in any other assignment operation, the variable on the left and the value on the right must be assignment-compatible. To be considered assignment-compatible, procedural types must have the same number of parameters, and parameters in corresponding positions must be of identical types; finally, the result types of functions must be identical. As mentioned previously, parameter names are of no significance when it comes to procedural-type compatibility.

In addition to being of a compatible type, a procedure or function must satisfy the following requirements if it is to be assigned to a procedural variable:

- It must be compiled in the {$F+} state.
- It cannot be
  - a standard procedure or function.
  - a nested procedure or function.
  - an **inline** procedure or function.
  - an **interrupt** procedure or function.

The easiest way to satisfy the {$F+} requirement is simply to place a {$F+} compiler directive at the beginning of the source text (or to set the **O/C/Force Far Calls** switch to On in the IDE).

Standard procedures and functions are the procedures and functions declared by the *System* unit, such as *Writeln*, *Readln*, *Chr*, and *Ord*. To use a standard procedure or function with a procedural variable, you will have to write a "shell" around it. For example, given the procedural type

```
type
  IntProc = procedure(N: integer);
```

the following is an assignment-compatible procedure to write an integer:

```
procedure WriteInt(Number: integer);
begin
  Write(Number);
end;
```

Nested procedures and function cannot be used with procedural variables. A procedure or function is nested when it is declared within another procedure or function. In the following example, *Inner* is nested within *Outer*, and *Inner* cannot therefore be assigned to a procedural variable.

```
program Nested;
procedure Outer;
procedure Inner;
begin
  Writeln('Inner is nested');
end;
begin
  Inner;
end;
begin
  Outer;
end.
```

The use of procedural types is not restricted to simple procedural variables. Like any other type, a procedural type can participate in the declaration of a structured type, as demonstrated by the following declarations:

```
type
  GotoProc  = procedure(X,Y: integer);
  ProcList  = array[1..10] of GotoProc;
  WindowPtr = ^WindowRec;
  WindowRec = record
                Next: WindowPtr;
                Header: string[31];
                Top,Left,Bottom,Right: integer;
                SetCursor: GotoProc;
              end;
var
  P: ProcList;
  W: WindowPtr;
```

Given the preceding declarations, the following statements are valid procedure calls:

```
P[3](1,1);
W^.SetCursor(10,10);
```

When a procedural value is assigned to a procedural variable, what physically takes place is that the address of the procedure is stored in the variable. In fact, a procedural variable is much like a pointer variable, except that instead of pointing to data, it points to a procedure or function. Like a pointer, a procedural variable occupies 4 bytes (two words), containing a memory address. The first word stores the offset part of the address, and the second word stores the segment part.

Procedural Type Parameters

Since procedural types are allowed in any context, it is possible to declare procedures or functions that take procedures or functions as parameters.

The following program demonstrates the use of a procedural type parameter to output three tables of different arithmetic functions:

```
program Tables;

type
  Func = function(X,Y: integer): integer;

{$F+}

function Add(X,Y: integer): integer;
begin
  Add := X + Y;
end;

function Multiply(X,Y: integer): integer;
begin
  Multiply := X * Y;
end;

function Funny(X,Y: integer): integer;
begin
  Funny := (X+Y) * (X-Y);
end;

{$F-}

procedure PrintTable(W,H: integer; Operation: Func);
var
  X,Y: integer;
begin
  for Y := 1 to H do
  begin
    for X := 1 to W do Write(Operation(X,Y):5);
    Writeln;
  end;
  Writeln;
end;

begin
  PrintTable(10,10,Add);
  PrintTable(10,10,Multiply);
  PrintTable(10,10,Funny);
end.
```

When run, the *Tables* program outputs three tables. The second one looks like this:

```
  1   2   3   4   5   6   7   8   9  10
  2   4   6   8  10  12  14  16  18  20
  3   6   9  12  15  18  21  24  27  30
  4   8  12  16  20  24  28  32  36  40
  5  10  15  20  25  30  35  40  45  50
  6  12  18  24  30  36  42  48  54  60
  7  14  21  28  35  42  49  56  63  70
```

```
 8  16  24  32  40  48  56  64  72   80
 9  18  27  36  45  54  63  72  81   90
10  20  30  40  50  60  70  80  90  100
```

Procedural type parameters are particularly useful in situations where a certain common action is to be carried out on a set of procedures or functions. In this case, the *PrintTable* procedure represents the common action to be carried out on the *Add*, *Multiply*, and *Funny* functions.

If a procedure or function is to be passed as a parameter, it must conform to the same type-compatibility rules as in an assignment. Thus, such procedures and functions must be compiled with {$F+}, they cannot be built-in routines, they cannot be nested, and they cannot be declared with the **inline** or **interrupt** attributes.

Procedural Types in Expressions

In general, the use of a procedural variable in a statement or an expression denotes a call of the procedure or function stored in the variable. There is however one exception: When Turbo Pascal sees a procedural variable on the left-hand side of an assignment statement, it knows that the right-hand side has to represent a procedural value. For example, consider the following program:

```
{$F+}

type
  IntFunc = function: integer;

var
  F: IntFunc;
  N: integer;

function ReadInt: integer;
var
  I: integer;
begin
  Read(I);
  ReadInt := I;
end;

begin
  F := ReadInt;                    { Assign procedural value }
  N := ReadInt;                    { Assign function result }
end.
```

The first statement in the main program assigns the procedural value (address of) *ReadInt* to the procedural variable *F*, where the second statement calls *ReadInt*, and assigns the returned value to *N*. The distinction

Chapter 8, Procedures and Functions   89

between getting the procedural value or calling the function is made by the type of the variable being assigned (*F* or *N*).

Unfortunately, there are situations where the compiler cannot determine the desired action from the context. For example, in the following statement, there is no obvious way the compiler can know if it should compare the procedural value in *F* to the procedural value of *ReadInt*, to determine if *F* currently points to *ReadInt*, or whether it should call *F* and *ReadInt*, and then compare the returned values.

```
if F = ReadInt then WriteLn('Equal');
```

However, standard Pascal syntax specifies that the occurrence of a function identifier in an expression denotes a call to that function, so the effect of the preceding statement is to call *F* and *ReadInt*, and then compare the returned values. To compare the procedural value in *F* to the procedural value of *ReadInt*, the following construct must be used:

```
if @F = @ReadInt then Writeln('Equal');
```

When applied to a procedural variable or a procedure or function identifier, the address (@) operator prevents the compiler from calling the procedure, and at the same time converts the argument into a pointer. Thus, @*F* converts *F* into an untyped pointer variable that contains an address, and @*ReadInt* returns the address of *ReadInt*; the two pointer values can then be compared to determine if *F* currently refers to *ReadInt*.

Note: To get the memory address of a procedural variable, rather than the address stored in it, a double address (@@) operator must be used. For example, where @*P* means convert *P* into an untyped pointer variable, @@*P* means return the physical address of the variable *P*.

Turbo Pascal fully supports variable typecasts involving procedural types. For example, given the declarations

```
type
  Func = function(X: integer): integer;
var
  F: Func;
  P: Pointer;
  N: integer;
```

you can construct the following assignments:

```
F := Func(P);            { Assign procedural value in P to F }
Func(P) := F;            { Assign procedural value in F to P }
@F := P;                 { Assign pointer value in P to F }
P := @F;                 { Assign pointer value in F to P }
N := F(N);               { Call function via F }
N := Func(P)(N);         { Call function via P }
```

In particular, notice that the address operator (@), when applied to a procedural variable, can be used on the left-hand side of an assignment. Also, notice the typecast on the last line to call a function via a pointer variable.

C H A P T E R 9

Programs and Units

Program Syntax

A Turbo Pascal program takes the form of a procedure declaration except for its heading and an optional **uses** clause.

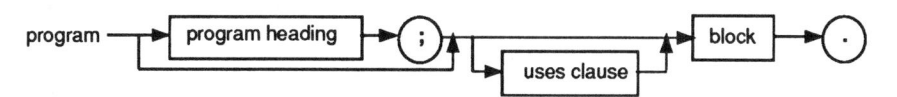

```
program → program heading → ; → uses clause → block → .
```

The Program Heading

The program heading specifies the program's name and its parameters.

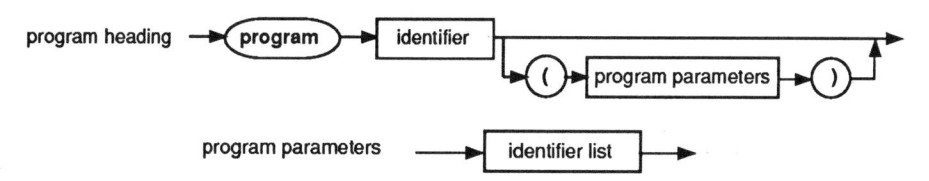

```
program heading → program → identifier → ( → program parameters → )

program parameters → identifier list
```

The program heading, if present, is purely decorative and is ignored by the compiler.

The Uses Clause

The **uses** clause identifies all units used by the program, including units used directly and units used by those units.

```
uses clause ──▶( uses )─┬─▶[ identifier ]─┬─▶( ; )─▶
                        ▲                 │
                        └──────( , )◀─────┘
```

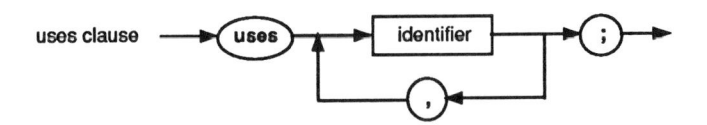

The *System* unit is always used automatically. *System* implements all low-level, run-time support routines to support such features as file I/O, string handling, floating point, dynamic memory allocation, and others.

Apart from *System*, Turbo Pascal implements many standard units, such as *Printer*, *Dos*, and *Crt*. These are not used automatically; you must include them in your **uses** clause, for instance,

    uses Dos,Crt;   { Can now access facilities in Dos and Crt }

The standard units are described in Chapter 12, "Standard Units."

To locate a unit specified in a **uses** clause, the compiler first checks the resident units—those units loaded into memory at startup from the TURBO.TPL file. If the unit is not among the resident units, the compiler assumes it must be on disk. The name of the file is assumed to be the unit name with extension .TPU. It is first searched for in the current directory, and then in the directories specified with the O/D/Unit Directories menu command or in a /U directive on the TPC command line. For instance, the construct

    uses Memory;

where *Memory* is not a resident unit, causes the compiler to look for the file MEMORY.TPU in the current directory, and then in each of the unit directories.

When the Compile/Make and Compile/Build commands compile the units specified in a **uses** clause, the source files are searched for in the same way as the .TPU files, and the name of a given unit's source file is assumed to be the unit name with extension .PAS.

Unit Syntax

Units are the basis of modular programming in Turbo Pascal. They are used to create libraries that you can include in various programs without making the source code available, and to divide large programs into logically related modules.

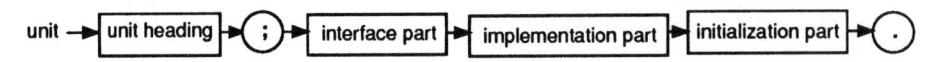

```
unit ──▶[ unit heading ]─▶( ; )─▶[ interface part ]─▶[ implementation part ]─▶[ initialization part ]─▶( . )
```

The Unit Heading

The unit heading specifies the unit's name.

```
unit heading ──▶( unit )──▶[ unit identifier ]──▶
```

The unit name is used when referring to the unit in a **uses** clause. The name must be unique—two units with the same name cannot be used at the same time.

The Interface Part

The interface part declares constants, types, variables, procedures, and functions that are *public*, that is, available to the host (the program or unit using the unit). The host can access these entities as if they were declared in a block that encloses the host.

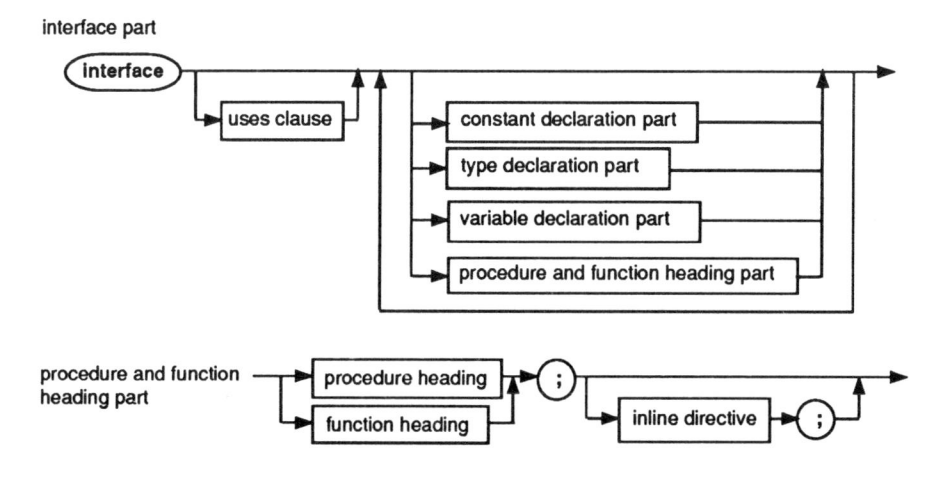

```
interface part

──( interface )──┬──────────────────────────────────────────┬──▶
                 ├─▶[ uses clause ]─┐                        │
                                    ├─▶[ constant declaration part ]─┤
                                    ├─▶[ type declaration part ]─────┤
                                    ├─▶[ variable declaration part ]─┤
                                    └─▶[ procedure and function heading part ]─┘
```

```
procedure and function     ┌─▶[ procedure heading ]─┐       ┌─▶[ inline directive ]─┐
heading part          ────┤                         ├─( ; )─┤                        ├─( ; )──▶
                           └─▶[ function heading ]──┘       └────────────────────────┘
```

Unless a procedure or function is **inline**, the interface part only lists the procedure or function heading. The block of the procedure or function follows in the implementation part.

The Implementation Part

The implementation part defines the block of all public procedures and functions. In addition, it declares constants, types, variables, procedures, and functions that are *private*, that is, not available to the host.

Chapter 9, Programs and Units

implementation part

```
─►(implementation)─┬─────────────────┬─►┌─ label declaration part ─┐
                   └─► uses clause ──┘  ├─ constant declaration part ─┤
                                        ├─ type declaration part ─┤
                                        ├─ variable declaration part ─┤
                                        └─ procedure and function declaration part ─┘
```

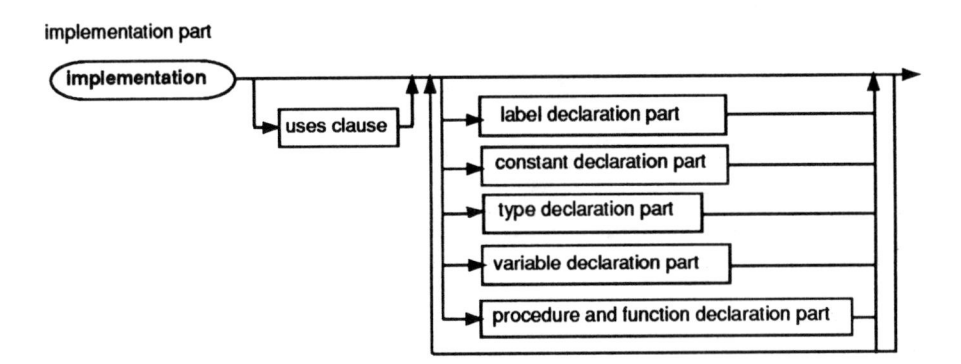

In effect, the procedure and function declarations in the interface part are like **forward** declarations, although the **forward** directive is not specified. Therefore, these procedures and functions can be defined and referenced in any sequence in the implementation part.

Note: Procedure and function headings can be duplicated from the interface part. You don't have to specify the formal parameter list, but if you do, the compiler will issue a compile-time error if the interface and implementation declarations don't match.

The Initialization Part

The initialization part is the last part of a unit. It consists either of the reserved word **end** (in which case the unit has no initialization code) or of a statement part to be executed in order to initialize the unit.

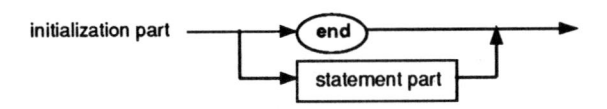

```
initialization part ──┬─►(end)──────────►
                      └─► statement part ─┘
```

The initialization parts of units used by a program are executed in the same order that the units appear in the **uses** clause.

Indirect Unit References

The **uses** clause in a module (program or unit) need only name the units used directly by that module. Consider the following example:

```
program Prog;
uses Unit2;
```

```
  const a = b;
begin end.
unit Unit2;
interface
uses Unit1;
const b = c;
implementation
end.
unit Unit1;
interface
const c = 1;
implementation
const d = 2;
end.
```

In the above example, *Unit2* is directly dependent on *Unit1*, and *Prog* is directly dependent on *Unit2*. Furthermore, *Prog* is indirectly dependent on *Unit1* (through *Unit2*), even though none of the identifiers declared in *Unit1* are available to *Prog*.

In order to compile a module, Turbo Pascal must be able to locate all units upon which the module depends (directly or indirectly). So, to compile *Prog* above, the compiler must be able to locate both *Unit1* and *Unit2*, or else an error occurs.

When changes are made in the interface part of a unit, other units using the unit must be recompiled. However, if changes are only made to the implementation or the initialization part, other units that use the unit *need not* be recompiled. In the preceding example, if the interface part of *Unit1* is changed (for example, c = 2) *Unit2* must be recompiled; changing the implementation part (for example, d = 1) doesn't require recompilation of *Unit2*.

When a unit is compiled, Turbo Pascal computes a *unit version number*, which is basically a checksum of the interface part. In the preceding example, when *Unit2* is compiled, the current version number of *Unit1* is saved in the compiled version of *Unit2*. When *Prog* is compiled, the version number of *Unit1* is checked against the version number stored in *Unit2*. If the version numbers do not match, indicating that a change was made in the interface part of *Unit1* since *Unit2* was compiled, the compiler shows an error or recompiles *Unit2*, depending on the mode of compilation.

Circular Unit References

Placing a **uses** clause in the implementation section of a unit allows you to further hide the inner details of the unit, since units used in the implementation section are not visible to users of the unit. More importantly, however, it also enables you to construct mutually dependent units.

The following program demonstrates how two units can "use" each other. The main program, *Circular*, uses a unit named *Display*. *Display* contains one routine in its interface section, *WriteXY*, which takes three parameters: an (*x*, *y*) coordinate pair and a text message to display. If the (*x*, *y*) coordinates are onscreen, *WriteXY* moves the cursor to (*x*, *y*) and displays the message there; otherwise, it calls a simple error-handling routine.

So far, there's nothing fancy here—*WriteXY* is taking the place of *Write*. Here's where the circular unit reference enters in: How is the error-handling routine going to display its error message? By using *WriteXY* again. Thus you have *WriteXY*, which calls the error-handling routine *ShowError*, which in turn calls *WriteXY* to put an error message onscreen. If your head is spinning in circles, let's look at the source code to this example, so you can see that it's really not that tricky.

The main program, *Circular*, clears the screen and makes three calls to *WriteXY*:

```
program Circular;
{ Display text using WriteXY }

uses
  Crt, Display;

begin
  ClrScr;
  WriteXY(1, 1, 'Upper left corner of screen');
  WriteXY(100, 100, 'Way off the screen');
  WriteXY(81 - Length('Back to reality'), 15, 'Back to reality');
end.
```

Look at the (*x*, *y*) coordinates of the second call to *WriteXY*. It's hard to display text at (100, 100) on an 80x25 line screen. Next, let's see how *WriteXY* works. Here's the source to the *Display* unit, which contains the *WriteXY* procedure. If the (*x*, *y*) coordinates are valid, it displays the message; otherwise, *WriteXY* displays an error message:

```
unit Display;
{ Contains a simple video display routine }

interface

procedure WriteXY(X, Y : integer; Message : string);

implementation
uses
  Crt, Error;

procedure WriteXY(X, Y : integer; Message : string);
begin
```

```
    if (X in [1..80]) and (Y in [1..25]) then
    begin
      GoToXY(X, Y);
      Write(Message);
    end
    else
      ShowError('Invalid WriteXY coordinates');
  end;

end.
```

The *ShowError* procedure called by *WriteXY* is declared in the following code in the *Error* unit. *ShowError* always displays its error message on the 25th line of the screen:

```
unit Error;
{ Contains a simple error-reporting routine }

interface

procedure ShowError(ErrMsg : string);

implementation

uses
  Display;

procedure ShowError(ErrMsg : string);
begin
  WriteXY(1, 25, 'Error: ' + ErrMsg);
end;

end.
```

Notice that the **uses** clause in the **implementation** sections of both *Display* and *Error* refer to each other. These two units can refer to each other in their **implementation** sections because Turbo Pascal can compile complete **interface** sections for both. In other words, the Turbo Pascal compiler will accept a reference to partially compiled unit *A* in the **implementation** section of unit *B*, as long as both *A* and *B*'s **interface** sections do not depend upon each other (and thus follow Pascal's strict rules for declaration order).

Sharing Other Declarations

What if you want to modify *WriteXY* and *ShowError* to take an additional parameter that specifies a rectangular window onscreen:

```
procedure WriteXY(SomeWindow : WindRec;
                  X, Y : integer;
                  Message : string);
procedure ShowError(SomeWindow : WindRec;
                    ErrMsg : string);
```

Remember these two procedures are in separate units. Even if you declared *WindData* in the **interface** of one, there would be no legal way to make that declaration available to the **interface** of the other. The solution is to declare a third module that contains only the definition of the window record:

```
unit WindData;
interface
type
  WinDRec = record
              X1, Y1, X2, Y2 : integer;
              ForeColor,
              BackColor      : byte;
              Active         : boolean;
            end;
implementation
end.
```

In addition to modifying the code to *WriteXY* and *ShowError* to make use of the new parameter, the **interface** sections of both the *Display* and *Error* units can now "use" *WindData*. This approach is legal because unit *WindData* has no dependencies in its **uses** clause, and units *Display* and *Error* refer to each other only in their respective **implementation** sections.

CHAPTER 10

Input and Output

This chapter briefly describes the standard (or built-in) input and output (I/O) procedures and functions of Turbo Pascal; for more detailed information, refer to Chapter 16.

An Introduction to I/O

A Pascal file variable is any variable whose type is a file type. There are three classes of Pascal files: *typed*, *text*, and *untyped*. The syntax for writing file types is given in the section "Structured Types" in Chapter 3.

Before a file variable can be used, it must be associated with an external file through a call to the *Assign* procedure. An external file is typically a named disk file, but it can also be a device, such as the keyboard or the display. The external file stores the information written to the file or supplies the information read from the file.

Once the association with an external file is established, the file variable must be "opened" to prepare it for input and/or output. An existing file can be opened via the *Reset* procedure, and a new file can be created and opened via the *Rewrite* procedure. Text files opened with *Reset* are read-only, and text files opened with *Rewrite* and *Append* are write-only. Typed files and untyped files always allow both reading and writing regardless of whether they were opened with *Reset* or *Rewrite*.

The standard text-file variables *Input* and *Output* are opened automatically when program execution begins. *Input* is a read-only file associated with the keyboard and *Output* is a write-only file associated with the display.

Every file is a linear sequence of components, each of which has the component type (or record type) of the file. Each component has a component number. The first component of a file is considered to be component zero.

Files are normally accessed *sequentially*; that is, when a component is read using the standard procedure *Read* or written using the standard procedure *Write*, the current file position moves to the next numerically-ordered file component. However, typed files and untyped files can also be accessed randomly via the standard procedure *Seek*, which moves the current file position to a specified component. The standard functions *FilePos* and *FileSize* can be used to determine the current file position and the current file size.

When a program completes processing a file, the file must be closed using the standard procedure *Close*. After closing a file completely, its associated external file is updated. The file variable can then be associated with another external file.

By default, all calls to standard I/O procedures and functions are automatically checked for errors: If an error occurs, the program terminates, displaying a run-time error message. This automatic checking can be turned on and off using the {$I+} and {$I-} compiler directives. When I/O checking is off—that is, when a procedure or function call is compiled in the {$I-} state—an I/O error does not cause the program to halt. To check the result of an I/O operation, you must instead call the standard function *IOResult*.

Standard Procedures and Functions for All Files

Here's a summary of the procedures and functions you can use in all files.

Procedures

Assign	Assigns the name of an external file to a file variable.
ChDir	Changes the current directory.
Close	Closes an open file.
Erase	Erases an external file.
GetDir	Returns the current directory of a specified drive.
MkDir	Creates a subdirectory.
Rename	Renames an external file.

Reset	Opens an existing file.
Rewrite	Creates and opens a new file.
RmDir	Removes an empty subdirectory.

Functions

Eof	Returns the end-of-file status of a file.
IOResult	Returns an integer value that is the status of the last I/O function performed.

Standard Procedures and Functions for Text Files

This section summarizes input and output using file variables of the standard type *Text*. Note that in Turbo Pascal the type *Text* is distinct from the type **file of** char.

When a text file is opened, the external file is interpreted in a special way: It is considered to represent a sequence of characters formatted into lines, where each line is terminated by an end-of-line marker (a carriage-return character, possibly followed by a line-feed character).

For text files, there are special forms of *Read* and *Write* that allow you to read and write values that are not of type char. Such values are automatically translated to and from their character representation. For example, *Read(f,i)*, where *i* is a type integer variable, will read a sequence of digits, interpret that sequence as a decimal integer, and store it in *i*.

As noted previously there are two standard text-file variables, *Input* and *Output*. The standard file variable *Input* is a read-only file associated with the operating system's standard input file (typically the keyboard), and the standard file variable *Output* is a write-only file associated with the operating system's standard output file (typically the display). *Input* and *Output* are automatically opened before a program begins execution, as if the following statements were executed:

```
Assign(Input,''); Reset(Input);
Assign(Output,''); Rewrite(Output);
```

Likewise, *Input* and *Output* are automatically closed after a program finishes executing.

Note: If a program uses the *Crt* standard unit, *Input* and *Output* will no longer by default refer to the standard input and standard output files. (For further details, refer to the description of the *Crt* unit in Chapter 12, "Standard Units").

Some of the standard procedures and functions listed in this section need not have a file variable explicitly given as a parameter. If the file parameter is omitted, *Input* or *Output* will be assumed by default, depending on whether the procedure or function is input- or output-oriented. For instance, *Read(x)* corresponds to *Read(Input,x)* and *Write(x)* corresponds to *Write(Output,x)*.

If you do specify a file when calling one of the procedures or functions in this section, the file must have been associated with an external file using *Assign*, and opened using *Reset*, *Rewrite*, or *Append*. An error message is generated if you pass a file that was opened with *Reset* to an output-oriented procedure or function. Likewise, it's an error to pass a file that was opened with *Rewrite* or *Append* to an input-oriented procedure or function.

Procedures

Append	Opens an existing file for appending.
Flush	Flushes the buffer of an output file.
Read	Reads one or more values from a text file into one or more variables.
Readln	Does what a *Read* does and then skips to the beginning of the next line in the file.
SetTextBuf	Assigns an I/O buffer to a text file.
Write	Writes one or more values to a text file.
Writeln	Does the same as a *Write*, and then writes an end-of-line marker to the file.

Functions

Eoln	Returns the end-of-line status of a file.
SeekEof	Returns the end-of-file status of a file.
SeekEoln	Returns the end-of-line status of a file.

Standard Procedures and Functions for Untyped Files

Untyped files are low-level I/O channels primarily used for direct access to any disk file regardless of type and structuring. An untyped file is declared with the word **file** and nothing more, for example:

var
  DataFile: **file;**

For untyped files, the *Reset* and *Rewrite* procedures allow an extra parameter to specify the record size used in data transfers.

For historical reasons, the default record size is 128 bytes. The preferred record size is 1, because that is the only value that correctly reflects the exact size of any file (no partial records are possible when the record size is 1).

Except for *Read* and *Write*, all typed file standard procedures and functions are also allowed on untyped files. Instead of *Read* and *Write*, two procedures called *BlockRead* and *BlockWrite* are used for high-speed data transfers.

BlockRead   Reads one or more records into a variable.

BlockWrite Writes one or more records from a variable.

With the exception of text files, the following procedures and functions may be used on a file variable of any type:

FilePos   Returns the current file position of a file.

FileSize   Returns the current size of a file.

Seek   Moves the current position of a file to a specified component.

Truncate   Truncates the file size at the current file position.

The FileMode Variable

The *FileMode* variable defined by the *System* unit determines the access code to pass to DOS when typed and untyped files (not text files) are opened using the *Reset* procedure.

The default *FileMode* is 2, which allows both reading and writing. Assigning another value to *FileMode* causes all subsequent *Resets* to use that mode.

The range of valid *FileMode* values depends on the version of DOS in use. However, for all versions, the following modes are defined:

- 0: Read only
- 1: Write only
- 2: Read/Write

DOS version 3.x defines additional modes, which are primarily concerned with file-sharing on networks. (For further details on these, please refer to your DOS Programmer's reference manual.)

Note: New files created using *Rewrite* are always opened in Read/Write mode, corresponding to *FileMode* = 2.

Devices in Turbo Pascal

Turbo Pascal and the DOS operating system regard external hardware, such as the keyboard, the display, and the printer, as *devices*. From the programmer's point of view, a device is treated as a file, and is operated on through the same standard procedures and functions as files.

Turbo Pascal supports two kinds of devices: DOS devices and text file devices.

DOS Devices

DOS devices are implemented through reserved file names that have a special meaning attached to them. DOS devices are completely transparent—in fact, Turbo Pascal is not even aware when a file variable refers to a device instead of a disk file. For example, the program

```
var
  Lst: Text;
begin
  Assign(Lst,'LPT1'); Rewrite(Lst);
  Writeln(Lst,'Hello World...');
  Close(Lst);
end.
```

will write the string `Hello World...` on the printer, even though the syntax for doing so is exactly the same as for a disk file.

The devices implemented by DOS are used for obtaining or presenting legible input or output. Therefore, DOS devices are normally used only in connection with text files. On rare occasions, untyped files can also be useful for interfacing with DOS devices.

Each of the DOS devices is described in the next section. Other DOS implementations can provide additional devices, and still others cannot provide all the ones described here.

The CON Device

CON refers to the CONsole device, in which output is sent to the display, and input is obtained from the keyboard. The *Input* and *Output* standard files and all files assigned an empty name refer to the CON device when input and/or output is not redirected.

Input from the CON device is line-oriented and uses the line-editing facilities described in the DOS manual. Characters are read from a line buffer, and when the buffer becomes empty, a new line is input.

An end-of-file character is generated by pressing *Ctrl-Z*, after which the *Eof* function will return True.

The LPT1, LPT2, and LPT3 Devices

The line printer devices are the three possible printers you can use. If only one printer is connected, it is usually referred to as LPT1, for which the synonym PRN can also be used.

The line printer devices are output-only devices—an attempt to *Reset* a file assigned to one of these generates an immediate end-of-file.

Note: The standard unit *Printer* declares a text-file variable called *Lst*, and makes it refer to the LPT1 device. To easily write something on the printer from one of your programs, include *Printer* in the program's **uses** clause, and use *Write(Lst,...)* and *Writeln(Lst,...)* to produce your output.

The COM1 and COM2 Devices

The communication port devices are the two serial communication ports. The synonym AUX can be used instead of COM1.

The NUL Device

The null device ignores anything written to it, and generates an immediate end-of-file when read from. You should use this when you don't want to create a particular file, but the program requires an input or output file name.

Text File Devices

Text file devices are used to implement devices unsupported by DOS or to make available another set of features other than those provided by a similar DOS device. A good example of a text file device is the CRT device implemented by the *Crt* standard unit. Its main function is to provide an interface to the display and the keyboard, just like the CON device in DOS. However, the CRT device is much faster and supports such invaluable features as color and windows (for further details on the CRT device, see Chapter 12, "Standard Units").

Contrary to DOS devices, text file devices have no reserved file names; in fact, they have no file names at all. Instead, a file is associated with a text file device through a customized *Assign* procedure. For instance, the *Crt* standard unit implements an *AssignCrt* procedure that associates text files with the CRT device.

In addition to the CRT device, Turbo Pascal allows you to write your own text file device drivers. A full description of this is given in the section "Text File Device Drivers" on page 210 of Chapter 15, "Inside Turbo Pascal."

CHAPTER 11

Standard Procedures and Functions

This chapter briefly describes all the standard (built-in) procedures and functions in Turbo Pascal, except for the I/O procedures and functions discussed in Chapter 10, "Input and Output." Additional procedures and functions are provided by the standard units described in Chapter 12, "Standard Units." For more detailed information, refer to Chapter 16, "Turbo Pascal Reference Lookup."

Standard procedures and functions are predeclared. Since all predeclared entities act as if they were declared in a block surrounding the program, no conflict arises from a declaration that redefines the same identifier within the program.

Flow Control Procedures

Exit   Exits immediately from the current block.
Halt   Stops program execution and returns to the operating system.
RunError Stops program execution and generates a run-time error.

Dynamic Allocation Procedures and Functions

These procedures and functions are used to manage the heap—a memory area that occupies all or some of the free memory left when a program is executed. A complete discussion of the techniques used to manage the heap is given in the section "The Heap Manager" on page 181 of Chapter 15, "Inside Turbo Pascal."

Procedures

Dispose	Disposes a dynamic variable.
FreeMem	Disposes a dynamic variable of a given size.
GetMem	Creates a new dynamic variable of a given size and sets a pointer variable to point to it.
Mark	Records the state of the heap in a pointer variable.
New	Creates a new dynamic variable and sets a pointer variable to point to it.
Release	Returns the heap to a given state.

Functions

MaxAvail	Returns the size of the largest contiguous free block in the heap, corresponding to the size of the largest dynamic variable that can be allocated at the time of the call to *MaxAvail*.
MemAvail	Returns the number of free bytes of heap storage available.

Transfer Functions

The procedures *Pack* and *Unpack*, as defined in standard Pascal, are not implemented by Turbo Pascal.

Chr	Returns a character of a specified ordinal number.
Ord	Returns the ordinal number of an ordinal-type value.
Round	Rounds a type real value to a type longint value.
Trunc	Truncates a type real value to a type longint value.

Arithmetic Functions

Note: When compiling in numeric processing mode, {$N+}, the return values of the floating-point routines in the *System* unit (*Sqrt, Pi, Sin,* and so on) are of type extended instead of real:

```
{$N+}
begin
```

```
              Writeln(Pi);                    { 3.14159265358979E+0000 }
  end.
  {$N-}
  begin
              Writeln(Pi)                     {   3.1415926536E+00    }
  end.
```

Abs	Returns the absolute value of the argument.
ArcTan	Returns the arctangent of the argument.
Cos	Returns the cosine of the argument.
Exp	Returns the exponential of the argument.
Frac	Returns the fractional part of the argument.
Int	Returns the integer part of the argument.
Ln	Returns the natural logarithm of the argument.
Pi	Returns the value of *Pi* (3.1415926535897932385).
Sin	Returns the sine of the argument.
Sqr	Returns the square of the argument.
Sqrt	Returns the square root of the argument.

Ordinal Procedures and Functions

Procedures

Dec	Decrements a variable.
Inc	Increments a variable.

Functions

Odd	Tests if the argument is an odd number.
Pred	Returns the predecessor of the argument.
Succ	Returns the successor of the argument.

String Procedures and Functions

Procedures

Delete   Deletes a substring from a string.

Insert   Inserts a substring into a string.

Str   Converts a numeric value to its string representation.

Val   Converts the string value to its numeric representation.

Functions

Concat   Concatenates a sequence of strings.

Copy   Returns a substring of a string.

Length   Returns the dynamic length of a string.

Pos   Searches for a substring in a string.

Pointer and Address Functions

Addr   Returns the address of a specified object.

CSeg   Returns the current value of the CS register.

DSeg   Returns the current value of the DS register.

Ofs   Returns the offset of a specified object.

Ptr   Converts a segment base and an offset address to a pointer-type value.

Seg   Returns the segment of a specified object.

SPtr   Returns the current value of the SP register.

SSeg   Returns the current value of the SS register.

Miscellaneous Procedures and Functions

Procedures

FillChar   Fills a specified number of contiguous bytes with a specified value.

Move	Copies a specified number of contiguous bytes from a source range to a destination range.
Randomize	Initializes the built-in random generator with a random value.

Functions

Hi	Returns the high-order byte of the argument.
Lo	Returns the low-order byte of the argument.
ParamCount	Returns the number of parameters passed to the program on the command line.
ParamStr	Returns a specified command-line parameter.
Random	Returns a random number.
SizeOf	Returns the number of bytes occupied by the argument.
Swap	Swaps the high- and low-order bytes of the argument.
UpCase	Converts a character to uppercase.

C H A P T E R

12

Standard Units

Chapter 11, "Standard Procedures and Functions," describes all the built-in procedures and functions of Turbo Pascal, which can be referred to without explicitly requesting them (as standard Pascal specifies). It's through Turbo Pascal's standard units, though, that you'll get the most programming power (see Chapter 16, "Turbo Pascal Reference Lookup," for more information).

Standard units are no different from the units you can write yourself. The following eight standard units are available to you:

Crt Exploits the full power of your PC's display and keyboard, including screen mode control, extended keyboard codes, color, windows, and sound.

Dos Supports numerous DOS functions, including date-and-time control, directory search, and program execution.

Graph A powerful graphics package with device-independent graphics support for CGA, EGA, VGA, HERC, IBM 3270 PC, MCGA, AT&T 6300, and IBM 8514.

Graph3 Implements Turbo Pascal 3.0 Turtlegraphics.

Overlay Implements 5.0's powerful overlay manager (refer to Chapter 13, "Overlays").

Printer Allows you to easily access your printer.

System Turbo Pascal's run-time library. This unit is automatically used by any unit or program.

Turbo3 Provides an even higher degree of compatibility with Turbo Pascal 3.0.

To use one of the standard units, simply include its name in your **uses** clause, for instance:

uses Dos,Crt,Graph;

The standard units usually all reside in the TURBO.TPL library, which is automatically loaded when you start up Turbo Pascal. To save memory, you can move seldom-used units, such as *Turbo3* and *Graph3*, out of the TURBO.TPL file by using the TPUMOVER utility.

Standard Unit Dependencies

Both the compatibility units, *Turbo3* and *Graph3*, depend on facilities made available by the *Crt* unit. So, when using *Turbo3* and *Graph3*, you must first specify *Crt* in your **uses** clause. Table 12.1 lists the standard units.

Table 12.1: Standard Units

Unit	Uses
Crt	None
Dos	None
Graph	None
Graph3	Crt
Overlay	None
Printer	None
System	None
Turbo3	Crt

We purposefully didn't indicate in the table that all units use the *System* unit; that's because *System* is always used implicitly, and need never be specified in a **uses** clause.

The System Unit

The *System* unit is, in fact, Turbo Pascal's run-time library. It implements low-level, run-time support routines for all built-in features, such as file I/O, string handling, 8087 emulation, floating point, overlay management, and dynamic memory allocation. The *System* unit is used automatically by any unit or program, and need never be referred to in a **uses** clause.

The procedures and functions provided by *System* are described in Chapters 10, "Input and Output," and 11, "Standard Procedures and Functions." A number of predeclared variables are also available, including:

```
const
  OvrCodeList: word = 0;              { Overlay code segment list }
  OvrHeapSize: word = 0;              { Initial overlay buffer size }
  OvrDebugPtr: pointer = nil;         { Overlay debugger hook }
  OvrHeapOrg: word = 0;               { Overlay buffer origin }
  OvrHeapPtr: word = 0;               { Overlay buffer pointer }
  OvrHeapEnd: word = 0;               { Overlay buffer end }
  OvrLoadList: word = 0;              { Loaded overlays list }
  OvrDosHandle: word = 0;             { Overlay DOS handle }
  OvrEmsHandle: word = 0;             { Overlay EMS handle }
  HeapOrg: pointer = nil;             { Heap origin }
  HeapPtr: pointer = nil;             { Heap pointer }
  FreePtr: pointer = nil;             { Free list pointer }
  FreeMin: word = 0;                  { Minimum free list size }
  HeapError: pointer = nil;           { Heap error function }
  ExitProc: pointer = nil;            { Exit procedure }
  ExitCode: integer = 0;              { Exit code }
  ErrorAddr: pointer = nil;           { Run-time error address }
  PrefixSeg: word = 0;                { Program segment prefix }
  StackLimit: word = 0;               { Minimum stack pointer }
  InOutRes: integer = 0;              { I/O result buffer }
  RandSeed: longint = 0;              { Random seed }
  FileMode: byte = 2;                 { File open mode }
  Test8087: byte = 0;                 { 8087 test result }

var
  Input: text;                        { Input standard file }
  Output: text;                       { Output standard file }
  SaveInt00: pointer;                 { Saved interrupt $00 }
  SaveInt02: pointer;                 { Saved interrupt $02 }
  SaveInt1B: pointer;                 { Saved interrupt $1B }
  SaveInt23: pointer;                 { Saved interrupt $23 }
  SaveInt24: pointer;                 { Saved interrupt $24 }
  SaveInt34: pointer;                 { Saved interrupt $34 }
  SaveInt35: pointer;                 { Saved interrupt $35 }
  SaveInt36: pointer;                 { Saved interrupt $36 }
  SaveInt37: pointer;                 { Saved interrupt $37 }
  SaveInt38: pointer;                 { Saved interrupt $38 }
  SaveInt39: pointer;                 { Saved interrupt $39 }
  SaveInt3A: pointer;                 { Saved interrupt $3A }
  SaveInt3B: pointer;                 { Saved interrupt $3B }
  SaveInt3C: pointer;                 { Saved interrupt $3C }
  SaveInt3D: pointer;                 { Saved interrupt $3D }
  SaveInt3E: pointer;                 { Saved interrupt $3E }
  SaveInt3F: pointer;                 { Saved interrupt $3F }
  SaveInt75: pointer;                 { Saved interrupt $75 }
```

The *Overlay* unit uses *OvrCodeList, OvrHeapSize, OvrDebugPtr, OvrHeapOrg, OvrHeapPtr, OvrHeapEnd, OvrLoadList, OvrDosHandle,* and *OvrEmsHandle* to implement Turbo Pascal's overlay manager. The overlay buffer resides between the stack segment and the heap, and *OvrHeapOrg* and *OvrHeapEnd* contain its starting and ending segment addresses. The default size of the overlay buffer corresponds to the size of the largest overlay in the program; if the program has no overlays, the size of the overlay buffer is zero. The size of the overlay buffer can be increased through a call to the *OvrSetBuf* routine in the *Overlay* unit; in that case, the size of the heap is decreased accordingly, by moving *HeapOrg* upwards.

The heap manager uses *HeapOrg*, *HeapPtr*, *FreePtr*, *FreeMin*, and *HeapError* to implement Turbo Pascal's dynamic memory allocation routines. The heap manager is described in full in Chapter 15, "Inside Turbo Pascal."

The *ExitProc*, *ExitCode*, and *ErrorAddr* variables implement exit procedures. This is also described in Chapter 15, "Inside Turbo Pascal."

PrefixSeg is a word variable containing the segment address of the Program Segment Prefix (PSP) created by DOS when the program was executed. For a complete description of the PSP, refer to your DOS manual.

StackLimit contains the offset of the bottom of the stack in the stack segment, corresponding to the lowest value the SP register is allowed to assume before it is considered a stack overflow. By default, *StackLimit* is zero, but in a program compiled with {$N+,E+}, the 8087 emulator will set it to 224 to reserve workspace at the bottom of the stack segment if no 8087 is present in the system.

The built-in I/O routines use *InOutRes* to store the value that the next call to the *IOResult* standard function will return.

RandSeed stores the built-in random number generator's seed. By assigning a specific value to *RandSeed*, the *Random* function can be made to generate a specific sequence of random numbers over and over. This is useful is applications that deal with data encryption, statistics, and simulations.

The *FileMode* variable allows you to change the access mode in which typed and untyped files are opened (by the *Reset* standard procedure). For further details, refer to Chapter 10, "Input and Output."

Test8087 stores the result of the coprocessor autodetection logic, which is executed at startup in a program compiled with {$N+}. For further details, refer to Chapter 14, "Using the 8087."

Input and *Output* are the standard I/O files required by every Pascal implementation. By default, they refer to the standard input and output files in DOS. For further details, refer to Chapter 10, "Input and Output."

The *System* unit takes over several interrupt vectors. Before installing its own interrupt handling routines, *System* stores the old vectors in the *SaveIntXX* variables.

Note that the *System* unit contains an INT 24 handler for trapping critical errors. In a Turbo Pascal program, a DOS critical error is treated like any other I/O error: In the {$I+} state, the program halts with a run-time error, and, in the {$I-} state, *IOResult* returns a nonzero value.

Here's a skeleton program that restores the original vector, and thereby the original critical error-handling logic:

```
program Restore;
uses Dos;
begin
  SetIntVec($24, SaveInt24);
  ...
end.
```

The *SwapVectors* routine in the *Dos* unit swaps the contents of the *SaveIntXX* variables with the current contents of the interrupt vectors. *SwapVectors* should be called just before and just after a call to the *Exec* routine, to ensure that the *Exec*'d process does not use any interrupt handlers installed by the current process, and vice versa. For more information, refer to page 384 for the entry on *SwapVectors* in Chapter 16 of the *Reference Guide*, "Turbo Pascal Reference Lookup."

The Printer Unit

The *Printer* unit is a very small unit designed to make life easier when you're using the printer from within a program. *Printer* declares a text file called *Lst*, and associates it with the LPT1 device. Using *Printer* saves you the trouble of declaring, assigning, opening, and closing a text file yourself. Here's an example of a short program using *Printer*:

```
program HelloPrinter;
uses Printer;
begin
  Writeln(Lst,'Hello Printer...');
end.
```

The Dos Unit

The *Dos* unit implements a number of very useful operating system and file-handling routines. None of the routines in the *Dos* unit are defined by standard Pascal, so they have been placed in their own module.

For a complete description of DOS operations, refer to the *IBM DOS Technical Manual*.

Constants, Types, and Variables

Each of the constants, types, and variables defined by the *Dos* unit are briefly discussed in this section. For more detailed information, see the descriptions of the procedures and functions that depend on these objects in Chapter 16, "Turbo Pascal Reference Lookup."

Flags Constants

The following constants test individual flag bits in the Flags register after a call to *Intr* or *MsDos*:

```
const
  FCarry     = $0001;
  FParity    = $0004;
  FAuxiliary = $0010;
  FZero      = $0040;
  FSign      = $0080;
  FOverflow  = $0800;
```

For instance, if *R* is a register's record, the tests

```
R.Flags and FCarry <> 0
R.Flags and FZero = 0
```

are True respectively if the Carry flag is set and if the Zero flag is clear.

File Mode Constants

The file-handling procedures use these constants when opening and closing disk files. The mode fields of Turbo Pascal's file variables will contain one of the values specified below.

```
const
  fmClosed = $D7B0;
  fmInput  = $D7B1;
  fmOutput = $D7B2;
  fmInOut  = $D7B3;
```

File Record Types

The record definitions used internally by Turbo Pascal are also declared in the *Dos* unit. *FileRec* is used for both typed and untyped files, while *TextRec* is the internal format of a variable of type text.

```
type
  { Typed and untyped files }
  FileRec = record
            Handle: word;
            Mode: word;
            RecSize: word;
            Private: array[1..26] of byte;
            UserData: array[1..16] of byte;
            Name: array[0..79] of char;
          end;
  { Textfile record }
  TextBuf = array[0..127] of char;
  TextRec = record
            Handle    : word;
            Mode      : word;
            BufSize   : word;
            Private   : word;
            BufPos    : word;
            BufEnd    : word;
            BufPtr    : ^TextBuf;
            OpenFunc  : pointer;
            InOutFunc : pointer;
            FlushFunc : pointer;
            CloseFunc : pointer;
            UserData  : array[1..16] of byte;
            Name      : array[0..79] of char;
            Buffer    : TextBuf;
          end;
```

File Attribute Constants

These constants test, set, and clear file attribute bits in connection with the *GetFAttr*, *SetFAttr*, *FindFirst*, and *FindNext* procedures:

```
const
  ReadOnly  = $01;
  Hidden    = $02;
  SysFile   = $04;
  VolumeID  = $08;
  Directory = $10;
  Archive   = $20;
  AnyFile   = $3F;
```

The constants are additive, that is, the statement

```
FindFirst('*.*', ReadOnly + Directory, S);
```

will locate all normal files as well as read-only files and subdirectories in the current directory. The *AnyFile* constant is simply the sum of all attributes.

The Registers Type

The *Intr* and *MsDos* procedures use variables of type *Registers* to specify the input register contents and examine the output register contents of a software interrupt.

```
type
  Registers = record
              case integer of
                0: (AX,BX,CX,DX,BP,SI,DI,DS,ES,Flags: word);
                1: (AL,AH,BL,BH,CL,CH,DL,DH: byte);
              end;
```

Notice the use of a variant record to map the 8-bit registers on top of their 16-bit equivalents.

The DateTime Type

Variables of *DateTime* type are used in connection with the *UnpackTime* and *PackTime* procedures to examine and construct 4-byte, packed date-and-time values for the *GetFTime*, *SetFTime*, *FindFirst*, and *FindNext* procedures.

```
type
  DateTime = record
             Year,Month,Day,Hour,Min,Sec: word;
             end;
```

Valid ranges are *Year* 1980..2099, *Month* 1..12, *Day* 1..31, *Hour* 0..23, *Min* 0..59, and *Sec* 0..59.

The SearchRec Type

The *FindFirst* and *FindNext* procedures use variables of type *SearchRec* to scan directories.

```
type
  SearchRec = record
              Fill: array[1..21] of byte;
              Attr: byte;
              Time: longint;
              Size: longint;
```

```
        Name: string[12];
      end;
```

The information for each file found by one of these procedures is reported back in a *SearchRec*. The *Attr* field contains the file's attributes (constructed from file attribute constants), *Time* contains its packed date and time (use *UnpackTime* to unpack), *Size* contains its size in bytes, and *Name* contains its name. The *Fill* field is reserved by DOS and should never be modified.

The File-Handling String Types

These string types are are defined by the *Dos* unit to handle file names and paths in connection with the string procedure *FSplit*:

```
ComStr  = string[127];                      { Command-line string }
PathStr = string[79];                       { Full file path string }
DirStr  = string[67];               { Drive and directory string }
NameStr = string[8];                             { File-name string }
ExtStr  = string[4];                        { File-extension string }
```

The DosError Variable

DosError is used by many of the routines in the *Dos* unit to report errors.

```
var DosError: integer;
```

The values stored in *DosError* are DOS error codes. A value of 0 indicates no error; other possible error codes include:

   2 = File not found
   3 = Path not found
   5 = Access denied
   6 = Invalid handle
   8 = Not enough memory
  10 = Invalid environment
  11 = Invalid format
  18 = No more files

Interrupt Support Procedures

Here's a brief listing of the interrupt support procedures:

GetIntVec   Returns the address stored in a specified interrupt vector.

Intr   Executes a specified software interrupt.

MsDos	Executes a DOS function call.
SetIntVec	Sets a specified interrupt vector to a specified address.

Date and Time Procedures

GetDate	Returns the current date set in the operating system.
GetFTime	Returns the date and time a file was last written.
GetTime	Returns the current time set in the operating system.
PackTime	Converts a *DateTime* record into a 4-byte, packed date-and-time character longint used by *SetFTime*. The fields of the *DateTime* record are not range-checked.
SetDate	Sets the current date in the operating system.
SetFTime	Sets the date and time a file was last written.
SetTime	Sets the current time in the operating system.
UnpackTime	Converts a 4-byte, packed date-and-time character longint returned by *GetFTime*, *FindFirst*, or *FindNext* into an unpacked *DateTime* record.

Disk Status Functions

DiskFree	Returns the number of free bytes of a specified disk drive.
DiskSize	Returns the total size in bytes of a specified disk drive.

File-Handling Procedures and Functions

Procedures

FindFirst	Searches the specified (or current) directory for the first entry matching the specified file name and set of attributes.
FindNext	Returns the next entry that matches the name and attributes specified in a previous call to *FindFirst*.
FSplit	Splits a file name into its three component parts (directory, file name, and extension).

GetFAttr	Returns the attributes of a file.
SetFAttr	Sets the attributes of a file.

Functions

FExpand	Takes a file name and returns a fully qualified file name (drive, directory, and extension).
FSearch	Searches for a file in a list of directories.

Process-Handling Procedures and Functions

Procedures

Exec	Executes a specified program with a specified command line.
Keep	*Keep* (or Terminate Stay Resident) terminates the program and makes it stay in memory.
SwapVectors	Swaps all saved interrupt vectors with the current vectors.

Functions

DosExitCode	Returns the exit code of a subprocess.

Environment-Handling Functions

EnvCount	Returns the number of strings contained in the DOS environment.
EnvStr	Returns a specified environment string.
GetEnv	Returns the value of a specified environment variable.

Miscellaneous Procedures and Function

Procedures

GetCBreak	Returns the state of *Ctrl-Break* checking in DOS.

Chapter 12, Standard Units

GetVerify	Returns the state of the verify flag in DOS.
SetCBreak	Sets the state of *Ctrl-Break* checking in DOS.
SetVerify	Sets the state of the verify flag in DOS.

Function

DosVersion	Returns the DOS version number.

The Crt Unit

The *Crt* unit implements a range of powerful routines that give you full control of your PC's features, such as screen mode control, extended keyboard codes, colors, windows, and sound. *Crt* can only be used in programs that run on IBM PCs, ATs, PS/2s, and true compatibles.

One of the major advantages to using *Crt* is the added speed and flexibility of screen output operations. Programs that do not use the *Crt* unit send their screen output through DOS, which adds a lot of overhead. With the *Crt* unit, output is sent directly to the BIOS or, for even faster operation, directly to video memory.

The Input and Output Files

The initialization code of the *Crt* unit assigns the *Input* and *Output* standard text files to refer to the CRT instead of to DOS's standard input and output files. This corresponds to the following statements being executed at the beginning of a program:

```
AssignCrt(Input); Reset(Input);
AssignCrt(Output); Rewrite(Output);
```

This means that I/O redirection of the *Input* and *Output* files is no longer possible unless these files are explicitly assigned back to standard input and output by executing

```
Assign(Input,''); Reset(Input);
Assign(Output,''); Rewrite(Output);
```

Windows

Crt supports a simple yet powerful form of windows. The *Window* procedure lets you define a window anywhere on the screen. When you write in such a window, the window behaves exactly as if you were using the entire screen, leaving the rest of the screen untouched. In other words, the screen outside the window is not accessible. Inside the window, lines can be inserted and deleted, the cursor wraps around at the right edge, and the text scrolls when the cursor reaches the bottom line.

All screen coordinates, except the ones used to define a window, are relative to the current window, and screen coordinates (1,1) correspond to the upper left corner of the screen.

The default window is the entire screen.

Turbo Pascal also supports screen modes for EGA (43 line) and VGA (50 line) (see the *TextMode* description in Chapter 16).

Special Characters

When writing to *Output* or to a file that has been assigned to the CRT, the following control characters have special meanings:

- **#7** Bell—emits a beep from the internal speaker.
- **#8** Backspace—moves the cursor left one character. If the cursor is already at the left edge of the current window, nothing happens.
- **#10** Line feed—moves the cursor one line down. If the cursor is already at the bottom of the current window, the window scrolls up one line.
- **#13** Carriage return—returns the cursor to the left edge of the current window.

All other characters will appear on the screen when written.

Line Input

When reading from *Input* or from a text file that has been assigned to *Crt*, text is input one line at a time. The line is stored in the text file's internal buffer, and when variables are read, this buffer is used as the input source. Whenever the buffer has been emptied, a new line is input.

When entering lines, the following editing keys are available:

BackSpace	Deletes the last character entered.
Esc	Deletes the entire input line.
Enter	Terminates the input line and stores the end-of-line marker (carriage return/line feed) in the buffer.

Ctrl-S	Same as *BackSpace*
Ctrl-D	Recalls one character from the last input line.
Ctrl-A	Same as *Esc*.
Ctrl-F	Recalls the last input line.
Ctrl-Z	Terminates the input line and generates an end-of-file marker.

Ctrl-Z will only generate an end-of-file marker if the *CheckEOF* variable has been set to True; it is False by default.

To test keyboard status and input single characters under program control, use the *KeyPressed* and *ReadKey* functions.

Constants, Types, and Variables

Each of the constants, types, and variables defined by the *Crt* unit are briefly discussed in this section.

Crt Mode Constants

The following constants are used as parameters to the *TextMode* procedure:

```
const
  BW40 = 0;              { 40x25 B/W on color adapter }
  BW80 = 2;              { 80x25 B/W on color adapter }
  Mono = 7;              { 80x25 B/W on monochrome adapter }
  C040 = 1;              { 40x25 color on color adapter }
  C080 = 3;              { 80x25 color on color adapter }
  Font8x8 = 256;         { For EGA/VGA 43 and 50 line }
  C40 = C040;            { For 3.0 compatibility }
  C80 = C080;            { For 3.0 compatibility }
```

BW40, C040, BW80, and *C080* represent the four color text modes supported by the IBM PC Color/Graphics Adapter (CGA). The *Mono* constant represents the single black-and-white text mode supported by the IBM PC Monochrome Adapter. *Font8x8* represents EGA/VGA 43- and 50-line modes. The *C40* and *C80* constants are for 3.0 compatibility. *LastMode* returns to the last active text mode after using graphics.

Text Color Constants

The following constants are used in connection with the *TextColor* and *TextBackground* procedures:

```
const
  Black        = 0;
  Blue         = 1;
  Green        = 2;
  Cyan         = 3;
  Red          = 4;
  Magenta      = 5;
  Brown        = 6;
  LightGray    = 7;
  DarkGray     = 8;
  LightBlue    = 9;
  LightGreen   = 10;
  LightCyan    = 11;
  LightRed     = 12;
  LightMagenta = 13;
  Yellow       = 14;
  White        = 15;
  Blink        = 128;
```

Colors are represented by the numbers between 0 and 15; to easily identify each color, you can use these constants instead of numbers. In the color text modes, the foreground of each character is selectable from 16 colors, and the background from 8 colors. The foreground of each character can also be made to blink.

Crt Variables

Here are the variables in *Crt*:

```
var
  CheckBreak  : boolean;
  CheckEof    : boolean;
  CheckSnow   : boolean;
  DirectVideo : boolean;
  LastMode    : word;
  TextAttr    : byte;
  WindMin     : word;
  WindMax     : word;
```

CheckBreak

Enables and disables checks for *Ctrl-Break*.

`var CheckBreak: boolean;`

When *CheckBreak* is True, pressing *Ctrl-Break* will abort the program when it next writes to the display. When *CheckBreak* is False, pressing *Ctrl-Break* has no effect. *CheckBreak* is True by default. (At run time, *Crt* stores the old *Ctrl-Break* interrupt vector, $1B, in a global pointer variable called *SaveInt1B*.)

CheckEOF

Enables and disables the end-of-file character:

var CheckEOF: boolean;

When *CheckEOF* is True, an end-of-file character is generated if you press *Ctrl-Z* while reading from a file assigned to the screen. When *CheckEOF* is False, pressing *Ctrl-Z* has no effect. *CheckEOF* is False by default.

CheckSnow

Enables and disables "snow-checking" when storing characters directly in video memory.

var CheckSnow: boolean;

On most CGAs, interference will result if characters are stored in video memory outside the horizontal retrace intervals. This does not occur with Monochrome Adapters or EGAs.

When a color text mode is selected, *CheckSnow* is set to True, and direct video-memory writes will occur only during the horizontal retrace intervals. If you are running on a newer CGA, you may want to set *CheckSnow* to False at the beginning of your program and after each call to *TextMode*. This will disable snow-checking, resulting in significantly higher output speeds.

CheckSnow has no effect when *DirectVideo* is False.

DirectVideo

Enables and disables direct memory access for *Write* and *Writeln* statements that output to the screen.

var DirectVideo: boolean;

When *DirectVideo* is True, *Write*s and *Writeln*s to files associated with the CRT will store characters directly in video memory instead of calling the BIOS to display them. When *DirectVideo* is False, all characters are written through BIOS calls, which is a significantly slower process.

DirectVideo always defaults to True. If, for some reason, you want characters displayed through BIOS calls, set *DirectVideo* to False at the beginning of your program and after each call to *TextMode*.

LastMode

Each time *TextMode* is called, the current video mode is stored in *LastMode*. In addition, *LastMode* is initialized at program startup to the then-active video mode.

    var LastMode: word;

TextAttr

Stores the currently selected text attributes.

    var TextAttr: byte;

The text attributes are normally set through calls to *TextColor* and *TextBackground*. However, you can also set them by directly storing a value in *TextAttr*. The color information is encoded in *TextAttr* as follows:

7	6 5 4	3 2 1 0
B	b b b	f f f f

where *ffff* is the 4-bit foreground color, *bbb* is the 3-bit background color, and *B* is the blink-enable bit. If you use the color constants for creating *TextAttr* values, note that the background color can only be selected from the first 8 colors, and that it must be multiplied by 16 to get it into the correct bit positions. The following assignment selects blinking yellow characters on a blue background:

    TextAttr := Yellow + Blue * 16 + Blink;

WindMin and WindMax

Store the screen coordinates of the current window.

    var WindMin, WindMax : word;

These variables are set by calls to the *Window* procedure. *WindMin* defines the upper left corner, and *WindMax* defines the lower right corner. The X coordinate is stored in the low byte, and the Y coordinate is stored in the high byte. For example, *Lo(WindMin)* produces the X coordinate of the left edge, and *Hi(WindMax)* produces the Y coordinate of the bottom edge. The upper left corner of the screen corresponds to (X,Y) = (0,0). Note, however, that for coordinates passed to *Window* and *GotoXY*, the upper left corner is at (1,1).

Procedures

AssignCrt	Associates a text file with the CRT.
ClrEol	Clears all characters from the cursor position to the end of the line without moving the cursor.
ClrScr	Clears the screen and places the cursor in the upper left-hand corner.
Delay	Delays a specified number of milliseconds.
DelLine	Deletes the line containing the cursor and moves all lines below that line one line up. The bottom line is cleared.
GotoXY	Positions the cursor. X is the horizontal position. Y is the vertical position.
HighVideo	Selects high-intensity characters.
InsLine	Inserts an empty line at the cursor position.
LowVideo	Selects low-intensity characters.
NormVideo	Selects normal characters.
NoSound	Turns off the internal speaker.
Sound	Starts the internal speaker.
TextBackground	Selects the background color.
TextColor	Selects the foreground character color.
TextMode	Selects a specific text mode.
Window	Defines a text window on the screen.

Functions

KeyPressed	Returns True if a key has been pressed on the keyboard, and False otherwise.
ReadKey	Reads a character from the keyboard.
WhereX	Returns the X-coordinate of the current cursor position, relative to the current window. X is the horizontal position.
WhereY	Returns the Y-coordinate of the current cursor position, relative to the current window. Y is the vertical position.

The Graph Unit

The *Graph* unit implements a complete library of more than 50 graphics routines that range from high-level calls, like *SetViewPort*, *Circle*, *Bar3D*, and *DrawPoly*, to bit-oriented routines, like *GetImage* and *PutImage*. Several fill and line styles are supported, and there are several fonts that may be magnified, justified, and oriented horizontally or vertically.

To compile a program that uses the *Graph* unit, you'll need your program's source code, the compiler, and access to the standard units in TURBO.TPL and the *Graph* unit in GRAPH.TPU. To run a program that uses the *Graph* unit, in addition to your .EXE program, you'll need one or more of the graphics drivers (.BGI files, see the next section). In addition, if your program uses any stroked fonts, you'll need one or more font (.CHR) files as well.

(Pursuant to the terms of the license agreement, you can distribute the .CHR and .BGI files along with your programs.)

Drivers

Graphics drivers are provided for the following graphics adapters (and true compatibles):

- CGA
- MCGA
- EGA
- VGA
- Hercules
- AT&T 400 line
- 3270 PC
- IBM 8514

Each driver contains code and data and is stored in a separate file on disk. At run time, the *InitGraph* procedure identifies the graphics hardware, loads and initializes the appropriate graphics driver, puts the system into graphics mode, and then returns control to the calling routine. The *CloseGraph* procedure unloads the driver from memory and restores the previous video mode. You can switch back and forth between text and graphics modes using the *RestoreCrtMode* and *SetGraphMode* routines. To load the driver files yourself or link them into your .EXE, refer to *RegisterBGIdriver* in Chapter 16.

Graph supports computers with dual monitors. When *Graph* is initialized by calling *InitGraph*, the correct monitor will be selected for the graphics driver and mode requested. When terminating a graphics program, the previous video mode will be restored. If autodetection of graphics hardware is requested on a dual monitor system, *InitGraph* will select the monitor and graphics card that will produce the highest quality graphics output.

CGA.BGI	Driver for IBM CGA, MCGA
EGAVGA.BGI	Driver for IBM EGA, VGA
HERC.BGI	Driver for Hercules monochrome
ATT.BGI	Driver for AT&T 6300 (400 line)
PC3270.BGI	Driver for IBM 3270 PC
IBM8514.BGI	Driver for IBM 8514

IBM 8514 Support

Turbo Pascal supports the IBM 8514 graphics card, which is a new, high-resolution graphics card capable of resolutions up to 1024 × 768 pixels, and a color palette of 256 colors from a list of 256K colors. The driver file name is IBM8514.BGI.

Turbo Pascal cannot properly autodetect the IBM 8514 graphics card (the autodetection logic recognizes it as VGA). Therefore, to use the IBM 8514 card, the *GraphDriver* variable must be assigned the value IBM8514 (which is defined in the *Graph* unit) when *InitGraph* is called. You should not use *DetectGraph* (or *Detect* with *InitGraph*) with the IBM 8514 unless you want the emulated VGA mode.

The supported modes of the IBM 8514 card are IBM8514LO (640×480 pixels), and IBM8514HI (1024×768 pixels). Both mode constants are defined in the interface for GRAPH.TPU.

The IBM 8514 uses three 6-bit values to define colors. There is a 6-bit Red, Green, and Blue component for each defined color. To allow you to define colors for the IBM 8514, a new routine was added to the BGI library. The routine is defined in GRAPH.TPU as follows:

procedure SetRGBPalette(ColorNum, Red, Green, Blue : word);

The argument *ColorNum* defines the palette entry to be loaded. *ColorNum* is an integer from 0-255 (decimal). The arguments *Red, Green,* and *Blue* define the component colors of the palette entry. Only the lower byte of these values is used, and out of this byte, only the 6 most-significant bits are loaded in the palette.

The other palette manipulation routines of the graphics library may not be used with the IBM 8514 driver (that is, *SetAllPalette, SetPalette, GetPalette*).

For compatibility with the balance of the IBM graphics adapters, the BGI driver defines the first 16 palette entries of the IBM 8514 to the default colors of the EGA/VGA. These values can be used as is, or changed using the *SetRGBPalette* routine.

The *FloodFill* routine will not work with the IBM 8514 driver.

These same restrictions apply when also using the VGA in 256-color mode.

Coordinate System

By convention, the upper left corner of the graphics screen is (0,0). The x values, or columns, increment to the right. The y values, or rows, increment downward. Thus, in 320×200 mode on a CGA, the screen coordinates for each of the four corners with a specified point in the middle of the screen would look like this:

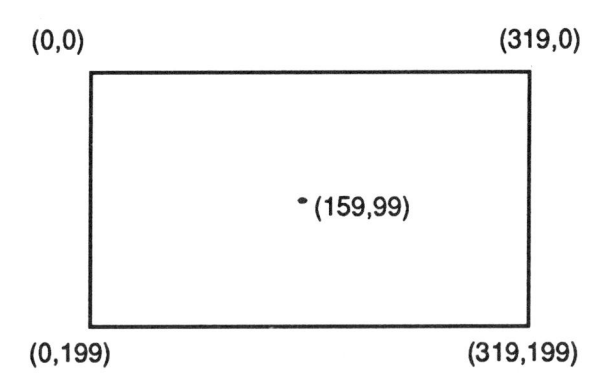

```
(0,0)                              (319,0)
    ┌─────────────────────────────┐
    │                             │
    │                             │
    │          • (159,99)         │
    │                             │
    │                             │
    └─────────────────────────────┘
(0,199)                          (319,199)
```

Current Pointer

Many graphics systems support the notion of a current pointer (CP). The CP is similar in concept to a text mode cursor except that the CP is not visible.

```
Write('ABC');
```

In text mode, the preceding *Write* statement will leave the cursor in the column immediately following the letter C. If the C is written in column 80, then the cursor will wrap around to column 1 of the next line. If the C is written in column 80 on the 25th line, the entire screen will scroll up one line, and the cursor will be in column 1 of line 25.

```
MoveTo(0,0)
LineTo(20,20)
```

In graphics mode, the preceding *LineTo* statement will leave the CP at the last point referenced (20,20). The actual line output would be clipped to the current viewport if clipping is active. Note that the CP is never clipped.

The *MoveTo* command is the equivalent of *GoToXY*. It's only purpose is to move the CP. Only the commands that use the CP move the CP: *InitGraph*,

MoveTo, MoveRel, LineTo, LineRel, OutText, SetGraphMode,* GraphDefaults,* ClearDevice,* SetViewPort,* and ClearViewPort*.

Note: The procedures with an asterisk (*) after their names in the preceding list move the CP to (0,0).)

Text

An 8×8 bit-mapped font and several "stroked" fonts are included for text output while in graphics mode. A bit-mapped character is defined by an 8×8 matrix of pixels. A stroked font is defined by a series of vectors that tell the graphics system how to draw the font.

The advantage to using a stroked font is apparent when you start to draw large characters. Since a stroked font is defined by vectors, it will still retain good resolution and quality when the font is enlarged.

When a bit-mapped font is enlarged, the matrix is multiplied by a scaling factor and, as the scaling factors becomes larger, the characters' resolution becomes coarser. For small characters, the bit-mapped font should be sufficient, but for larger text you will want to select a "stroked" font.

The justification of graphics text is controlled by the *SetTextJustify* procedure. Scaling and font selection is done with the *SetTextStyle* procedure. Graphics text is output by calling either the *OutText* or *OutTextXY* procedures. Inquiries about the current text settings are made by calling the *GetTextSettings* procedure. The size of stroked fonts can be customized by the *SetUserCharSize* procedure.

Stroked fonts are each kept in a separate file on disk with a .CHR file extension. Font files can be loaded from disk automatically by the *Graph* unit at run time (as described), or they can also be linked in or loaded by the user program and "registered" with the *Graph* unit.

A special utility, BINOBJ.EXE, is provided that converts a font file (or any binary data file, for that matter) to an .OBJ file that can be linked into a unit or program using the {$L} compiler directive. This makes it possible for a program to have all its font files built into the .EXE file. (Read the comments at the beginning of the GRLINK.PAS sample program on the distribution disks.)

Figures and Styles

All kinds of support routines are provided for drawing and filling figures, including points, lines, circles, arcs, ellipses, rectangles, polygons, bars, 3-D bars, and pie slices. Use *SetLineStyle* to control whether lines are thick or thin, or whether they are solid, dotted, or built using your own pattern.

Use *SetFillStyle* and *SetFillPattern*, *FillPoly* and *FloodFill* to fill a region or a polygon with cross-hatching or other intricate patterns.

Viewports and Bit Images

The *ViewPort* procedure makes all output commands operate in a rectangular region on the screen. Plots, lines, figures—all graphics output—are viewport-relative until the viewport is changed. Other routines are provided to clear a viewport and read the current viewport definitions. If clipping is active, all graphics output is clipped to the current port. Note that the CP is never clipped.

GetPixel and *PutPixel* are provided for reading and plotting pixels. *GetImage* and *PutImage* can be used to save and restore rectangular regions on the screen. They support the full complement of *BitBlt* operations (copy, **xor, or, and, not**).

Paging and Colors

There are many other support routines, including support for multiple graphic pages (EGA, VGA, and Hercules only; especially useful for doing animation), palettes, colors, and so on.

Error-Handling

Internal errors in the *Graph* unit are returned by the function *GraphResult*. *GraphResult* returns an error code that reports the status of the last graphics operation. The following error return codes are defined:

- 0: No error
- −1: (BGI) graphics not installed (use *InitGraph*)
- −2: Graphics hardware not detected
- −3: Device driver file not found
- −4: Invalid device driver file
- −5: Not enough memory to load driver
- −6: Out of memory in scan fill
- −7: Out of memory in flood fill
- −8: Font file not found
- −9: Not enough memory to load font

- –10: Invalid graphics mode for selected driver
- –11: Graphics error
- –12: Graphics I/O error
- –13: Invalid font file
- –14: Invalid font number

The following routines set *GraphResult*:

Bar	*ImageSize*	*SetFillPattern*
Bar3D	*InitGraph*	*SetFillStyle*
ClearViewPort	*InstallUserDriver*	*SetGraphBufSize*
CloseGraph	*InstallUserFont*	*SetGraphMode*
DetectGraph	*PieSlice*	*SetLineStyle*
DrawPoly	*RegisterBGIdriver*	*SetPalette*
FillPoly	*RegisterBGIfont*	*SetTextJustify*
FloodFill	*SetAllPalette*	*SetTextStyle*
GetGraphMode		

Note that *GraphResult* is reset to zero after it has been called. Therefore, the user should store the value of *GraphResult* into a temporary variable and then test it. The following return code constants are defined:

```
const
  { GraphResult error return codes }
  grOk             =   0;
  grNoInitGraph    =  -1;
  grNotDetected    =  -2;
  grFileNotFound   =  -3;
  grInvalidDriver  =  -4;
  grNoLoadMem      =  -5;
  grNoScanMem      =  -6;
  grNoFloodMem     =  -7;
  grFontNotFound   =  -8;
  grNoFontMem      =  -9;
  grInvalidMode    = -10;
  grError          = -11;
  grIOError        = -12;
  grInvalidFont    = -13;
  grInvalidFontNum = -14;
```

Getting Started

Here's a simple graphics program:

```
1  program GraphTest;
2  uses
3    Graph;
4  var
```

```
5    GraphDriver : integer;
6    GraphMode   : integer;
7    ErrorCode   : integer;
8  begin
9    GraphDriver := Detect;                          { Set flag: do detection }
10   InitGraph(GraphDriver, GraphMode, 'C:\DRIVERS');
11   ErrorCode := GraphResult;
12   if ErrorCode <> grOk then                                       { Error? }
13   begin
14     Writeln('Graphics error: ', GraphErrorMsg(ErrorCode));
15     Writeln('Program aborted...');
16     Halt(1);
17   end;
18   Rectangle(0, 0, GetMaxX, GetMaxY);            { Draw full screen box }
19   SetTextJustify(CenterText, CenterText);              { Center text }
20   SetTextStyle(DefaultFont, HorizDir, 3);
21   OutTextXY(GetMaxX div 2, GetMaxY div 2,           { Center of screen }
22             'Borland Graphics Interface (BGI)');
23   Readln;
24   CloseGraph;
25 end.  { GraphTest }
```

The program begins with a call to *InitGraph,* which autodetects the hardware and loads the appropriate graphics driver (located in C:\DRIVERS). If no graphics hardware is recognized or an error occurs during initialization, an error message is displayed and the program terminates. Otherwise, a box is drawn along the edge of the screen and text is displayed in the center of the screen.

Note: Neither the AT&T 400 line card nor the IBM 8514 graphics adapter is autodetected. You can still use these drivers by overriding autodection and passing *InitGraph* the driver code and a valid graphics mode. To use the AT&T driver, for example, replace lines 9 and 10 in the preceding example with the following three lines of code:

```
GraphDriver := ATT400;
GraphMode := ATT400Hi;
InitGraph(GraphDriver, GraphMode, 'C:\DRIVERS');
```

This instructs the graphics system to load the AT&T 400 line driver located in C:\DRIVERS and set the graphics mode to 640 by 400.

Here's another example that demonstrates how to switch back and forth between graphics and text modes:

```
 1  program GraphTest;
 2  uses
 3    Graph;
 4  var
 5    GraphDriver : integer;
 6    GraphMode   : integer;
 7    ErrorCode   : integer;
 8  begin
 9    GraphDriver := Detect;                              { Set flag: do detection }
10    InitGraph(GraphDriver, GraphMode, 'C:\DRIVERS');
11    ErrorCode := GraphResult;
12    if ErrorCode <> grOk then                           { Error? }
13    begin
14      Writeln('Graphics error: ', GraphErrorMsg(ErrorCode));
15      Writeln('Program aborted...');
16      Halt(1);
17    end;
18    OutText('In Graphics mode. Press <RETURN>');
19    Readln;
20    RestoreCRTMode;
21    Write('Now in text mode. Press <RETURN>');
22    Readln;
23    SetGraphMode(GraphMode);
24    OutText('Back in Graphics mode. Press <RETURN>');
25    Readln;
26    CloseGraph;
27  end. { GraphTest }
```

Note that the *SetGraphMode* call on line 23 resets all the graphics parameters (palette, current pointer, foreground, and background colors, and so on) to the default values.

The call to *CloseGraph* restores the video mode that was detected initially by *InitGraph* and frees the heap memory that was used to hold the graphics driver.

User-Written Heap Management Routines

Two heap management routines are used by the *Graph* unit: *GraphGetMem* and *GraphFreeMem*. *GraphGetMem* allocates memory for graphics device drivers, stroked fonts, and a scan buffer. *GraphFreeMem* deallocates the memory allocated to the drivers. The standard routines take the following form:

```
procedure GraphGetMem(var P : pointer; Size : word);
{ Allocate memory for graphics }

procedure GraphFreeMem(var P : pointer; Size : word);
{ Deallocate memory for graphics }
```

Two pointers are defined by *Graph* that by default point to the two standard routines described here. The pointers are defined as follows:

```
var
  GraphGetMemPtr  : pointer;        { Pointer to memory allocation routine }
  GraphFreeMemPtr : pointer         { Pointer to memory deallocation routine }
```

The heap management routines referenced by *GraphGetMemPtr* and *GraphFreeMemPtr* are called by the *Graph* unit to allocate and deallocate memory for three different purposes:

- a multi-purpose graphics buffer whose size can be set by a call to *SetGraphBufSize* (default = 4K)
- a device driver that is loaded by *InitGraph* (*.BGI files)
- a stroked font file that is loaded by *SetTextStyle* (*.CHR files)

The graphics buffer is always allocated on the heap. The device driver is allocated on the heap unless your program loads or links one in and calls *RegisterBGIdriver*, and the font file is allocated on the heap when you select a stroked font using *SetTextStyle*—unless your program loads or links one in and calls *RegisterBGIfont*.

Upon initialization of the *Graph* unit, these pointers point to the standard graphics allocation and deallocation routines that are defined in the implementation section of the *Graph* unit. You can insert your own memory management routines by assigning these pointers the address of your routines. The user-defined routines must have the same parameter lists as the standard routines and must be *far* procedures. The following is an example of user-defined allocation and deallocation routines; notice the use of *MyExitProc* to automatically call *CloseGraph* when the program terminates:

```
program UserHeapManagement;
{ Illustrates how the user can steal the heap }
{ management routines used by the Graph unit. }

uses
  Graph;
var
  GraphDriver, GraphMode : integer;
  ErrorCode              : integer;    { Used to store GraphResult return code }
  PreGraphExitProc       : pointer;        { Used to save original exit proc }
{$F+} { User routines must be far call model }
procedure MyGetMem(var P : pointer; Size : word);
{ Allocate memory for graphics device drivers, fonts, and scan buffer }
begin
  GetMem(P, Size)
end; { MyGetMem }

procedure MyFreeMem(var P : pointer; Size : word);
```

Chapter 12, Standard Units

```
                            { Deallocate memory for graphics device drivers, fonts, and scan buffer }
                            begin
                              if P <> nil then                               { Don't free Nil pointers! }
                              begin
                                FreeMem(P, Size);
                                P := nil;
                              end;
                            end; { MyFreeMem }

                            procedure MyExitProc;
                            { Always gets called when program terminates }
                            begin
                              ExitProc := PreGraphExitProc;                 { Restore original exit proc }
                              CloseGraph;                                        { Do heap clean up }
                            end; { MyExitProc }
                            {$F-}
                            begin
                              { Install clean-up routine }
                              PreGraphExitProc := ExitProc;
                              ExitProc := @MyExitProc;

                              GraphGetMemPtr := @MyGetMem;                  { Control memory allocation }
                              GraphFreeMemPtr := @MyFreeMem;                { Control memory deallocation }

                              GraphDriver := Detect;
                              InitGraph(GraphDriver, GraphMode, '');
                              ErrorCode := GraphResult;
                              if ErrorCode <> grOk then
                              begin
                                Writeln('Graphics error: ', GraphErrorMsg(ErrorCode));
                                Readln;
                                Halt(1);
                              end;
                              Line(0, 0, GetMaxX, GetMaxY);
                              OutTextXY(1, 1, 'Press <Return>:');
                              Readln;
                            end. { UserHeapManagment }
```

Graph Unit Constants, Types and Variables

Constants

The following error values are returned by *GraphResult*:

```
const
  grOk              =   0;
  grNoInitGraph     =  -1;
  grNotDetected     =  -2;
  grFileNotFound    =  -3;
  grInvalidDriver   =  -4;
  grNoLoadMem       =  -5;
  grNoScanMem       =  -6;
  grNoFloodMem      =  -7;
  grFontNotFound    =  -8;
  grNoFontMem       =  -9;
  grInvalidMode     = -10;
  grError           = -11;   { generic error }
  grIOerror         = -12;
  grInvalidFont     = -13;
  grInvalidFontNum  = -14;
```

Use these driver and mode constants with *InitGraph*, *DetectGraph*, and *GetModeRange*:

```
const
  Detect        =    0;                    { Requests autodetection }
  CGA           =    1;
  MCGA          =    2;
  EGA           =    3;
  EGA64         =    4;
  EGAMono       =    5;
  IBM8514       =    6;
  HercMono      =    7;
  ATT400        =    8;
  VGA           =    9;
  PC3270        =   10;
  CurrentDriver = -128;                    { Passed to GetModeRange }

  CGAC0     = 0;     { 320x200 palette 0: LightGreen, LightRed, Yellow; 1 page }
  CGAC1     = 1;     { 320x200 palette 1: LightCyan, LightMagenta, White; 1 page }
  CGAC2     = 2;            { 320x200 palette 2: Green, Red, Brown; 1 page }
  CGAC3     = 3;         { 320x200 palette 3: Cyan, Magenta, LightGray; 1 page }
  CGAHi     = 4;                                      { 640x200 1 page }
  MCGAC0    = 0;     { 320x200 palette 0: LightGreen, LightRed, Yellow; 1 page }
  MCGAC1    = 1;     { 320x200 palette 1: LightCyan, LightMagenta, White; 1 page }
  MCGAC2    = 2;            { 320x200 palette 2: Green, Red, Brown; 1 page }
  MCGAC3    = 3;         { 320x200 palette 3: Cyan, Magenta, LightGray; 1 page }
  MCGAMed   = 4;                                      { 640x200 1 page }
  MCGAHi    = 5;                                      { 640x480 1 page }
  EGALo     = 0;                                 { 640x200 16 color 4 page }
  EGAHi     = 1;                                 { 640x350 16 color 2 page }
  EGA64Lo   = 0;                                 { 640x200 16 color 1 page }
  EGA64Hi   = 1;                                 { 640x350 4 color 1 page }
  EGAMonoHi = 3;        { 640x350 64K on card, 1 page; 256K on card, 2 page }
  HercMonoHi = 0;                                     { 720x348 2 page }
```

Chapter 12, Standard Units

```
ATT400C0    = 0;    { 320x200 palette 0: LightGreen, LightRed, Yellow; 1 page }
ATT400C1    = 1;    { 320x200 palette 1: LightCyan, LightMagenta, White; 1 page }
ATT400C2    = 2;    { 320x200 palette 2: Green, Red, Brown; 1 page }
ATT400C3    = 3;    { 320x200 palette 3: Cyan, Magenta, LightGray; 1 page }
ATT400Med   = 4;                                       { 640x200 1 page }
ATT400Hi    = 5;                                       { 640x400 1 page }
VGALo       = 0;                              { 640x200 16 color 4 page }
VGAMed      = 1;                              { 640x350 16 color 2 page }
VGAHi       = 2;                              { 640x480 16 color 1 page }
PC3270Hi    = 0;                                       { 720x350 1 page }
IBM8514LO   = 0;                                  { 640x480 256 colors }
IBM8514HI   = 1;                                 { 1024x768 256 colors }
```

Use these color constants with *SetPalette* and *SetAllPalette*:

```
const
  Black        = 0;
  Blue         = 1;
  Green        = 2;
  Cyan         = 3;
  Red          = 4;
  Magenta      = 5;
  Brown        = 6;
  LightGray    = 7;
  DarkGray     = 8;
  LightBlue    = 9;
  LightGreen   = 10;
  LightCyan    = 11;
  LightRed     = 12;
  LightMagenta = 13;
  Yellow       = 14;
  White        = 15;
```

These color constants can be used with *SetRGBPalette* to select the standard EGA colors on an IBM 8514 graphics adapter:

```
const
  EGABlack        = 0;        { dark colors }
  EGABlue         = 1;
  EGAGreen        = 2;
  EGACyan         = 3;
  EGARed          = 4;
  EGAMagenta      = 5;
  EGABrown        = 20;
  EGALightgray    = 7;
  EGADarkgray     = 56;       { light colors }
  EGALightblue    = 57;
  EGALightgreen   = 58;
  EGALightcyan    = 59;
  EGALightred     = 60;
  EGALightmagenta = 61;
```

```
EGAYellow           = 62;
EGAWhite            = 63;
```

Use these line style constants with *GetLineSettings* and *SetLineStyle*:

```
const
  SolidLn    = 0;
  DottedLn   = 1;
  CenterLn   = 2;
  DashedLn   = 3;
  UserBitLn  = 4;                              { User-defined line style }

  NormWidth  = 1;
  ThickWidth = 3;
```

Use these font control constants with *GetTextSettings* and *SetTextStyle*:

```
const
  DefaultFont    = 0;                          { 8x8 bit mapped font }
  TriplexFont    = 1;                          { "Stroked" fonts }
  SmallFont      = 2;
  SansSerifFont  = 3;
  GothicFont     = 4;

  HorizDir       = 0;                          { Left to right }
  VertDir        = 1;                          { Bottom to top }

  UserCharSize   = 0;                          { User-defined char size }
```

These constants control horizontal and vertical justification for *SetTextJustify*:

```
const
  LeftText   = 0;
  CenterText = 1;
  RightText  = 2;

  BottomText = 0;
{ CenterText = 1; already defined above }
  TopText    = 2;
```

Use these constants with *SetViewPort* to control clipping. With clipping on, graphics output is clipped at the viewport boundaries:

```
const
  ClipOn  = true;
  ClipOff = false;
```

These constants may be used with *Bar3D* to specify whether a 3-D top should be drawn on top of the bar (allows for stacking bars and only drawing a top on the topmost bar):

```
const
  TopOn  = true;
  TopOff = false;
```

These fill pattern constants are used by *GetFillSettings* and *SetFillStyle*. Use *SetFillPattern* to define your own fill pattern; then call

```
SetFillStyle(UserFill, SomeColor)
```

and make your fill pattern the active style:

```
const
  EmptyFill      = 0;   { Fills area in background color }
  SolidFill      = 1;   { Fills area in solid fill color }
  LineFill       = 2;   { --- fill }
  LtSlashFill    = 3;   { /// fill }
  SlashFill      = 4;   { /// fill with thick lines }
  BkSlashFill    = 5;   { \\\ fill with thick lines }
  LtBkSlashFill  = 6;   { \\\ fill }
  HatchFill      = 7;   { Light hatch fill }
  XHatchFill     = 8;   { Heavy cross hatch fill }
  InterleaveFill = 9;   { Interleaving line fill }
  WideDotFill    = 10;  { Widely spaced dot fill }
  CloseDotFill   = 11;  { Closely spaced dot fill }
  UserFill       = 12;  { User-defined fill }
```

Use these BitBlt operators with both *PutImage* and *SetWriteMode*:

```
const
  CopyPut = 0;   { MOV }
  XORPut  = 1;   { XOR }
```

These BitBlt operators are used by *PutImage* only:

```
const
  OrPut   = 2;   { OR }
  AndPut  = 3;   { AND }
  NotPut  = 4;   { NOT }
```

This constant is used by *GetPalette, GetDefaultPalette, SetAllPalette*, and to define the *PaletteType* record:

```
const
  MaxColors = 15;
```

Types

This record is used by *GetPalette, GetDefaultPalette*, and *SetAllPalette*:

```
type
  PaletteType = record
    Size   : byte;
    Colors : array[0..MaxColors] of shortint;
  end;
```

This record is used by by *GetLineSettings*:

```
type
  LineSettingsType = record
    LineStyle : word;
    Pattern   : word;
    Thickness : word;
  end;
```

This record is used by by *GetTextSettings*:

```
type
  TextSettingsType = record
    Font      : word;
    Direction : word;
    CharSize  : word;
    Horiz     : word;
    Vert      : word;
  end;
```

This record is used by by *GetFillSettings*:

```
type
  FillSettingsType = record
    Pattern : word;
    Color   : word;
  end;
```

This record is used by *GetFillPattern* and *SetFillPattern*:

```
type
  FillPatternType = array[1..8] of byte;  { User-defined fill style }
```

This type is defined for your convenience. Note that both fields are of type integer (not word):

```
type
  PointType = record
    X, Y : integer;
  end;
```

This record is used by *GetViewSettings* to report the status of the current viewport:

```
type
  ViewPortType = record
    x1, y1, x2, y2 : integer;
    Clip           : boolean;
  end;
```

This record is used by by *GetArcCoords* and can be used to retrieve information about the last call to *Arc* or *Ellipse*:

Chapter 12, Standard Units   147

```
type
  ArcCoordsType = record
    X, Y           : integer;
    Xstart, Ystart : integer;
    Xend, Yend     : integer;
  end;
```

Variables

These variables initially point to the Graph unit's heap management routines. If your program does its own heap management, assign the addresses of your allocation and deallocation routines to *GraphGetMemPtr* and *GraphFreeMemPtr* respectively:

```
GraphGetMemPtr  : pointer;        { Allows user to steal heap allocation }
GraphFreeMemPtr : pointer;        { Allows user to steal heap deallocation }
```

Procedures

Arc	Draws a circular arc from start angle to end angle, using (x,y) as the center point.
Bar	Draws a bar using the current fill style and color.
Bar3D	Draws a 3-D bar using the current fill style and color.
Circle	Draws a circle using (x,y) as the center point.
ClearDevice	Clears the currently selected output device and homes the current pointer.
ClearViewPort	Clears the current viewport.
CloseGraph	Shuts down the graphics system.
DetectGraph	Checks the hardware and determines which graphics driver and mode to use.
DrawPoly	Draws the outline of a polygon using the current line style and color.
Ellipse	Draws an elliptical arc from start angle to end angle, using (X,Y) as the center point.
FillEllipse	Draws a filled ellipse using (X,Y) as a center point and *XRadius* and *YRadius* as the horizontal and vertical axes.
FillPoly	Fills a polygon, using the scan converter.

FloodFill	Fills a bounded region using the current fill pattern and fill color.
GetArcCoords	Allows the user to inquire about the coordinates of the last *Arc* command.
GetAspectRatio	Returns the effective resolution of the graphics screen from which the aspect ratio (*Xasp:Yasp*) can be computed.
GetFillPattern	Returns the last fill pattern set by a call to *SetFillPattern*.
GetFillSettings	Allows the user to inquire about the current fill pattern and color as set by *SetFillStyle* or *SetFillPattern*.
GetImage	Saves a bit image of the specified region into a buffer.
GetLineSettings	Returns the current line style, line pattern, and line thickness as set by *SetLineStyle*.
GetModeRange	Returns the lowest and highest valid graphics mode for a given driver.
GetPalette	Returns the current palette and its size.
GetTextSettings	Returns the current text font, direction, size, and justification as set by *SetTextStyle* and *SetTextJustify*.
GetViewSettings	Allows the user to inquire about the current viewport and clipping parameters.
GraphDefaults	Homes the current pointer (CP) and resets the graphics system.
InitGraph	Initializes the graphics system and puts the hardware into graphics mode.
Line	Draws a line from the (*x1, y1*) to (*x2, y2*).
LineRel	Draws a line to a point that is a relative distance from the current pointer (CP).
LineTo	Draws a line from the current pointer to (*x,y*).
MoveRel	Moves the current pointer (CP) a relative distance from its current position.
MoveTo	Moves the current graphics pointer (CP) to (*x,y*).
OutText	Sends a string to the output device at the current pointer.

OutTextXY	Sends a string to the output device.
PieSlice	Draws and fills a pie slice, using (X,Y) as the center point and drawing from start angle to end angle.
PutImage	Puts a bit image onto the screen.
PutPixel	Plots a pixel at *x,y*.
Rectangle	Draws a rectangle using the current line style and color.
RestoreCrtMode	Restores the original screen mode before graphics is initialized.
Sector	Draws and fills an elliptical sector.
SetActivePage	Set the active page for graphics output.
SetAllPalette	Changes all palette colors as specified.
SetAspectRatio	Changes the default aspect ratio.
SetBkColor	Sets the current background color using the palette.
SetColor	Sets the current drawing color using the palette.
SetFillPattern	Selects a user-defined fill pattern.
SetFillStyle	Sets the fill pattern and color.
SetGraphBufSize	Allows you to change the size of the buffer used for scan and flood fills.
SetGraphMode	Sets the system to graphics mode and clears the screen.
SetLineStyle	Sets the current line width and style.
SetPalette	Changes one palette color as specified by *ColorNum* and *Color*.
SetRGBPalette	Allows you to modify palette entries for the IBM 8514 and the VGA drivers.
SetTextJustify	Sets text justification values used by *OutText* and *OutTextXY*.
SetTextStyle	Sets the current text font, style, and character magnification factor.
SetUserCharSize	Lets you change the character width and height for stroked fonts.
SetViewPort	Sets the current output viewport or window for graphics output.

SetVisualPage	Sets the visual graphics page number.
SetWriteMode	Sets the writing mode (copy or XOR) for lines drawn by *DrawPoly, Line, LineRel, LineTo,* and *Rectangle.*

Functions

GetBkColor	Returns the current background color.
GetColor	Returns the current drawing color.
GetDefaultPalette	Returns the default hardware palette in a record of *PaletteType.*
GetDriverName	Returns a string containing the name of the current driver.
GetGraphMode	Returns the current graphics mode.
GetMaxColor	Returns the highest color that can be passed to *SetColor.*
GetMaxMode	Returns the maximum mode number for the currently loaded driver.
GetMaxX	Returns the rightmost column (*x* resolution) of the current graphics driver and mode.
GetMaxY	Returns the bottommost row (*y* resolution) of the current graphics driver and mode.
GetModeName	Returns a string containing the name of the specified graphics mode.
GetPaletteSize	Returns the size of the palette color lookup table.
GetPixel	Gets the pixel value at *X,Y.*
GetX	Returns the X coordinate of the current position (CP).
GetY	Returns the Y coordinate of the current position (CP).
GraphErrorMsg	Returns an error message string for the specified *ErrorCode.*
GraphResult	Returns an error code for the last graphics operation.
ImageSize	Returns the number of bytes required to store a rectangular region of the screen.

InstallUserDriver	Installs a vendor-added device driver to the BGI device driver table.
InstallUserFont	Installs a new font file that is not built into the BGI system.
RegisterBGIdriver	Registers a valid BGI driver with the graphics system.
RegisterBGIfont	Registers a valid BGI font with the graphics system.
TextHeight	Returns the height of a string in pixels.
TextWidth	Returns the width of a string in pixels.

For a detailed description of each procedure or function, refer to Chapter 16, "Turbo Pascal Reference Lookup."

The Turbo3 Unit

Every routine in this unit is duplicated or improved upon in other standard units. The *Turbo3* unit is provided for backward compatibility only. By using *Turbo3*, you gain more 3.0-compatibility, but lose direct access to important new features built into some of the standard routines duplicated here. (Note that you can still call these standard routines by using the unit override syntax; for example, *Turbo3*'s *MemAvail* calls the *System.MemAvail* function even if you are using the *Turbo3* unit in your program. For more information about referring to routines with the same name in other units, look at Chapter 4 in the *User's Guide*, "Units and Related Mysteries.")

Note: The routines that follow are *not* described in Chapter 16. For more detailed information about *Turbo3* routines, refer to your Turbo Pascal 3.0 reference manual.

Interface Section

Here's a look at the **interface** section of the *Turbo3* unit:

```
unit Turbo3;
interface
uses Crt;
var
  Kbd    : Text;
  CBreak : boolean absolute CheckBreak;

function MemAvail: integer;
function MaxAvail: integer;
function LongFileSize(var F): real;
```

```
function LongFilePos(var F): real;
procedure LongSeek(var F; Pos: real);
procedure HighVideo;
procedure NormVideo;
procedure LowVideo;
function IOResult : integer;
```

As you can see, there are two global variables, five functions, and four procedures declared in the *Turbo3* unit.

Kbd

This is provided for Turbo Pascal 3.0 programs that read from the keyboard device; for example, *Read(Kbd, CharVar)*. Note that there is now a function in the *Crt* unit called *ReadKey* that should be used in place of *Read(Kbd, CharVar)*. Here are two programs that read a character and report whether an extended key was typed (*F1, F2, Left arrow*, and so on):

In version 3.0:

```
program TestKbd;
uses Crt, Turbo3;
var
  c : char;
begin
  Read(Kbd, c);
  if (c = #27) and KeyPressed then
  begin
    Read(Kbd, c);
    Writeln('Extended key: ', c);
  end
  else
    Writeln(c);
end.
```

Notice that the *Kbd* device handler converts extended keys from (null + character) to (ESC + second character). Since *Esc* (#27) is a perfectly valid key to enter from the keyboard, a call to *KeyPressed* must be made to determine whether the #27 is the first key from an extended key or an actual *Esc* typed on the keyboard. If an *Esc* is typed, followed quickly by another character before the program detected the *Esc*, the two keys would be mistaken as an extended keystroke.

In version 5.0:

```
program TestReadKey;
uses Crt;
var
  c : char;
```

```
begin
  c := ReadKey;
  if (c = #0) then
    Writeln('Extended key: ', ReadKey);
  else
    Writeln(c);
end.
```

The code in 5.0 is smaller (and faster), and contains none of the ambiguity about the leading character of an extended keystroke. (It is impossible to generate a null character from the keyboard except when using the extended keys.)

CBreak

CBreak has been renamed to *CheckBreak* in version 5.0. Backward compatibility is achieved by giving *CBreak* the same address as *CheckBreak*, which is declared in the *Crt* unit. The statement *CBreak := False* turns off *Ctrl-Break* checking; *CBreak := True* turns it back on.

Procedures

HighVideo	Sets the video attribute to yellow on black (color systems) or white on black (black and white, mono systems).
LongSeek	Moves the current position of a file to a specified component. Uses a real number parameter to specify the component number.
LowVideo	Sets the video attribute to *LightGray* on black.
NormVideo	Same as *HighVideo*. Sets the video attribute to yellow on black (color systems) or white on black (black and white, mono systems).

Functions

IOResult	Returns an integer value that is the status of the last I/O operation performed. The *Turbo3 IOResult* function returns 3.0-compatible return codes wherever possible.
LongFilePos	Returns the current file position of a file. The value returned is a real number.
LongFileSize	Returns the size of the file. The value returned is a real number.

MaxAvail	Returns the size of the largest contiguous free block in the heap (in paragraphs).
MemAvail	Returns the number of free paragraphs of heap storage available.

The Graph3 Unit

The *Graph3* unit is a direct implementation of the turtlegraphics driver provided by Turbo Pascal 3.0. In Turbo Pascal 3.0, the turtlegraphics driver was made up of two files, GRAPH.P and GRAPH.BIN that supported the IBM CGA and compatibles. GRAPH.P actually defines the external machine code routines contained in GRAPH.BIN.

Graph3 combines Turbo Pascal 3.0's GRAPH.P and GRAPH.BIN into a single unit, still retaining the same functionality. The only modification you need to make to a Turbo Pascal 3.0 program that uses the turtlegraphics driver is to remove the {$I GRAPH.P} compiler directive, replacing it with a reference to *Crt* and *Graph3* in your program's **uses** clause.

Note: The routines that follow are *not* described in Chapter 16. For more detailed information about *Graph3* routines, refer to your Turbo Pascal 3.0 reference manual.

Here are *Graph3*'s constants:

```
const
  North = 0;
  East  = 90;
  South = 180;
  West  = 270;
```

Procedures

Arc	Draws an arc using the given parameters.
Back	Moves the turtle backward by the given distance. (Turtlegraphics)
Circle	Draws a circle.
ClearScreen	Clears the active window and homes the turtle. (Turtlegraphics)
ColorTable	Defines a color translation table that lets the current color of any given point determine the new color of that point when it is redrawn.

Draw	Draws a line between the specified endpoints and in the specified color.
FillPattern	Fills a rectangular area with the current pattern using the specified color.
FillScreen	Fills the entire active window with the indicated color.
FillShape	Fills an area of any shape with the specified color.
Forwd	Moves the turtle forward by the given distance. (Turtlegraphics)
GetDotColor	Returns the color value of the dot at the indicated location.
GetPic	Copies the contents of an area on the screen into a buffer; the contents can later be restored using *PutPic*.
GraphBackground	Sets background color of screen.
GraphColorMode	Sets you in 320x200 color graphics mode.
GraphMode	Sets you in 320x200 black-and-white graphics mode.
GraphWindow	Lets you define an area of the screen as the active window in any of the graphics modes.
Heading	Returns the current heading of the turtle. (Turtlegraphics)
HideTurtle	Hides the turtle. (Turtlegraphics)
HiRes	Sets screen in 640x200 high-resolution graphics mode.
HiResColor	Selects the color used for drawing in high-resolution graphics.
Home	Puts the turtle in its home position. (Turtlegraphics)
NoWrap	Disables "wrapping" for the turtle. (Turtlegraphics)
Palette	Activates the color palette specified.
Pattern	Defines an 8x8 pattern to be used by *FillPattern*.
PenDown	Puts the turtle's pen "down" so that any movement of the turtle results in drawing. (Turtlegraphics)

PenUp	Puts the turtle's pen "up" so that the turtle can be moved without drawing. (Turtlegraphics)
Plot	Plots a point at the specified coordinates and in the specified color.
PutPic	Copies the contents of a buffer.
SetHeading	Turns the turtle to the specified angle. (Turtlegraphics)
SetPenColor	Sets the color used for the turtle's pen. (Turtlegraphics)
SetPosition	Moves the turtle to the given coordinates without drawing a line. (Turtlegraphics)
ShowTurtle	Makes the turtle visible. (Turtlegraphics)
TurnLeft	Turns the turtle's heading to the left (counterclockwise). (Turtlegraphics)
TurnRight	Turns the turtle's heading to the right (clockwise). (Turtlegraphics)
TurtleDelay	Sets a delay between each step of the turtle. (Turtlegraphics)
TurtleThere	Tests if the turtle is visible and in the active window. (Turtlegraphics)
TurtleWindow	Defines an area of the screen as the active turtle graphics screen. (Turtlegraphics)
Wrap	Forces wraparound when the turtle attempts to move past the boundaries of the active window. (Turtlegraphics)
XCor	Returns the current X-coordinate of the turtle. (Turtlegraphics)
YCor	Returns the current Y-coordinate of the turtle. (Turtlegraphics)

CHAPTER

13

Overlays

Overlays are parts of a program that share a common memory area. Only the parts of the program that are required for a given function reside in memory at the same time; they can overwrite each other during execution.

Overlays can significantly reduce a program's total run-time memory requirements. In fact, with overlays you can execute programs that are much larger than the total available memory, since only parts of the program reside in memory at any given time.

Turbo Pascal manages overlays at the unit level; this is the smallest part of a program that can be made into an overlay. When an overlaid program is compiled, Turbo Pascal generates an overlay file (extension .OVR) in addition to the executable file (extension .EXE). The .EXE file contains the static (non-overlaid) parts of the program, and the .OVR file contains all the overlaid units that will be swapped in and out of memory during program execution.

Except for a few programming rules, an overlaid unit is identical to a non-overlaid unit. In fact, as long as you observe these rules, you don't even need to recompile a unit to make it into an overlay. The decision of whether or not a unit is overlaid is made by the program that uses the unit.

When an overlay is loaded into memory, it is placed in the overlay buffer, which resides in memory between the stack segment and the heap. By default, the size of the overlay buffer is as small as possible, but it may be easily increased at run-time by allocating additional space from the heap. Like the data segment and the minimum heap size, the default overlay buffer size is allocated when the .EXE is loaded. If enough memory isn't available, an error message will be displayed by DOS (Program too big to fit in memory) or by the IDE (Not enough memory to run program).

One very important option of the overlay manager is the ability to load the overlay file into expanded memory when sufficient space is available. Turbo Pascal supports version 3.2 or later of the Lotus/Intel/Microsoft Expanded Memory Specification (EMS) for this purpose. Once placed into EMS, the overlay file is closed, and subsequent overlay loads are reduced to fast in-memory transfers.

The Overlay Unit

Turbo Pascal's overlay manager is implemented by the *Overlay* standard unit. The buffer management techniques used by the *Overlay* unit are very advanced, and always guarantee optimal performance in the available memory. For example, the overlay manager always keeps as many overlays as possible in the overlay buffer, to reduce the chance of having to read an overlay from disk. Once an overlay is loaded, a call to one of its routines executes just as fast as a call to a non-overlaid routine. Furthermore, when the overlay manager needs to dispose of an overlay to make room for another, it attempts to first dispose of overlays that are inactive (ones that have no active routines at that point in time).

To implement its advanced overlay management techniques, Turbo Pascal requires that you observe two important rules when writing overlaid programs:

- All overlaid units must include a {$O+} directive, which causes the compiler to ensure that the generated code can be overlaid.
- At any call to an overlaid procedure or function, you must guarantee that all currently active procedures and functions use the FAR call model.

Both rules are explained further in a section entitled "Designing Overlaid Programs," beginning on page 164. For now, just note that you can easily satisfy these requirements by placing a {$O+,F+} compiler directive at the beginning of all overlaid units, and a {$F+} compiler directive at the beginning of all other units and the main program.

Note: Failing to observe the FAR call requirement in an overlaid program will cause unpredictable and possibly catastrophic results when the program is executed.

The {$O *unitname*} compiler directive is used in a program to indicate which units to overlay. This directive must be placed after the program's **uses** clause, and the **uses** clause must name the *Overlay* standard unit before any of the overlaid units. An example follows:

```
program Editor;

{$F+}                       { Force FAR calls for all procedures & functions }
```

uses
  Overlay,Crt,Dos,EdInOut,EdFormat,EdPrint,EdFind,EdMain;
{$O EdInOut}
{$O EdFormat}
{$O EdPrint}
{$O EdFind}
{$O EdMain}

Note: The compiler reports an error if you attempt to overlay a unit that wasn't compiled in the {$O+} state. Of the standard units, the only one that can be overlaid is *Dos*; the other standard units, *System, Overlay, Crt, Graph, Turbo3,* and *Graph3,* cannot be overlaid. In addition, programs containing overlaid units must be compiled to disk; the compiler reports an error if you attempt to compile such programs to memory.

Constants and Variables

The constants and variables defined by the *Overlay* unit are briefly discussed in this section.

The OvrResult Variable

Before returning, each of the procedures in the *Overlay* unit stores a result code in the *OvrResult* variable.

  var OvrResult: Integer;

The possible return codes are defined in the constant declaration in the next section. In general, a value of zero indicates success.

The *OvrResult* variable resembles the *IOResult* standard function except that *OvrResult* is *not* set to zero once it is accessed. Thus, there is no need to copy *OvrResult* into a local variable before it is examined.

Result Codes

Errors in the *Overlay* unit are reported through the *OvrResult* variable. The following result codes are defined:

```
const
  ovrOk = 0;                             { Success }
  ovrError = -1;                         { Overlay manager error }
  ovrNotFound = -2;                      { Overlay file not found }
  ovrNoMemory = -3;          { Not enough memory for overlay buffer }
  ovrIOError = -4;                       { Overlay file I/O error }
  ovrNoEMSDriver = -5;                   { EMS driver not installed }
  ovrNoEMSMemory = -6;                   { Not enough EMS memory }
```

Procedures and Functions

The *Overlay* unit defines the procedures *OvrInit*, *OvrInitEMS*, *OvrSetBuf*, and *OvrClearBuf*, and the function *OvrGetBuf*. Here is a brief description of each; for more detailed information, see Chapter 8, "Procedures and Functions."

OvrInit

procedure OvrInit(FileName:**string**);

Initializes the overlay manager and opens the overlay file. If the *FileName* parameter does not specify a drive or a subdirectory, the overlay manager searches for the file in the current directory, in the directory that contains the .EXE file (if running under DOS 3.x), and in the directories specified in the DOS PATH environment variable. Possible error return codes are *ovrError* and *ovrNotFound*. In case of error, the overlay manager remains uninstalled, and an attempt to call an overlaid routine will produce run-time error 208.

Note: The *OvrInit* procedure *must* be called before any of the other overlay manager procedures.

OvrInitEMS

procedure OvrInitEMS;

If possible, loads the overlay file into EMS. If successful, the overlay file is closed, and all subsequent overlay loads are reduced to fast in-memory transfers. Possible error return codes are *ovrError*, *ovrIOError*, *ovrNoEMSDriver*, and *ovrNoEMSMemory*. The overlay manager will continue to function if *OvrInitEMS* returns an error, but overlays will be read from disk.

Note: Using *OvrInitEMS* to place the overlay file in EMS does not eliminate the need for an overlay buffer. Overlays still have to be copied from EMS into "normal" memory in the overlay buffer before they can be executed. However, since such in-memory transfers are significantly faster than disk reads, the need to increase the size of the overlay buffer becomes less apparent.

OvrSetBuf

procedure OvrSetBuf(Size:longint);

Sets the size of the overlay buffer. The specified size must be larger than or equal to the initial size of the overlay buffer, and less than or equal to *MemAvail* plus the current size of the overlay buffer. If the specified size is larger than the current size, additional space is allocated from the beginning of the heap (thus decreasing the size of the heap). Likewise, if the specified size is less than the current size, excess space is returned to the heap. *OvrSetBuf* requires that the heap be empty; an error is returned if dynamic variables have already been allocated using *New* or *GetMem*. Possible error return codes are *ovrError* and *ovrNoMemory*. The overlay manager will continue to function if *OvrSetBuf* returns an error, but the size of the overlay buffer will remain unchanged.

OvrGetBuf

function OvrGetBuf:longint;

Returns the current size of the overlay buffer. Initially, the overlay buffer is as small as possible, corresponding to the size of the largest overlay. A buffer of this size is automatically allocated when an overlaid program is executed. (**Note**: The initial buffer size may be larger than 64K, since it includes both code and fix-up information for the largest overlay.)

OvrClearBuf

procedure OvrClearBuf;

Clears the overlay buffer. All currently loaded overlays are disposed from the overlay buffer, forcing subsequent calls to overlaid routines to reload the overlays from the overlay file (or from EMS). If *OvrClearBuf* is called from an overlay, that overlay will immediately be reloaded upon return from *OvrClearBuf*. The overlay manager never requires you to call *OvrClearBuf*; in fact, doing so will decrease performance of your application, since it forces overlays to be reloaded. *OvrClearBuf* is solely intended for special use, such as temporarily reclaiming the memory occupied by the overlay buffer.

Designing Overlaid Programs

This section provides some important information on designing programs with overlays. Look it over carefully, since a number of the issues discussed are vital to well-behaved overlaid applications.

Overlay Code Generation

Turbo Pascal only allows a unit to be overlaid if it was compiled with {$O+}. In this state, the code generator takes special precautions when passing string and set constant parameters from one overlaid procedure or function to another. For example, if *UnitA* contains a procedure with the following header:

```
procedure WriteStr(S: string);
```

and if *UnitB* contains the statement

```
WriteStr('Hello world...');
```

then Turbo Pascal places the string constant 'Hello world...' in *UnitB*'s code segment, and passes a pointer to it to the *WriteStr* procedure. However, if both units are overlaid, this would not work, since at the call to *WriteStr*, *UnitB*'s code segment may be overwritten by *UnitA*'s, thus rendering the string pointer invalid. The {$O+} directive is used to avoid such problems; whenever Turbo Pascal detects a call from one unit compiled with {$O+} to another unit compiled with {$O+}, the compiler makes sure to copy all code-segment-based constants into stack temporaries before passing pointers to them.

The use of {$O+} in a unit does not force you to overlay that unit. It just instructs Turbo Pascal to ensure that the unit can be overlaid, if so desired. If you develop units that you plan to use in overlaid as well as non-overlaid applications, then compiling them with {$O+} ensures that you can indeed do both with just one version of the unit.

The FAR Call Requirement

As mentioned previously, at any call to an overlaid procedure or function in another module, you *must* guarantee that all currently active procedures or functions use the FAR call model.

This is best illustrated by example: Assume that *OvrA* is a procedure in an overlaid unit, and that *MainB* and *MainC* are procedures in the main program. If the main program calls *MainC*, which calls *MainB*, which then calls *OvrA*, then at the call to *OvrA*, *MainB* and *MainC* are active (they have not yet returned), and are thus required to use the FAR call model. Being declared in the main program, *MainB* and *MainC* would normally use the NEAR call model; in this case, though, a {$F+} compiler directive must be used to force the FAR call model into effect.

The easiest way to satisfy the FAR call requirement is of course to place a {$F+} directive at the beginning of the main program and each unit. Alternatively, you can change the default $F setting to {$F+} using a /$F+ command-line directive (TPC.EXE) or the O/C/Force Far Calls menu command in the IDE. Compared to mixed NEAR and FAR calls, the added cost of FAR calls exclusively is usually quite limited: One extra word of stack space per active procedure, and one extra byte per call.

Initializing the Overlay Manager

Here we'll take a look at some examples of how to initialize the overlay manager. The initialization code must be placed before the first call to an overlaid routine, and would typically be done at the beginning of the program's statement part.

The following piece of code shows just how little you need to initialize the overlay manager:

```
begin
  OvrInit('EDITOR.OVR');
end;
```

No error checks are made, so if there is not enough memory for the overlay buffer or if the overlay file was not found, run-time error 208 (Overlay manager not installed) will occur when you attempt to call an overlaid routine.

Here's another simple example that expands on the previous one:

```
begin
  OvrInit('EDITOR.OVR');
  OvrInitEMS;
end;
```

In this case, provided there is enough memory for the overlay buffer and that the overlay file can be located, the overlay manager checks to see if EMS memory is available and, if so, loads the overlay file into EMS.

As mentioned previously, the initial overlay buffer size is as small as possible, or rather, just big enough to contain the largest overlay. This may prove adequate for some applications, but imagine a situation where a particular function of a program is implemented through two or more units, each of which are overlaid. If the total size of those units is larger than the largest overlay, a substantial amout of swapping will occur if the units make frequent calls to each other.

Obviously, the solution is to increase the size of the overlay buffer so that enough memory is available at any given time to contain all overlays that make frequent calls to each other. The following code demonstrates the use of *OvrSetBuf* to increase the overlay buffer size:

```
const
  OvrMaxSize = 80000;
begin
  OvrInit('EDITOR.OVR');
  OvrInitEMS;
  OvrSetBuf(OvrMaxSize);
end;
```

There is no general formula for determining the ideal overlay buffer size. Only an intimate knowledge of the application and a bit of experimenting will provide a suitable value.

Note: Using *OvrInitEMS* to place the overlay file in EMS does not eliminate the need for an overlay buffer. Overlays must still be copied from EMS into "normal" memory in the overlay buffer before they can be executed. However, since as such in-memory transfers are significantly faster than disk reads, the need to increase the size of the overlay buffer becomes less apparent.

Remember, *OvrSetBuf* will expand the overlay buffer by shrinking the heap. Therefore, the heap must be empty or *OvrSetBuf* will have no effect. If you are using the *Graph* unit, make sure you call *OvrSetBuf before* you call *InitGraph*, which allocates memory on the heap.

Here's a rather elaborate example of overlay manager initialization with full error-checking:

```
const
  OvrMaxSize = 80000;
var
  OvrName: string[79];
  Size: LongInt;
begin
  OvrName:='EDITOR.OVR';
  repeat
    OvrInit(OvrName);
    if OvrResult=ovrNotFound then
    begin
      WriteLn('Overlay file not found: ',OvrName,'.');
      Write('Enter correct overlay file name: ');
      ReadLn(OvrName);
    end;
  until OvrResult<>ovrNotFound;
```

```
    if OvrResult<>ovrOk then
    begin
      WriteLn('Overlay manager error.');
      Halt(1);
    end;
    OvrInitEMS;
    if OvrResult<>OvrOK then
    begin
      case OvrResult of
        ovrIOError:     Write('Overlay file I/O error');
        ovrNoEMSDriver: Write('EMS driver not installed');
        ovrNoEMSMemory: Write('Not enough EMS memory');
      end;
      Write('. Press Enter...');
      ReadLn;
    end;
    OvrSetBuf(OvrMaxSize);
  end;
```

First, if the default overlay file name is not correct, the user is repeatedly prompted for a correct file name.

Next, a check is made for other errors that might have occurred during initialization. If an error is detected, the program halts, since errors in *OvrInit* are fatal. (If they are ignored, a run-time error will occur upon the first call to an overlaid routine.)

Assuming successful initialization, a call to *OvrInitEMS* is made to load the overlay file into EMS if possible. In case of error, a diagnostic message is displayed, but the program is not halted. Instead, it will just continue to read overlays from disk.

Finally, *OvrSetBuf* is called to set the overlay buffer size to a suitable value, determined through analysis and experimentation with the particular application. Errors from *OvrSetBuf* are ignored, although *OvrResult* might return an error code of –3 (*OvrNoMemory*). If there is not enough memory, the overlay manager will just continue to use the minimum buffer that was allocated when the program started.

Initialization Sections in Overlaid Units

Like static units, overlaid units may have an initialization section. Although overlaid initialization code is no different from normal overlaid code, the overlay manager must be initialized first so it can load and execute overlaid units.

Referring to the earlier *Editor* program, assume that the *EdInOut* and *EdMain* units have initialization code. This requires that *OvrInit* is called before *EdInOut*'s initialization code, and the only way to do that is to create an additional non-overlaid unit, which goes before *EdInOut* and calls *OvrInit* in its initialization section:

```
unit EdInit;
interface
implementation
uses Overlay;
const
  OvrMaxSize = 80000;
begin
  OvrInit('EDITOR.OVR');
  OvrInitEMS;
  OvrSetBuf(OvrMaxSize);
end.
```

The *EdInit* unit must be listed in the program's **uses** clause before any of the overlaid units:

```
program Editor;

{$F+}

uses
  Overlay,Crt,Dos,EdInit,EdInOut,EdFormat,EdPrint,EdFind,EdMain;

{$O EdInOut}
{$O EdFormat}
{$O EdPrint}
{$O EdFind}
{$O EdMain}
```

In general, although initialization code in overlaid units is indeed possible, it should be avoided for a number of reasons.

First, the initialization code, even though it is only executed once, is a part of the overlay, and will occupy overlay buffer space whenever the overlay is loaded. Second, if a number of overlaid units have initialization code, each of them will have to be read into memory when the program starts.

A much better approach is to gather all the initialization code into an overlaid initialization unit, which is called once at the beginning of the program, and then never referenced again.

What Not to Overlay

Certain units cannot be overlaid. In particular, don't try to overlay the following:

- Units compiled in the {$O-} state. The compiler reports an error if you attempt to overlay a unit that wasn't compiled with {$O+}. Such non-overlay units include *System, Overlay, Crt, Graph, Turbo3,* and *Graph3*.
- Units that contain interrupt handlers. Due to the non-reentrant nature of the DOS operating system, units that implement **interrupt** procedures should not be overlaid. An example of such a unit is the *Crt* standard unit, which implements a *Ctrl-Break* interrupt handler.
- BGI drivers or fonts registered with calls to *RegisterBGIdriver* or *RegisterBGIfont*.

Calling overlaid routines via procedure pointers is fully supported by Turbo Pascal's overlay manager. Examples of the use of procedure pointers include exit procedures and text file device drivers.

Likewise, passing overlaid procedures and functions as procedural parameters, and assigning overlaid procedures and functions to procedural type variables is fully supported.

Debugging Overlays

Most debuggers have very limited overlay debugging capabilities, if any at all. Not so with Turbo Pascal and Turbo Debugger. The integrated debugger fully supports single-stepping and breakpoints in overlays in a manner completely transparent to you. By using overlays, you can easily engineer and debug huge applications—all from inside the IDE or by using Turbo Debugger.

External Routines in Overlays

Like normal Pascal procedures and functions, **external** assembly language routines must observe certain programming rules to work correctly with the overlay manager.

If an assembly language routine makes calls to *any* overlaid procedures or functions, the assembly language routine must use the FAR model, and it must set up a stack frame using the BP register. For example, assuming that *OtherProc* is an overlaid procedure in another unit, and that the assembly language routine *ExternProc* calls it, then *ExternProc* must be FAR and set up a stack frame as the following demonstrates:

```
ExternProc      PROC    FAR
        PUSH    bp                      ;Save BP
        mov     bp,sp                   ;Set up stack frame
        SUB     sp,LocalSize            ;Allocate local variables
```

```
            ...
            CALL    OtherProc       ;Call another overlaid unit
            ...
            mov     sp,bp           ;Dispose local variables
            pop     bp              ;Restore BP
            RET     ParamSize       ;Return
ExternProc  ENDP
```

where *LocalSize* is the size of the local variables, and *ParamSize* is the size of the parameters. If *LocalSize* is zero, the two lines to allocate and dispose local variables can be omitted.

These requirements are the same if *ExternProc* makes *indirect* references to overlaid procedures or functions. For example, if *OtherProc* makes calls to overlaid procedures or functions, but is not itself overlaid, *ExternProc* must still use the FAR model and still has to set up a stack frame.

In the case where an assembly language routine doesn't make any direct or indirect references to overlaid procedures or functions, there are no special requirements; the assembly language routine is free to use the NEAR model and it does not have to set up a stack frame.

Overlaid assembly language routines should *not* create variables in the code segment, since any modifications made to an overlaid code segment are lost when the overlay is disposed. Likewise, pointers to objects based in an overlaid code segment cannot be expected to remain valid across calls to other overlays, since the overlay manager freely moves around and disposes overlaid code segments.

CHAPTER

14

Using the 8087

There are two kinds of numbers you can work with in Turbo Pascal: integers (shortint, integer, longint, byte, word) and reals (real, single, double, extended, comp). Reals are also known as floating-point numbers. The 8086 processor is designed to easily handle integer values, but it takes considerably more time and effort to handle reals. To improve floating-point performance, the 8086 family of processors has a corresponding family of math coprocessors, the 8087s.

The 8087 is a special hardware numeric processor that can be installed in your PC. It executes floating-point instructions very quickly, so if you use floating point a lot, you'll probably want a coprocessor.

Turbo Pascal provides optimal floating-point performance whether or not you have an 8087.

- For programs running on any PC, with or without an 8087, Turbo Pascal provides the real type and an associated library of software routines that handle floating-point operations. The real type occupies 6 bytes of memory, providing a range of 2.9×10^{-39} to 1.7×10^{38} with 11 to 12 significant digits. The software floating-point library is optimized for speed and size, trading in some of the fancier features provided by the 8087 processor.

- If you need the added precision and flexibility of the 8087, you can instruct Turbo Pascal to produce code that uses the 8087 chip. This gives you access to four additional real types (single, double, extended, and comp), and an extended floating-point range of 3.4×10^{-4951} to 1.1×10^{4932} with 19 to 20 significant digits.

You switch between the two different models of floating-point code generation using the $N compiler directive or the O/C/Numeric

Processing command. The default state is {$N-}, and in this state, the compiler uses the 6-byte floating-point library, allowing you to operate only on variables of type real. In the {$N+} state, the compiler generates code for the 8087, giving you increased precision and access to the four additional real types.

Note: When compiling in numeric processing mode, {$N+}, the return values of the floating-point routines in the *System* unit (*Sqrt, Pi, Sin,* and so on) are of type extended instead of real:

```
{$N+}
begin
  Writeln(Pi);                            { 3.14159265358979E+0000 }
end.
{$N-}
begin
  Writeln(Pi)                             { 3.1415926536E+00 }
end.
```

Even if you don't have an 8087 in your machine, you can instruct Turbo Pascal to include a run-time library that emulates the numeric coprocessor. In that case, if an 8087 is present, it is used. If it's not present, it is emulated by the run-time library, at the cost of running somewhat slower.

The $E compiler directive and the O/C/Emulation menu are used to enable and disable 8087 emulation. The default state is {$E+}, and in this state, the full 8087 emulator is automatically included in programs that use the 8087. In the {$E-} state, a substantially smaller floating-point library is used, and the final .EXE file can only be run on machines with an 8087.

Note: The $E compiler directive has no effect if used in a unit; it only applies to the compilation of a program. Furthermore, if the program is compiled in the {$N-} state, and if all the units used by the program were compiled with {$N-}, then an 8087 run-time library is not required, and the $E compiler directive is ignored.

The remainder of this chapter discusses special issues concerning Turbo Pascal programs that use the 8087 coprocessor.

The 8087 Data Types

For programs that use the 8087, Turbo Pascal provides four floating-point types in addition to the type real.

- The single type is the smallest format you can use with floating-point numbers. It occupies 4 bytes of memory, providing a range of 1.5×10^{-45} to 3.4×10^{38} with 7 to 8 significant digits.

- The double type occupies 8 bytes of memory, providing a range of 5.0×10^{-324} to 1.7×10^{308} with 15 to 16 significant digits.
- The extended type is the largest floating-point type supported by the 8087. It occupies 10 bytes of memory, providing a range of 3.4×10^{-4932} to 1.1×10^{4932} with 19 to 20 significant digits. Any arithmetic involving real-type values is performed with the range and precision of the extended type.
- The comp type stores integral values in 8 bytes, providing a range of $-2^{63}+1$ to $2^{63}-1$, which is approximately -9.2×10^{18} to 9.2×10^{18}. Comp may be compared to a double-precision longint, but it is considered a real type because all arithmetic done with comp uses the 8087 coprocessor. Comp is well suited for representing monetary values as integral values of cents or mils (thousandths) in business applications.

Whether or not you have an 8087, the 6-byte real type is always available, so you need not modify your source code when switching to the 8087, and you can still read data files generated by programs that use software floating point.

Note, however, that 8087 floating-point calculations on variables of type real are slightly slower than on other types. This is because the 8087 cannot directly process the real format—instead, calls must be made to library routines to convert real values to extended before operating on them. If you are concerned with optimum speed and never need to run on a system without an 8087, you may want to use the single, double, extended, and comp types exclusively.

Extended Range Arithmetic

The extended type is the basis of all floating-point computations with the 8087. Turbo Pascal uses the extended format to store all non-integer numeric constants and evaluates all non-integer numeric expressions using extended precision. The entire right side of the following assignment, for instance, will be computed in extended before being converted to the type on the left side:

```
{$N+}
var
  X,A,B,C : real;
begin
  X := (B + Sqrt(B * B - A * C)) / A;
end;
```

With no special effort by the programmer, Turbo Pascal performs computations using the precision and range of the extended type. The added precision means smaller round-off errors, and the additional range means overflow and underflow are less common.

You can go beyond Turbo Pascal's automatic *extended* capabilities. For example, you can declare variables used for intermediate results to be of type extended. The following example computes a sum of products:

```
var
  Sum : single;
  X,Y : array[1..100] of single;
  I   : integer;
  T   : extended;                    { For intermediate results }
begin
  T := 0.0;
  for I := 1 to 100 do T := T + X[I] * Y[I];
  Sum := T;
end;
```

Had *T* been declared single, the assignment to *T* would have caused a round-off error at the limit of single precision at each loop entry. But because *T* is extended, all round-off errors are at the limit of extended precision, except for the one resulting from the assignment of *T* to *Sum*. Fewer round-off errors mean more accurate results.

You can also declare formal value parameters and function results to be of type extended. This avoids unnecessary conversions between numeric types, which can result in loss of accuracy. For example,

```
function Area(Radius: extended): extended;
begin
  Area := Pi * Radius * Radius;
end;
```

Comparing Reals

Because real-type values are approximations, the results of comparing values of different real types are not always as expected. For example, if *X* is a variable of type single and *Y* is a variable of type double, then the following statements will output False:

```
X := 1/3;
Y := 1/3;
Writeln(X = Y);
```

The reason is that *X* is accurate only to 7 to 8 digits, where *Y* is accurate to 15 to 16 digits, and when both are converted to extended, they will differ after 7 to 8 digits. Similarly, the statements

```
X := 1/3;
```

Turbo Pascal Reference Guide

```
Writeln(X = 1/3);
```

will output False, since the result of 1/3 in the *Writeln* statement is calculated with 20 significant digits.

The 8087 Evaluation Stack

The 8087 coprocessor has an internal evaluation stack that can be up to eight levels deep. Accessing a value on the 8087 stack is much faster than accessing a variable in memory; so to achieve the best possible performance, Turbo Pascal uses the 8087's stack for storing temporary results.

In theory, very complicated real-type expressions can cause an 8087 stack overflow. However, this is not likely to occur, since it would require the expression to generate more than eight temporary results.

A more tangible danger lies in recursive function calls. If such constructs are not coded correctly, they can very well cause an 8087 stack overflow.

Consider the following procedure that calculates Fibonacci numbers using recursion:

```
function Fib(N: integer): extended;
begin
  if N = 0 then
    Fib := 0.0
  else
    if N = 1 then
      Fib := 1.0
    else
      Fib := Fib(N-1) + Fib(N-2);
end;
```

A call to this version of *Fib* will cause an 8087 stack overflow for values of N larger than 8. The reason is that the calculation of the last assignment requires a temporary on the 8087 stack to store the result of *Fib(N-1)*. Each recursive invocation allocates one such temporary, causing an overflow the ninth time. The correct construct in this case is

```
function Fib(N: integer): extended;
var
  F1,F2: extended;
begin
  if N = 0 then
    Fib := 0.0
  else
    if N = 1 then
      Fib := 1.0
    else
```

```
    begin
      F1 := Fib(N-1); F2 := Fib(N-2);
      Fib := F1 + F2;
    end;
end;
```

The temporary results are now stored in variables allocated on the 8086 stack. (The 8086 stack can of course also overflow, but this would typically require significantly more recursive calls.)

Writing Reals with the 8087

In the {$N+} state, the *Write* and *Writeln* standard procedures output four digits, not two, for the exponent in a floating-point decimal string to provide for the extended numeric range. Likewise, the *Str* standard procedure returns a four-digit exponent when floating-point format is selected.

Units Using the 8087

Units that use the 8087 can only be used by other units or programs that are compiled in the {$N+} state.

The fact that a unit uses the 8087 is determined by whether it contains 8087 instructions—not by the state of the $N compiler directive at the time of its compilation. This makes the compiler more forgiving in cases where you accidentally compile a unit (that doesn't use the 8087) in the {$N+} state.

Detecting the 8087

The Turbo Pascal 8087 run-time library built into your program (compiled with {$N+}) includes startup code that automatically detects the presence of an 8087 chip. If an 8087 is available, then the program will use it. If one is not present, the program will use the emulation run-time library. If the program was compiled in the {$E-} state, and an 8087 could not be detected at startup, the program displays `Numeric coprocessor required`, and terminates.

There are some instances in which you might want to override this default autodetection behavior. For example, your own system may have an 8087, but you want to verify that your program will work as intended on systems without a coprocessor. Or your program may need to run on a PC-compatible system, but that particular system returns incorrect information to the autodetection logic (saying that an 8087 is present when it's not, or vice versa).

Turbo Pascal provides an option for overriding the startup code's default autodetection logic; this option is the *87* environment variable.

You set the *87* environment variable at the DOS prompt with the SET command, like this:

```
SET 87=Y
```

or

```
SET 87=N
```

Setting the *87* environment variable to *N* (for no) tells the startup code that you do not want to use the 8087, even though it might be present in the system. Conversely, setting the *87* environment variable to *Y* (for yes) means that the coprocessor is there, and you want the program to use it. **Beware:** If you set *87=Y* when, in fact, there is no 8087 available, your program will either crash or hang!

If the *87* environment variable has been defined (to any value) but you want to undefine it, enter

```
SET 87=
```

at the DOS prompt and then press *Enter* immediately.

If an *87=Y* entry is present in the DOS environment, or if the autodetection logic succeeds in detecting a coprocessor, the startup code executes further checks to determine what kind of coprocessor it is (8087, 80287, or 80387). This is required so that Turbo Pascal can correctly handle certain incompatibilities that exist between the different coprocessors.

The result of the autodetection and the coprocessor classification is stored in the *Test8087* variable (which is declared by the *System* unit). The following values are defined:

```
0 = No coprocessor detected
1 = 8087 detected
2 = 80287 detected
3 = 80387 detected
```

Your program may examine the *Test8087* variable to determine the characteristics of the system it is running on. In particular, *Test8087* may be examined to determine whether floating-point instructions are being emulated or truly executed.

Using 8087 Emulation in Assembly Language

When linking in object files using {*$L filename*} directives, make sure that these object files were compiled with the 8087 emulation enabled. For example, if you are using 8087 instructions in assembly language **external** procedures, make sure to enable emulation when you assemble the .ASM files into .OBJ files. Otherwise, the 8087 instructions cannot be emulated on machines without an 8087. Use Turbo Assembler's */E* command-line switch to enable emulation.

C H A P T E R

15

Inside Turbo Pascal

In this chapter, we provide technical information for advanced Turbo Pascal programmers. We'll cover such topics as memory maps, the heap manager, internal data formats, calling conventions, and more.

Figure 15.1 (on page 180) depicts the memory map of a Turbo Pascal program.

The Program Segment Prefix (PSP) is a 256-byte area built by MS-DOS when the .EXE file is loaded. The segment address of PSP is stored in the predeclared word variable *PrefixSeg*.

Each module (which includes the main program and each unit) has its own code segment. The main program occupies the first code segment; the code segments that follow it are occupied by the units (in reverse order from how they are listed in the **uses** clause), and the last code segment is occupied by the run-time library (the *System* unit). The size of a single code segment cannot exceed 64K, but the total size of the code is limited only by the available memory.

Top of DOS Memory

```
                 ┌─────────────────────────────────┐
                 │  Free List (grows downward)     │
                 │              ↓                  │
    FreePtr  →   ├ ─ ─ ─ ─ ─ ─ ─ ─ ─ ─ ─ ─ ─ ─ ─ ─ ┤
                 │        Free Memory              │
    HeapPtr  →   ├ ─ ─ ─ ─ ─ ─ ─ ─ ─ ─ ─ ─ ─ ─ ─ ─ ┤
                 │              ↑                  │
                 │    Heap (grows upward)          │
    HeapOrg  →   ├─────────────────────────────────┤ ← OvrHeapEnd
                 │       Overlay Buffer            │
                 │                                 │ ← OvrHeapOrg
                 ├─────────────────────────────────┤
                 │   Stack (grows downward)        │
                 │              ↓                  │
    SSeg:Sptr →  ├ ─ ─ ─ ─ ─ ─ ─ ─ ─ ─ ─ ─ ─ ─ ─ ─ ┤
                 │         Free Stack              │
    SSeg:0000 →  ├─────────────────────────────────┤
                 │       Global Variables          │
                 ├ ─ ─ ─ ─ ─ ─ ─ ─ ─ ─ ─ ─ ─ ─ ─ ─ ┤
                 │       Typed Constants           │
    DSeg:0000 →  ├─────────────────────────────────┤
                 │    System Unit Code Segment     │
                 ├ ─ ─ ─ ─ ─ ─ ─ ─ ─ ─ ─ ─ ─ ─ ─ ─ ┤
                 │    First Unit Code Segment      │    Contents
                 │              ⋮                  │      of an
                 │              ⋮                  │    .EXE file
                 ├ ─ ─ ─ ─ ─ ─ ─ ─ ─ ─ ─ ─ ─ ─ ─ ─ ┤      image
                 │    Last Unit Code Segment       │
                 ├─────────────────────────────────┤
                 │    Main Program Code Segment    │
                 ├─────────────────────────────────┤
                 │   Program Segment Prefix (PSP)  │
    PrefixSeg →  └─────────────────────────────────┘
```

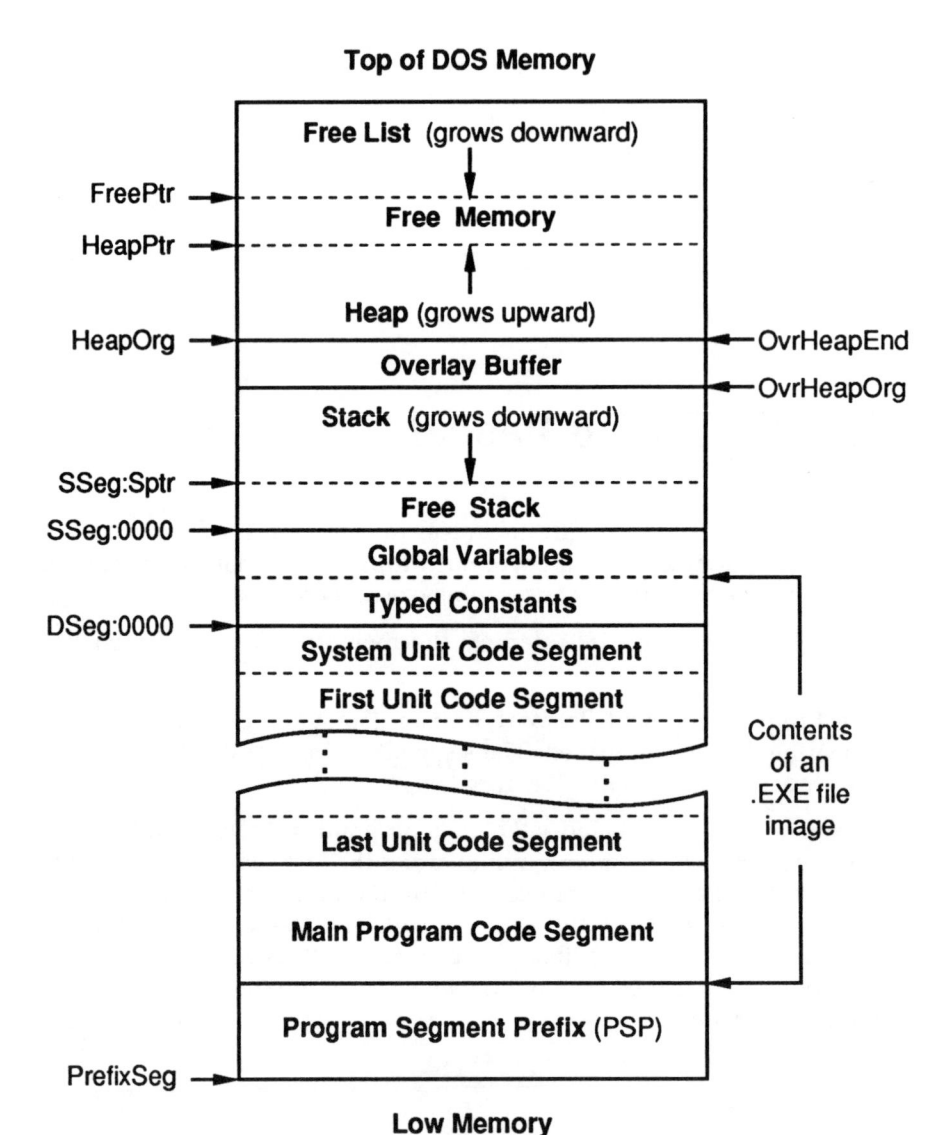

Low Memory

Figure 15.1: Turbo Pascal Memory Map

The data segment (addressed through DS) contains all typed constants followed by all global variables. The DS register is never changed during program execution. The size of the data segment cannot exceed 64K.

On entry to the program, the stack segment register (SS) and the stack pointer (SP) are loaded so that SS:SP points to the first byte past the stack segment. The SS register is never changed during program execution, but SP can move downward until it reaches the bottom of the segment. The size of the stack segment cannot exceed 64K; the default size is 16K, but this can be changed with a $M compiler directive.

The overlay buffer is used by the *Overlay* standard unit to store overlaid code. The default size of the overlay buffer corresponds to the size of the largest overlay in the program; if the program has no overlays, the size of the overlay buffer is zero. The size of the overlay buffer can be increased through a call to the *OvrSetBuf* routine in the *Overlay* unit; in that case, the size of the heap is decreased accordingly, by moving *HeapOrg* upwards.

The heap stores *dynamic variables*, that is, variables allocated through calls to the *New* and *GetMem* standard procedures. It occupies all or some of the free memory left when a program is executed. The actual size of the heap depends on the minimum and maximum heap values, which can be set with the $M compiler directive. Its size is guaranteed to be at least the minimum heap size and never more than the maximum heap size. If the minimum amount of memory is not available, the program will not execute. The default heap minimum is 0 bytes, and the default heap maximum is 640 Kb; this means that by default the heap will occupy all remaining memory.

As you might expect, the heap manager (which is part of Turbo Pascal's run-time library) manages the heap. It is described in detail in the following section.

The Heap Manager

The heap is a stack-like structure that grows from low memory in the heap segment. The bottom of the heap is stored in the variable *HeapOrg*, and the top of the heap, corresponding to the bottom of free memory, is stored in the variable *HeapPtr*. Each time a dynamic variable is allocated on the heap (via *New* or *GetMem*), the heap manager moves *HeapPtr* upward by the size of the variable, in effect stacking the dynamic variables on top of each other.

HeapPtr is always normalized after each operation, thus forcing the offset part into the range $0000 to $000F. The maximum size of a single variable that can be allocated on the heap is 65519 bytes (corresponding to $10000 minus $000F), since every variable must be completely contained in a single segment.

Disposal Methods

The dynamic variables stored on the heap are disposed of in one of two ways: (1) through *Dispose* or *FreeMem* or (2) through *Mark* and *Release*. The simplest scheme is that of *Mark* and *Release*; for example, if the following statements are executed:

```
New(Ptr1);
New(Ptr2);
Mark(P);
New(Ptr3);
New(Ptr4);
New(Ptr5);
```

the layout of the heap will then look like Figure 15.2.

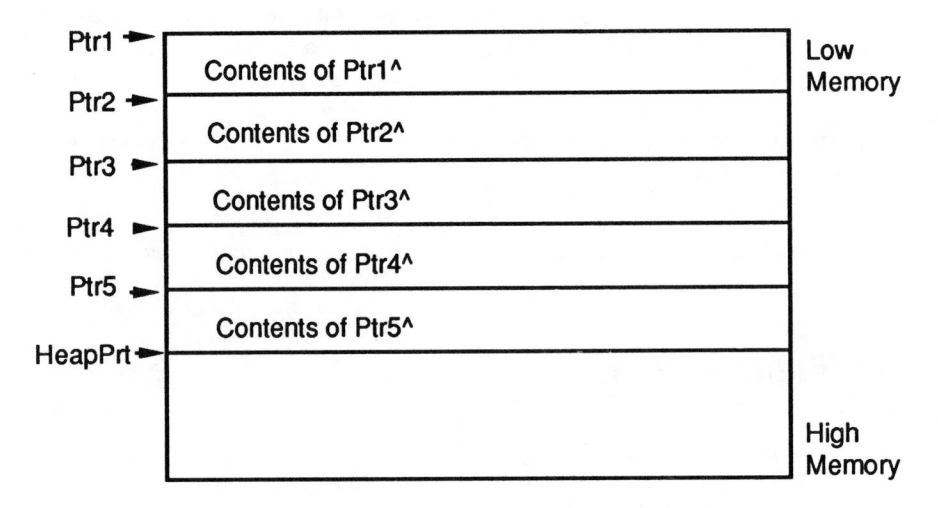

```
Ptr1 →  ┌─────────────────────┐  Low
        │  Contents of Ptr1^  │  Memory
Ptr2 →  ├─────────────────────┤
        │  Contents of Ptr2^  │
Ptr3 →  ├─────────────────────┤
        │  Contents of Ptr3^  │
Ptr4 →  ├─────────────────────┤
        │  Contents of Ptr4^  │
Ptr5 →  ├─────────────────────┤
        │  Contents of Ptr5^  │
HeapPrt→├─────────────────────┤
        │                     │
        │                     │  High
        └─────────────────────┘  Memory
```

Figure 15.2: Disposal Method Using Mark and Release

The *Mark(P)* statement marks the state of the heap just before *Ptr3* is allocated (by storing the current *HeapPtr* in *P*). If the statement *Release(P)* is executed, the heap layout becomes like that of Figure 15.3, effectively disposing of all pointers allocated since the call to *Mark*.

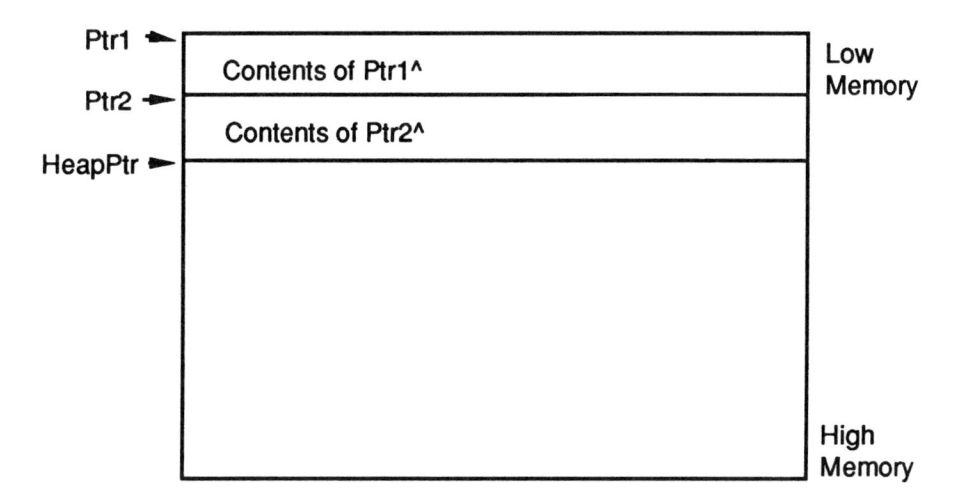

```
Ptr1  ──▶ ┌─────────────────────────┐  Low
          │   Contents of Ptr1^     │  Memory
Ptr2  ──▶ ├─────────────────────────┤
          │   Contents of Ptr2^     │
HeapPtr ▶ ├─────────────────────────┤
          │                         │
          │                         │
          │                         │
          │                         │
          │                         │  High
          └─────────────────────────┘  Memory
```

Figure 15.3: Heap Layout with Release(P) Executed

Note: Executing *Release(HeapOrg)* completely disposes of the entire heap because *HeapOrg* points to the bottom of the heap.

For applications that dispose of pointers in exactly the reverse order of allocation, the *Mark* and *Release* procedures are very efficient. Yet most programs tend to allocate and dispose of pointers in a more random manner, requiring the more-sophisticated management technique implemented by *Dispose* and *FreeMem*. These procedures allow an application to dispose of any pointer at any time.

When a dynamic variable that is not the topmost variable on the heap is disposed of through *Dispose* or *FreeMem*, the heap becomes fragmented. Assuming that the same statement sequence has been executed, then after executing *Dispose(Ptr3)*, a "hole" is created in the middle of the heap (see Figure 15.4).

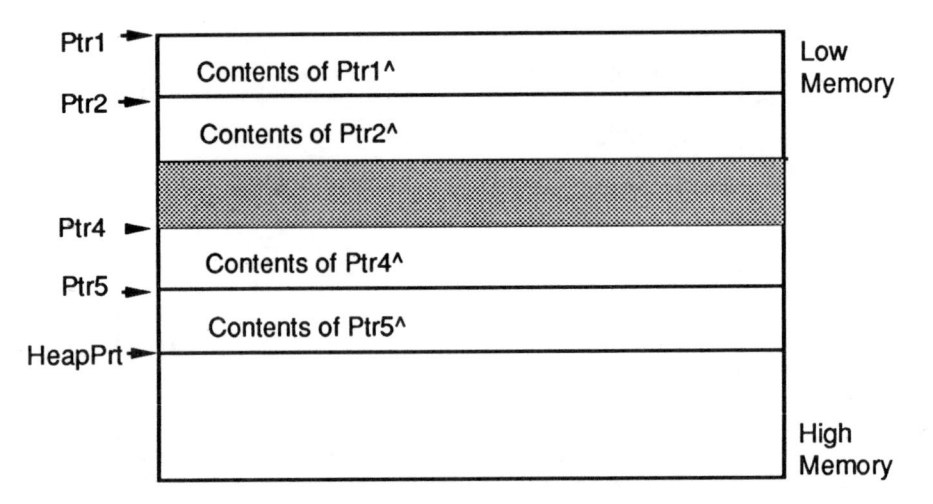

Figure 15.4: Creating a "Hole" in the Heap

If at this time *New(Ptr3)* has been executed, it would again occupy the same memory area. On the other hand, executing *Dispose(Ptr4)* enlarges the free block, since *Ptr3* and *Ptr4* were neighboring blocks (see Figure 15.5).

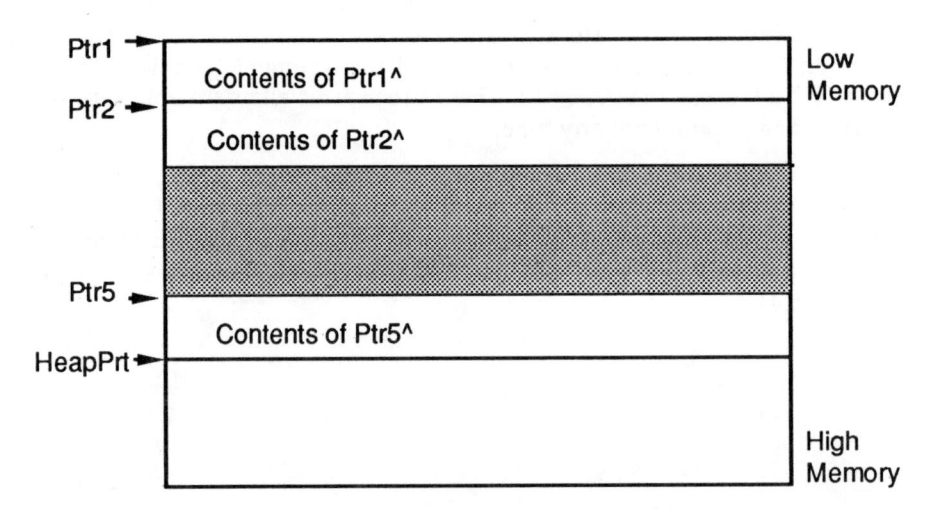

Figure 15.5: Enlarging the Free Block

Finally, executing *Dispose(Ptr5)* first creates an even bigger free block, and then lowers *HeapPtr*. This, in effect, releases the free block, since the last valid pointer is now *Ptr2* (see Figure 15.6).

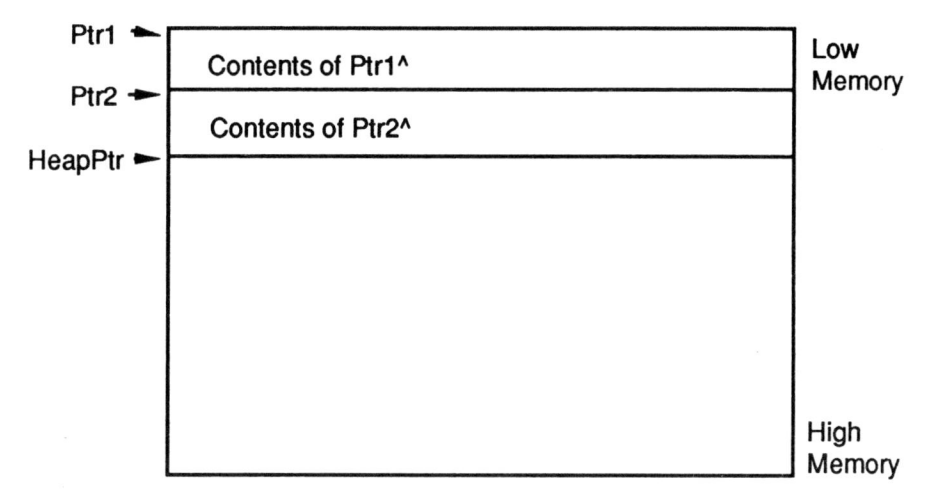

```
      Ptr1  ▶ ┌─────────────────────────────┐   Low
               │     Contents of Ptr1^       │   Memory
      Ptr2  ▶ ├─────────────────────────────┤
               │     Contents of Ptr2^       │
    HeapPtr ▶ ├─────────────────────────────┤
               │                             │
               │                             │
               │                             │
               │                             │   High
               └─────────────────────────────┘   Memory
```

Figure 15.6: Releasing the Free Block

The heap is now in the same state as it would be after executing *Release(P)*, as shown in Figure 15.3. However, the free blocks created and destroyed in the process were tracked for possible reuse.

The Free List

The addresses and sizes of the free blocks generated by *Dispose* and *FreeMem* operations are kept on a *free list*, which grows downward from high memory in the heap segment. Whenever a dynamic variable is allocated, the free list is checked before the heap is expanded. If a free block of adequate size (greater than or equal to the size of the requested block size) exists, it is used.

Note: The *Release* procedure always clears the free list, thus causing the heap manager to "forget" about any free blocks that might exist below the heap pointer. If you mix calls to *Mark* and *Release* with calls to *Dispose* and *FreeMem*, you must ensure that no such free blocks exist.

The free list pointer is stored in a variable called *FreePtr*. Although declared to be of type *pointer*, *FreePtr* is actually a pointer to an array of free-list records, as indicated by the *FreeListP* type:

```
type
  FreeRec  = record
               OrgPtr,EndPtr: pointer;
             end;
  FreeList = array[0..8190] of FreeRec;
```

Chapter 15, Inside Turbo Pascal   185

```
FreeListP = ^FreeList;
```

The *OrgPtr* and *EndPtr* fields of each record define the origin and end of each free block. (*EndPtr* is in fact a pointer to the first byte after the block.) Both are normalized pointers. The number of entries in the *FreeList* array is calculated from

```
FreeCount = (8192 - Ofs(FreePtr^) div 8) mod 8192
```

This means that there can be up to 8191 entries in the free list. When the offset part of *FreePtr* is 0, the free list is empty. *FreePtr* can be compared to the stack pointer in the sense that it grows downward, and that all bytes from *FreePtr* to the end of the heap segment are part of the "free stack."

Note: Trying to dispose of a pointer when the free list is full causes a run-time error. However, a full free list is a highly unlikely situation—it would require 8191 completely noncontiguous blocks to be disposed of and not reused.

FreePtr also serves to mark the top of free memory in the heap (the bottom of which is pointed to by *HeapPtr*). Note, though, that when the offset part of *FreePtr* is 0, $1000 must be added to the segment part to produce the true top-of-heap pointer. (In fact, the segment part of *FreePtr* always contains the segment address of top-of-memory minus $1000.)

When disposing of a range of noncontiguous pointers, the free list grows (expands downward) to make room for an entry for each block. As long as there is enough room between *HeapPtr* and *FreePtr*, this presents no problem. However, when the heap is almost full, there may not be enough room to cater to the larger free list, in which case a run-time error will occur.

In particular, imagine that the free list is empty and that the heap is almost full. In that situation, disposing of a range of pointers other than the topmost pointer will cause a block expansion of the free list.

To prevent, or foresee, such problems, the heap manager provides a word variable *FreeMin* that can be set to control the minimum allowable size of the memory region between *HeapPtr* and *FreePtr*. You cannot use *New* or *GetMem* to allocate a variable that would make the size of that region less than *FreeMin*. Likewise, *MemAvail* and *MaxAvail* will subtract *FreeMin* from the size of that region before returning their results.

The value stored in *FreeMin* is in bytes. To ensure room for a specific number of free-list entries, multiply that number by 8 and store it in *FreeMin*.

A final note on the free list concerns a potential problem with "granularity." The granularity of Turbo Pascal's heap manager is 1 byte; that is, if you allocate 1 byte, it will only occupy that 1 byte. In most situations, and especially when using *Mark* and *Release* or when not disposing of anything at all, this guarantees optimum use of the memory available. However, it can also be deceiving.

When randomly allocating and disposing of a lot of blocks of differing sizes, such as line records in a text-processing program, a number of very small free blocks can result and possibly cause the free list to overflow. As an example, assume a block of 50 bytes is allocated and disposed of, thus becoming an entry on the free list. If the next allocation request is for a block of 49 bytes, that block will be reused, leaving a 1-byte free block entry on the free list. Until one of the neighboring blocks are disposed of (thereby merging the 1-byte block into a bigger block), the 1-byte block is very unlikely to become reallocated. Thus, it will occupy a free-list entry for a long time, if not for the program's duration.

If a free list overflow occurs because of this, you can introduce a "resolution factor" to round upward the size specified by each call to *GetMem* and *FreeMem* to a factor of some number. In general, the higher the number, the less likely unusable free blocks will occur. To do this you would write your own *GetMem* and *FreeMem* routines that would modify the *Size* parameter and then call *System.GetMem* or *System.FreeMem*:

```
procedure GetMem(var P : pointer; Size : word);
begin
  System.GetMem(P, (Size + 15) and $FFF0);            { 16 byte blocks }
end;

procedure FreeMem(var P : pointer; Size : word);
begin
  System.FreeMem(P, (Size + 15) and $FFF0);           { 16 byte blocks }
end;
```

The Heap Error Function

The *HeapError* variable allows you to install a heap error function, which gets called whenever the heap manager cannot complete an allocation request. *HeapError* is a pointer that points to a function with the following header:

```
{$F+} function HeapFunc(Size: word): integer; {$F-}
```

Note that the {$F+} compiler directive forces the heap error function to use the FAR call model.

The heap error function is installed by assigning its address to the *HeapError* variable:

```
HeapError:=@HeapFunc;
```

The heap error function gets called whenever a call to *New* or *GetMem* cannot complete the request. The *Size* parameter contains the size of the block that could not be allocated, and the heap error function should attempt to free a block of at least that size.

Depending on its success, the heap error function should return 0, 1, or 2. A return of 0 indicates failure, causing a run-time error to occur immediately. A return of 1 also indicates failure, but instead of a run-time error, it causes *New* or *GetMem* to return a **nil** pointer. Finally, a return of 2 indicates success and causes a retry (which could also cause another call to the heap error function).

The standard heap error function always returns 0, thus causing a run-time error whenever a call to *New* or *GetMem* cannot be completed. However, for many applications, the simple heap error function that follows is more appropriate:

```
{$F+} function HeapFunc(Size: word) : integer; {$F-}
begin
   HeapFunc:=1;
end;
```

When installed, this function causes *New* or *GetMem* to return **nil** when they cannot complete the request, instead of aborting the program.

Internal Data Formats

Integer Types

The format selected to represent an integer-type variable depends on its minimum and maximum bounds:

- If both bounds are within the range –128..127 (shortint), the variable is stored as a signed byte.
- If both bounds are within the range 0..255 (byte), the variable is stored as an unsigned byte.
- If both bounds are within the range –32768..32767 (integer), the variable is stored as a signed word.
- If both bounds are within the range 0..65535 (word), the variable is stored as an unsigned word.
- Otherwise, the variable is stored as a signed double word (longint).

Char Types

A char, or a subrange of a char type, is stored as an unsigned byte.

Boolean Types

A boolean type is stored as a byte that can assume the value of 0 (False) or 1 (True).

Enumerated Types

An enumerated type is stored as an unsigned byte if the enumeration has 256 or fewer values; otherwise, it is stored as an unsigned word.

Floating-Point Types

The floating-point types (real, single, double, extended, and comp) store the binary representations of a sign (+ or –), an *exponent*, and a *significand*. A represented number has the value

$$+/-\ significand \times 2^{exponent}$$

where the significand has a single bit to the left of the binary decimal point (that is, $0 <= significand < 2$).

Note: In the figures that follow, *msb* means most significant bit, and *lsb* means least significant bit. The leftmost items are stored at the highest addresses. For example, for a real-type value, *e* is stored in the first byte, *f* in the following five bytes, and *s* in the most significant bit of the last byte.

The Real Type

A 6-byte (48-bit) *Real* number is divided into three fields:

```
     1            39                8    width
   ┌───┬──────────────────────┬──────────┐
   │ s │          f           │    e     │
   └───┴──────────────────────┴──────────┘
   msb                   lsb msb    lsb  order
```

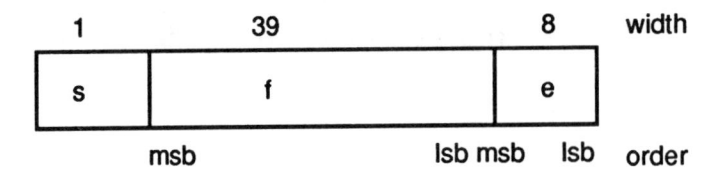

The value v of the number is determined by

if $0 < e <= 255$, **then** $v = (-1)^s * 2^{(e-129)} * (1.f)$.
if $e = 0$, **then** $v = 0$.

Note: The real type cannot store denormals, NaNs, and infinities. Denormals become zero when stored in a real, and NaNs and infinities produce an overflow error if an attempt is made to store them in a real.

The Single Type

A 4-byte (32-bit) *Single* number is divided into three fields:

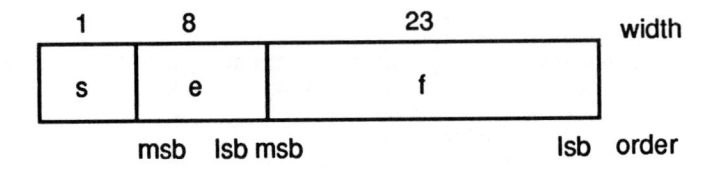

```
     1     8              23         width
   ┌───┬───────┬───────────────────┐
   │ s │   e   │         f         │
   └───┴───────┴───────────────────┘
   msb   lsb msb              lsb   order
```

The value v of the number is determined by

if $0 < e < 255$,   **then** $v = (-1)^s * 2^{(e-127)} * (1.f)$.
if $e = 0$ **and** $f <> 0$, **then** $v = (-1)^s * 2^{(-126)} * (0.f)$.
if $e = 0$ **and** $f = 0$, **then** $v = (-1)^s * 0$.
if $e = 255$ **and** $f = 0$, **then** $v = (-1)^s * \text{Inf}$.
if $e = 255$ **and** $f <> 0$, **then** v is a NaN.

The Double Type

An 8-byte (64-bit) *Double* number is divided into three fields:

```
    1      11              52            width
  ┌───┬─────────┬──────────────────────┐
  │ s │    e    │          f           │
  └───┴─────────┴──────────────────────┘
   msb    lsb msb                   lsb  order
```

The value v of the number is determined by

if $0 < e < 2047$,   **then** $v = (-1)^s * 2^{(e-1023)} * (1.f)$.
if $e = 0$ **and** $f <> 0$, **then** $v = (-1)^s * 2^{(-1022)} * (0.f)$.
if $e = 0$ **and** $f = 0$, **then** $v = (-1)^s * 0$.
if $e = 2047$ **and** $f = 0$, **then** $v = (-1)^s * \text{Inf}$.
if $e = 2047$ **and** $f <> 0$, **then** v is a NaN.

The Extended Type

A 10-byte (80-bit) *Extended* number is divided into four fields:

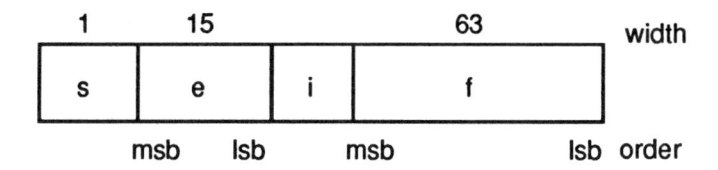

```
    1       15              63         width
  ┌───┬─────────┬───┬──────────────────┐
  │ s │    e    │ i │        f         │
  └───┴─────────┴───┴──────────────────┘
   msb      lsb  msb               lsb  order
```

The value v of the number is determined by

if $0 <= e < 32767$,   **then** $v = (-1)^s * 2^{(e-16383)} * (i.f)$.
if $e = 32767$ **and** $f = 0$, **then** $v = (-1)^s * \text{Inf}$.
if $e = 32767$ **and** $f <> 0$, **then** v is a NaN.

The Comp Type

An 8-byte (64-bit) *Comp* number is divided into two fields:

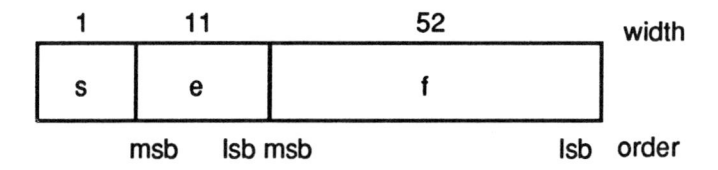

Chapter 15, Inside Turbo Pascal

```
 1        63              width
┌───┬──────────────────┐
│ s │       d          │
└───┴──────────────────┘
 msb                lsb  order
```

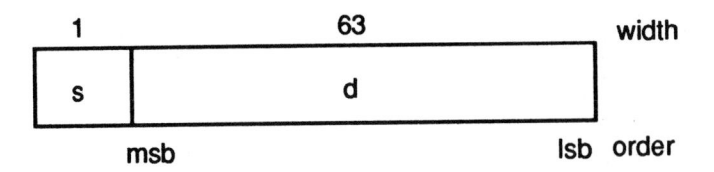

The value v of the number is determined by

if s = 1 **and** d = 0, **then** v is a NaN

Otherwise, v is the two's complement 64-bit value.

Pointer Types

A pointer type is stored as a double word, with the offset part in the low word and the segment part in the high word. The pointer value **nil** is stored as a double-word zero.

String Types

A string occupies as many bytes as its maximum length plus one. The first byte contains the current dynamic length of the string, and the following bytes contain the characters of the string. The length byte and the characters are considered unsigned values. Maximum string length is 255 characters plus a length byte (**string**[255]).

Set Types

A set is a bit array, where each bit indicates whether an element is in the set or not. The maximum number of elements in a set is 256, so a set never occupies more than 32 bytes. The number of bytes occupied by a particular set is calculated as

    ByteSize = (Max div 8) - (Min div 8) + 1

where *Min* and *Max* are the lower and upper bounds of the base type of that set. The byte number of a specific element *E* is

    ByteNumber = (E div 8) - (Min div 8)

and the bit number within that byte is

```
BitNumber = E mod 8
```

where *E* denotes the ordinal value of the element.

Array Types

An array is stored as a contiguous sequence of variables of the component type of the array. The components with the lowest indexes are stored at the lowest memory addresses. A multidimensional array is stored with the rightmost dimension increasing first.

Record Types

The fields of a record are stored as a contiguous sequence of variables. The first field is stored at the lowest memory address. If the record contains variant parts, then each variant starts at the same memory address.

File Types

File types are represented as records. Typed files and untyped files occupy 128 bytes, which are laid out as follows:

```
type
  FileRec = record
              Handle   : word;
              Mode     : word;
              RecSize  : word;
              Private  : array[1..26] of byte;
              UserData : array[1..16] of byte;
              Name     : array[0..79] of char;
            end;
```

Text files occupy 256 bytes, which are laid out as follows:

```
type
  TextBuf = array[0..127] of char;
  TextRec = record
              Handle   : word;
              Mode     : word;
              BufSize  : word;
              Private  : word;
              BufPos   : word;
              BufEnd   : word;
              BufPtr   : ^TextBuf;
```

```
        OpenFunc  : pointer;
        InOutFunc : pointer;
        FlushFunc : pointer;
        CloseFunc : pointer;
        UserData  : array[1..16] of byte;
        Name      : array[0..79] of char;
        Buffer    : TextBuf;
     end;
```

Handle contains the file's handle (when open) as returned by MS-DOS.

The *Mode* field can assume one of the following "magic" values:

```
const
   fmClosed = $D7B0;
   fmInput  = $D7B1;
   fmOutput = $D7B2;
   fmInOut  = $D7B3;
```

fmClosed indicates that the file is closed. *fmInput* and *fmOutput* indicate that the file is a text file that has been reset (*fmInput*) or rewritten (*fmOutput*). *fmInOut* indicates that the file variable is a typed or an untyped file that has been reset or rewritten. Any other value indicates that the file variable has not been assigned (and thereby not initialized).

The *UserData* field is never accessed by Turbo Pascal, and is free for user-written routines to store data in.

Name contains the file name, which is a sequence of characters terminated by a null character (#0).

For typed files and untyped files, *RecSize* contains the record length in bytes, and the *Private* field is unused but reserved.

For text files, *BufPtr* is a pointer to a buffer of *BufSize* bytes, *BufPos* is the index of the next character in the buffer to read or write, and *BufEnd* is a count of valid characters in the buffer. *OpenFunc*, *InOutFunc*, *FlushFunc*, and *CloseFunc* are pointers to the I/O routines that control the file. The upcoming section entitled "Text File Device Drivers" provides information on that subject.

Procedural Types

A procedural type is stored as a double word, with the offset part of the referenced procedure in the low word and the segment part in the high word.

Calling Conventions

Parameters are transferred to procedures and functions via the stack. Before calling a procedure or function, the parameters are pushed onto the stack in their order of declaration. Before returning, the procedure or function removes all parameters from the stack.

The skeleton code for a procedure or function call looks like this:

```
PUSH    Param1
PUSH    Param2
  :
PUSH    ParamX
CALL    ProcOrFunc
```

Parameters are passed either by *reference* or by *value*. When a parameter is passed by reference, a pointer that points to the actual storage location is pushed onto the stack. When a parameter is passed by value, the actual value is pushed onto the stack.

Variable Parameters

Variable parameters (**var** parameters) are always passed by reference—a pointer points to the actual storage location.

Value Parameters

Value parameters are passed by value or by reference depending on the type and size of the parameter. In general, if the value parameter occupies 1, 2, or 4 bytes, the value is pushed directly onto the stack. Otherwise a pointer to the value is pushed, and the procedure or function then copies the value into a local storage location.

Note: The 8086 does not support byte-sized PUSH and POP instructions, so byte-sized parameters are always transferred onto the stack as words. The low-order byte of the word contains the value, and the high-order byte is unused (and undefined).

An integer type or parameter is passed as a byte, a word, or a double word, using the same format as an integer-type variable. (For double words, the high-order word is pushed before the low-order word so that the low-order word ends up at the lowest address.)

A char-type parameter is passed as an unsigned byte.

A boolean-type parameter is passed as a byte with the value 0 or 1.

An enumerated-type parameter is passed as an unsigned byte if the enumeration has 256 or fewer values; otherwise it is passed as an unsigned word.

A real-type parameter (type real) is passed as 6 bytes on the stack, thus being an exception to the rule that only 1, 2, and 4 byte values are passed directly on the stack.

A floating-point type parameter (real, single, double, extended, and comp) is passed as 4, 6, 8, or 10 bytes on the stack, thus being an exception to the rule that only 1, 2, and 4-byte values are passed directly on the stack.

Note: Version 4.0 of Turbo Pascal passed 8087-type parameters (single, double, extended, and comp) on the internal stack of the 8087 numeric coprocessor. For reasons of compatibility with other languages, and to avoid 8087 stack overflows, Version 5.0 uses the 8086 stack.

A pointer-type parameter is passed as a double word (the segment part is pushed before the offset part so that the offset part ends up at the lowest address).

A string-type parameter is passed as a pointer to the value.

A set-type parameter is passed as a pointer to an "unpacked" set that occupies 32 bytes.

Arrays and records with 1, 2, or 4 bytes are passed directly onto the stack. Other arrays and records are passed as pointers to the value.

Function Results

Ordinal-type function results (integer, char, boolean, and enumeration types) are returned in the CPU registers: Bytes are returned in AL, words are returned in AX, and double words are returned in DX:AX (high-order word in DX, low-order word in AX).

Real-type function results (type real) are returned in the DX:BX:AX registers (high-order word in DX, middle word in BX, low-order word in AX).

8087-type function results (type single, double, extended, and comp) are returned in the 8087 coprocessor's top-of-stack register (ST(0)).

Pointer-type function results are returned in DX:AX (segment part in DX, offset part in AX).

For a string-type function result, the caller pushes a pointer to a temporary storage location before pushing any parameters, and the function returns a string value in that temporary location. The function must not remove the pointer.

NEAR and FAR Calls

The 8086 CPU supports two kinds of call and return instructions: *NEAR* and *FAR*. The **NEAR** instructions transfer control to another location within the same code segment, and the **FAR** instructions allow a change of code segment.

A **NEAR CALL** instruction pushes a 16-bit return address (offset only) onto the stack, and a **FAR CALL** instruction pushes a 32-bit return address (both segment and offset). The corresponding **RET** instructions pop only an offset or both an offset and a segment.

Turbo Pascal will automatically select the correct call model based on the procedure's declaration. Procedures declared in the **interface** section of a unit are FAR—they can be called from other units. Procedures declared in a program or in the **implementation** section of a unit are NEAR—they can only be called from within that program or unit.

For some specific purposes, a procedure may be required to be FAR. For example, in an overlaid application, all procedures and functions are generally required to be FAR; likewise, if a procedure or function is to be assigned to a procedural variable, it has to be FAR. The *$F* compiler directive is used to override the compiler's automatic call model selection. Procedures and functions compiled in the {$F+} state are always FAR; in the {$F-} state, Turbo Pascal automatically selects the correct model. The default state is {$F-}.

Nested Procedures and Functions

A procedure or function is said to be nested when it is declared within another procedure or function. By default, nested procedures and functions always use the NEAR call model, since they are only "visible" within a specific procedure or function in the same code segment. However, in an overlaid application, a {$F+} directive is generally used to force all procedures and functions to be FAR, including those that are nested.

When calling a nested procedure or function, the compiler generates a **PUSH BP** instruction just before the **CALL**, in effect passing the caller's BP as an additional parameter. Once the called procedure has set up its own BP, the caller's BP is accessible as a word stored at [BP+4], or at [BP+6] if the procedure is FAR. Using this link at [BP+4] or [BP+6], the called procedure can access the local variables in the caller's stack frame. If the caller itself is also a nested procedure, it also has a link at [BP+4] or [BP+6], and so on. The following example demonstrates how to access local variables from an **inline** statement in a nested procedure:

```
{$F-}
procedure PA;
var IntA: integer;
{$F+}
  procedure B;
  var IntB: integer;
  {$F-}
    procedure C;
    var IntC: integer;
    begin
      inline(
        $8B/$46/<IntC/        { MOV  AX,[BP+IntC]    ;AX = IntC }
        $8B/$5E/$04/          { MOV  BX,[BP+4]       ;BX = B's stack frame }
        $36/$8B/$47/<IntB/    { MOV  AX,SS:[BX+IntB] ;AX = IntB }
        $8B/$5E/$04/          { MOV  BX,[BP+4]       ;BX = B's stack frame }
        $36/$8B/$5F/$06/      { MOV  BX,SS:[BX+6]    ;BX = A's stack frame }
        $36/$8B/$47/<IntA);   { MOV  AX,SS:[BX+IntA] ;AX = IntA }
    end;
  begin end;
begin end;
```

Note: Nested procedures and functions cannot be declared with the **external** directive, and they cannot be procedural parameters.

Entry and Exit Code

Each Pascal procedure and function begins and ends with standard entry and exit code that creates and removes its activation.

The standard entry code is

```
    push  bp              ;Save BP
    mov   bp,sp           ;Set up stack frame
    sub   sp,Localsize    ;Allocate local variables
```

where *LocalSize* is the size of the local variables. The **SUB** instruction is only present if *LocalSize* is not 0. If the procedure's call model is NEAR, the parameters start at BP + 4; if it is FAR, they start at BP + 6.

The standard exit code is

```
    mov   sp,bp           ;Deallocate local variables
    pop   bp              ;Restore BP
    ret   ParamSize       ;Remove parameters and return
```

where *ParamSize* is the size of the parameters. The **RET** instruction is either a **NEAR** or a **FAR** return, depending on the procedure's call model.

Register-Saving Conventions

Procedures and functions should preserve the BP, SP, SS, and DS registers. All other registers may be modified.

Linking with Assembly Language

Procedures and functions written in assembly language can be linked with Turbo Pascal programs or units using the $L compiler directive. The assembly language source file must be assembled into an object file (extension .OBJ) using an assembler like Turbo Assembler. Multiple object files can be linked with a program or unit through multiple $L directives.

Procedures and functions written in assembly language must be declared as **external** in the Pascal program or unit, for example,

```
function LoCase(Ch: char): char; external;
```

In the corresponding assembly language source file, all procedures and functions must appear in a segment named **CODE**, and the names of the external procedures and functions must appear in **PUBLIC** directives. (**CSEG** is also accepted as a segment name in place of **CODE**.)

You must ensure that an assembly language procedure or function matches its Pascal definition with respect to call model (NEAR or FAR), number of parameters, types of parameters, and result type.

An assembly language source file can declare variables in a segment named **DATA**. Such variables are private to the assembly language source file and cannot be referenced from the Pascal program or unit. However, they reside in the same segment as the Pascal globals, and can be accessed through the DS segment register. (**DSEG** is also accepted as a segment name in place of **DATA**.)

All procedures, functions, and variables declared in the Pascal program or unit, and the ones declared in the **interface** section of the used units, can be referenced from the assembly language source file through **EXTRN** directives. Again, it is up to you to supply the correct type in the **EXTRN** definition.

When an object file appears in a $L directive, Turbo Pascal converts the file from the Intel relocatable object module format (.OBJ) to its own internal relocatable format. This conversion is possible only if certain rules are observed:

- All procedures and functions must be placed in a segment named **CODE**, and all private variables must be placed in a segment named **DATA**. All other segments are ignored, and so are **GROUP** directives. The segment definitions can specify **BYTE** or **WORD** alignment; when linked, they are always word-aligned. The segment definitions can optionally specify **PUBLIC** (which is ignored), but they should not specify a class name. (**CSEG** is also accepted as a segment name in place of **CODE**, and **DSEG** is accepted as a segment name in place of **DATA**.)

- When declaring variables in the **DATA** or **DSEG** segment, always use a question mark (?) to specify the value, for instance:

```
Count   DW  ?
Buffer  DB  128 DUP(?)
```

Turbo Pascal ignores any request to create initialized variables in the **DATA** or **DSEG** segment.

- When referring to **EXTRN** procedures and functions, do not specify an offset. For example, the following construct is not allowed:

```
EXTRN   MyProc : NEAR
CALL    MyProc + 8
```

Note that this restriction does not apply to **EXTRN** variables.

- Byte-sized references to **EXTRN** symbols are not allowed. For example, this means that the assembly language **HIGH** and **LOW** operators cannot be used with **EXTRN** symbols.

Turbo Assembler and Turbo Pascal

Turbo Assembler (TASM) makes it much easier to program routines in assembly language and interface them into your Turbo Pascal programs. Turbo Assembler provides simplified segmentation, memory model, and language support for Turbo Pascal programmers.

Using **TPASCAL** with the **.MODEL** directive sets up Pascal calling conventions, defines the segment names, does the **PUSH BP** and **MOV BP,SP**, and it also sets up the return with **POP BP** and **RET** *N* (where *N* is the number of parameter bytes).

The **PROC** directive lets you define your parameters in the same order as they are defined in your Pascal program. If you are defining a function that returns a string, notice that the **PROC** directive has a **RETURNS** option that lets you access the temporary string pointer on the stack without affecting the number of parameter bytes added to the **RET** statement.

Here's an example coded to use the **.MODEL** and **PROC** directives:

```
        .MODEL TPASCAL
        .CODE
MyProc PROC    FAR i:BYTE,j:BYTE RETURNS result:DWORD
        PUBLIC MyProc
```

```
        les   di,result      ;get address of temporary string
        mov   al,i            ;get first parameter i
        mov   bl,j            ;get second parameter j
        .
        .
        .
        ret
```

The Pascal function definition would look like this:

function MyProc(i,j : char) : **string**; external;

For more information about interfacing Turbo Assembler and Turbo Pascal, refer to Chapter 7 of the *Turbo Assembler User's Guide.*

Examples of Assembly Language Routines

The following code is an example of a unit that implements two assembly language string-handling routines. The *UpperCase* function converts all characters in a string to uppercase, and the *StringOf* function returns a string of characters of a specified length.

```
unit Strings;
interface
function UpperCase(S: string): string;
function StringOf(Ch: char; Count: byte): string;
implementation
{$L STRS}
function UpperCase; external;
function StringOf; external;
end.
```

The assembly language file that implements the *UpperCase* and *StringOf* routines is shown next. It must be assembled into a file called STRS.OBJ before the *Strings* unit can be compiled. Note that the routines use the FAR call model because they are declared in the **interface** section of the unit.

```
CODE       SEGMENT BYTE PUBLIC
           ASSUME  CS:CODE
           PUBLIC  UpperCase,StringOf      ;Make them known

; function UpperCase(S: string): string

UpperRes        EQU     DWORD PTR [BP+10]
UpperStr        EQU     DWORD PTR [BP+6]

UpperCase       PROC FAR
         push   bp                  ;Save BP
         mov    bp,sp               ;Set up stack frame
         push   ds                  ;Save DS
         lds    si,UpperStr         ;Load string address
```

```
            les     di,UpperRes         ;Load result address
            cld                         ;Forward string-ops
            lodsb                       ;Load string length
            stosb                       ;Copy to result
            mov     cl,al               ;String length to CX
            xor     ch,ch
            jcxz    U3                  ;Skip if empty string
    U1:     lodsb                       ;Load character
            cmp     al,'a'              ;Skip if not 'a'..'z'
            jb      U2
            cmp     al,'z'
            ja      U2
            sub     al,'a'-'A'          ;Convert to uppercase
    U2:     stosb                       ;Store in result
            loop    U1                  ;Loop for all characters
    U3:     pop     ds                  ;Restore DS
            pop     bp                  ;Restore BP
            ret     4                   ;Remove parameter and return
    UpperCase   ENDP

    ; procedure StringOf(var S: string; Ch: char; Count: byte)

    StrOfS      EQU     DWORD PTR [BP+10]
    StrOfchar   EQU     BYTE PTR [BP+8]
    StrOfCount  EQU     BYTE PTR [BP+6]

    StringOf    PROC FAR
            push    bp                  ;Save BP
            mov     bp,sp               ;Set up stack frame
            les     di,StrOfRes         ;Load result address
            mov     al,StrOfCount       ;Load count
            cld                         ;Forward string-ops
            stosb                       ;Store length
            mov     cl,al               ;Count to CX
            xor     ch,ch
            mov     al,StrOfChar        ;Load character
            rep     STOSB               ;Store string of characters
            pop     bp                  ;Restore BP
            ret     8                   ;Remove parameters and return
    StringOf    ENDP
    CODE    ENDS
            END
```

To assemble the example and compile the unit, use the following commands:

```
TASM STR5
TPC strings
```

The next example shows how an assembly language routine can refer to Pascal routines and variables. The Numbers program reads up to 100 integer values, and then calls an assembly language procedure to check the range of each of these values. If a value is out of range, the assembly language procedure calls a Pascal procedure to print it.

```
program Numbers;
{$L CHECK}
var
  Buffer : array[1..100] of integer;
  Count  : integer;

procedure RangeError(N: integer);
begin
  Writeln('Range error: ',N);
end;

procedure CheckRange(Min,Max: integer); external;

begin
  Count := 0;
  while not Eof and (Count<100) do
  begin
  { Ends when you type Ctrl-Z or after 100 iterations }
  Count := Count+1; Readln(Buffer[Count]);
  end;
  CheckRange(-10,10);
end.
```

The assembly language file that implements the *CheckRange* procedure is shown next. It must be assembled into a file called CHECK.OBJ before the Numbers program can be compiled. Note that the procedure uses the NEAR call model because it is declared in a program.

```
DATA      SEGMENT WORD PUBLIC
          EXTRN   Buffer:WORD,Count:WORD    ;Pascal variables
DATA      ENDS
CODE      SEGMENT BYTE PUBLIC
          ASSUME  CS:CODE,DS:Buffer
          EXTRN   RangeError:NEAR           ;Implemented in Pascal
          PUBLIC  CheckRange                ;Implemented here
CheckRange          PROC    NEAR
          mov     bx,sp                     ;Get parameters pointer
          mov     ax,ss:[BX+4]              ;Load Min
          mov     dx,ss:[BX+2]              ;Load Max
          xor     bx,bx                     ;Clear Data index
          mov     cx,count                  ;Load Count
          jcxz    SD4                       ;Skip if zero
SD1:      cmp     Buffer[BX],AX             ;Too small?
          jl      SD2                       ;Yes, jump
          cmp     Buffer[BX],DX             ;Too large?
          jle     SD3                       ;No, jump
SD2:      push    ax                        ;Save registers
```

Chapter 15, Inside Turbo Pascal 203

```
            push    bx
            push    cx
            push    dx
            push    Buffer[BX]      ;Pass offending value to Pascal
            call    RangeError      ;Call Pascal procedure
            pop     dx              ;Restore registers
            pop     cx
            pop     bx
            pop     ax
    SD3:    inc     bx              ;Point to next element
            inc     bx
            loop    SD1             ;Loop for each item
    SD4:    ret     4               ;Clean stack and return

    CheckRange      ENDP
    CODE    ENDS
            END
```

Turbo Assembler Example

Here's a Turbo Assembler version of the previous assembly language example that takes advantage of TASM's support for Turbo Pascal:

```
            .MODEL  TPASCAL                 ;Turbo Pascal code model
            LOCALS  @@                      ;Define local labels prefix
            .DATA                           ;Data segment
            EXTRN   Buffer:WORD,Count:WORD  ;Pascal variables

            .CODE                           ;Code segment
            EXTRN   RangeError:NEAR         ;Implemented in Pascal
            PUBLIC  CheckRange              ;Implemented here

    CheckRange      PROC NEAR Min:WORD,Max:WORD
            mov     ax,Min          ;Keep Min in AX
            mov     dx,Max          ;Keep Max in DX
            xor     bx,BX           ;Clear Buffer index
            mov     cx,Count        ;Load Count
            jcxz    @@4             ;Skip if zero
    @@1:    cmp     ax,Buffer[BX]   ;Too small?
            jg      @@2             ;Yes, goto CR2
            cmp     dx,Buffer[BX]   ;Too large?
            jge     @@3             ;No, goto CR3
    @@2:    push    ax              ;Save registers
            push    bx
            push    cx
            push    dx
            push    Buffer[BX]      ;Pass offending value to Pascal
            call    RangeError      ;Call Pascal procedure
            pop     dx              ;Restore registers
            pop     cx
```

```
              pop      bx
              pop      ax
      @@3:    inc      bx              ;Point to next element
              inc      bx
              loop     @@1             ;Loop for each item
      @@4:    ret                      ;Done
      CheckRange       ENDP
              END
```

Notice that with .MODEL TPASCAL Turbo Assembler automatically generates entry code before the first instruction, and generates exit code upon seeing the RET.

Inline Machine Code

For very short assembly language subroutines, Turbo Pascal's **inline** statements and directives are very convenient. They allow you to insert machine code instructions directly into the program or unit text instead of through an object file.

Inline Statements

An **inline** statement consists of the reserved word **inline** followed by one or more inline elements, separated by slashes and enclosed in parentheses:

```
inline(10/$2345/Count+1/Data-Offset);
```

Here's the syntax of an inline statement:

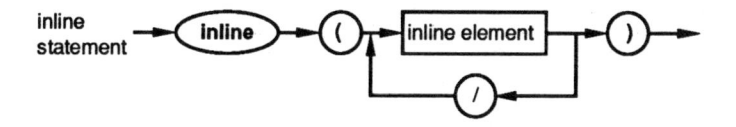

Each inline element consists of an optional size specifier, < or >, and a constant or a variable identifier, followed by zero or more offset specifiers (see the syntax that follows). An offset specifier consists of a + or a − followed by a constant.

inline element ──→─┬─────────────────┬──┬─→ constant ─────────────┬──→
                   │ ┌─< ←─┐   │ │   │
                   │ └─> ←─┘   │ │   │
                   └─→ variable identifier ──┬──→ sign → constant ─┘
                                             └←────────────────────┘

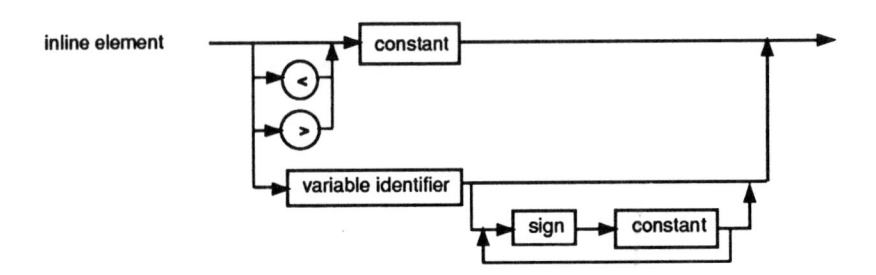

Each inline element generates 1 byte or one word of code. The value is computed from the value of the first constant or the offset of the variable identifier, to which is added or subtracted the value of each of the constants that follow it.

An inline element generates 1 byte of code if it consists of constants only and if its value is within the 8-bit range (0..255). If the value is outside the 8-bit range or if the inline element refers to a variable, one word of code is generated (least-significant byte first).

The < and > operators can be used to override the automatic size selection we described earlier. If an inline element starts with a < operator, only the least-significant byte of the value is coded, even if it is a 16-bit value. If an inline element starts with a > operator, a word is always coded, even though the most-significant byte is 0. For example, the statement

```
inline(<$1234/>$44);
```

generates 3 bytes of code: $34,$44,$00.

The value of a variable identifier in an inline element is the offset address of the variable within its base segment. The base segment of global variables—variables declared at the outermost level in a program or a unit—and typed constants is the data segment, which is accessible through the DS register. The base segment of local variables—variables declared within the current subprogram—is the stack segment. In this case the variable offset is relative to the BP register, which automatically causes the stack segment to be selected.

Note: Registers BP, SP, SS, and DS must be preserved by **inline** statements; all other registers can be modified.

The following example of an **inline** statement generates machine code for storing a specified number of words of data in a specified variable. When called, procedure *FillWord* stores *Count* words of the value *Data* in memory, starting at the first byte occupied by *Dest*.

```
procedure FillWord(var Dest;Count,Data: word);
begin
```

```
  inline(
    $C4/$BE/Dest/                    { LES DI,Dest[BP] }
    $8B/$8E/Count/                   { MOV CX,Count[BP] }
    $8B/$86/Data/                    { MOV AX,Data[BP] }
    $FC/                             { CLD }
    $F3/$AB);                        { REP STOSW }
  end;
```

Inline statements can be freely mixed with other statements throughout the statement part of a block.

Inline Directives

Inline directives let you write procedures and functions that expand into a given sequence of machine code instructions whenever they are called. These are comparable to macros in assembly language. The syntax for an inline directive is the same as that of an inline statement:

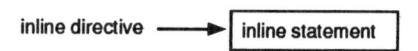

inline directive ⟶ inline statement

When a normal procedure or function is called (including one that contains **inline** statements), the compiler generates code that pushes the parameters (if any) onto the stack, and then generates a **CALL** instruction to call the procedure or function. However, when you call an inline procedure or function, the compiler generates code from the inline directive instead of the **CALL**. Here's a short example of two inline procedures:

```
  procedure DisableInterrupts; inline($FA);    { CLI }
  procedure EnableInterrupts; inline($FB);     { STI }
```

When *DisableInterrupts* is called, it generates 1 byte of code—a **CLI** instruction.

Procedures and functions declared with inline directives can have parameters; however, the parameters cannot be referred to symbolically in the inline directive (other variables can, though). Also, because such procedures and functions are in fact macros, there is no automatic entry and exit code, nor should there be any return instruction.

The following function multiplies two integer values, producing a longint result:

```
  function LongMul(X,Y : integer): longint;
  inline(
    $5A/                             { POP AX ;Pop X }
    $58/                             { POP DX ;Pop Y }
    $F7/$EA);                        { IMUL DX ;DX : AX = X*Y }
```

Note the lack of entry and exit code and the missing return instruction. These are not required, because the 4 bytes are inserted into the instruction stream when *LongMul* is called.

Inline directives are intended for very short (less than 10 bytes) procedures and functions only.

Because of the macro-like nature of inline procedures and functions, they cannot be used as arguments to the @ operator and the *Addr*, *Ofs*, and *Seg* functions.

Direct Memory and Port Access

The Mem, MemW, and MemL Arrays

Turbo Pascal implements three predefined arrays, *Mem*, *MemW*, and *MemL*, which are used to directly access memory. Each component of *Mem* is a byte, each component of *MemW* is a word, and each component of *MemL* is a longint.

The *Mem* arrays use a special syntax for indexes: Two expressions of the integer-type word, separated by a colon, are used to specify the segment base and offset of the memory location to access. Some examples include

```
Mem[$0040:$0049] := 7;
Data := MemW[Seg(V):Ofs(V)];
MemLong := MemL[64:3*4];
```

The first statement stores the value 7 in the byte at $0040:$0049. The second statement moves the word value stored in the first 2 bytes of the variable *V* into the variable *Data*. The third statement moves the longint value stored at $0040:$000C into the variable *MemLong*.

The Port and PortW Arrays

For access to the 80x86 CPU data ports, Turbo Pascal implements two predefined arrays, *Port* and *PortW*. Both are one-dimensional arrays, and each element represents a data port, whose port address corresponds to its index. The index type is the integer-type word. Components of the *Port* array are of type byte, and components of the *PortW* array are of type word.

When a value is assigned to a component of *Port* or *PortW*, the value is output to the selected port. When a component of *Port* or *PortW* is referenced in an expression, its value is input from the selected port. Some examples include:

```
    Port[$20] := $20;
    Port[Base] := Port[Base] xor Mask;
    while Port[$B2] and $80 = 0 do                                    { Wait };
```

Use of the *Port* and *PortW* arrays is restricted to assignment and reference in expressions only, that is, components of *Port* and *PortW* cannot be used as variable parameters. Furthermore, references to the entire *Port* or *PortW* array (reference without index) are not allowed.

Interrupt Handling

The Turbo Pascal run-time library and the code generated by the compiler are fully interruptible. Also, most of the run-time library is reentrant, which allows you to write interrupt service routines in Turbo Pascal.

Writing Interrupt Procedures

Interrupt procedures are declared with the **interrupt** directive. Every interrupt procedure must specify the following procedure header (or a subset of it, as explained later):

```
procedure IntHandler(Flags,CS,IP,AX,BX,CX,DX,SI,DI,DS,ES,BP: word);
interrupt;
begin
  :
  :
end;
```

As you can see, all the registers are passed as pseudo-parameters so you can use and modify them in your code. You can omit some or all of the parameters, starting with *Flags* and moving towards *BP*. It is an error to declare more parameters than are listed in the preceding example or to omit a specific parameter without also omitting the ones before it (although no error is reported). For example:

```
procedure IntHandler(DI,ES,BP : word);              { Invalid call }
procedure IntHandler(SI,DI,DS,ES,BP : word);        { Valid call }
```

On entry, an interrupt procedure automatically saves all registers (regardless of the procedure header) and initializes the DS register:

```
    push    ax
    push    bx
    push    cx
    push    dx
    push    si
    push    di
```

Chapter 15, Inside Turbo Pascal   209

```
        push    ds
        push    es
        push    bp
        mov     bp,sp
        sub     sp,LocalSize
        mov     ax,SEG DATA
        mov     ds,ax
```

Notice the lack of a STI instruction to enable further interrupts. You should code this yourself (if required) using an inline statement. The exit code restores the registers and executes an interrupt-return instruction:

```
        mov     sp,bp
        pop     bp
        pop     es
        pop     ds
        pop     di
        pop     si
        pop     dx
        pop     cx
        pop     bx
        pop     ax
        iret
```

An interrupt procedure can modify its parameters. Changing the declared parameters will modify the corresponding register when the interrupt handler returns. This can be useful when you are using an interrupt handler as a user service, much like the DOS INT 21H services.

Interrupt procedures that handle hardware-generated interrupts should refrain from using any of Turbo Pascal's input and output or dynamic memory allocation routines, because they are not reentrant. Likewise, no DOS functions can be used, because DOS is not reentrant.

Text File Device Drivers

As mentioned in Chapter 10, "Input and Output," Turbo Pascal allows you to define your own text file device drivers. A *text file device driver* is a set of four functions that completely implement an interface between Turbo Pascal's file system and some device.

The four functions that define each device driver are *Open, InOut, Flush,* and *Close*. The function header of each function is

   function DeviceFunc(**var** F: TextRec): integer;

where *TextRec* is the text file record type defined in the earlier section, "File Types," on page 193. Each function must be compiled in the {$F+} state to force it to use the FAR call model. The return value of a device interface function becomes the value returned by *IOResult*. The return value of 0 indicates a successful operation.

To associate the device interface functions with a specific file, you must write a customized *Assign* procedure (like the *AssignCrt* procedure in the *Crt* unit). The *Assign* procedure must assign the addresses of the four device interface functions to the four function pointers in the text file variable. In addition, it should store the *fmClosed* "magic" constant in the *Mode* field, store the size of the text file buffer in *BufSize*, store a pointer to the text file buffer in *BufPtr*, and clear the *Name* string.

Assuming, for example, that the four device interface functions are called *DevOpen*, *DevInOut*, *DevFlush*, and *DevClose*, the *Assign* procedure might look like this:

```
procedure AssignDev(var F: Text);
begin
  with TextRec(F) do
  begin
    Mode      := fmClosed;
    BufSize   := SizeOf(Buffer);
    BufPtr    := @Buffer;
    OpenFunc  := @DevOpen;
    InOutFunc := @DevInOut;
    FlushFunc := @DevFlush;
    CloseFunc := @DevClose;
    Name[0]   := #0;
  end;
end;
```

The device interface functions can use the *UserData* field in the file record to store private information. This field is not modified by the Turbo Pascal file system at any time.

The Open Function

The *Open* function is called by the *Reset*, *Rewrite*, and *Append* standard procedures to open a text file associated with a device. On entry, the *Mode* field contains *fmInput*, *fmOutput*, or *fmInOut* to indicate whether the *Open* function was called from *Reset*, *Rewrite*, or *Append*.

The *Open* function prepares the file for input or output, according to the *Mode* value. If *Mode* specified *fmInOut* (indicating that *Open* was called from *Append*), it must be changed to *fmOutput* before *Open* returns.

Open is always called before any of the other device interface functions. For that reason, *Assign* only initializes the *OpenFunc* field, leaving initialization of the remaining vectors up to *Open*. Based on *Mode*, *Open* can then install pointers to either input- or output-oriented functions. This saves the *InOut*, *Flush*, and *Close* functions from determining the current mode.

The InOut Function

The *InOut* function is called by the *Read*, *Readln*, *Write*, *Writeln*, *Eof*, *Eoln*, *SeekEof*, *SeekEoln*, and *Close* standard procedures and functions whenever input or output from the device is required.

When *Mode* is *fmInput*, the *InOut* function reads up to *BufSize* characters into *BufPtr^*, and returns the number of characters read in *BufEnd*. In addition, it stores 0 in *BufPos*. If the *InOut* function returns 0 in *BufEnd* as a result of an input request, *Eof* becomes True for the file.

When *Mode* is *fmOutput*, the *InOut* function writes *BufPos* characters from *BufPtr^*, and returns 0 in *BufPos*.

The Flush Function

The *Flush* function is called at the end of each *Read*, *Readln*, *Write*, and *Writeln*. It can optionally flush the text file buffer.

If *Mode* is *fmInput*, the *Flush* function can store 0 in *BufPos* and *BufEnd* to flush the remaining (un-read) characters in the buffer. This feature is seldom used.

If *Mode* is *fmOutput*, the *Flush* function can write the contents of the buffer, exactly like the *InOut* function, which ensures that text written to the device appears on the device immediately. If *Flush* does nothing, the text will not appear on the device until the buffer becomes full or the file is closed.

The Close Function

The *Close* function is called by the *Close* standard procedure to close a text file associated with a device. (The *Reset*, *Rewrite*, and *Append* procedures also call *Close* if the file they are opening is already open.) If *Mode* is *fmOutput*, then before calling *Close*, Turbo Pascal's file system calls *InOut* to ensure that all characters have been written to the device.

Examples of Text File Device Drivers

The following unit implements a text file device driver for the communication ports (serial ports) of an IBM PC:

```pascal
unit AuxInOut;
interface
uses Dos;
procedure AssignAux(var F: Text; Port,Params: word);
implementation
{$R-,S-}
type
  AuxRec = record
             Port,Params: word;
             Unused: array[1..12] of byte;
           end;
procedure AuxInit(Port,Params: word);
inline(
  $58/                        { POP AX    ;Pop parameters }
  $5A/                        { POP DX    ;Pop port number }
  $B4/$00/                    { MOV AH,0  ;Code for initialize }
  $CD/$14);                   { INT 14H   ;Call BIOS }
function AuxInChar(Port: word): char;
inline(
  $5A/                        { POP DX    ;Pop port number }
  $B4/$02/                    { MOV AH,2  ;Code for input }
  $CD/$14);                   { INT 14H   ;Call BIOS }
procedure AuxOutChar(Port: word; Ch: char);
inline(
  $58/                        { POP AX    ;Pop character }
  $5A/                        { POP DX    ;Pop port number }
  $B4/$01/                    { MOV AH,1  ;Code for output }
  $CD/$14);                   { INT 14H   ;Call BIOS }
function AuxInReady(Port: word): boolean;
inline(
  $5A/                        { POP DX    ;Pop port number }
  $B4/$03/                    { MOV AH,3  ;Code for status }
  $CD/$14/                    { INT 14H   ;Call BIOS }
  $88/$E0/                    { MOV AL,AH ;Get line status in AH }
  $24/$01);                   { AND AL,1  ;Isolate Data Ready bit }

{$F+}

function AuxInput(var F: TextRec): integer;
var
  P: word;
begin
  with F,AuxRec(UserData) do
  begin
    P := 0;
    while AuxInReady(Port) and (P<BufSize) do
    begin
      BufPtr^[P] := AuxInChar(Port); Inc(P);
    end;
```

```pascal
      BufPos := 0; Bufend := P;
    end;
    AuxInput := 0;
end;

function AuxOutput(var F: TextRec): integer;
var
  P: word;
begin
  with F,AuxRec(UserData) do
   begin
    P := 0;
    while P<BufPos do
    begin
      AuxOutChar(Port,BufPtr^[P]); Inc(P);
    end;
    BufPos := 0;
   end;
  AuxOutput := 0;
end;

function AuxIgnore(var F: TextRec): integer;
begin
  AuxIgnore := 0;
end;

function AuxOpen(var F: TextRec): integer;
begin
  with F,AuxRec(UserData) do
   begin
    AuxInit(Port,Params);
    if Mode=fmInput then
    begin
      InOutFunc := @AuxInput;
      FlushFunc := @AuxIgnore;
    end
    else
    begin
      Mode := fmOutput;
      InOutFunc := @AuxOutput;
      FlushFunc := @AuxOutput;
    end;
    CloseFunc := @AuxIgnore;
   end;
  AuxOpen := 0;
end;

{$F-}

procedure AssignAux;
begin
  with TextRec(F) do
   begin
```

```
      Handle := $FFFF;
      Mode := fmClosed;
      BufSize := Sizeof(Buffer);
      BufPtr := @Buffer;
      OpenFunc := @AuxOpen;
      AuxRec(UserData).Port := Port;
      AuxRec(UserData).Params := Params;
      Name[0] := #0;
    end;
  end;
end.
```

The *TextRec* record is defined in the *Dos* unit. The first two words of the 16-byte *UserData* array are used for storing the communications port number and parameter byte. The remaining 12 bytes are not used. Note that the *AuxRec* record is used only for typecasting.

The *AuxInit* procedure initializes a specified communications port according to a specified parameter byte. The *AuxInChar* function reads a character from the specified port. The *AuxOutChar* procedure outputs a character to the specified port. The *AuxInReady* function returns True if a character is ready to be read from the specified port. Notice the use of inline directives to implement these procedures and functions. For further details on the communication ports, refer to the *IBM PC Technical Reference Manual*.

AssignAux initializes a specified text file variable to refer to a specified communication port with a specified parameter byte. Port numbers 0 and 1 correspond to COM1 and COM2. The parameter byte is described in the *IBM PC Technical Reference Manual*.

AuxOpen initializes the selected communication port and sets up the function pointers according to the *Mode* field. Note that for output, *FlushFunc* is set to the same address as *InOutFunc*, causing the text file buffer to be flushed after each *Write* or *Writeln*.

AuxInput inputs up to *BufSize* characters from the selected port, and *AuxOutput* outputs the contents of the buffer to the selected port.

AuxIgnore is used in those cases where no special action is required, such as for *Close* and for *Flush* (when in input mode).

The following short program uses the *AuxInOut* unit to write a string to one of the communication ports. Through the *AssignAux* procedure, the Com1 file is associated with the COM1 port using 1200 baud, no parity, 1 stop bit, and 8 data bits:

```
program TestAux;
uses AuxInOut;
var
  Com1: Text;
begin
```

```
    AssignAux(Com1,0,$83);
    Rewrite(Com1);
    Writeln(Com1,'Device Drivers are fun!');
    Close(Com1);
end.
```

Exit Procedures

By installing an exit procedure, you can gain control over a program's termination process. This is useful when you want to make sure specific actions are carried out before a program terminates; a typical example is updating and closing files.

The *ExitProc* pointer variable allows you to install an exit procedure. The exit procedure always gets called as a part of a program's termination, whether it is a normal termination, a termination through a call to *Halt*, or a termination due to a run-time error.

An exit procedure takes no parameters, and must be compiled in the {$F+} state to force it to use the FAR call model.

When implemented properly, an exit procedure actually becomes part of a chain of exit procedures. This chain makes it possible for units as well as programs to install exit procedures. Some units install an exit procedure as part of their initialization code, and then rely on that specific procedure to be called to clean up after the unit; for instance, to close files or to restore interrupt vectors. The procedures on the exit chain get executed in reverse order of installation. This ensures that the exit code of one unit does not get executed before the exit code of any units that depend upon it.

To keep the exit chain intact, you must save the current contents of *ExitProc* before changing it to the address of your own exit procedure. Furthermore, the first statement in your exit procedure must reinstall the saved value of *ExitProc*. The following program demonstrates a skeleton method of implementing an exit procedure:

```
program Testexit;
var
  ExitSave: pointer;

{$F+}
procedure MyExit;
begin
  ExitProc := ExitSave;                   { Always restore old vector first }
  :
  :
end;
{$F-}
```

```
begin
  ExitSave := ExitProc;
  ExitProc := @MyExit;
  :
  :
end.
```

On entry, the program saves the contents of *ExitProc* in *ExitSave*, and then installs the *MyExit* exit procedure. After having been called as part of the termination process, the first thing *MyExit* does is reinstall the previous exit procedure.

The termination routine in the run-time library keeps calling exit procedures until *ExitProc* becomes **nil**. To avoid infinite loops, *ExitProc* is set to **nil** before every call, so the next exit procedure is called only if the current exit procedure assigns an address to *ExitProc*. If an error occurs in an exit procedure, it will not be called again.

An exit procedure may learn the cause of termination by examining the *ExitCode* integer variable and the *ErrorAddr* pointer variable.

In case of normal termination, *ExitCode* is zero and *ErrorAddr* is **nil**. In case of termination through a call to *Halt*, *ExitCode* contains the value passed to *Halt* and *ErrorAddr* is **nil**. Finally, in case of termination due to a run-time error, *ExitCode* contains the error code and *ErrorAddr* contains the address of the statement in error.

The last exit procedure (the one installed by the run-time library) closes the *Input* and *Output* files, and restores the interrupt vectors that were captured by Turbo Pascal. In addition, if *ErrorAddr* is not **nil**, it outputs a run-time error message.

If you wish to present run-time error messages yourself, install an exit procedure that examines *ErrorAddr* and outputs a message if it is not **nil**. In addition, before returning, make sure to set *ErrorAddr* to **nil**, so that the error is not reported again by other exit procedures.

Once the run-time library has called all exit procedures, it returns to DOS, passing as a return code the value stored in *ExitCode*.

Automatic Optimizations

Turbo Pascal performs several different types of code optimizations, ranging from constant folding and short-circuit Boolean expression evaluation all the way up to smart linking. The following sections describe some of the types of optimizations performed.

Constant Folding

If the operand(s) of an operator are constants, Turbo Pascal evaluates the expression at compile time. For example, X := 3 + 4 * 2 generates the same code as X := 11, and S := 'In' + 'Out' generates the same code as S := 'InOut'.

Likewise, if an operand of an *Abs, Chr, Hi, Length, Lo, Odd, Ord, Pred, Ptr, Round, Succ, Swap,* or *Trunc* function call is a constant, the function is evaluated at compile time.

If an array index expression is a constant, the address of the component is evaluated at compile time. For example, accessing *Data[5,5]* is just as efficient as accessing a simple variable.

Constant Merging

Using the same string constant two or more times in a statement part generates only one copy of the constant. For example, two or more *Write('Done')* statements in the same statement part will reference the same copy of the string constant *'Done'*.

Short-Circuit Evaluation

Turbo Pascal implements short-circuit Boolean evaluation, which means that evaluation of a Boolean expression stops as soon as the result of the entire expression becomes evident. This guarantees minimum execution time, and usually minimum code size. Short-circuit evaluation also makes possible the evaluation of constructs that would not otherwise be legal; for instance:

```
while (I<=Length(S)) and (S[I]<>' ') do Inc(I);
while (P<>nil) and (P^.Value<>5) do P:=P^.Next;
```

In both cases, the second test is not evaluated if the first test is False.

The opposite of short-circuit evaluation is complete evaluation, which is selected through a {$B+} compiler directive. In this state, every operand of a Boolean expression is guaranteed to be evaluated.

Order of Evaluation

As permitted by the Pascal standards, operands of an expression are frequently evaluated differently from the left to right order in which they are written. For example, the statement

```
I:=F(J) div G(J);
```

where *F* and *G* are functions of type integer, causes *G* to be evaluated before *F*, since this enables the compiler to produce better code. Because of this, it is important that an expression never depend on any specific order of evaluation of the embedded functions. Referring to the previous example, if *F* must be called before *G*, use a temporary
variable:

```
T:=F(J); I:=T div G(J);
```

Note: As an exception to this rule, when short-circuit evaluation is enabled (the {$B-} state), boolean operands grouped with **and** or **or** are *always* evaluated from left to right.

Range-Checking

Assignment of a constant to a variable and use of a constant as a value parameter is range-checked at compile time; no run-time range-check code is generated. For example, X:=999, where *X* is of type *Byte*, causes a compile-time error.

Shift Instead of Multiply

The operation *X * C*, where *C* is a constant and a power of 2, is coded using a Shl instruction.

Likewise, when the size of an array's components is a power of 2, a Shl instruction (not a Mul instruction) is used to scale the index expression.

Automatic Word Alignment

By default, Turbo Pascal aligns all variables and typed constants larger than 1 byte on a machine-word boundary. On all 16-bit 80x86 CPUs, word alignment means faster execution, since word-sized items on even addresses are accessed faster than words on odd addresses.

Data alignment is controlled through the *$A* compiler directive. In the default {$A+} state, variables and typed constants are aligned as described above. In the {$A-} state, no alignment measures are taken. For further details, refer to Appendix B, "Compiler Directives".

Dead Code Removal

Statements that are known never to execute do not generate any code. For example, these constructs don't generate any code:

```
if False then statement
while False do statement
```

Smart Linking

Turbo Pascal 5.0's built-in linker automatically removes unused code and data when building an .EXE file. Procedures, functions, variables, and typed constants that are part of the compilation, but never get referenced, are removed in the .EXE file. The removal of unused code takes place on a per procedure basis, and the removal of unused data takes place on a per declaration section basis.

Consider the following program:

```
program SmartLink;

const
  H: array[0..15] of char = '0123456789ABCDEF';

var
  I,J: integer;
  X,Y: real;

var
  S: string[79];

var
  A: array[1..10000] of integer;

procedure P1;
begin
  A[1] := 1;
end;

procedure P2;
begin
  I := 1;
end;
```

```
procedure P3;
begin
  S := 'Turbo Pascal';
  P2;
end;

begin
  P3;
end.
```

The main program calls *P3*, which calls *P2*, so both *P2* and *P3* are included in the .EXE file; and since *P2* references the first **var** declaration section, and *P3* references the second **var** declaration, *I*, *J*, *X*, *Y*, and *S* are also included in the .EXE file. However, no references are made to *P1*, and none of the included procedures reference *H* and *A*, so these objects are removed.

Smart linking is especially valuable in connection with units that implement procedure/function libraries. An example of such a unit is the *Dos* standard unit: It contains a number of procedures and functions, all of which are seldom used by the same program. If a program uses only one or two procedures from *Dos*, then only these procedures are included in the final .EXE file, and the remaining ones are removed, greatly reducing the size of the .EXE file.

Note: When compiling to memory, Turbo Pascal's smart linker is disabled. This explains why some programs become smaller when compiled to disk.

CHAPTER

16

Turbo Pascal Reference Lookup

This chapter describes all the procedures and functions of Turbo Pascal 5.0. For your convenience, they're arranged alphabetically. For a list of what procedures and functions are new and modified in Turbo Pascal 5.0, refer to Appendix A in the *User's Guide*, "Differences Between Turbo Pascal 3.0, 4.0, and 5.0." Here's a sample layout so you can easily understand the format of the lookup; note that only the relevant items are listed in each entry.

Sample procedure — What unit it occupies

Function	What it does
Declaration	How it's declared; italicized items are user-defined
Result type	What it returns if it's a function
Remarks	General information about the procedure or function
Restrictions	Things to be aware of
Differences	From 3.0 and 4.0
See also	Related procedures/functions, and so on.
Example	Sample program or code fragment

Note: When you compile in numeric processing mode ({$N+}), the return values of the floating-point routines in the *System* unit—*Sqrt, Pi, Sin,* and so on—are of type extended instead of real.

Abs function

Function	Returns the absolute value of the argument.
Declaration	`Abs(x)`
Result type	Same type as parameter.
Remarks	*x* is an integer-type or real-type expression. The result, of the same type as *x*, is the absolute value of *x*.

Example
```
var
  r: real;
  i: integer;
begin
  r := Abs(-2.3);      { 2.3 }
  i := Abs(-157);      { 157 }
end.
```

Addr function

Function	Returns the address of a specified object.
Declaration	`Addr(x)`
Result type	pointer
Remarks	*x* is any variable, or a procedure or function identifier. The result is a pointer that points to *x*. Like **nil**, the result of *Addr* is assignment compatible with all pointer types.
	Note: The @ operator produces the same result as *Addr*.
See also	*Ofs*, *Ptr*, *Seg*

Example
```
var p: pointer;
begin
  p := Addr(p);        { Now points to itself }
end.
```

Append procedure

Function Opens an existing file for appending.

Declaration Append(**var** f: text)

Remarks *f* is a text-file variable that must have been associated with an external file using *Assign*.

Append opens the existing external file with the name assigned to *f*. It is an error if there is no existing external file of the given name. If *f* was already open, it is first closed and then re-opened. The current file position is set to the end of the file.

If a *Ctrl-Z* (ASCII 26) is present in the last 128-byte block of the file, the current file position is set to overwrite the first *Ctrl-Z* in the block. In this way, text can be appended to a file that terminates with a *Ctrl-Z*.

If *f* was assigned an empty name, such as *Assign(f,'')*, then, after the call to *Append*, *f* will refer to the standard output file (standard handle number 1).

After a call to *Append*, *f* becomes write-only, and the file pointer is at end-of-file.

With {$I-}, *IOResult* will return a 0 if the operation was successful; otherwise, it will return a nonzero error code.

See also *Assign, Close, Reset, Rewrite*

Example
```
var f: text;
begin
  Assign(f, 'TEST.TXT');
  Rewrite(f);                        { Create new file }
  Writeln(f, 'original text');
  Close(f);                          { Close file, save changes }
  Append(f);                         { Add more text onto end }
  Writeln(f, 'appended text');
  Close(f);                          { Close file, save changes }
end.
```

Chapter 16, Turbo Pascal Reference Lookup

Arc procedure   Graph

Function	Draws a circular arc from start angle to end angle, using (x,y) as the center point.
Declaration	`Arc(X, Y: integer; StAngle, EndAngle, Radius: word)`
Remarks	Draws a circular arc around (x,y), with a radius of *Radius*. The *Arc* travels from *StAngle* to *EndAngle* and is drawn in the current drawing color.
	Each graphics driver contains an aspect ratio that is used by *Circle*, *Arc*, and *PieSlice*. A start angle of 0 and an end angle of 360 will draw a complete circle. The angles for *Arc*, *Ellipse*, and *PieSlice* are counterclockwise with 0 degrees at 3 o'clock, 90 degrees at 12 o'clock, and so on. Information about the last call to *Arc* can be retrieved with a call to *GetArcCoords*.
	A similar routine exists in Turbo C 2.0.
Restrictions	Must be in graphics mode.
See also	*Circle, Ellipse, FillEllipse, GetArcCoords, GetAspectRatio, PieSlice, Sector, SetAspectRatio*
Example	

```
uses Graph;
var
  Gd, Gm: integer;
  Radius: integer;
begin
  Gd := Detect;
  InitGraph(Gd, Gm, '');
  if GraphResult <> grOk then
    Halt(1);
  for Radius := 1 to 5 do
    Arc(100, 100, 0, 90, Radius*10);
  Readln;
  CloseGraph;
end.
```

ArcTan function

Function	Returns the arctangent of the argument.
Declaration	`ArcTan(x: real)`
Result type	real

ArcTan function

Remarks *x* is a real-type expression. The result is the principal value, in radians, of the arctangent of *x*.

See also *Cos, Sin*

Example
```
var r: real;
begin
  r := ArcTan(Pi);
end.
```

Assign procedure

Function Assigns the name of an external file to a file variable.

Declaration `Assign(var f; name: string)`

Remarks *f* is a file variable of any file type, and *name* is a string-type expression. All further operations on *f* will operate on the external file with the file name *name*.

After a call to *Assign*, the association between *f* and the external file continues to exist until another *Assign* is done on *f*.

A file name consists of a path of zero or more directory names separated by backslashes, followed by the actual file name:

`Drive:\DirName\...\DirName\FileName`

If the path begins with a backslash, it starts in the root directory; otherwise, it starts in the current directory.

Drive is a disk drive identifier (A-Z). If *Drive* and the colon are omitted, the default drive is used. *\DirName\ ...\DirName* is the root directory and subdirectory path to the file name. *FileName* consists of a name of up to eight characters, optionally followed by a period and an extension of up to three characters.

The maximum length of the entire file name is 79 characters.

A special case arises when *name* is an empty string; that is, when *Length(name)* is zero. In that case, *f* becomes associated with the standard input or standard output file. These special files allow a program to utilize the I/O redirection feature of the DOS operating system. If assigned an empty name, then after a call to *Reset(f)*, *f*

Assign procedure

will refer to the standard input file, and after a call to *Rewrite(f), f* will refer to the standard output file.

Restrictions   *Assign* must never be used on an open file.

See also   *Append, Close, Reset, Rewrite*

Example
```
{ Try redirecting this program from DOS
  to PRN, disk file, etc. }
var f: text;
begin
  Assign(f, '');                          { Standard output }
  Rewrite(f);
  Writeln(f, 'standard output...');
  Close(f);
end.
```

AssignCrt procedure   Crt

Function   Associates a text file with the CRT.

Declaration   AssignCrt(**var** f: Text)

Remarks   *AssignCrt* works exactly like the *Assign* standard procedure except that no file name is specified. Instead, the text file is associated with the CRT.

This allows faster output (and input) than would normally be possible using standard output (or input).

Example
```
uses Crt;
var f: text;
begin
  Write('Output to screen or printer [S, P]? ');
  if UpCase(ReadKey) = 'P' then
    Assign(f, 'PRN')                      { Output to printer }
  else
    AssignCrt(f);   { Output to screen, use fast CRT routines }
  Rewrite(f);
  Writeln(f, 'Fast output via CRT routines...');
  Close(f);
end.
```

Bar procedure   Graph

Function   Draws a bar using the current fill style and color.

Declaration   `Bar(x1, y1, x2, y2: integer)`

Remarks   Draws a filled-in rectangle (used in bar charts, for example). Uses the pattern and color defined by *SetFillStyle* or *SetFillPattern*. To draw an outlined bar, call *Bar3D* with a depth of zero.

A similar routine exists in Turbo C 2.0.

Restrictions   Must be in graphics mode.

See also   *Bar3D, GraphResult, SetFillStyle, SetFillPattern, SetLineStyle*

Example
```
uses Graph;
var
  Gd, Gm : integer;
  I, Width: integer;
begin
  Gd := Detect;
  InitGraph(Gd, Gm, '');
  if GraphResult <> grOk then
    Halt(1);
  Width := 10;
  for I := 1 to 5 do
    Bar(I*Width, I*10, Succ(I)*Width, 200);
  Readln;
  CloseGraph;
end.
```

Bar3D procedure   Graph

Function   Draws a 3-D bar using the current fill style and color.

Declaration   `Bar3D(x1, y1, x2, y2: integer; Depth: word; Top: boolean)`

Remarks   Draws a filled-in, three-dimensional bar. Uses the pattern and color defined by *SetFillStyle* or *SetFillPattern*. The 3-D outline of the bar is drawn in the current line style and color as set by *SetLineStyle* and *SetColor*. *Depth* is the number of pixels deep of the 3-D outline. If *Top* is True, a 3-D top is put on the bar; if *Top* is False, no top is

Bar3D procedure

put on the bar (making it possible to stack several bars on top one another).

A typical depth could be calculated by taking 25% of the width of the bar:

```
Bar3d(x1,y1,x2,y2,(x2-x1+1) div 4, TopOn);
```

The following constants are defined:

```
const
  TopOn  = True;
  TopOff = False;
```

A similar routine exists in Turbo C 2.0.

Restrictions Must be in graphics mode.

See also *Bar, GraphResult, SetFillPattern, SetFillStyle, SetLineStyle*

Example
```
uses Graph;
var
  Gd, Gm: integer;
  y0, y1, y2, x1, x2: integer;
begin
  Gd := Detect;
  InitGraph(Gd, Gm, '');
  if GraphResult <> grOk then
    Halt(1);
  y0 := 10;
  y1 := 60;
  y2 := 110;
  x1 := 10;
  x2 := 50;
  Bar3D(x1, y0, x2, y1, 10, TopOn);
  Bar3D(x1, y1, x2, y2, 10, TopOff);
  Readln;
  CloseGraph;
end.
```

BlockRead procedure

Function Reads one or more records into a variable.

Declaration BlockRead(**var** f: **file;** **var** buf; count: word
              [; **var** result: word])

Remarks *f* is an untyped file variable, *buf* is any variable, *count* is an expression of type word, and *result* is a variable of type word.

BlockRead procedure

BlockRead reads *count* or less records from the file *f* into memory, starting at the first byte occupied by *buf*. The actual number of complete records read (less than or equal to *count*) is returned in the optional parameter *result*. If *result* is not specified, an I/O error will occur if the number read is not equal to *count*.

The entire block transferred occupies at most *count* * *recsize* bytes, where *recsize* is the record size specified when the file was opened (or 128 if it was omitted). It's an error if *count* * *recsize* is greater than 65535 (64 Kb).

result is an optional parameter. Here is how it works: If the entire block was transferred, *result* will be equal to *count* on return. Otherwise, if *result* is less than *count*, the end of the file was reached before the transfer was completed. In that case, if the file's record size is greater than one, *result* returns the number of complete records read; that is, a possible last partial record is not included in *result*.

The current file position is advanced by *result* records as an effect of the *BlockRead*.

With {$I-}, *IOResult* will return a 0 if the operation was successful; otherwise, it will return a nonzero error code.

Restrictions	File must be open.
Differences	3.0 read partial records; 5.0 discards them.
See also	*BlockWrite*
Example	

```
program CopyFile;
{ Simple, fast file copy program with NO error-checking }
var
  FromF, ToF: file;
  NumRead, NumWritten: word;
  buf: array[1..2048] of char;
begin
  Assign(FromF, ParamStr(1));           { Open input file }
  Reset(FromF, 1);                      { Record size = 1 }
  Assign(ToF, ParamStr(2));             { Open output file }
  Rewrite(ToF, 1);                      { Record size = 1 }
  Writeln('Copying ', FileSize(FromF), ' bytes...');
  repeat
    BlockRead(FromF,buf,SizeOf(buf),NumRead);
    BlockWrite(ToF,buf,NumRead,NumWritten);
  until (NumRead = 0) or (NumWritten <> NumRead);
```

Chapter 16, Turbo Pascal Reference Lookup

```
        Close(FromF);
        Close(ToF);
end.
```

BlockWrite procedure

Function	Writes one or more records from a variable.
Declaration	BlockWrite(BlockWrite(**var** f: **file**; **var** buf; count: word [; **var** result: word])
Remarks	*f* is an untyped file variable, *buf* is any variable, *count* is an expression of type word, and *result* is a variable of type word.

BlockWrite writes *count* or less records to the file *f* from memory, starting at the first byte occupied by *buf*. The actual number of complete records written (less than or equal to *count*) is returned in the optional parameter *result*. If *result* is not specified, an I/O error will occur if the number written is not equal to *count*.

The entire block transferred occupies at most *count * recsize* bytes, where *recsize* is the record size specified when the file was opened (or 128 if it was omitted). It is an error if *count * recsize* is greater than 65535 (64K).

result is an optional parameter. Here is how it works: If the entire block was transferred, *result* will be equal to *count* on return. Otherwise, if *result* is less than *count*, the disk became full before the transfer was completed. In that case, if the file's record size is greater than one, *result* returns the number of complete records written; that is, it's possible a remaining partial record is not included in *result*.

The current file position is advanced by *result* records as an effect of the *BlockWrite*.

With {$I-}, *IOResult* will return a 0 if the operation was successful; otherwise, it will return a nonzero error code.

Restrictions	File must be open.
Differences	3.0 read partial records; 5.0 discards them.
See also	*BlockRead*
Example	See example for *BlockRead*.

ChDir procedure

Function Changes the current directory.

Declaration ChDir(s: **string**)

Remarks *s* is a string-type expression. The current directory is changed to a path specified by *s*. If *s* specifies a drive letter, the current drive is also changed.

With {$I-}, *IOResult* will return a 0 if the operation was successful; otherwise, it will return a nonzero error code.

See also *GetDir, MkDir, RmDir*

Example
```
begin
  {$I-}
  { Get directory name from command line }
  ChDir(ParamStr(1));
  if IOResult <> 0 then
    Writeln('Cannot find directory');
end.
```

Chr function

Function Returns a character with a specified ordinal number.

Declaration Chr(x: byte)

Result type char

Remarks *x* is an integer-type expression. The result is the character with an ordinal value (ASCII value) of *x*.

See also *Ord*

Example
```
uses Printer;
begin
  Writeln(Lst, Chr(12));      { Send form feed to printer }
end.
```

Chapter 16, Turbo Pascal Reference Lookup

Circle procedure   Graph

Function   Draws a circle using (X,Y) as the center point.

Declaration   `Circle(X, Y: integer; Radius: word)`

Remarks   The circle is drawn in the current color set by *SetColor*. Each graphics driver contains an aspect ratio that is used by *Circle*, *Arc*, and *PieSlice* to make circles.

A similar routine exists in Turbo C 2.0.

Restrictions   Must be in graphics mode.

See also   *Arc, Ellipse, FillEllipse, GetArcCoords, GetAspectRatio, PieSlice, Sector, SetAspectRatio*

Example

```
uses Graph;
var
  Gd, Gm: integer;
  Radius: integer;
begin
  Gd := Detect;
  InitGraph(Gd, Gm, '');
  if GraphResult <> grOk then
    Halt(1);
  for Radius := 1 to 5 do
    Circle(100, 100, Radius*10);
  Readln;
  CloseGraph;
end.
```

ClearDevice procedure   Graph

Function   Clears the graphics screen and prepares it for output.

Declaration   `ClearDevice`

Remarks   *ClearDevice* moves the current pointer to (0,0), clears the screen using the background color set by *SetBkColor*, and prepares it for output.

A similar routine exists in Turbo C 2.0.

Restrictions   Must be in graphics mode.

See also   *ClearViewPort, CloseGraph, GraphDefaults, InitGraph, RestoreCrtMode, SetGraphMode*

Example

```
uses Crt, Graph;
var
  Gd, Gm: integer;
begin
  Gd := Detect;
  InitGraph(Gd, Gm, '');
  if GraphResult <> grOk then
    Halt(1);
  Randomize;
  repeat
    LineTo(Random(200), Random(200));
  until KeyPressed;
  ClearDevice;
  Readln;
  CloseGraph;
end.
```

ClearViewPort procedure   Graph

Function   Clears the current viewport.

Declaration   `ClearViewPort`

Remarks   Sets the fill color to the background color (*Palette*[0]), calls *Bar*, and moves the current pointer to (0,0).

A similar routine exists in Turbo C 2.0.

Restrictions   Must be in graphics mode.

See also   *Bar, ClearDevice, GetViewSettings, SetViewPort*

Example

```
uses Graph;
var
  Gd, Gm: integer;
begin
  Gd := Detect;
  InitGraph(Gd, Gm, '');
  if GraphResult <> grOk then
    Halt(1);
  Rectangle(19, 19, GetMaxX-19, GetMaxY-19);
  SetViewPort(20, 20, GetMaxX-20, GetMaxY-20, ClipOn);
  OutTextXY(0, 0, '<ENTER> clears viewport:');
  Readln;
  ClearViewPort;
  OutTextXY(0, 0, '<ENTER> to quit:');
  Readln;
  CloseGraph;
end.
```

Close procedure

Function Closes an open file.

Declaration Close(**var** f)

Remarks *f* is a file variable of any file type that was previously opened with *Reset*, *Rewrite*, or *Append*. The external file associated with *f* is completely updated and then closed, and its DOS file handle is freed for reuse.

With {$I-}, *IOResult* will return a 0 if the operation was successful; otherwise, it will return a nonzero error code.

See also *Append, Assign, Reset, Rewrite*

Example
```
var f: file;
begin
  Assign(f, '\AUTOEXEC.BAT');            { Open file }
  Reset(f, 1);
  Writeln('File size = ', FileSize(f));
  Close(f);                              { Close file }
end.
```

CloseGraph procedure   Graph

Function Shuts down the graphics system.

Declaration CloseGraph

Remarks *CloseGraph* restores the original screen mode before graphics was initialized and frees the memory allocated on the heap for the graphics scan buffer. *CloseGraph* also deallocates driver and font memory buffers if they were allocated by calls to *GraphGetMem* and *GraphFreeMem*.

A similar routine exists in Turbo C 2.0.

Restrictions Must be in graphics mode.

See also *DetectGraph, GetGraphMode, InitGraph, RestoreCrtMode, SetGraphMode*

Example
```
uses Graph;
var
  Gd, Gm: integer;
begin
  Gd := Detect;
```

CloseGraph procedure

```
    InitGraph(Gd, Gm, '');
    if GraphResult <> grOk then
      Halt(1);
    Line(0, 0, GetMaxX, GetMaxY);
    Readln;
    CloseGraph;                              { Shut down graphics }
end.
```

ClrEol procedure   Crt

Function   Clears all characters from the cursor position to the end of the line without moving the cursor.

Declaration   ClrEol

Remarks   All character positions are set to blanks with the currently defined text attributes. Thus, if *TextBackground* is not black, the column from the cursor to the right edge of the screen becomes the background color.

This procedure is window-relative:

```
Window(1,1,60,20);
ClrEol;
```

will clear from the current cursor position (1,1) to the right edge of the active window (60,1).

See also   *ClrScr, Window*

Example
```
uses Crt;
begin
  TextBackground(LightGray);
  ClrEol;    { Changes cleared columns to LightGray background }
end.
```

ClrScr procedure   Crt

Function   Clears the active window and places the cursor in the upper left-hand corner.

Declaration   ClrScr

Remarks   All character positions are set to blanks with the currently defined text attributes. Thus, if *TextBackground* is

ClrScr procedure

not black, the entire screen becomes the background color. This also applies to characters cleared by *ClrEol*, *InsLine*, and *DelLine*, as well as empty lines created by scrolling.

This procedure is window-relative:

```
Window(1,1,60,20);
ClrScr;
```

will clear a 60 × 20 rectangle beginning at (1,1).

See also *ClrEol, Window*

Example
```
uses Crt;
begin
  TextBackground(LightGray);
  ClrScr;     { Changes entire window to LightGray background }
end.
```

Concat function

Function   Concatenates a sequence of strings.

Declaration Concat(s1 [, s2, ..., sn]: **string**)

Result type string

Remarks   Each parameter is a string-type expression. The result is the concatenation of all the string parameters. If the resulting string is longer than 255 characters, it is truncated after the 255th character. Using the plus (+) operator returns the same results as using the *Concat* function:

```
S := 'ABC' + 'DEF';
```

See also *Copy, Delete, Insert, Length, Pos*

Example
```
var s: string;
begin
  s := Concat('ABC', 'DEF');              { 'ABCDEF' }
end.
```

238 Turbo Pascal Reference Guide

Copy function

Function	Returns a substring of a string.
Declaration	`Copy(s: string; index: integer; count: integer)`
Result type	string
Remarks	*s* is a string-type expression. *index* and *count* are integer-type expressions. *Copy* returns a string containing *count* characters starting with the *index*th character in *s*. If *index* is larger than the length of *s*, an empty string is returned. If *count* specifies more characters than remain starting at the *index*th position, only the remainder of the string is returned.
See also	*Concat, Delete, Insert, Length, Pos*
| **Example** | ```
var s: string;
begin
  s := 'ABCDEF';
  s := Copy(s, 2, 3);           { 'BCD' }
end.
``` |

Cos function

Function	Returns the cosine of the argument.
Declaration	`Cos(x: real)`
Result type	real
Remarks	*x* is a real-type expression. The result is the cosine of *x*. *x* is assumed to represent an angle in radians.
See also	*ArcTan, Sin*
| **Example** | ```
var r: real;
begin
  r := Cos(Pi);
end.
``` |

CSeg function

Function	Returns the current value of the CS register.
Declaration	CSeg
Result type	word
Remarks	The result of type word is the segment address of the code segment within which *CSeg* was called.
See also	*DSeg, SSeg*

Dec procedure

Function	Decrements a variable.
Declaration	Dec(**var** x [; n: longint])
Remarks	*x* is an ordinal-type variable, and *n* is an integer-type expression. *x* is decremented by 1, or by *n* if *n* is specified; that is, *Dec(x)* corresponds to *x := x-1*, and *Dec(x,n)* corresponds to *x := x-n*.
	Dec generates optimized code and is especially useful in a tight loop.
See also	*Inc, Pred, Succ*
Example	

```
var
  IntVar: integer;
  LongintVar: longint;
begin
  Dec(IntVar);              { IntVar := IntVar - 1 }
  Dec(LongintVar, 5);       { LongintVar := LongintVar - 5 }
end.
```

Delay procedure   Crt

Function	Delays a specified number of milliseconds.
Declaration	Delay(ms: word)
Remarks	*ms* specifies the number of milliseconds to wait.

Delay is an approximation, so the delay period will not last exactly *ms* milliseconds.

Delete procedure

Function	Deletes a substring from a string.
Declaration	`Delete(`**`var`**` s: `**`string`**`; index: integer; count: integer)`
Remarks	*s* is a string-type variable. *index* and *count* are integer-type expressions. *Delete* deletes *count* characters from *s* starting at the *index*th position. If *index* is larger than the length of *s*, no characters are deleted. If *count* specifies more characters than remain starting at the *index*th position, the remainder of the string is deleted.
See also	*Concat, Copy, Insert, Length, Pos*

DelLine procedure   Crt

Function	Deletes the line containing the cursor.
Declaration	`DelLine`
Remarks	The line containing the cursor is deleted, and all lines below are moved one line up (using the BIOS scroll routine). A new line is added at the bottom.

All character positions are set to blanks with the currently defined text attributes. Thus, if *TextBackground* is not black, the new line becomes the background color.

This procedure is window-relative:

```
Window(1,10,60,20);
DelLine;
```

will delete the first line in the window, which is the tenth line on the screen.

See also   *Insline, Window*

DetectGraph procedure — Graph

Function Checks the hardware and determines which graphics driver and mode to use.

Declaration DetectGraph(**var** GraphDriver, GraphMode: integer)

Remarks Returns the detected driver and mode value that can be passed to *InitGraph*, which will then load the correct driver. If no graphics hardware was detected, the *GraphDriver* parameter and *GraphResult* will return a value of –2 (*grNotDetected*).

The following constants are defined:

```
const
  Detect   = 0;        { Request autodetection }
  CGA      = 1;
  MCGA     = 2;
  EGA      = 3;
  EGA64    = 4;
  EGAMono  = 5;
  IBM8514  = 6;
  HercMono = 7;
  ATT400   = 8;
  VGA      = 9;
  PC3270   = 10;
```

Unless instructed otherwise, *InitGraph* calls *DetectGraph*, finds and loads the correct driver, and initializes the graphics system. The only reason to call *DetectGraph* directly is to override the driver that *DetectGraph* recommends. The example that follows identifies the system as a 64K or 256K EGA, and loads the CGA driver instead. Note that when you pass *InitGraph* a *GraphDriver* other than *Detect*, you must also pass in a valid *GraphMode* for the driver requested.

A similar routine exists in Turbo C 2.0.

Restrictions You should not use *DetectGraph* (or *Detect* with *InitGraph*) with the IBM 8514 unless you want the emulated VGA mode.

See also *CloseGraph, GraphResult, InitGraph*

Example
```
uses Graph;
var
  GraphDriver, GraphMode: integer;
begin
```

DetectGraph procedure

```
DetectGraph(GraphDriver, GraphMode);
if (GraphDriver = EGA) or
   (GraphDriver = EGA64) then
begin
  GraphDriver := CGA;
  GraphMode := CGAHi;
end;
InitGraph(GraphDriver,GraphMode,'');
if GraphResult <> grOk then
  Halt(1);
Line(0, 0, GetMaxX, GetMaxY);
Readln;
CloseGraph;
end.
```

DiskFree function   Dos

Function	Returns the number of free bytes on a specified disk drive.
Declaration	DiskFree(Drive: byte)
Result type	longint
Remarks	A *Drive* of 0 indicates the default drive, 1 indicates drive A, 2 indicates B, and so on. *DiskFree* returns –1 if the drive number is invalid.
See also	*DiskSize, GetDir*
| **Example** | ```
uses Dos;
begin
  Writeln(DiskFree(0) div 1024, ' k-bytes free ');
end.
``` |

DiskSize function   Dos

Function	Returns the total size in bytes on a specified disk drive.
Declaration	DiskSize(Drive: byte)
Result type	longint
Remarks	A *Drive* of 0 indicates the default drive, 1 indicates drive A, 2 indicates B, and so on. *DiskSize* returns –1 if the drive number is invalid.

Chapter 16, Turbo Pascal Reference Lookup
```

DiskSize function

See also
: *DiskFree, GetDir*

Example
: ```
uses Dos;
begin
  Writeln(DiskSize(0) div 1024, ' k-bytes capacity');
end.
```

# Dispose procedure

Function
: Disposes a dynamic variable.

Declaration
: Dispose(**var** p: pointer)

Remarks
: *p* is a pointer variable of any pointer type that was previously assigned by the *New* procedure or was assigned a meaningful value by an assignment statement. *Dispose* destroys the variable referenced by *p* and returns its memory region to the heap. After a call to *Dispose*, the value of *p* becomes undefined, and it is an error to subsequently reference *p^*.

Restrictions
: If *p* does not point to a memory region in the heap, a run-time error occurs.

    *Dispose* and *FreeMem* cannot be used interchangeably with *Mark* and *Release* unless certain rules are observed. For a complete discussion of this topic, refer to the section "The Heap Manager" on page 181.

See also
: *FreeMem, GetMem, Mark, New, Release*

Example
: ```
type
  Str18 = string[18];
var
  p: ^Str18;
begin
  New(p);
  p^ := 'Now you see it...';
  Dispose(p);                    { Now you don't... }
end.
```

DosExitCode function   Dos

Function	Returns the exit code of a subprocess.
Declaration	`DosExitCode`
Result type	word
Remarks	The low byte is the code sent by the terminating process. The high byte is set to

- 0 for normal termination
- 1 if terminated by *Ctrl-C*
- 2 if terminated due to a device error
- 3 if terminated by the *Keep* procedure

See also	*Exec, Keep*

DosVersion function   Dos

Function	Returns the DOS version number.
Declaration	`DosVersion`
Result type	word
Remarks	*DosVersion* returns the DOS version number. The low byte of the result is the major version number, and the high byte is the minor version number. For example, DOS 3.20 returns 3 in the low byte, and 20 in the high byte.
Example	

```
uses Dos;
var
  Ver: word;
begin
  Ver:=DosVersion;
  Writeln('This is DOS version ',Lo(Ver),'.',Hi(Ver));
end.
```

DrawPoly procedure   Graph

Function   Draws the outline of a polygon using the current line style and color.

Declaration   DrawPoly(NumPoints: word; **var** PolyPoints)

Remarks   *PolyPoints* is an untyped parameter that contains the coordinates of each intersection in the polygon. *NumPoints* specifies the number of coordinates in *PolyPoints*. A coordinate consists of two words, an *x* and a *y* value.

DrawPoly uses the current line style and color. Use *SetWriteMode* to determine whether the polygon is copied to or XOR'd to the screen.

Note that in order to draw a closed figure with *n* vertices, you must pass *N* + 1 coordinates to *DrawPoly*, and where *PolyPoints[n+1]* = *PolyPoints[1]* (see the example that follows). In order to draw a triangle, for example, four coordinates must be passed to *DrawPoly*.

A similar routine exists in Turbo C 2.0.

Restrictions   Must be in graphics mode.

See also   *FillPoly, GetLineSettings, GraphResult, SetColor, SetLineStyle, SetWriteMode*

Example
```
uses Graph;
const
  Triangle: array[1..4] of PointType = ((x:  50; y: 100),
                                        (x: 100; y: 100),
                                        (x: 150; y: 150),
                                        (x:  50; y: 100));
var
  Gd, Gm: integer;
begin
  Gd := Detect;
  InitGraph(Gd, Gm, '');
  if GraphResult <> grOk then
    Halt(1);
  DrawPoly(SizeOf(Triangle) div SizeOf(PointType),
           Triangle);                                        { 4 }
  Readln;
  CloseGraph;
end.
```

DSeg function

Function	Returns the current value of the DS register.
Declaration	DSeg
Result type	word
Remarks	The result of type word is the segment address of the data segment.
See also	*CSeg, SSeg*

Ellipse procedure   Graph

Function	Draws an elliptical arc from start angle to end angle, using (X,Y) as the center point.
Declaration	`Ellipse(X, Y: integer; StAngle, EndAngle: word;` `        XRadius, YRadius: word)`
Remarks	Draws an elliptical arc using (X,Y) as a center point, and *XRadius* and *YRadius* as the horizontal and vertical axes. The ellipse travels from *StAngle* to *EndAngle* and is drawn in the current color.
	A start angle of 0 and an end angle of 360 will draw a complete oval. The angles for *Arc*, *Ellipse*, and *PieSlice* are counterclockwise with 0 degrees at 3 o'clock, 90 degrees at 12 o'clock, and so on. Information about the last call to *Ellipse* can be retrieved with a call to *GetArcCoords*.
	A similar routine exists in Turbo C 2.0.
Restrictions	Must be in graphics mode.
See also	*Arc, Circle, FillEllipse, GetArcCoords, GetAspectRatio, PieSlice, Sector, SetAspectRatio*
| **Example** | ```
uses Graph;
var
  Gd, Gm: integer;
begin
  Gd := Detect;
  InitGraph(Gd, Gm, '');
  if GraphResult <> grOk then
    Halt(1);
``` |

Chapter 16, Turbo Pascal Reference Lookup
```

Ellipse procedure

```
    Ellipse(100,100,0,360,30,50);
    Ellipse(100,100,0,180,50,30);
    Readln;
    CloseGraph;
end.
```

EnvCount function   Dos

Function   Returns the number of strings contained in the DOS environment.

Declaration   EnvCount

Result type   integer

Remarks   *EnvCount* returns the number of strings contained in the DOS environment. Each environment string is of the form *VAR=VALUE*. The strings can be examined with the *EnvStr* function.

For more information about the DOS environment, refer to your DOS manuals.

See also   *EnvStr, GetEnv*

Example
```
uses Dos;
var
  I: integer;
begin
  for I := 1 to EnvCount do
   Writeln(EnvStr(I));
end.
```

EnvStr function   Dos

Function   Returns a specified environment string.

Declaration   EnvStr(Index: integer)

Result type   string

Remarks   *EnvStr* returns a specified string from the DOS environment. The string *EnvStr* returns is of the form *VAR=VALUE*. The index of the first string is one. If *Index* is less than one or greater than *EnvCount*, *EnvStr* returns an empty string.

Eof function (text files)

For more information about the DOS environment, refer to your DOS manuals.

See also   *EnvCount, GetEnv*

Eof function (text files)

Function   Returns the end-of-file status of a text file.

Declaration   Eof [(**var** f: text)]

Result type   boolean

Remarks   *f*, if specified, is a text-file variable. If *f* is omitted, the standard file variable *Input* is assumed. *Eof(f)* returns True if the current file position is beyond the last character of the file or if the file contains no components; otherwise, *Eof(f)* returns False.

With {$I-}, *IOResult* will return a 0 if the operation was successful; otherwise, it will return a nonzero error code.

See also   *Eoln, SeekEof*

Example
```
var
  f : text;
  ch: char;
begin
  { Get file to read from command line }
  Assign(f, ParamStr(1));
  Reset(f);
  while not Eof(f) do
  begin
    Read(f,ch);
    Write(ch);                        { Dump text file }
  end;
end.
```

Eof function (typed, untyped files)

Function   Returns the end-of-file status of a typed or untyped file.

Declaration   Eof(**var** f)

Result type   boolean

Chapter 16, Turbo Pascal Reference Lookup

Eof function (typed, untyped files)

Remarks *f* is a file variable. *Eof(f)* returns True if the current file position is beyond the last component of the file or if the file contains no components; otherwise, *Eof(f)* returns False.

With {$I-}, *IOResult* will return a 0 if the operation was successful; otherwise, it will return a nonzero error code.

Eoln function

Function Returns the end-of-line status of a file.

Declaration `Eoln [ (var f: text) ]`

Result type boolean

Remarks *f*, if specified, is a text-file variable. If *f* is omitted, the standard file variable *Input* is assumed. *Eoln(f)* returns True if the current file position is at an end-of-line marker or if *Eof(f)* is True; otherwise, *Eoln(f)* returns False.

When checking *Eoln* on standard input that has not been redirected, the following program will wait for a carriage return to be entered before returning from the call to *Eoln*:

```
begin
  { Tells program to wait for keyboard input }
  Writeln(Eoln);
end.
```

With {$I-}, *IOResult* will return a 0 if the operation was successful; otherwise, it will return a nonzero error code.

See also *Eof, SeekEoln*

Erase procedure

Function Erases an external file.

Declaration `Erase(var f)`

Remarks *f* is a file variable of any file type. The external file associated with *f* is erased.

Erase procedure

	With {$I-}, *IOResult* will return a 0 if the operation was successful; otherwise, it will return a nonzero error code.
Restrictions	*Erase* must never be used on an open file.
See also	*Rename*
| Example | ```
var
  f : file;
  ch: char;
begin
  { Get file to delete from command line }
  Assign(f, ParamStr(1));
  {$I-}
  Reset(f);
  {$I+}
  if IOResult <> 0 then
    Writeln('Cannot find ', ParamStr(1))
  else
  begin
    Close(f);
    Write('Erase ', ParamStr(1), '? ');
    Readln(ch);
    if UpCase(ch) = 'Y' then
      Erase(f);
  end;
end.
``` |

Exec procedure   Dos

Function	Executes a specified program with a specified command line.
Declaration	Exec(Path, CmdLine: **string**)
Remarks	The program name is given by the *Path* parameter, and the command line is given by *CmdLine*. To execute a DOS internal command, run COMMAND.COM; for instance,

```
Exec('\COMMAND.COM','/C DIR *.PAS');
```

The /C in front of the command is a requirement of COMMAND.COM (but not of other applications). Errors are reported in *DosError*; possible error codes are 2, 8, 10, and 11. The exit code of any child process is reported by the *DosExitCode* function.
```

Exec procedure

It is recommended that *SwapVectors* be called just before and just after the call to *Exec*. *SwapVectors* swaps the contents of the *SaveIntXX* pointers in the *System* unit with the current contents of the interrupt vectors. This ensures that the *Exec*'d process does not use any interrupt handlers installed by the current process, and vice versa.

Exec does not change the memory allocation state before executing the program. Therefore, when compiling a program that uses *Exec*, be sure to reduce the "maximum" heap size; otherwise, there won't be enough memory (*DosError* = 8).

Restrictions   Versions of the Novell Network system software earlier than 2.01 or 2.02 do not support a DOS call used by *Exec*. If you are using the integrated development environment to run a program that uses *Exec*, and you have early Novell system software, set Compile/Destination to Disk and run your program from DOS (you can use the File/OS Shell command to do this).

See also   *DosExitCode, SwapVectors*

Example
```
{$M $4000,0,0 }      { 16K stack, no heap required or reserved }
uses Dos;
var
  ProgramName, CmdLine: string;
begin
  Write('Program to Exec (include full path): ');
  Readln(ProgramName);
  Write('Command line to pass to ', ProgramName, ': ');
  Readln(CmdLine);
  Writeln('About to Exec...');
  SwapVectors;
  Exec(ProgramName, CmdLine);
  SwapVectors;
  Writeln('...back from Exec');
  if DosError <> 0 then                                  { Error? }
    Writeln('Dos error #', DosError)
  else
    Writeln('Exec successful. ',
            'Child process exit code = ',
            DosExitCode);
end.
```

Exit procedure

Function	Exits immediately from the current block.
Declaration	Exit
Remarks	When *Exit* is executed in a subroutine (procedure or function), it causes the subroutine to return. When it is executed in the statement part of a program, it causes the program to terminate. A call to *Exit* is analogous to a **goto** statement addressing a label just before the **end** of a block.
See also	*Halt*
Example	

```
uses Crt;
procedure WasteTime;
begin
  repeat
    if KeyPressed then Exit;
    Write('Xx');
  until False;
end;
begin
  WasteTime;
end.
```

Exp function

Function	Returns the exponential of the argument.
Declaration	Exp(x: real)
Result type	real
Remarks	x is a real-type expression. The result is the exponential of x; that is, the value e raised to the power of x, where e is the base of the natural logarithms.
See also	*Ln*

FExpand function   Dos

Function   Expands a file name into a fully qualified file name.

Declaration   FExpand(Path: PathStr)

Result type   *PathStr*

Remarks   Expands the file name in *Path* into a fully qualified file name. The resulting name is converted to uppercase and consists of a drive letter, a colon, a root relative directory path, and a file name. Embedded '.' and '..' directory references are removed.

The *PathStr* type is defined in the *Dos* unit as **string**[79].

Assuming that the current drive and directory is C:\SOURCE\PAS, the following *FExpand* calls would produce these values:

```
FExpand('test.pas')         = 'C:\SOURCE\PAS\TEST.PAS'
FExpand('..\*.TPU')         = 'C:\SOURCE\*.TPU'
FExpand('c:\bin\turbo.exe') = 'C:\BIN\TURBO.EXE'
```

The *FSplit* procedure may be used to split the result of *FExpand* into a drive/directory string, a file name string, and an extension string.

See also   *FindFirst, FindNext, FSplit*

FilePos function

Function   Returns the current file position of a file.

Declaration   FilePos(**var** f)

Result type   longint

Remarks   *f* is a file variable. If the current file position is at the beginning of the file, *FilePos(f)* returns 0. If the current file position is at the end of the file—that is, if *Eof(f)* is True—*FilePos(f)* is equal to *FileSize(f)*.

With {$I-}, *IOResult* will return a 0 if the operation was successful; otherwise, it will return a nonzero error code.

Restrictions   Cannot be used on a text file. File must be open.

254   *Turbo Pascal Reference Guide*

Differences	The result type in 3.0 was an integer.
See also	*FileSize, Seek*

FileSize function

Function	Returns the current size of a file.
Declaration	FileSize(**var** f)
Result type	longint
Remarks	*f* is a file variable. *FileSize(f)* returns the number of components in *f*. If the file is empty, *FileSize(f)* returns 0.

With {$I-}, *IOResult* will return a 0 if the operation was successful; otherwise, it will return a nonzero error code. |
Restrictions	Cannot be used on a text file. File must be open.
Differences	The result type in 3.0 was an integer.
See also	*FilePos*
| Example | ```
var
  f: file of byte;
begin
  { Get file name from command line }
  Assign(f, ParamStr(1));
  Reset(f);
  Writeln('File size in bytes: ', FileSize(f));
  Close(f);
end.
``` |

FillChar procedure

Function	Fills a specified number of contiguous bytes with a specified value.
Declaration	FillChar(**var** x; count: word; value)
Remarks	*x* is a variable reference of any type. *count* is an expression of type word. *value* is any ordinal-type expression. *FillChar* writes *count* contiguous bytes of memory into *value*, starting at the first byte occupied by *x*. No range-checking is performed, so be careful.
```

FillChar procedure

Whenever possible, use the *SizeOf* function to specify the count parameter. When using *FillChar* on strings, remember to set the length byte after the fill.

See also *Move*

Example
```
var s: string[80];
begin
  { Set a string to all spaces }
  FillChar(s, SizeOf(s), ' ');
  s[0] := #80;                        { Set length byte }
end.
```

FillEllipse procedure   Graph

Function   Draws a filled ellipse.

Declaration   `FillEllipse(X, Y: integer; XRadius, YRadius: word)`

Remarks   Draws a filled ellipse using (*X,Y*) as a center point, and *XRadius* and *YRadius* as the horizontal and vertical axes. The ellipse is filled with the current fill color and fill style, and is bordered with the current color.

A similar routine exists in Turbo C 2.0.

Restrictions Must be in graphics mode.

See also   *Arc, Circle, Ellipse, GetArcCoords, GetAspectRatio, PieSlice, Sector, SetAspectRatio*

Example
```
uses
  Graph;
const
  R = 30;
var
  Driver, Mode : integer;
  Xasp, Yasp : word;
begin
  Driver := Detect;                  { Put in graphics mode }
  InitGraph(Driver, Mode, '');
  if GraphResult < 0 then
    Halt(1);
  { Draw ellipse }
  FillEllipse(GetMaxX div 2, GetMaxY div 2, 50, 50);
  GetAspectRatio(Xasp, Yasp);
  { Circular ellipse }
  FillEllipse(R, R, R, R * LongInt(Xasp) div Yasp);
```

```
    Readln;
    Closegraph;
end.
```

FillPoly procedure — Graph

Function Draws and fills a polygon, using the scan converter.

Declaration `FillPoly(NumPoints: word; var PolyPoints)`

Remarks *PolyPoints* is an untyped parameter that contains the coordinates of each intersection in the polygon. *NumPoints* specifies the number of coordinates in *PolyPoints*. A coordinate consists of two words, an *x* and a *y* value.

FillPoly calculates all the horizontal intersections, and then fills the polygon using the current fill style and color defined by *SetFillStyle* or *SetFillPattern*. The outline of the polygon is drawn in the current line style and color as set by *SetLineStyle*.

If an error occurs while filling the polygon, *GraphResult* will return a value of –6 (*grNoScanMem*).

A similar routine exists in Turbo C 2.0.

Restrictions Must be in graphics mode.

See also *DrawPoly, GetFillSettings, GetLineSettings, GraphResult, SetFillPattern, SetFillStyle, SetLineStyle*

Example
```
uses Graph;
const
  Triangle : array[1..3] of PointType = ((x:  50; y: 100),
                                         (x: 100; y: 100),
                                         (x: 150; y: 150));
var
  Gd, Gm : integer;
begin
  Gd := Detect;
  InitGraph(Gd, Gm, '');
  if GraphResult <> grOk then
    Halt(1);
  FillPoly(SizeOf(Triangle) div SizeOf(PointType), Triangle);
```

```
    Readln;
    CloseGraph;
end.
```

FindFirst procedure — Dos

Function Searches the specified (or current) directory for the first entry matching the specified file name and set of attributes.

Declaration FindFirst(Path: **string**; Attr: word; **var** S: SearchRec)

Remarks *Path* is the directory mask (for example, * . *). The *Attr* parameter specifies the special files to include (in addition to all normal files). Here are the file attributes as they are declared in the *Dos* unit:

```
const
  ReadOnly  = $01;
  Hidden    = $02;
  SysFile   = $04;
  VolumeID  = $08;
  Directory = $10;
  Archive   = $20;
  AnyFile   = $3F;
```

The result of the directory search is returned in the specified search record. *SearchRec* is declared in the *Dos* unit:

```
type
  SearchRec = record
                Fill: array[1..21] of byte;
                Attr: byte;
                Time: longint;
                Size: longint;
                Name: string[12];
              end;
```

Errors are reported in *DosError*; possible error codes are 3 (Directory Not Found) and 18 (No More Files).

See also *FExpand, FindNext*

Example
```
uses Dos;
var
  DirInfo: SearchRec;
begin
  FindFirst('*.PAS', Archive, DirInfo);  { Same as DIR *.PAS }
```

```
    while DosError = 0 do
    begin
      Writeln(DirInfo.Name);
      FindNext(DirInfo);
    end;
end.
```

FindNext procedure   Dos

Function   Returns the next entry that matches the name and attributes specified in a previous call to *FindFirst*.

Declaration   `FindNext(var S: SearchRec)`

Remarks   *S* must be the same one Passed to *FindFirst* (*SearchRec* is declared in *Dos* unit; see *FindFirst*). Errors are reported in *DosError*; the only possible error code is 18, which indicates no more files.

See also   *FindFirst, FExpand*

Example   See the example for *FindFirst*.

FloodFill procedure   Graph

Function   Fills a bounded region with the current fill pattern.

Declaration   `FloodFill(x, y: integer; Border: word)`

Remarks   This procedure is called to fill an enclosed area on bitmap devices. (*x,y*) is a seed within the enclosed area to be filled. The current fill pattern, as set by *SetFillStyle* or *SetFillPattern*, is used to flood the area bounded by *Border* color. If the seed point is within an enclosed area, then the inside will be filled. If the seed is outside the enclosed area, then the exterior will be filled.

If an error occurs while flooding a region, *GraphResult* will return a value of –7 (*grNoFloodMem*).

Note that *FloodFill* stops after two blank lines have been output. This can occur with a sparse fill pattern and a small polygon. In the following program, the rectangle is not completely filled:

FloodFill procedure

```
program StopFill;
uses Graph;
var
  Driver, Mode: integer;
begin
  Driver := Detect;
  InitGraph(Driver, Mode, 'c:\bgi');
  if GraphResult <> grOk then
    Halt(1);
  SetFillStyle(LtSlashFill, GetMaxColor);
  Rectangle(0, 0, 8, 20);
  FloodFill(1, 1, GetMaxColor);
  Readln;
  CloseGraph;
end.
```

In this case, using a denser fill pattern like *SlashFill* will completely fill the figure.

A similar routine exists in Turbo C 2.0.

Restrictions Use *FillPoly* instead of *FloodFill* whenever possible so that you can maintain code compatibility with future versions. Must be in graphics mode. This procedure is not available when using the IBM 8514 graphics driver (IBM8514.BGI).

See also *FillPoly, GraphResult, SetFillPattern, SetFillStyle*

Example
```
uses Graph;
var
  Gd, Gm: integer;
begin
  Gd := Detect;
  InitGraph(Gd, Gm, '');
  if GraphResult <> grOk then
    Halt(1);
  SetColor(GetMaxColor);
  Circle(50, 50, 20);
  FloodFill(50,50,GetMaxColor);
  Readln;
  CloseGraph;
end.
```

Flush procedure

Function	Flushes the buffer of a text file open for output.
Declaration	Flush(**var** f: text)
Remarks	*f* is a text-file variable.

When a text file has been opened for output using *Rewrite* or *Append*, a call to *Flush* will empty the file's buffer. This guarantees that all characters written to the file at that time have actually been written to the external file. *Flush* has no effect on files opened for input.

With {$I-}, *IOResult* will return a 0 if the operation was successful; otherwise, it will return a nonzero error code.

Frac function

Function	Returns the fractional part of the argument.
Declaration	Frac(x: real)
Result type	real
Remarks	*x* is a real-type expression. The result is the fractional part of *x*, that is, *Frac(x) = x – Int(x)*.
See also	*Int*
Example	

```
var r: real;
begin
  r := Frac(123.456);    { 0.456 }
  r :=Frac(-123.456);    { -0.456 }
end.
```

FreeMem procedure

Function	Disposes a dynamic variable of a given size.
Declaration	FreeMem(**var** p: pointer; size: word)
Remarks	*p* is a pointer variable of any pointer type that was previously assigned by the *GetMem* procedure or was

FreeMem procedure

assigned a meaningful value by an assignment statement. *Size* is an expression of type word, specifying the size in bytes of the dynamic variable to dispose; it must be *exactly* the number of bytes previously allocated to that variable by *GetMem*. *FreeMem* destroys the variable referenced by *p* and returns its memory region to the heap. If *p* does not point to a memory region in the heap, a run-time error occurs. After a call to *FreeMem*, the value of *p* becomes undefined, and it is an error to subsequently reference *p*^.

Restrictions *Dispose* and *FreeMem* cannot be used interchangeably with *Mark* and *Release* unless certain rules are observed. For a complete discussion of this topic, refer to the section "The Heap Manager" on page 181.

Differences In 3.0, *size* was an integer.

See also *Dispose, GetMem, Mark, New, Release*

FSearch function   Dos

Function Searches for a file in a list of directories.

Declaration `FSearch(Path: PathStr; DirList:` **string**`)`

Result type *PathStr*

Remarks Searches for the file given by *Path* in the list of directories given by *DirList*. The directories in *DirList* must be separated by semicolons, just like the directories specified in a PATH command in DOS. The search always starts with the current directory of the current drive. The returned value is a concatenation of one of the directory paths and the file name, or an empty string if the file could not be located.

The *PathStr* type is defined in the *Dos* unit as **string**[79].

To search the PATH used by DOS to locate executable files, call *GetEnv*('PATH') and pass the result to *FSearch* as the *DirList* parameter.

The result of *FSearch* can be passed to *FExpand* to convert it into a fully qualified file name, that is, an uppercase file name that includes both a drive letter and a root-relative directory path. In addition, you can use

FSearch function

FSplit to split the file name into a drive/directory string, a file name string, and an extension string.

See also *FExpand, FSplit, GetEnv*

Example
```
uses Dos;
var
  S: PathStr;
begin
  S := FSearch('TURBO.EXE',GetEnv('PATH'));
  if S = '' then
    Writeln('TURBO.EXE not found')
  else
    Writeln('Found as ',FExpand(S));
end.
```

FSplit procedure   Dos

Function   Splits a file name into its three components.

Declaration FSplit(Path: PathStr; **var** Dir: DirStr;
                    var Name: NameStr; **var** Ext: ExtStr)

Remarks   Splits the file name specified by *Path* into its three components. *Dir* is set to the drive and directory path with any leading and trailing backslashes, *Name* is set to the file name, and *Ext* is set to the extension with a preceding dot. Each of the component strings may possibly be empty, if *Path* contains no such component.

The *PathStr, DirStr, NameStr,* and *ExtStr* types are defined in the *Dos* unit as follows:

```
type
  PathStr = string[79];
  DirStr  = string[67];
  NameStr = string[8];
  ExtStr  = string[4];
```

FSplit never adds or removes characters when it splits the file name, and the concatenation of the resulting *Dir, Name,* and *Ext* will always equal the specified *Path*.

See also *FExpand, FindFirst, FindNext*

Example
```
uses Dos;
var
  P: PathStr;
  D: DirStr;
```

FSplit procedure

```
            N: NameStr;
            E: ExtStr;
          begin
            Write('Filename (WORK.PAS): ');
            ReadLn(P);
            FSplit(P, D, N, E);
            if N = '' then N:='WORK';
            if E = '' then E:='.PAS';
            P := D + N + E;
            Writeln('Resulting name is ', P);
          end.
```

GetArcCoords procedure   Graph

Function   Allows the user to inquire about the coordinates of the last *Arc* command.

Declaration   GetArcCoords(**var** ArcCoords: ArcCoordsType)

          A similar routine exists in Turbo C 2.0.

Remarks   *GetArcCoords* returns a variable of type *ArcCoordsType*. *ArcCoordsType* is predeclared as follows:

```
          type
            ArcCoordsType = record
                              X, Y: integer;
                              Xstart, Ystart: integer;
                              Xend, Yend: integer;
                            end;
```

          GetArcCoords returns a variable containing the center point (*X,Y*), the starting position (*Xstart,Ystart*), and the ending position (*Xend,Yend*) of the last *Arc* or *Ellipse* command. These values are useful if you need to connect a line to the end of an ellipse.

Restrictions Must be in graphics mode.

See also   *Arc, Circle, Ellipse, FillEllipse, PieSlice, PieSliceXY, Sector*

Example
```
          uses Graph;
          var
            Gd, Gm : integer;
            ArcCoords : ArcCoordsType;
          begin
            Gd := Detect;
            InitGraph(Gd, Gm, '');
            if GraphResult <> grOk then
```

```
    Halt(1);
Arc(100,100,0,270,30);
GetArcCoords(ArcCoords);
with ArcCoords do
  Line(Xstart, Ystart, Xend, Yend);
Readln;
CloseGraph;
end.
```

GetAspectRatio procedure   Graph

Function Returns the effective resolution of the graphics screen from which the aspect ratio (*Xasp:Yasp*) can be computed.

Declaration `GetAspectRatio(var Xasp, Yasp: word)`

Remarks Each driver and graphics mode has an aspect ratio associated with it (maximum *y* resolution divided by maximum *x* resolution). This ratio can be computed by making a call to *GetAspectRatio* and then dividing the *Xasp* parameter by the *Yasp* parameter. This ratio is used to make circles, arcs, and pie slices round.

A similar routine exists in Turbo C 2.0.

Restrictions Must be in graphics mode.

See also *Arc, Circle, Ellipse, GetMaxX, GetMaxY, PieSlice, SetAspectRatio*

Example
```
uses Graph;
var
  Gd, Gm : integer;
  Xasp, Yasp : word;
  XSideLength, YSideLength : integer;
begin
  Gd := Detect;
  InitGraph(Gd, Gm, '');
  if GraphResult <> grOk then
    Halt(1);
  GetAspectRatio(Xasp, Yasp);
  XSideLength := 20;

  { Adjust Y length for aspect ratio }
  YSideLength := Round((Xasp/Yasp) * XSideLength);
```

```
  { Draw a "square" rectangle on the screen }
  Rectangle(0, 0, XSideLength, YSideLength);
  Readln;
  CloseGraph;
end.
```

GetBkColor function   Graph

Function   Returns the index into the palette of the current background color.

Declaration   GetBkColor

Result type   word

Remarks   Background colors can range from 0 to 15, depending on the current graphics driver and current graphics mode.

GetBkColor will return 0 if the 0th palette entry is changed by a call to *SetPalette* or *SetAllPalette*.

A similar routine exists in Turbo C 2.0.

Restrictions Must be in graphics mode.

See also   *GetColor, GetPalette, InitGraph, SetAllPalette, SetBkColor, SetColor, SetPalette*

Example
```
uses Crt, Graph;
var
  Gd, Gm: integer;
  Color: word;
  Pal: PaletteType;
begin
  Gd := Detect;
  InitGraph(Gd, Gm, '');
  if GraphResult <> grOk then
    Halt(1);
  Randomize;
  GetPalette(Pal);
  if Pal.Size <> 1 then
    begin
      repeat                              { Cycle through colors }
        Color := Succ(GetBkColor);
        if Color > Pal.Size-1 then
          Color := 0;
        SetBkColor(Color);
        LineTo(Random(GetMaxX), Random(GetMaxY));
      until KeyPressed;
```

```
      end
    else
      Line(0, 0, GetMaxX, GetMaxY);
    Readln;
    CloseGraph;
end.
```

GetCBreak procedure   Dos

Function   Returns the state of *Ctrl-Break* checking in DOS.

Declaration   `GetCBreak(var Break: boolean)`

Remarks   *GetCBreak* returns the state of *Ctrl-Break* checking in DOS. When off (False), DOS only checks for *Ctrl-Break* during I/O to console, printer, or communication devices. When on (True), checks are made at every system call.

See also   *SetCBreak*

GetColor function   Graph

Function   Returns the color value passed to the previous successful call to *SetColor*.

Declaration   `GetColor`

Result type   word

Remarks   Drawing colors can range from 0 to 15, depending on the current graphics driver and current graphics mode.

A similar routine exists in Turbo C 2.0.

Restrictions Must be in graphics mode.

See also   *GetBkColor, GetPalette, InitGraph, SetAllPalette, SetColor, SetPalette*

Example
```
uses Graph;
var
  Gd, Gm: integer;
  Color: word;
  Pal: PaletteType;
begin
  Gd := Detect;
```

GetColor function

```
    InitGraph(Gd, Gm, '');
    if GraphResult <> grOk then
      Halt(1);
    Randomize;
    GetPalette(Pal);
    repeat
      Color := Succ(GetColor);
      if Color > Pal.Size-1 then
        Color := 0;
      SetColor(Color);
      LineTo(Random(GetMaxX), Random(GetMaxY));
    until KeyPressed;
    CloseGraph;
  end.
```

GetDate procedure   Dos

Function   Returns the current date set in the operating system.

Declaration   GetDate(**var** Year, Month, Day, DayofWeek: word)

Remarks   Ranges of the values returned are *Year* 1980..2099, *Month* 1..12, *Day* 1..31, and *DayOfWeek* 0..6 (where 0 corresponds to Sunday).

See also   *GetTime, SetDate, SetTime*

GetDefaultPalette function   Graph

Function   Returns the palette definition record.

Declaration   GetDefaultPalette (**var** Palette : PaletteType)

Result type   *PaletteType*

Remarks   *GetDefaultPalette* returns a *PaletteType* record, which contains the palette as the driver initialized it during *InitGraph*:

```
    const
      MaxColors = 15;
    type
      PaletteType = record
                      Size : byte;
                      Colors : array[0..MaxColor] of shortint;
                    end;
```

GetDefaultPalette function

	A similar routine exists in Turbo C 2.0.
Restrictions	Must be in graphics mode.
See also	*InitGraph, GetPalette, SetAllPalette, SetPalette*
Example	

```
uses
  Crt, Graph;
var
  Driver, Mode,
  i : integer;
  MyPal, OldPal : PaletteType;
begin
  DirectVideo := false;
  Randomize;
  Driver := Detect;                      { Put in graphics mode }
  InitGraph(Driver, Mode, '');
  if GraphResult < 0 then
    Halt(1);
  GetDefaultPalette(OldPal);                 { Preserve old one }
  MyPal := OldPal;                      { Duplicate and modify }
  { Display something }
  for i := 0 to MyPal.Size - 1 do
  begin
    SetColor(i);
    OutTextXY(10, i * 10, '...Press any key...');
  end;

  repeat            { Change palette until a key is pressed }
    with MyPal do
      Colors[Random(Size)] := Random(Size + 1);
    SetAllPalette(MyPal);
  until KeyPressed;
  SetAllPalette(OldPal);              { Restore original palette }
  ClearDevice;
  OutTextXY(10, 10, 'Press <Return>...');
  Readln;
  Closegraph;
end.
```

GetDir procedure

Function	Returns the current directory of a specified drive.
Declaration	GetDir(d: byte; **var** s: **string**)
Remarks	*d* is an integer-type expression, and *s* is a string-type variable. The current directory of the drive specified by

Chapter 16, Turbo Pascal Reference Lookup

GetDir procedure

d is returned in *s*. *d* = 0 indicates the current drive, 1 indicates drive *A*, 2 indicates drive *B*, and so on.

With {$I-}, *IOResult* will return a 0 if the operation was successful; otherwise, it will return a nonzero error code.

See also ChDir, DiskFree, DiskSize, MkDir, RmDir

GetDriverName function   Graph

Function	Returns a string containing the name of the current driver.
Declaration	GetDriverName
Result type	string
Remarks	After a call to *InitGraph*, returns the name of the active driver.
	A similar routine exists in Turbo C 2.0.
Restrictions	Must be in graphics mode.
See also	GetModeName, InitGraph
Example	

```
uses
  Graph;
var
  Driver, Mode : integer;
begin
  Driver := Detect;                    { Put in graphics mode }
  InitGraph(Driver, Mode, '');
  if GraphResult < 0 then
    Halt(1);
  OutText('Using driver ' + GetDriverName);
  Readln;
  Closegraph;
end.
```

GetEnv function   Dos

Function	Returns the value of a specified environment variable.
Declaration	GetEnv(EnvVar: **string**)
Result type	string

GetEnv function

Remarks *GetEnv* returns the value of a specified variable. The variable name can be in either uppercase or lowercase, but it must not include the equal sign (=) character. If the specified environment variable does not exist, *GetEnv* returns an empty string.

For more information about the DOS environment, refer to your DOS manuals.

See also *EnvCount, EnvStr*

Example
```
{$M 8192,0,0}
uses Dos;
var
  Command: string[79];
begin
  Write('Enter DOS command: ');
  Readln(Command);
  if Command <> '' then
    Command := '/C ' + Command;
  SwapVectors;
  Exec(GetEnv('COMSPEC'), Command);
  SwapVectors;
  if DosError <> 0 then
    Writeln('Could not execute COMMAND.COM');
end.
```

GetFAttr procedure   Dos

Function Returns the attributes of a file.

Declaration `GetFAttr(var f; var Attr: word);`

Remarks *F* must be a file variable (typed, untyped, or text file) that has been assigned but not opened. The attributes are examined by **anding** them with the file attribute masks defined as constants in the *Dos* unit:

```
const
  ReadOnly  = $01;
  Hidden    = $02;
  SysFile   = $04;
  VolumeID  = $08;
  Directory = $10;
  Archive   = $20;
  AnyFile   = $3F;
```

GetFAttr procedure

Errors are reported in *DosError*; possible error codes are:

- 3 (Invalid Path)
- 5 (File Access Denied)

Restrictions *f* cannot be open.

See also *GetFTime, SetFAttr, SetFTime*

Example
```
uses Dos;
var
  f: file;
  attr: word;

begin
  { Get file name from command line }
  Assign(f, ParamStr(1));
  GetFAttr(f, attr);
  Writeln(ParamStr(1));
  if DosError <> 0 then
    Writeln('Dos error code = ', DosError)
  else
  begin
    Write('Attribute = ', attr, 'to:'to);
    { Determine file attribute type
      using flags in Dos unit }
    if attr and ReadOnly <> 0 then
      Writeln('read only file');
    if attr and Hidden <> 0 then
      Writeln('hidden file');
    if attr and SysFile <> 0 then
      Writeln('system file');
    if attr and VolumeID <> 0 then
      Writeln('volume ID');
    if attr and Directory <> 0 then
      Writeln('directory name');
    if attr and Archive <> 0 then
      Writeln('archive (normal file)');
  end; { else }
end.
```

GetFillPattern procedure   Graph

Function Returns the last fill pattern set by a previous call to *SetFillPattern*.

Declaration `GetFillPattern(var FillPattern: FillPatternType);`

Remarks *FillPatternType* is declared in the *Graph* unit:

```
type
  FillPatternType = array[1..8] of byte;
```

If no user call has been made to *SetFillPattern*, *GetFillPattern* will return an array filled with *$FF*.

A similar routine exists in Turbo C 2.0.

Restrictions	Must be in graphics mode.
See also	*GetFillSettings, SetFillPattern, SetFillStyle*

GetFillSettings procedure   Graph

Function	Returns the last fill pattern and color set by a previous call to *SetFillPattern* or *SetFillStyle*.
Declaration	`GetFillSettings(var FillInfo: FillSettingsType)`
Remarks	*GetFillSettings* returns a variable of type *FillSettingsType*. *FillSettingsType* is predeclared as follows:

```
type
  FillSettingsType = record
                       Pattern: word;
                       Color: word;
                     end;
```

The *Pattern* field reports the current fill pattern selected. The *Color* field reports the current fill color selected. Both the fill pattern and color can be changed by calling the *SetFillStyle* or *SetFillPattern* procedure. If *Pattern* is equal to *UserFill*, use *GetFillPattern* to get the user-defined fill pattern that is selected.

A similar routine exists in Turbo C 2.0.

Restrictions	Must be in graphics mode.
See also	*FillPoly, GetFillPattern, SetFillPattern, SetFillStyle*
Example	```

```
uses Graph;
var
  Gd, Gm : integer;
  FillInfo: FillSettingsType;
begin
  Gd := Detect;
  InitGraph(Gd, Gm, '');
  if GraphResult <> grOk then
    Halt(1);
```

GetFillSettings procedure

```
        GetFillSettings(FillInfo);      { Save fill style and color }
        Bar(0, 0, 50, 50);
        SetFillStyle(XHatchFill, GetMaxColor);         { New style }
        Bar(50, 0, 100, 50);
        with FillInfo do
          SetFillStyle(Pattern, Color);     { Restore old fill style }
        Bar(100, 0, 150, 50);
        Readln;
        CloseGraph;
      end.
```

GetFTime procedure   Dos

Function   Returns the date and time a file was last written.

Declaration   `GetFTime(var f; var Time: longint);`

Remarks   *f* must be a file variable (typed, untyped, or text file) that has been assigned and opened. The time returned in the *Time* parameter may be unpacked through a call to *UnpackTime*. Errors are reported in *DosError*; the only possible error code is 6 (Invalid File Handle).

Restrictions *f* must be open.

See also   *PackTime, SetFAttr, SetFTime, UnpackTime*

GetGraphMode function   Graph

Function   Returns the current graphics mode.

Declaration   `GetGraphMode`

Result type   integer

Remarks   *GetGraphMode* returns the current graphics mode set by *InitGraph* or *SetGraphMode*. The *Mode* value is an integer from 0 to 5, depending on the current driver.

GetGraphMode function

The following mode constants are defined:

Graphics Driver	Constant Name	Value	Column x Row	Palette	Pages
CGA	CGAC0	0	320x200	C0	1
	CGAC1	1	320x200	C1	1
	CGAC2	2	320x200	C2	1
	CGAC3	3	320x200	C3	1
	CGAHi	4	640x200	2 color	1
MCGA	MCGAC0	0	320x200	C0	1
	MCGAC1	1	320x200	C1	1
	MCGAC2	2	320x200	C2	1
	MCGAC3	3	320x200	C3	1
	MCGAMed	4	640x200	2 color	1
	MCGAHi	5	640x480	2 color	1
EGA	EGALo	0	640x200	16 color	4
	EGAHi	1	640x350	16 color	2
EGA64	EGA64Lo	0	640x200	16 color	1
	EGA64Hi	1	640x350	4 color	1
EGA-MONO	EGAMonoHi	3	640x350	2 color	1*
	EGAMonoHi	3	640x350	2 color	2**
HERC	HercMonoHi	0	720x348	2 color	2
ATT400	ATT400C0	0	320x200	C0	1
	ATT400C1	1	320x200	C1	1
	ATT400C2	2	320x200	C2	1
	ATT400C3	3	320x200	C3	1
	ATT400Med	4	640x200	2 color	1
	ATT400Hi	5	640x400	2 color	1
VGA	VGALo	0	640x200	16 color	2
	VGAMed	1	640x350	16 color	2
	VGAHi	2	640x480	16 color	1
PC3270	PC3270Hi	0	720x350	2 color	1
8514	IBM8514Lo	0	640x480	256 color	1
8514	IBM8514Hi	0	1024x768	256 color	1

* 64K on EGAMono card
** 256K on EGAMono card

A similar routine exists in Turbo C 2.0.

Restrictions   Must be in graphics mode.

GetGraphMode function

See also   *ClearDevice, DetectGraph, InitGraph, RestoreCrtMode, SetGraphMode*

Example
```
uses Graph;
var
  Gd, Gm: integer;
  Mode  : integer;
begin
  Gd := Detect;
  InitGraph(Gd, Gm, '');
  if GraphResult <> grOk then
    Halt(1);
  OutText('<ENTER> to leave graphics:');
  Readln;
  RestoreCRTMode;
  Writeln('Now in text mode');
  Write('<ENTER> to enter graphics mode:');
  Readln;
  SetGraphMode(GetGraphMode);
  OutTextXY(0, 0, 'Back in graphics mode');
  OutTextXY(0, TextHeight('H'), '<ENTER> to quit:');
  Readln;
  CloseGraph;
end.
```

GetImage procedure   Graph

Function   Saves a bit image of the specified region into a buffer.

Declaration   `GetImage(x1, y1, x2, y2: integer; var BitMap);`

Remarks   *x1, y1, x2,* and *y2* define a rectangular region on the screen. *BitMap* is an untyped parameter that must be greater than or equal to 6 plus the amount of area defined by the region. The first two words of *BitMap* store the width and height of the region. The third word is reserved.

The remaining part of *BitMap* is used to save the bit image itself. Use the *ImageSize* function to determine the size requirements of *BitMap*.

A similar routine exists in Turbo C 2.0.

Restrictions   Must be in graphics mode. The memory required to save the region must be less than 64K.

See also   *ImageSize, PutImage*

GetImage procedure

Example
```
uses Graph;
var
  Gd, Gm : integer;
  P      : pointer;
  Size   : word;
begin
  Gd := Detect;
  InitGraph(Gd, Gm, '');
  if GraphResult <> grOk then
    Halt(1);
  Bar(0, 0, GetMaxX, GetMaxY);
  Size := ImageSize(10,20,30,40);
  GetMem(P, Size);                    { Allocate memory on heap }
  GetImage(10,20,30,40,P^);
  Readln;
  ClearDevice;
  PutImage(100, 100, P^, NormalPut);
  Readln;
  CloseGraph;
end.
```

GetIntVec procedure — Dos

Function Returns the address stored in a specified interrupt vector.

Declaration GetIntVec(IntNo: byte; **var** Vector: pointer)

Remarks *IntNo* specifies the interrupt vector number (0..255), and the address is returned in *Vector*.

See also *SetIntVec*

GetLineSettings procedure — Graph

Function Returns the current line style, line pattern, and line thickness as set by *SetLineStyle*.

Declaration GetLineSettings(**var** LineInfo: LineSettingsType)

Remarks The following type and constants are defined:

```
type
  LineSettingsType = record
                       LineStyle: word;
                       Pattern: word;
```

Chapter 16, Turbo Pascal Reference Lookup

GetLineSettings procedure

```
                              Thickness: word;
                        end;
         const
           { Line styles }
           SolidLn   = 0;
           DottedLn  = 1;
           CenterLn  = 2;
           DashedLn  = 3;
           UserBitLn = 4;                    { User-defined line style }

           { Line widths }
           NormWidth = 1;
           ThickWidth = 3;
```

A similar routine exists in Turbo C 2.0.

Restrictions Must be in graphics mode.

See also *DrawPoly, SetLineStyle*

Example
```
uses Graph;
var
  Gd, Gm  : integer;
  OldStyle: LineSettingsType;
begin
  Gd := Detect;
  InitGraph(Gd, Gm, '');
  if GraphResult <> grOk then
    Halt(1);
  Line(0, 0, 100, 0);
  GetLineSettings(OldStyle);
  SetLineStyle(DottedLn, 0, ThickWidth);        { New style }
  Line(0, 10, 100, 10);
  with OldStyle do                    { Restore old line style }
    SetLineStyle(LineStyle, Pattern, Thickness);
  Line(0, 20, 100, 20);
  Readln;
  CloseGraph;
end.
```

GetMaxColor function   Graph

Function Returns the highest color that can be passed to the *SetColor* procedure.

Declaration GetMaxColor

Result type word

GetMaxColor function

Remarks As an example, on a 256K EGA, *GetMaxColor* will always return 15, which means that any call to *SetColor* with a value from 0..15 is valid. On a CGA in high-resolution mode or on a Hercules monochrome adapter, *GetMaxColor* returns a value of 1 because these adapters only support draw colors of 0 or 1.

A similar routine exists in Turbo C 2.0.

Restrictions Must be in graphics mode.

See also *SetColor*

GetMaxMode function — Graph

Function Returns the maximum mode number for the currently loaded driver.

Declaration `GetMaxMode`

Result type word

Remarks *GetMaxMode* lets you find out the maximum mode number for the current driver, directly *from* the driver. (Formerly, *GetModeRange* was the only way you could get this number; *GetModeRange* is still supported, but only for the Borland drivers.)

The value returned by *GetMaxMode* is the maximum value that may be passed to *SetGraphMode*. Every driver supports modes 0..*GetMaxMode*.

A similar routine exists in Turbo C 2.0.

Restrictions Must be in graphics mode.

See also *GetModeRange, SetGraphMode*

Example
```
uses
  Graph;
var
  Driver, Mode : integer;
  i : integer;
begin
  Driver := Detect;                     { Put in graphics mode }
  InitGraph(Driver, Mode, '');
  if GraphResult < 0 then
    Halt(1);
  for i := 0 to GetMaxMode do           { Display all mode names }
```

```
            OutTextXY(10, 10 * Succ(i), GetModeName(i));
        Readln;
        Closegraph;
    end.
```

GetMaxX function   Graph

Function   Returns the rightmost column (*x* resolution) of the current graphics driver and mode.

Declaration GetMaxX

Result type integer

Remarks   Returns the maximum *x* value for the current graphics driver and mode. On a CGA in 320×200 mode; for example, *GetMaxX* will return 319.

GetMaxX and *GetMaxY* are invaluable for centering, determining the boundries of a region on the screen, and so on.

A similar routine exists in Turbo C 2.0.

Restrictions Must be in graphics mode.

See also   *GetMaxY, GetX, GetY, MoveTo*

Example
```
uses Graph;
var
  Gd, Gm: integer;
begin
  Gd := Detect;
  InitGraph(Gd, Gm, '');
  if GraphResult <> grOk then
    Halt(1);
  Rectangle(0,0,GetMaxX,GetMaxY);   { Draw a full-screen box }
  Readln;
  CloseGraph;
end.
```

GetMaxY function — Graph

Function	Returns the bottommost row (*y* resolution) of the current graphics driver and mode.
Declaration	GetMaxY
Result type	integer
Remarks	Returns the maximum *y* value for the current graphics driver and mode. On a CGA in 320×200 mode; for example, *GetMaxY* will return 199.
	GetMaxX and *GetMaxY* are invaluable for centering, determining the boundaries of a region on the screen, and so on.
	A similar routine exists in Turbo C 2.0.
Restrictions	Must be in graphics mode.
See also	*GetMaxX, GetX, GetY, MoveTo*
| **Example** | ```
uses Graph;
var
  Gd, Gm: integer;
begin
  Gd := Detect;
  InitGraph(Gd, Gm, '');
  if GraphResult <> grOk then
    Halt(1);
  Rectangle(0,0,GetMaxX,GetMaxY);   { Draw a full-screen box }
  Readln;
  CloseGraph;
end.
``` |

GetMem procedure

Function	Creates a new dynamic variable of the specified size, and puts the address of the block in a pointer variable.
Declaration	GetMem(**var** p: pointer; size: word)
Remarks	*p* is a pointer variable of any pointer type. *Size* is an expression of type word specifying the size in bytes of the dynamic variable to allocate. The newly created variable can be referenced as *p*^.
```

GetMem procedure

	If there isn't enough free space in the heap to allocate the new variable, a run-time error occurs. (It is possible to avoid a run-time error; see "The Heap Error Function" on page 187.)
Restrictions	The largest block that can be allocated on the heap at one time is 65521 bytes (64Kb-$F). If the heap is not fragmented, for example at the beginning of a program, successive calls to *GetMem* will return neighboring blocks of memory.
Differences	In 3.0, *size* was an integer.
See also	*Dispose, FreeMem, Mark, New, Release*

GetModeName function   Graph

Function	Returns a string containing the name of the specified graphics mode.
Declaration	`GetModeName(ModeNumber : integer)`
Result type	string
Remarks	The mode names are embedded in each driver. The return values (320 x 200 CGA P1, 640 x 200 CGA, etc.) are useful for building menus, display status, etc.
	A similar routine exists in Turbo C 2.0.
Restrictions	Must be in graphics mode.
See also	*GetDriverName, GetMaxMode, GetModeRange*
Example	

```
uses
  Graph;
var
  Driver, Mode : integer;
  i : integer;
begin
  Driver := Detect;                      { Put in graphics mode }
  InitGraph(Driver, Mode, '');
  if GraphResult < 0 then
    Halt(1);
  for i := 0 to GetMaxMode do            { Display all mode names }
    OutTextXY(10, 10 * Succ(i), GetModeName(i));
  Readln;
  Closegraph;
end.
```

GetModeRange procedure   Graph

Function   Returns the lowest and highest valid graphics mode for a given driver.

Declaration   GetModeRange(GraphDriver : integer;
                   var LoMode, HiMode: integer);

Remarks   The output from the following program:

```
uses Graph;
var
  Lowest, Highest : integer;
begin
  GetModeRange(EGA64, Lowest, Highest);
  Write('Lowest = ', Lowest);
  Write(' Highest = ', Highest);
end.
```

will be *Lowest* = 0 and *Highest* = 1.

If the value of *GraphDriver* is invalid, the return parameters are set to –1.

A similar routine exists in Turbo C 2.0.

See also   *GetGraphMode, SetGraphMode, InitGraph, DetectGraph*

GetPalette procedure   Graph

Function   Returns the current palette and its size.

Declaration   GetPalette(**var** Palette: PaletteType)

Remarks   Returns the current palette and its size in a variable of type *PaletteType*. *PaletteType* is defined as follows:

```
const
  MaxColors = 15;
type
  PaletteType = record
                  Size: byte;
                  Colors: array[0..MaxColors] of shortint;
                end;
```

The size field reports the number of colors in the palette for the current driver in the current mode. *Colors* contains the actual colors 0..*Size*-1.

Chapter 16, Turbo Pascal Reference Lookup

GetPalette procedure

	A similar routine exists in Turbo C 2.0.
Restrictions	Must be in graphics mode, and can only be used with EGA, EGA 64, or VGA (not the IBM 8514 or the VGA in 256-color mode).
See also	*GetDefaultPalette, GetPaletteSize, SetAllPalette, SetPalette*
Example	

```
uses Graph;
var
  Gd, Gm : integer;
  Color  : word;
  Palette: PaletteType;
begin
  Gd := Detect;
  InitGraph(Gd, Gm, '');
  if GraphResult <> grOk then
    Halt(1);
  GetPalette(Palette);
  if Palette.Size <> 1 then
    for Color := 0 to Pred(Palette.Size) do
    begin
      SetColor(Color);
      Line(0, Color*5, 100, Color*5);
    end
  else
    Line(0, 0, 100, 0);
  Readln;
  CloseGraph;
end.
```

GetPaletteSize function   Graph

Function	Returns the the size of the palette color lookup table.
Declaration	`GetPaletteSize`
Result type	integer
Remarks	*GetPaletteSize* reports how many palette entries can be set for the current graphics mode; for example, the EGA in color mode will return a value of 16.
	A similar routine exists in Turbo C 2.0.
Restrictions	Must be in graphics mode.
See also	*GetMaxColor, GetDefaultPalette, GetPalette, SetPalette*

GetPixel function — Graph

Function	Gets the pixel value at *X,Y*.
Declaration	`GetPixel(X,Y: integer)`
Result type	word
Remarks	Gets the pixel color at (*X,Y*).
	A similar routine exists in Turbo C 2.0.
Restrictions	Must be in graphics mode.
See also	*PutPixel, GetImage, PutImage, SetWriteMode*
Example	

```
uses Graph;
var
  Gd, Gm    : integer;
  PixelColor: word;
begin
  Gd := Detect;
  InitGraph(Gd, Gm, '');
  if GraphResult <> grOk then
    Halt(1);
  PixelColor := GetPixel(10,10);
  if PixelColor = 0 then
    PutPixel(10, 10, GetMaxColor);
  Readln;
  CloseGraph;
end.
```

GetTextSettings procedure — Graph

Function	Returns the current text font, direction, size, and justification as set by *SetTextStyle* and *SetTextJustify*.
Declaration	`GetTextSettings(var TextInfo: TextSettingsType)`
Remarks	The following type and constants are defined:

```
type
  TextSettingsType = record
                       Font: word;
                       Direction: word;
                       CharSize: word;
                       Horiz: word;
                       Vert: word;
                     end;
```

GetTextSettings procedure

```
const
  DefaultFont    = 0;               { 8x8 bit mapped font }
  TriplexFont    = 1;                   { "Stroked" fonts }
  SmallFont      = 2;
  SansSerifFont  = 3;
  GothicFont     = 4;
  HorizDir       = 0;                   { Left to right }
  VertDir        = 1;                   { Bottom to top }
```

A similar routine exists in Turbo C 2.0.

Restrictions Must be in graphics mode.

See also *InitGraph, SetTextJustify, SetTextStyle, TextHeight, TextWidth*

Example
```
uses Graph;
var
  Gd, Gm : integer;
  OldStyle: TextSettingsType;
begin
  Gd := Detect;
  InitGraph(Gd, Gm, '');
  if GraphResult <> grOk then
    Halt(1);
  GetTextSettings(OldStyle);
  OutTextXY(0, 0, 'Old text style');
  SetTextJustify(LeftText, CenterText);
  SetTextStyle(TriplexFont, VertDir, 4);
  OutTextXY(GetMaxX div 2, GetMaxY div 2, 'New Style');
  with OldStyle do
  begin                             { Restore old text style }
    SetTextJustify(Horiz, Vert);
    SetTextStyle(Font, Direction, CharSize);
  end;
  OutTextXY(0, TextHeight('H'), 'Old style again');
  Readln;
  CloseGraph;
end.
```

GetTime procedure — Dos

Function Returns the current time set in the operating system.

Declaration GetTime(**var** Hour, Minute, Second, Sec100: word)

Remarks Ranges of the values returned are *Hour* 0..23, *Minute* 0..59, *Second* 0..59, and *Sec*100 (hundredths of seconds) 0..99.

See also *GetDate, SetDate, SetTime, UnpackTime*

GetVerify procedure — Dos

Function Returns the state of the verify flag in DOS.

Declaration GetVerify(**var** Verify: boolean)

Remarks *GetVerify* returns the state of the verify flag in DOS. When off (False), disk writes are not verified. When on (True), all disk writes are verified to ensure proper writing.

See also *SetVerify*

GetViewSettings procedure — Graph

Function Returns the current viewport and clipping parameters, as set by *SetViewPort*.

Declaration GetViewSettings(**var** ViewPort: ViewPortType)

Remarks *GetViewSettings* returns a variable of type *ViewPortType*. *ViewPortType* is predeclared as follows:

```
type
  ViewPortType = record
                   x1, y1, x2, y2: integer;
                   Clip: boolean;
                 end;
```

The points (*x1*, *y1*) and (*x2*, *y2*) are the dimensions of the active viewport and are given in absolute screen coordinates. *Clip* is a Boolean variable that controls whether clipping is active.

GetViewSettings procedure

	A similar routine exists in Turbo C 2.0.
Restrictions	Must be in graphics mode.
See also	*ClearViewPort, SetViewPort*
| **Example** | ```
uses Graph;
var
  Gd, Gm  : integer;
  ViewPort: ViewPortType;
begin
  Gd := Detect;
  InitGraph(Gd, Gm, '');
  if GraphResult <> grOk then
    Halt(1);
  GetViewSettings(ViewPort);
  with ViewPort do
  begin
    Rectangle(0, 0, x2-x1, y2-y1);
    if Clip then
      OutText('Clipping is active.')
    else
      OutText('No clipping today.');
  end;
  Readln;
  CloseGraph;
end.
``` |

GetX function   Graph

Function	Returns the X coordinate of the current position (CP).
Declaration	GetX
Result type	integer
Remarks	*GetX* is viewport-relative. In the following example:

1 `SetViewPort(0,0,GetMaxX,GetMaxY,True);`
2 `MoveTo(5,5);`
3 `SetViewPort(10,10,100,100,True);`
4 `MoveTo(5,5);`

- Line 1 moves CP to absolute (0,0), and *GetX* would also return a value of 0.

- Line 2 moves CP to absolute (5,5), and *GetX* would also return a value of 5.

288   Turbo Pascal Reference Guide
```

GetX function

- Line 3 moves CP to absolute (10,10), but *GetX* would return a value of 0.
- Line 4 moves CP to absolute (15,15), but *GetX* would return a value of 5.

A similar routine exists in Turbo C 2.0.

Restrictions   Must be in graphics mode.

See also   *GetViewSettings, GetY, InitGraph, MoveTo, SetViewPort*

Example
```
uses Graph;
var
  Gd, Gm: integer;
  X, Y: integer;
begin
  Gd := Detect;
  InitGraph(Gd, Gm, '');
  if GraphResult <> grOk then
    Halt(1);
  OutText('Starting here. ');
  X := GetX;
  Y := GetY;
  OutTextXY(20, 10, 'Now over here...');
  OutTextXY(X, Y, 'Now back over here.');
  Readln;
  CloseGraph;
end.
```

GetY function   Graph

Function   Returns the Y coordinate of the current position (CP).

Declaration   GetY

Result type   integer

Remarks   *GetY* is viewport-relative. In the following example:

    1 SetViewPort(0,0,GetMaxX,GetMaxY,True);
    2 MoveTo(5,5);
    3 SetViewPort(10,10,100,100,True);
    4 MoveTo(5,5);

- Line 1 moves CP to absolute (0,0), and *GetY* would also return a value of 0.
- Line 2 moves CP to absolute (5,5), and *GetY* would also return a value of 5.

GetY function

- Line 3 moves CP to absolute (10,10), but *GetY* would return a value of 0.
- Line 4 moves CP to absolute (15,15), but *GetY* would return a value of 5.

A similar routine exists in Turbo C 2.0.

Restrictions   Must be in graphics mode.

See also   *GetViewSettings, GetX, InitGraph, MoveTo, SetViewPort*

Example
```
uses Graph;
var
  Gd, Gm: integer;
  X, Y: integer;
begin
  Gd := Detect;
  InitGraph(Gd, Gm, '');
  if GraphResult <> grOk then
    Halt(1);
  OutText('Starting here. ');
  X := GetX;
  Y := GetY;
  OutTextXY(20, 10, 'Now over here...');
  OutTextXY(X, Y, 'Now back over here.');
  Readln;
  CloseGraph;
end.
```

GotoXY procedure   Crt

Function   Positions the cursor.

Declaration   GotoXY(X, Y: byte)

Remarks   The cursor is moved to the position within the current window specified by *X* and *Y* (*X* is the column, *Y* is the row). The upper left corner is (1,1).

This procedure is window-relative:

```
Window(1,10,60,20);
GotoXY(1,1);
```

and will move the cursor to the upper left corner of the active window (absolute coordinates (1,10)).

Restrictions   If the coordinates are in any way invalid, the call to *GotoXY* is ignored.

See also   Window, WhereX, WhereY

GraphDefaults procedure   Graph

Function   Resets the graphics settings.

Declaration   `GraphDefaults`

Remarks   Homes the current pointer (CP) and resets the graphics system to the default values for

- viewport
- palette
- draw and background colors
- line style and line pattern
- fill style, fill color, and fill pattern
- active font, text style, text justification, and user char size

A similar routine exists in Turbo C 2.0.

Restrictions   Must be in graphics mode.

See also   *InitGraph*

GraphErrorMsg function   Graph

Function   Returns an error message string for the specified *ErrorCode*.

Declaration   `GraphErrorMsg(ErrorCode: integer)`

Result type   string

Remarks   This function returns a string containing an error message that corresponds with the error codes in the graphics system. This makes it easy for a user program to display a descriptive error message ("Device driver not found" instead of "error code –3").

A similar routine exists in Turbo C 2.0.

See also   *DetectGraph, GraphResult, InitGraph*

Example
```
uses Graph;
var
  GraphDriver, GraphMode: integer;
```

GraphErrorMsg function

```
      ErrorCode: integer;
begin
  GraphDriver := Detect;
  InitGraph(GraphDriver, GraphMode, '');
  ErrorCode := GraphResult;
  if ErrorCode <> grOk then
  begin
    Writeln('Graphics error: ', GraphErrorMsg(ErrorCode));
    Readln;
    Halt(1);
  end;
  Line(0, 0, GetMaxX, GetMaxY);
  Readln;
  CloseGraph;
end.
```

GraphResult function   Graph

Function   Returns an error code for the last graphics operation.

Declaration   GraphResult

Result type   integer

Remarks   Returns an error code for the last graphics operation. The following error return codes are defined:

GraphResult function

Error Code	Graphics Error Constant	Corresponding Error Message String
0	grOk	No error
−1	grNoInitGraph	(BGI) graphics not installed (use *InitGraph*)
−2	grNotDetected	Graphics hardware not detected
−3	grFileNotFound	Device driver file not found
−4	grInvalidDriver	Invalid device driver file
−5	grNoLoadMem	Not enough memory to load driver
−6	grNoScanMem	Out of memory in scan fill
−7	grNoFloodMem	Out of memory in flood fill
−8	grFontNotFound	Font file not found
−9	grNoFontMem	Not enough memory to load font
−10	grInvalidMode	Invalid graphics mode for selected driver
−11	grError	Graphics error
−12	grIOerror	Graphics I/O error
−13	grInvalidFont	Invalid font file
−14	grInvalidFontNum	Invalid font number

The following routines set *GraphResult*:

Bar	*ImageSize*	*SetFillPattern*
Bar3D	*InitGraph*	*SetFillStyle*
ClearViewPort	*InstallUserDriver*	*SetGraphBufSize*
CloseGraph	*InstallUserFont*	*SetGraphMode*
DetectGraph	*PieSlice*	*SetLineStyle*
DrawPoly	*RegisterBGIdriver*	*SetPalette*
FillPoly	*RegisterBGIfont*	*SetTextJustify*
FloodFill	*SetAllPalette*	*SetTextStyle*
GetGraphMode		

Note that *GraphResult* is reset to zero after it has been called (similar to *IOResult*). Therefore, the user should store the value of *GraphResult* into a temporary variable and then test it.

A string function, *GraphErrorMsg*, is provided to return a string that corresponds with each error code.

A similar routine exists in Turbo C 2.0.

See also *GraphErrorMsg*

Chapter 16, Turbo Pascal Reference Lookup 293

GraphResult function

Example

```
uses Graph;
var
  ErrorCode: integer;
  GrDriver, GrMode: integer;
begin
  GrDriver := Detect;
  InitGraph(GrDriver, GrMode, '');
  ErrorCode := GraphResult;              { Check for errors }
  if ErrorCode <> grOk then
  begin
    Writeln('Graphics error:');
    Writeln(GraphErrorMsg(ErrorCode));
    Writeln('Program aborted...');
    Halt(1);
  end;

  { Do some graphics... }
  ClearDevice;
  Rectangle(0, 0, GetMaxX, GetMaxY);
  Readln;
  CloseGraph;
end.
```

Halt procedure

Function	Stops program execution and returns to the operating system.
Declaration	Halt [(exitcode: word)]
Remarks	*exitcode* is an optional expression of type word that specifies the exit code of the program. *Halt* without a parameter corresponds to *Halt(0)*. The exit code can be examined by a parent process using the *DosExitCode* function in the *Dos* unit or through an ERRORLEVEL test in a DOS batch file.
	Note that *Halt* will initiate execution of any unit *Exit* procedures (see Chapter 15).
See also	*Exit, RunError*

Hi function

Function	Returns the high-order byte of the argument.
Declaration	`Hi(x)`
Result type	byte
Remarks	*x* is an expression of type integer or word. *Hi* returns the high-order byte of *x* as an unsigned value.
See also	*Lo, Swap*
| **Example** | ```
var w: word;
begin
  w := Hi($1234);    { $12 }
end.
``` |

HighVideo procedure   Crt

Function	Selects high-intensity characters.
Declaration	`HighVideo`
Remarks	There is a byte variable in *Crt*—*TextAttr*—that is used to hold the current video attribute. *HighVideo* sets the high intensity bit of *TextAttr*'s foreground color, thus mapping colors 0-7 onto colors 8-15.
Differences	In 3.0, *HighVideo* always selected yellow on black (white on black in mono and BW80 video modes).
See also	*LowVideo, NormVideo, TextBackground, TextColor*
| **Example** | ```
uses Crt;
begin
  TextAttr := LightGray;
  HighVideo;                    { Color is now white }
end.
``` |

ImageSize function   Graph

Function   Returns the number of bytes required to store a rectangular region of the screen.

Declaration   ImageSize(x1, y1, x2, y2: integer)

Result type   word

Remarks   *x1, y1, x2,* and *y2* define a rectangular region on the screen. *ImageSize* determines the number of bytes necessary for *GetImage* to save the specified region of the screen. The image size includes space for three words. The first stores the width of the region, the second stores the height, and the third is reserved.

If the memory required to save the region is greater than or equal to 64K, a value of 0 is returned and *GraphResult* will return –11 (*grError*).

A similar routine exists in Turbo C 2.0.

Restrictions Must be in graphics mode.

See also   *GetImage, PutImage*

Example
```
uses Graph;
var
  Gd, Gm: integer;
  P: pointer;
  Size: word;
begin
  Gd := Detect;
  InitGraph(Gd, Gm, '');
  if GraphResult <> grOk then
    Halt(1);
  Bar(0, 0, GetMaxX, GetMaxY);
  Size := ImageSize(10,20,30,40);
  GetMem(P, Size);                  { Allocate memory on heap }
  GetImage(10,20,30,40,P^);
  Readln;
  ClearDevice;
  PutImage(100, 100, P^, NormalPut);
  Readln;
  CloseGraph;
end.
```

Inc procedure

Function Increments a variable.

Declaration `Inc(var x [ ; n: longint ] )`

Remarks *x* is an ordinal-type variable, and *n* is an integer-type expression. *x* is incremented by 1, or by *n* if *n* is specified; that is, *Inc(x)* corresponds to *x := x+1*, and *Inc(x,n)* corresponds to *x := x+n*.

Inc generates optimized code and is especially useful for use in tight loops.

See also *Dec, Pred, Succ*

Example
```
var
  IntVar: integer;
  LongintVar: longint;
begin
  Inc(IntVar);                 { IntVar := IntVar + 1 }
  Inc(LongintVar, 5);          { LongintVar := LongintVar + 5 }
end.
```

InitGraph procedure Graph

Function Initializes the graphics system and puts the hardware into graphics mode.

Declaration `InitGraph(var GraphDriver: integer;`
`           var GraphMode: integer; PathToDriver: string)`

Remarks Both *GraphDriver* and *GraphMode* are **var** parameters.

If *GraphDriver* is equal to *Detect (0)*, a call is made to any user-defined autodetect routines (see *InstallUserDriver*) and then *DetectGraph*. If graphics hardware is detected, the appropriate graphics driver is initialized, and a graphics mode is selected.

If *GraphDriver* is not equal to 0, the value of *GraphDriver* is assumed to be a driver number; that driver is selected, and the system is put into the mode specified by *GraphMode*. If you override autodetection in this manner, you must supply a valid *GraphMode* parameter for the driver requested.

InitGraph procedure

PathToDriver specifies the directory path where the graphics drivers can be found. If *PathToDriver* is null, the driver files must be in the current directory.

Normally, *InitGraph* loads a graphics driver by allocating memory for the driver (through *GraphGetMem*), then loads the appropriate .BGI file from disk. As an alternative to this dynamic loading scheme, you can link a graphics driver file (or several of them) directly into your executable program file. You do this by first converting the .BGI file to an .OBJ file (using the BINOBJ utility), then placing calls to *RegisterBGIdriver* in your source code (before the call to *InitGraph*) to register the graphics driver(s). When you build your program, you must link the .OBJ files for the registered drivers. You can also load a BGI driver onto the heap and then register it using *RegisterBGIdriver*.

If memory for the graphics driver is allocated on the heap using *GraphGetMem*, that memory is released when a call is made to *CloseGraph*.

After calling *InitGraph*, *GraphDriver* will be set to the current graphics driver, and *GraphMode* will be set to the current graphics mode.

If an error occurred, both *GraphDriver* and *GraphResult* (a function) will return one of the following values:

–2	Cannot detect a graphics card
–3	Cannot find driver file
–4	Invalid driver
–5	Insufficient memory to load driver
–10	Invalid graphics mode for selected driver

InitGraph resets all graphics settings to their defaults (current pointer, palette, color, viewport, etc.).

You can use *InstallDriver* to install a vendor-supplied graphics driver (see *InstallUserDriver* for more information).

Several useful constants are defined for each graphics driver supported:

InitGraph procedure

Error Code	Graphics Error Constant	Corresponding Error Message String
0	grOk	No error
–1	grNoInitGraph	(BGI) graphics not installed (use *InitGraph*)
–2	grNotDetected	Graphics hardware not detected
–3	grFileNotFound	Device driver file not found
–4	grInvalidDriver	Invalid device driver file
–5	grNoLoadMem	Not enough memory to load driver
–6	grNoScanMem	Out of memory in scan fill
–7	grNoFloodMem	Out of memory in flood fill
–8	grFontNotFound	Font file not found
–9	grNoFontMem	Not enough memory to load font
–10	grInvalidMode	Invalid graphics mode for selected driver
–11	grError	Graphics error
–12	grIOerror	Graphics I/O error
–13	grInvalidFont	Invalid font file
–14	grInvalidFontNum	Invalid font number

A similar routine exists in Turbo C 2.0.

Restrictions   Must be in graphics mode. If you use the Borland Graphics Interface (BGI) on a Zenith Z-449 card, Turbo Pascal's autodetection code will always select the 640x480 enhanced EGA mode. If this mode isn't compatible with your monitor, select a different mode in the *InitGraph* call. Also, Turbo Pascal cannot autodetect the IBM 8514 graphics card (the autodetection logic recognizes it as VGA). Therefore, to use the IBM 8514 card, the *GraphDriver* variable must be assigned the value IBM8514 (which is defined in the *Graph* unit) when *InitGraph* is called. You should not use *DetectGraph* (or *Detect* with *InitGraph*) with the IBM 8514 unless you want the emulated VGA mode.

See also   *CloseGraph, DetectGraph, InstallUserDriver, RestoreCrtMode, SetGraphMode, GraphResult, SetGraphBufSize, RegisterBGIdriver, RegisterBGIfont, GraphDefaults*

Example
```
uses Graph;
var
```

InitGraph procedure

```
    grDriver: integer;
    grMode  : integer;
    ErrCode : integer;
begin
    grDriver := Detect;
    InitGraph(grDriver,grMode,'');
    ErrCode := GraphResult;
    if ErrCode = grOk then
      begin  { Do graphics }
        Line(0, 0, GetMaxX, GetMaxY);
        Readln;
        CloseGraph;
      end
    else
      Writeln('Graphics error:', GraphErrorMsg(ErrCode));
end.
```

Insert procedure

Function	Inserts a substring into a string.
Declaration	Insert(source: **string**; **var** s: **string**; index: integer)
Remarks	*source* is a string-type expression. *s* is a string-type variable of any length. *index* is an integer-type expression. *Insert* inserts *source* into *s* at the *index*th position. If the resulting string is longer than 255 characters, it is truncated after the 255th character.
See also	*Delete, Copy, Concat, Length, Pos*
| **Example** | ```
var
  s: string;
begin
  s := 'Honest Lincoln';
  Insert('Abe ', s, 8);           { 'Honest Abe Lincoln' }
end.
``` |

InsLine procedure   Crt

Function	Inserts an empty line at the cursor position.
Declaration	InsLine
```

InsLine procedure

Remarks All lines below the inserted line are moved down one line, and the bottom line scrolls off the screen (using the BIOS scroll routine).

All character positions are set to blanks with the currently defined text attributes. Thus, if *TextBackground* is not black, the new line becomes the background color.

This procedure is window-relative:

```
Window(1,10,60,20);
InsLine;
```

and will insert a line 60 columns wide at absolute coordinates (1,10).

See also *DelLine, Window*

InstallUserDriver function   Graph

Function Installs a vendor-added device driver to the BGI device driver table.

Declaration
```
InstallUserDriver(Name : string;
                  AutoDetectPtr : pointer)
```

Result type integer

Remarks *InstallUserDriver* allows you to use a vendor-added device driver. The *Name* parameter is the file name of the new device driver. *AutoDetectPtr* is a pointer to an optional autodetect function that may accompany the new driver. This autodetect function takes no parameters and returns an integer value.

If the internal driver table is full, *InstallUserDriver* returns a value of –11 (*grError*); otherwise *InstallUserDriver* assigns and returns a driver number for the new device driver.

There are two ways to use this vendor-supplied driver. Let's assume you have a new video card called the Spiffy Graphics Array (SGA) and that the SGA manufacturer provided you with a BGI device driver (SGA.BGI). The easiest way to use this driver is to install it by calling *InstallUserDriver* and then passing the return value (the assigned driver number) directly to *InitGraph*:

InstallUserDriver function

```
var
  Driver, Mode : integer;
begin
  Driver := InstallUserDriver('SGA', Nil);
  if Driver = grError then              { Table full? }
    Halt(1);
  Mode := 0;              { Every driver supports mode of 0 }
  InitGraph(Driver, Mode, '');    { Override autodetection }
  ...                                   { Do graphics ... }
end.
```

The **nil** value for the *AutoDetectPtr* parameter in the *InstallUserDriver* call indicates there isn't an autodetect function for the SGA.

The other, more general way to use this driver is to link in an autodetect function that will be called by *InitGraph* as part of its hardware-detection logic. Presumably, the manufacturer of the SGA gave you an autodetect function that looks something like this:

```
{$F+}
function DetectSGA : integer;
var Found : boolean;
begin
  DetectSGA := grError;           { Assume it's not there }
  Found := ...                    { Look for the hardware }
  if not Found then
    Exit;                                { Returns -11 }
  DetectSGA := 3; { Return recommended default video mode }
end;
{$F-}
```

DetectSGA's job is to look for the SGA hardware at run time. If an SGA is not detected, *DetectSGA* returns a value of –11 (*grError*); otherwise, the return value is the default video mode for the SGA (usually the best mix of color and resolution available on this hardware).

Note that this function takes no parameters, returns a signed, integer-type value, and *must* be a far call. When you install the driver (by calling *InstallUserDriver*), you pass the address of *DetectSGA* along with the device driver's file name:

InstallUserDriver function

```
var
  Driver, Mode : integer;
begin
  Driver := InstallUserDriver('SGA', @DetectSGA);
  if Driver = grError then                   { Table full? }
    Halt(1);
  Driver := Detect;
  { Discard SGA driver #; trust autodetection }
  InitGraph(Driver, Mode, '');
  ...
end.
```

After you install the device driver file name and the SGA autodetect function, you call *InitGraph* and let it go through its normal autodetection process. Before InitGraph calls its built-in autodetection function (*DetectGraph*), it first calls *DetectSGA*. If *DetectSGA* doesn't find the SGA hardware, it returns a value of –11 (*grError*) and *InitGraph* proceeds with its normal hardware detection logic (which may include calling any other vendor-supplied autodetection functions in the order in which they were "installed"). If, however, *DetectSGA* determines that an SGA is present, it returns a nonnegative mode number, and *InitGraph* locates and loads SGA.BGI, puts the hardware into the default graphics mode recommended by *DetectSGA*, and finally returns control to your program.

A similar routine exists in Turbo C 2.0.

See also *GraphResult, InitGraph, InstallUserFont, RegisterBGIfont, RegisterBGIdriver*

Example

```
uses
  Graph;
var
  Driver, Mode,
  TestDriver,
  ErrCode  : integer;

{$F+}
function TestDetect : integer;
{ Autodetect function: assume hardware is always present;
  return value = recommended default mode }
begin
  TestDetect := 1;                         { Default mode = 1 }
end;
{$F-}

begin
  { Install the driver }
```

Chapter 16, Turbo Pascal Reference Lookup 303

InstallUserDriver function

```
      TestDriver := InstallUserDriver('TEST', @TestDetect);
      if GraphResult <> grOk then
      begin
        Writeln('Error installing TestDriver');
        Halt(1);
      end;
      Driver := Detect;                    { Put in graphics mode }
      InitGraph(Driver, Mode, '');
      ErrCode := GraphResult;
      if ErrCode <> grOk then
      begin
        Writeln('Error during Init: ', ErrCode);
        Halt(1);
      end;
      OutText('Installable drivers supported...');
      Readln;
      Closegraph;
    end.
```

InstallUserFont function   Graph

Function Installs a new font not built into the BGI system.

Declaration **function** InstallUserFont(FontFileName : **string**)

Result type integer

Remarks *FontFileName* is the file name of a stroked font. *InstallUserFont* returns the font ID number that can be passed to *SetTextStyle* to select this font. If the internal font table is full, a value of 0 (*DefaultFont*) will be returned.

A similar routine exists in Turbo C 2.0.

See also *InstallUserDriver, RegisterBGIdriver, RegisterBGIfont, SetTextStyle*

Example
```
    uses
      Graph;
    var
      Driver, Mode : integer;
      TestFont : integer;
    begin
      TestFont := InstallUserFont('TEST');    { Install the font }
      if GraphResult <> grOk then
      begin
        Writeln('Error installing TestFont (using DefaultFont)');
        Readln;
```

InstallUserFont function

```
      end;
      Driver := Detect;                        { Put in graphics mode }
      InitGraph(Driver, Mode, '');
      if GraphResult <> grOk then
        Halt(1);
      SetTextStyle(TestFont, HorizDir, 2);     { Use new font }
      OutText('Installable fonts supported...');
      Readln;
      Closegraph;
    end.
```

Int function

Function	Returns the integer part of the argument.
Declaration	Int(x: real)
Result type	real
Remarks	*x* is a real-type expression. The result is the integer part of *x*, that is, *x* rounded toward zero.
See also	*Frac, Round, Trunc*
Example	

```
var r: real;
begin
  r := Int(123.456);     { 123.0 }
  r := Int(-123.456);    { -123.0 }
end.
```

Intr procedure   Dos

Function	Executes a specified software interrupt.
Declaration	Intr(IntNo: byte; var Regs: Registers)
Remarks	*IntNo* is the software interrupt number (0..255). *Registers* is a record defined in DOS:

```
type
  Registers = record
                case integer of
                  0: (AX,BX,CX,DX,BP,SI,DI,DS,ES,
                      Flags: word);
                  1: (AL,AH,BL,BH,CL,CH,DL,DH: byte);
              end;
```

Chapter 16, Turbo Pascal Reference Lookup   305

Intr procedure

Before executing the specified software interrupt, *Intr* loads the 8086 CPU's AX, BX, CX, DX, BP, SI, DI, DS, and ES registers from the *Regs* record. When the interrupt completes, the contents of the AX, BX, CX, DX, BP, SI, DI, DS, ES, and Flags registers are stored back into the *Regs* record.

For details on writing interrupt procedures, refer to the section "Interrupt Handling" in Chapter 15, "Inside Turbo Pascal."

Restrictions   Software interrupts that depend on specific values in SP or SS on entry, or modify SP and SS on exit, cannot be executed using this procedure.

Differences   In 3.0, the *Registers* variable passed to *Intr* was a user-defined type. In 5.0, the *Registers* variable must be of type *Registers* defined in the *Dos* unit.

See also   *MsDos*

IOResult function

Function   Returns an integer value that is the status of the last I/O operation performed.

Declaration   IOResult

Result type   word

Remarks   I/O-checking must be off—{$I-}—in order to trap I/O errors using *IOResult*. If an I/O error occurs and I/O-checking is off, all subsequent I/O operations are ignored until a call is made to *IOResult*. A call to *IOResult* clears its internal error flag.

The codes returned are summarized in Appendix D, "Error Messages and Codes." A value of 0 reflects a successful I/O operation.

Differences   In 3.0, return codes were mapped differently.

Example
```
var f: file of byte;
begin
  { Get file name command line }
  Assign(f, ParamStr(1));
  {$I-}
  Reset(f);
```

IOResult function

```
{$I+}
if IOResult = 0 then
  Writeln('File size in bytes: ', FileSize(f))
else
  Writeln('File not found');
end.
```

Keep procedure   Dos

Function	*Keep* (or Terminate Stay Resident) terminates the program and makes it stay in memory.
Declaration	`Keep(ExitCode: word)`
Remarks	The entire program stays in memory—including data segment, stack segment, and heap—so be sure to specify a maximum size for the heap using the $M compiler directive. The *ExitCode* corresponds to the one passed to the *Halt* standard procedure.
Restrictions	Use with care! Terminate Stay Resident (TSR) programs are complex and *no* other support for them is provided. Refer to the MS-DOS technical documentation for more information.
See also	*DosExitCode*

KeyPressed function   Crt

Function	Returns True if a key has been pressed on the keyboard; False otherwise.
Declaration	`KeyPressed`
Result type	boolean
Remarks	The character (or characters) is left in the keyboard buffer. *KeyPressed* does not detect shift keys like *Shift, Alt, NumLock,* and so on.
Differences	In 3.0, break-checking {$C-} had to be off; 5.0 has no such restriction.
See also	*ReadKey*

Length function

| Example | ```
uses Crt;
begin
  repeat
    Write('Xx');      { Fill the screen until a key is typed }
  until KeyPressed;
end.
``` |

Length function

Function	Returns the dynamic length of a string.
Declaration	Length(s: **string**)
Result type	integer
Remarks	s is a string-type expression. The result is the length of s.
See also	*Concat, Copy, Delete, Insert, Pos*
| Example | ```
var f: text; s: string;
begin
  Assign(f, 'gary.pas');
  Reset(f);
  Readln(f, s);
  Writeln('"', s, '"');
  Writeln('length = ', length(s));
end.
``` |

Line procedure   Graph

Function	Draws a line from the (x1, y1) to (x2, y2).
Declaration	Line(x1, y1, x2, y2: integer)
Remarks	Draws a line in the style and thickness defined by *SetLineStyle* and uses the color set by *SetColor*. Use *SetWriteMode* to determine whether the line is copied or XOR'd to the screen.

Note that

```
MoveTo(100,100);
LineTo(200,200);
```

is equivalent to

```
Line(100,100,200,200);
```

Line procedure

```
MoveTo(200,200);
```

Use *LineTo* when the current pointer is at one endpoint of the line. If you want the current pointer updated automatically when the line is drawn, use *LineRel* to draw a line a relative distance from the CP. Note that *Line* doesn't update the current pointer.

A similar routine exists in Turbo C 2.0.

Restrictions Must be in graphics mode. Also, for drawing a horizontal line, *Bar* is faster than *Line*.

See also *GetLineStyle, LineRel, LineTo, MoveTo, Rectangle, SetColor, SetLineStyle, SetWriteMode*

Example
```
uses Crt, Graph;
var
  Gd, Gm: integer;
begin
  Gd := Detect;
  InitGraph(Gd, Gm, '');
  if GraphResult <> grOk then
    Halt(1);
  Randomize;
  repeat
    Line(Random(200),Random(200),Random(200),Random(200));
  until KeyPressed;
  Readln;
  CloseGraph;
end.
```

LineRel procedure   Graph

Function Draws a line to a point that is a relative distance from the current pointer (CP).

Declaration `LineRel(Dx, Dy: integer);`

Remarks *LineRel* will draw a line from the current pointer to a point that is a relative (*Dx,Dy*) distance from the current pointer. The current line style and pattern, as set by *SetLineStyle*, are used for drawing the line and uses the color set by *SetColor*. Relative move and line commands are useful for drawing a shape on the screen whose starting point can be changed to draw the same shape in a different location on the screen. Use *SetWriteMode* to

LineRel procedure

determine whether the line is copied or XOR'd to the screen.

The current pointer is set to the last point drawn by *LineRel*.

Restrictions Must be in graphics mode.

A similar routine exists in Turbo C 2.0.

See also *GetLineStyle, Line, LineTo, MoveRel, MoveTo, SetLineStyle, SetWriteMode*

Example
```
uses Graph;
var
  Gd, Gm: integer;
begin
  Gd := Detect;
  InitGraph(Gd, Gm, '');
  if GraphResult <> grOk then
    Halt(1);
  MoveTo(1,2);
  LineRel(100, 100);         { Draw to the point (101,102) }
  Readln;
  CloseGraph;
end.
```

LineTo procedure Graph

Function Draws a line from the current pointer to (*x,y*).

Declaration `LineTo(x, y: integer)`

Remarks Draws a line in the style and thickness defined by *SetLineStyle* and uses the color set by *SetColor*. Use *SetWriteMode* to determine whether the line is copied or XOR'd to the screen.

Note that
```
MoveTo(100,100);
LineTo(200,200);
```
is equivalent to
```
Line(100,100,200,200);
```

The first method is slower and uses more code. Use *LineTo* only when the current pointer is at one endpoint of the line. Use *LineRel* to draw a line a relative distance

LineTo procedure

from the CP. Note that the second method doesn't change the value of the current pointer.

LineTo moves the current pointer to (*x,y*).

A similar routine exists in Turbo C 2.0.

Restrictions Must be in graphics mode.

See also *Line, LineRel, MoveTo, MoveRel, SetLineStyle, GetLineStyle, SetWriteMode*

Example
```
uses Crt, Graph;
var
  Gd, Gm: integer;
begin
  Gd := Detect;
  InitGraph(Gd, Gm, '');
  if GraphResult <> grOk then
    Halt(1);
  Randomize;
  repeat
    LineTo(Random(200),Random(200));
  until KeyPressed;
  Readln;
  CloseGraph;
end.
```

Ln function

Function	Returns the natural logarithm of the argument.
Declaration	Ln(x: real)
Result type	real
Remarks	*x* is a real-type expression. The result is the natural logarithm of *x*.
See Also	*Exp*

Chapter 16, Turbo Pascal Reference Lookup

Lo function

Function	Returns the low-order byte of the argument.
Declaration	Lo(x)
Result type	byte
Remarks	*x* is an expression of type integer or word. *Lo* returns the low-order byte of *x* as an unsigned value.
See also	*Hi, Swap*
| **Example** | ```
var w: word;
begin
  w := Lo($1234);   { $34 }
end.
``` |

LowVideo procedure   Crt

Function	Selects low-intensity characters.
Declaration	LowVideo
Remarks	There is a byte variable in *Crt—TextAttr—*that is used to hold the current video attribute. *LowVideo* clears the high-intensity bit of *TextAttr*'s foreground color, thus mapping colors 8-15 onto colors 0-7.
Differences	In 3.0, *LowVideo* always selected *LightGray* on black.
See also	*HighVideo, NormVideo, TextBackground, TextColor*
| **Example** | ```
uses Crt;
begin
  TextAttr := White;
  LowVideo;                  { Color is now light gray }
end.
``` |

Mark procedure

Function	Records the state of the heap in a pointer variable.
Declaration	Mark(**var** p: pointer)
Remarks	*p* is a pointer variable of any pointer type. The current value of the heap pointer is recorded in *p*, and can later be used as an argument to *Release*.
Restrictions	*Mark* and *Release* cannot be used interchangeably with *Dispose* and *FreeMem* unless certain rules are observed. For a complete discussion of this topic, refer to the section "The Heap Manager" on page 181.
See also	*Dispose, FreeMem, GetMem, New, Release*

MaxAvail function

Function	Returns the size of the largest contiguous free block in the heap, corresponding to the size of the largest dynamic variable that can be allocated at that time.
Declaration	MaxAvail
Result type	longint
Remarks	This number is calculated by comparing the sizes of all free blocks below the heap pointer to the size of free memory above the heap pointer. To find the total amount of free memory on the heap, call *MemAvail*. Your program can specify minimum and maximum heap requirements using the $M compiler directive (see Appendix B, "Compiler Directives").
Differences	In 3.0, the returned value was an integer that represented the size of the largest free block in paragraphs.
See also	*MemAvail*
| **Example** | ```
type
  FriendRec = record
                Name: string[30];
                Age : byte;
              end;
var
  p: pointer;
``` |

Chapter 16, Turbo Pascal Reference Lookup
```

MaxAvail function

```
begin
  if MaxAvail < SizeOf(FriendRec) then
    Writeln('Not enough memory')
  else
  begin
    { Allocate memory on heap }
    GetMem(p, SizeOf(FriendRec));
    :
    :
  end;
end.
```

MemAvail function

Function	Returns the sum of all free blocks in the heap.
Declaration	`MemAvail`
Result type	longint
Remarks	This number is calculated by adding the sizes of all free blocks below the heap pointer to the size of free memory above the heap pointer. Note that unless *Dispose* and *FreeMem* were never called, a block of storage the size of the returned value is unlikely to be available due to fragmentation of the heap. To find the largest free block, call *MaxAvail*. Your program can specify minimum and maximum heap requirements using the $M compiler directive (see Appendix B, "Compiler Directives").
Differences	In 3.0, the returned value was an integer that represented the number of free paragraphs.
See also	*MaxAvail*
Example	```begin
Writeln(MemAvail, ' bytes available');
Writeln('Largest free block is ', MaxAvail, ' bytes');
end.```

MkDir procedure

Function	Creates a subdirectory.
Declaration	`MkDir(s: string)`

MkDir procedure

Remarks s is a string-type expression. A new subdirectory with the path specified by s is created. The last item in the path cannot be an existing file name.

With {$I-}, *IOResult* will return a 0 if the operation was successful; otherwise, it will return a nonzero error code.

See also *RmDir, ChDir, GetDir*

Example
```
begin
  {$I-}
  { Get directory name from command line }
  MkDir(ParamStr(1));
  if IOResult <> 0 then
    Writeln('Cannot create directory')
  else
    Writeln('New directory created');
end.
```

Move procedure

Function Copies a specified number of contiguous bytes from a source range to a destination range.

Declaration `Move(var source, dest; count: word)`

Remarks *source* and *dest* are variable references of any type. *count* is an expression of type word. *Move* copies a block of *count* bytes from the first byte occupied by *source* to the first byte occupied by *dest*. No checking is performed, so be careful with this procedure.

Note: When *source* and *dest* are in the same segment, that is, when the segment parts of their addresses are equal, *Move* automatically detects and compensates for any overlap. Intrasegment overlaps never occur on statically and dynamically allocated variables (unless they are deliberately forced), and they are therefore not detected.

Whenever possible, use the *SizeOf* function to determine the *count*.

See also *FillChar*

MoveRel procedure

Example
```pascal
var
  a: array[1..4] of char;
  b: longint;
begin
  Move(a, b, SizeOf(a));         { SizeOf = safety! }
end.
```

MoveRel procedure   Graph

Function   Moves the current pointer (CP) a relative distance from its current location.

Declaration MoveRel(Dx, Dy: integer)

Remarks   *MoveRel* moves the current pointer (CP) to a point that is a relative (*Dx,Dy*) distance from the current pointer. Relative move and line commands are useful for drawing a shape on the screen whose starting point can be changed to draw the same shape in a different location on the screen.

A similar routine exists in Turbo C 2.0.

Restrictions Must be in graphics mode.

See also   *GetMaxX, GetMaxY, GetX, GetY, LineRel, LineTo, MoveTo*

Example
```pascal
uses Graph;
var
  Gd, Gm: integer;
begin
  Gd := Detect;
  InitGraph(Gd, Gm, '');
  if GraphResult <> grOk then
    Halt(1);
  MoveTo(1,2);
  MoveRel(10,10);                { Move to the point (11, 12) }
  PutPixel(GetX, GetY, GetMaxColor);
  Readln;
  CloseGraph;
end.
```

MoveTo procedure   Graph

Function   Moves the current pointer (CP) to (x,y).

Declaration   `MoveTo(x, y: integer)`

Remarks   The CP is similar to a text mode cursor except that the CP is not visible. The following routines move the CP:

    ClearDevice   *MoveRel*
    ClearViewPort   *MoveTo*
    GraphDefaults   *OutText*
    InitGraph   *SetGraphMode*
    LineRel   *SetViewPort*
    LineTo

If a viewport is active, the CP will be viewport-relative (the *x* and *y* values will be added to the viewport's *x*1 and *y*1 values). The CP is never clipped at the current viewport's boundaries.

A similar routine exists in Turbo C 2.0.

See also   *GetMaxX, GetMaxY, GetX, GetY, MoveRel*

Example
```
uses Graph;
var
  Gd, Gm: integer;
begin
  Gd := Detect;
  InitGraph(Gd, Gm, '');
  if GraphResult <> grOk then
    Halt(1);
  MoveTo(0,0);               { Upper left corner of viewport }
  LineTo(GetMaxX, GetMaxY);
  Readln;
  CloseGraph;
end.
```

Chapter 16, Turbo Pascal Reference Lookup

MsDos procedure   Dos

Function   Executes a DOS function call.

Declaration   MsDos(**var** Regs: Registers)

Remarks   The effect of a call to *MsDos* is the same as a call to *Intr* with an *IntNo* of $21. *Registers* is a record declared in the *Dos* unit:

```
type
  Registers = record
                case integer of
                  0: (AX,BX,CX,DX,BP,SI,DI,DS,ES,
                      Flags: word);
                  1: (AL,AH,BL,BH,CL,CH,DL,DH: byte);
              end;
```

Restrictions   Software interrupts that depend on specific calls in SP or SS on entry or modify SP and SS on exit cannot be executed using this procedure.

Differences   In 3.0, no type-checking was performed on the *Registers* parameter.

See also   *Intr*

New procedure

Function   Creates a new dynamic variable and sets a pointer variable to point to it.

Declaration   New(**var** p: pointer)

Remarks   *p* is a pointer variable of any pointer type. The size of the allocated memory block corresponds to the size of the type that *p* points to. The newly created variable can be referenced as *p^*. If there isn't enough free space in the heap to allocate the new variable, a run-time error occurs. (It is possible to avoid a run-time error in this case; see "The Heap Error Function" on page 187.)

See also   *Dispose, FreeMem, GetMem, Release*

NormVideo procedure   Crt

Function	Selects the original text attribute read from the cursor location at startup.
Declaration	NormVideo
Remarks	There is a byte variable in *Crt*—*TextAttr*—that is used to hold the current video attribute. *NormVideo* restores *TextAttr* to the value it had when the program was started.
Differences	In 3.0, *NormVideo* and *HighVideo* were identical; see *HighVideo*.
See also	*HighVideo, LowVideo, TextColor, TextBackground*

NoSound procedure   Crt

Function	Turns off the internal speaker.
Declaration	NoSound
Remarks	The following program fragment emits a 440-hertz tone for half a second:

```
Sound(440); Delay(500); NoSound;
```

See also	*Sound*

Odd function

Function	Tests if the argument is an odd number.
Declaration	Odd(x: longint)
Result type	boolean
Remarks	*x* is a longint-type expression. The result is True if *x* is an odd number, and False if *x* is an even number.

Chapter 16, Turbo Pascal Reference Lookup

Ofs function

Function	Returns the offset of a specified object.
Declaration	Ofs(x)
Result type	word
Remarks	*x* is any variable, or a procedure or function identifier. The result of type word is the offset part of the address of *x*.
See also	*Addr, Seg*

Ord function

Function	Returns the ordinal number of an ordinal-type value.
Declaration	Ord(x)
Result type	longint
Remarks	*x* is an ordinal-type expression. The result is of type longint and its value is the ordinality of *x*.
See also	*Chr*

OutText procedure   Graph

Function	Sends a string to the output device at the current pointer.
Declaration	OutText(TextString: **string**)
Remarks	*TextString* is output at the current pointer using the current justification settings. *TextString* is always truncated at the viewport border if it is too long. If one of the stroked fonts is active, *TextString* is truncated at the screen boundary if it is too long. If the default (bit-mapped) font is active and the string is too long to fit on the screen, no text is displayed.

OutText uses the font set by *SetTextStyle*. In order to maintain code compatibility when using several fonts, |

OutText procedure

use the *TextWidth* and *TextHeight* calls to determine the dimensions of the string.

OutText uses the output options set by *SetTextJustify* (justify, center, rotate 90 degrees, and so on).

The current pointer (CP) is only updated by *OutText* if the direction is horizontal, and the horizontal justification is left. Text output direction is set by *SetTextStyle* (horizontal or vertical); text justification is set by *SetTextJustify* (CP at the left of the string, centered around CP, or CP at the right of the string—written above CP, below CP, or centered around CP). In the following example, block #1 outputs *ABCDEF* and moves CP (text is both horizontally output and left-justified); block #2 outputs *ABC* with *DEF* written right on top of it because text is right-justified; similarly, block #3 outputs *ABC* with *DEF* written right on top of it because text is written vertically.

```
program CPupdate;
uses Graph;
var
  Driver, Mode: integer;
begin
  Driver := Detect;
  InitGraph(Driver, Mode, '');
  if GraphResult < 0 then
    Halt(1);
  { #1 }
  MoveTo(0, 0);
  SetTextStyle(DefaultFont, HorizDir, 1);    { CharSize = 1 }
  SetTextJustify(LeftText, TopText);
  OutText('ABC');                             { CP is updated }
  OutText('DEF');                             { CP is updated }
  { #2 }
  MoveTo(100, 50);
  SetTextStyle(DefaultFont, HorizDir, 1);    { CharSize = 1 }
  SetTextJustify(RightText, TopText);
  OutText('ABC');                             { CP is updated }
  OutText('DEF');                             { CP is updated }
  { #3 }
  MoveTo(100, 100);
  SetTextStyle(DefaultFont, VertDir, 1);     { CharSize = 1 }
  SetTextJustify(LeftText, TopText);
  OutText('ABC');                             { CP is NOT updated }
  OutText('DEF');                             { CP is NOT updated }
  Readln;
  CloseGraph;
end.
```

OutText procedure

The CP is never updated by *OutTextXY*.

The default font (8×8 bit-mapped) is not clipped at the screen edge. Instead, if any part of the string would go off the screen, no text is output. For example, the following statements would have no effect:

```
SetViewPort(0, 0, GetMaxX, GetMaxY, ClipOn);
SetTextJustify(LeftText, TopText);
OutTextXY(-5, 0);                        { -5,0 not on screen }
OutTextXY(GetMaxX - 1, 0, 'ABC');             { Part of 'A', }
                                         { All of 'BC' off screen }
```

The "stroked" fonts are clipped at the screen edge, however.

A similar routine exists in Turbo C 2.0.

Restrictions Must be in graphics mode.

See also *OutTextXY, SetTextStyle, SetTextJustify, GetTextSettings, TextHeight, TextWidth, SetUserCharSize*

Example
```
uses Graph;
var
  Gd, Gm: integer;
begin
  Gd := Detect;
  InitGraph(Gd, Gm, '');
  if GraphResult <> grOk then
    Halt(1);
  OutText('Easy to use');
  Readln;
  CloseGraph;
end.
```

OutTextXY procedure   Graph

Function Sends a string to the output device.

Declaration `OutTextXY(X,Y: integer; TextString: string)`

Remarks *TextString* is output at (X,Y). *TextString* is always truncated at the viewport border if it is too long. If one of the stroked fonts is active, *TextString* is truncated at the screen boundary if it is too long. If the default (bit-mapped) font is active and the string is too long to fit on the screen, no text is displayed.

OutTextXY procedure

Use *OutText* to output text at the current pointer; use *OutTextXY* to output text elsewhere on the screen.

OutTextXY uses the font set by *SetTextStyle*. In order to maintain code compatibility when using several fonts, use the *TextWidth* and *TextHeight* calls to determine the dimensions of the string.

OutTextXY uses the output options set by *SetTextJustify* (justify, center, rotate 90 degrees, and so forth).

A similar routine exists in Turbo C 2.0.

Restrictions Must be in graphics mode.

See also *OutText, SetTextStyle, SetTextJustify, GetTextSetting, TextHeight, TextWidth, SetUserCharSize*

Example
```
uses Graph;
var
  Gd, Gm: integer;
begin
  Gd := Detect;
  InitGraph(Gd, Gm, '');
  if GraphResult <> grOk then
    Halt(1);
  MoveTo(0, 0);
  OutText('Inefficient');
  Readln;
  OutTextXY(GetX, GetY, 'Also inefficient');
  Readln;
  ClearDevice;
  OutTextXY(0, 0, 'Perfect!');         { Replaces above }
  Readln;
  CloseGraph;
end.
```

OvrClearBuf procedure   Overlay

Function Clears the overlay buffer.

Declaration `OvrClearBuf`

Remarks Upon a call to *OvrClearBuf*, all currently loaded overlays are disposed from the overlay buffer. This forces subsequent calls to overlaid routines to reload the overlays from the overlay file (or from EMS). If *OvrClearBuf* is called from an overlay, that overlay will

OvrClearBuf procedure

immediately be reloaded upon return from *OvrClearBuf*. The overlay manager never requires you to call *OvrClearBuf*; in fact, doing so will decrease performance of your application, since it forces overlays to be reloaded. *OvrClearBuf* is solely intended for special use, such as temporarily reclaiming the memory occupied by the overlay buffer.

See also *OvrGetBuf, OvrSetBuf*

OvrGetBuf function — Overlay

Function Returns the current size of the overlay buffer.

Declaration OvrGetBuf

Result type longint

Remarks The size of the overlay buffer is set through a call to *OvrSetBuf*. Initially, the overlay buffer is as small as possible, corresponding to the size of the largest overlay. A buffer of this size is automatically allocated when an overlaid program is executed. (**Note:** The initial buffer size may be larger than 64K, since it includes both code and fix-up information for the largest overlay.)

See also *OvrInit, OvrInitEMS, OvrSetBuf*

Example
```
{$M 16384,65536,655360}
uses Overlay;
const
  ExtraSize = 49152; {48K}
begin
   OvrInit('EDITOR.OVR');
   Writeln('Initial size of overlay buffer is ',
           OvrGetBuf,' bytes.');
   OvrSetBuf(OvrGetBuf+ExtraSize);
   Writeln('Overlay buffer now increased to ',
           OvrGetBuf,' bytes.');
end.
```

OvrInit procedure   Overlay

Function Initializes the overlay manager and opens the overlay file.

Declaration OvrInit(FileName: **string**)

Remarks If the file name parameter does not specify a drive or a subdirectory, the overlay manager searches for the file in the current directory, in the directory that contains the .EXE file (if running under DOS 3.x), and in the directories specified in the PATH environment variable.

Errors are reported in the *OvrResult* variable. *ovrOk* indicates success. *ovrError* means that the overlay file is of an incorrect format, or that the program has no overlays. *ovrNotFound* means that the overlay file could not be located.

In case of error, the overlay manager remains uninstalled, and an attempt to call an overlaid routine will produce run-time error 208 (Overlay manager not installed).

OvrInit must be called before any of the other overlay manager procedures.

See also *OvrGetBuf, OvrInitEMS, OvrSetBuf*

Example
```
uses Overlay;
begin
  OvrInit('EDITOR.OVR');
  if OvrResult<>ovrOk then
  begin
    case OvrResult of
      ovrError:    Writeln('Program has no overlays.');
      ovrNotFound: Writeln('Overlay file not found.');
    end;
    Halt(1);
  end;
end.
```

OvrInitEMS procedure   Overlay

Function Loads the overlay file into EMS if possible.

Declaration OvrInitEMS

OvrInitEMS procedure

Remarks If an EMS driver can be detected and if enough EMS memory is available, *OvrInitEMS* loads all overlays into EMS and closes the overlay file. Subsequent overlay loads are reduced to fast in-memory transfers. *OvrInitEMS* installs an exit procedure, which automatically deallocates EMS memory upon termination of the program.

Errors are reported in the *OvrResult* variable. *ovrOk* indicates success. *ovrError* means that *OvrInit* failed or was not called. *ovrIOError* means that an I/O error occurred while reading the overlay file. *ovrNoEMSDriver* means that an EMS driver could not be detected. *ovrNoEMSMemory* means that there is not enough free EMS memory available to load the overlay file.

In case of error, the overlay manager will continue to function, but overlays will be read from disk.

The EMS driver must conform to the Lotus/Intel/Microsoft Expanded Memory Specification (EMS). If you are using an EMS-based RAM disk, make sure that the command in the CONFIG.SYS file that loads the RAM-disk driver leaves some unallocated EMS memory for your overlaid applications.

See also *OvrGetBuf, OvrInit, OvrSetBuf*

Example
```
uses Overlay;
begin
  OvrInit('EDITOR.OVR');
  if OvrResult<>ovrOk then
  begin
    Writeln('Overlay manager initialization failed.');
    Halt(1);
  end;
  OvrInitEMS;
  case OvrResult of
    ovrIOError:     Writeln('Overlay file I/O error.');
    ovrNoEMSDriver: Writeln('EMS driver not installed.');
    ovrNoEMSMemory: Writeln('Not enough EMS memory.');
  else
    Writeln('Using EMS for faster overlay swapping.');
  end;
end;
```

OvrSetBuf procedure   Overlay

Function Sets the size of the overlay buffer.

Declaration `OvrSetBuf(BufSize: longint)`

Remarks *BufSize* must be larger than or equal to the initial size of the overlay buffer, and less than or equal to *MemAvail* + *OvrGetBuf*. The initial size of the overlay buffer is the size returned by *OvrGetBuf* before any calls to *OvrSetBuf*.

If the specified size is larger than the current size, additional space is allocated from the beginning of the heap, thus decreasing the size of the heap. Likewise, if the specified size is less than the current size, excess space is returned to the heap.

OvrSetBuf requires that the heap be empty; an error is returned if dynamic variables have already been allocated using *New* or *GetMem*. For this reason, make sure to call *OvrSetBuf* before the *Graph* unit's *InitGraph* procedure; *InitGraph* allocates memory on the heap and—once it has done so—all calls to *OvrSetBuf* will be ignored.

If you are using *OvrSetBuf* to increase the size of the overlay buffer, you should also include a *$M* compiler directive in your program to increase the minimum size of the heap accordingly.

Errors are reported in the *OvrResult* variable. *ovrOk* indicates success. *ovrError* means that *OvrInit* failed or was not called, that *BufSize* is too small, or that the heap is not empty. *ovrNoMemory* means that there is not enough heap memory to increase the size of the overlay buffer.

See also *OvrGetBuf, OvrInit, OvrInitEMS*

Example
```
{$M 16384,65536,655360}
uses Overlay;
const
  ExtraSize = 49152; {48K}
begin
  OvrInit('EDITOR.OVR');
  OvrSetBuf(OvrGetBuf+ExtraSize);
end.
```

PackTime procedure   Dos

Function	Converts a *DateTime* record into a 4-byte, packed date-and-time longint used by *SetFTime*.
Declaration	`PackTime(`**`var`**` DT: DateTime; `**`var`**` Time: longint)`
Remarks	*DateTime* is a record declared in the *Dos* unit:

```
DateTime = record
             Year, Month, Day, Hour, Min, Sec: word;
           end;
```

The fields of the *DateTime* record are not range-checked.

See also	*UnpackTime, GetFTime, SetFTime, GetTime, SetTime*

ParamCount function

Function	Returns the number of parameters passed to the program on the command line.
Declaration	`ParamCount`
Result type	word
Remarks	Blanks and tabs serve as separators.
See also	*ParamStr*
Example	

```
begin
  if ParamCount < 1 then
    Writeln('No parameters on command line')
  else
    Writeln(ParamCount, ' parameter(s)');
end.
```


ParamStr function

Function	Returns a specified command-line parameter.
Declaration	`ParamStr(index)`
Result type	string

ParamStr function

Remarks	*index* is an expression of type word. *ParamStr* returns the *index*th parameter from the command line, or an empty string if *index* is zero or greater than *ParamCount*. With DOS 3.0 or later, *ParamStr(0)* returns the path and file name of the executing program (for example, C:\TP\MYPROG.EXE).
See also	*ParamCount*
Example	```var i: word;
begin
for i := 1 to ParamCount do
Writeln(ParamStr(i));
end.```

Pi function

Function	Returns the value of Pi (3.1415926535897932385).
Declaration	Pi
Result type	real
Remarks	Precision varies, depending on whether the compiler is in 8087 (80287, 80387) or software-only mode.
Differences	In 3.0, *Pi* was a constant.

PieSlice procedure   Graph

Function	Draws and fills a pie slice, using (X,Y) as the center point and drawing from start angle to end angle.
Declaration	PieSlice(x, y: integer; StAngle, EndAngle, Radius: word)
Remarks	The pie slice is outlined using the current color, and filled using the pattern and color defined by *SetFillStyle* or *SetFillPattern*.
	Each graphics driver contains an aspect ratio that is used by *Circle*, *Arc*, and *PieSlice*. A start angle of 0 and an end angle of 360 will draw and fill a complete circle. The angles for *Arc*, *Ellipse*, and *PieSlice* are counterclockwise with 0 degrees at 3 o'clock, 90 degrees at 12 o'clock, and so on.

PieSlice procedure

If an error occurs while filling the pie slice, *GraphResult* will return a value of –6 (*grNoScanMem*).

A similar routine exists in Turbo C 2.0.

Restrictions Must be in graphics mode.

See also *Arc, Circle, Ellipse, FillEllipse, GetArcCoords, GetAspectRatio, Sector, SetFillStyle, SetFillPattern, SetGraphBufSize*

Example
```
uses Graph;
const
  Radius = 30;
var
  Gd, Gm: integer;
begin
  Gd := Detect;
  InitGraph(Gd, Gm, '');
  if GraphResult <> grOk then
    Halt(1);
  PieSlice(100, 100, 0, 270, Radius);
  Readln;
  CloseGraph;
end.
```

Pos function

Function Searches for a substring in a string.

Declaration Pos(substr, s: **string**)

Result type byte

Remarks *substr* and *s* are string-type expressions. *Pos* searches for *substr* within *s*, and returns an integer value that is the index of the first character of *substr* within *s*. If *substr* is not found, *Pos* returns zero.

See also *Concat, Copy, Delete, Insert, Length*

Example
```
var s: string;
begin
  s := '   123.5';
  { Convert spaces to zeroes }
  while Pos(' ', s) > 0 do
    s[Pos(' ', s)] := '0';
end.
```

Pred function

Function	Returns the predecessor of the argument.
Declaration	Pred(x)
Result type	Same type as parameter.
Remarks	*x* is an ordinal-type expression. The result, of the same type as *x*, is the predecessor of *x*.
See also	*Succ, Dec, Inc*

Ptr function

Function	Converts a segment base and an offset address to a pointer-type value.
Declaration	Ptr(Seg, Ofs: word)
Result type	pointer
Remarks	*Seg* and *Ofs* are expressions of type word. The result is a pointer that points to the address given by *Seg* and *Ofs*. Like **nil**, the result of *Ptr* is assignment-compatible with all pointer types.

The function result may be dereferenced and typecast:

```
if Byte(Ptr($40, $49)^) = 7 then
   Writeln('Video mode = mono');
```

See also	*Addr, Ofs, Seg*
| **Example** | ```
var p: ^byte;
begin
  p := Ptr($40, $49);
  Writeln('Current video mode is ', p^);
end.
``` |

PutImage procedure   Graph

Function	Puts a bit image onto the screen.
Declaration	PutImage(x, y: integer; **var** BitMap; BitBlt: word)

Chapter 16, Turbo Pascal Reference Lookup
```

PutImage procedure

Remarks (x,y) is the upper left corner of a rectangular region on the screen. *BitMap* is an untyped parameter that contains the height and width of the region, and the bit image that will be put onto the screen. *BitBlt* specifies which binary operator will be used to put the bit image onto the screen.

The following constants are defined:

```
const
  CopyPut = 0;    { MOV }
  XORPut  = 1;    { XOR }
  OrPut   = 2;    { OR  }
  AndPut  = 3;    { AND }
  NotPut  = 4;    { NOT }
```

Each constant corresponds to a binary operation. For example, *PutImage(x,y,BitMap,NormalPut)* puts the image stored in *BitMap* at (x,y) using the assembly language MOV instruction for each byte in the image.

Similarly, *PutImage(x,y,BitMap,XORPut)* puts the image stored in *BitMap* at (x,y) using the assembly language XOR instruction for each byte in the image. This is an often-used animation technique for "dragging" an image around the screen.

PutImage(x,y,Bitmap,NotPut) inverts the bits in *BitMap* and then puts the image stored in *BitMap* at (x, y) using the assembly language MOV for each byte in the image. Thus, the image appears in inverse video of the original *BitMap*.

Note that *PutImage* is never clipped to the viewport boundary. Moreover—with one exception—it is not actually clipped at the screen edge either. Instead, if any part of the image would go off the screen, no image is output. In the following example, the first image would be output, but the middle three *PutImage* statements would have no effect:

```
program NoClip;
uses graph;
var
  Driver, Mode: integer;
  p: pointer;
begin
  Driver := Detect;
  InitGraph(Driver, Mode, '');
  if GraphResult < 0 then
```

PutImage procedure

```
         Halt(1);
      SetViewPort(0, 0, GetMaxX, GetMaxY, clipon);
      GetMem(p, ImageSize(0, 0, 99, 49));
      PieSlice(50, 25, 0, 360, 45);
      GetImage(0, 0, 99, 49, p^);      { Width = 100, height = 50 }
      ClearDevice;
      PutImage(GetMaxX - 99, 0,            { Will barely fit }
               p^, NormalPut);
      PutImage(GetMaxX - 98, 0,        { x + height > GetMaxX }
               p^, NormalPut);
      PutImage(-1, 0,                      { -1,0 not on screen }
               p^, NormalPut);
      PutImage(0, -1,                      { 0,-1 not on screen }
               p^, NormalPut);
      PutImage(0, GetMaxY - 30,        { Will output 31 "lines" }
               p^, NormalPut);
      Readln;
      CloseGraph;
   end.
```

In the last *PutImage* statement, the height is clipped at the lower screen edge, and a partial image is displayed. This is the only time any clipping is performed on *PutImage* output.

A similar routine exists in Turbo C 2.0.

Restrictions Must be in graphics mode.

See also *GetImage, ImageSize*

Example
```
uses Graph;
var
  Gd, Gm: integer;
  P: pointer;
  Size: word;
begin
  Gd := Detect;
  InitGraph(Gd, Gm, '');
  if GraphResult <> grOk then
    Halt(1);
  Bar(0, 0, GetMaxX, GetMaxY);
  Size := ImageSize(10,20,30,40);
  GetMem(P, Size);                   { Allocate memory on heap }
  GetImage(10,20,30,40,P^);
  Readln;
  ClearDevice;
  PutImage(100, 100, P^, NormalPut);
  Readln;
  CloseGraph;
end.
```

PutPixel procedure   Graph

Function	Plots a pixel at *x,y*.
Declaration	`PutPixel(X, y: integer; Pixel: word)`
Remarks	Plots a point in the color defined by *Pixel* at (*x,y*).
	A similar routine exists in Turbo C 2.0.
Restrictions	Must be in graphics mode.
See also	*GetImage, GetPixel, PutImage*
Example	

```
uses Crt, Graph;
var
  Gd, Gm: integer;
  Color : word;
begin
  Gd := Detect;
  InitGraph(Gd, Gm, '');
  if GraphResult <> grOk then
    Halt(1);
  Color := GetMaxColor;
  Randomize;
  repeat
    PutPixel(Random(100),Random(100),Color);   { Plot "stars" }
    Delay(10);
  until KeyPressed;
  Readln;
  CloseGraph;
end.
```

Random function

Function	Returns a random number.
Declaration	`Random [ ( range: word) ]`
Result type	real or word, depending on the parameter
Remarks	If *range* is not specified, the result is a *Real* random number within the range $0 <= x < 1$. If *range* is specified, it must be an expression of type integer, and the result is a word random number within the range $0 <= x <$ *range*. If *range* equals 0, a value of 0 will be returned.

Random function

The *Random* number generator should be initialized by making a call to *Randomize*, or by assigning a value to *RandSeed*.

See also *Randomize*

Example
```
uses Crt;
begin
  Randomize;
  repeat
    { Write text in random colors }
    TextAttr := Random(256);
    Write('!');
  until KeyPressed;
end.
```

Randomize procedure

Function   Initializes the built-in random generator with a random value.

Declaration Randomize

Remarks   The random value is obtained from the system clock.

Note: The random-number generator's seed is stored in a predeclared longint variable called *RandSeed*. By assigning a specific value to *RandSeed*, a specific sequence of random numbers can be generated over and over. This is particularly useful in applications that use data encryption.

See also *Random*

Read procedure (text files)

Function   Reads one or more values from a text file into one or more variables.

Declaration Read([**var** f: text;] v1 [, v2,...,vn])

Remarks   *f*, if specified, is a text-file variable. If *f* is omitted, the standard file variable *Input* is assumed. Each *v* is a variable of type char, integer, real, or string.

Read procedure (text files)

With a type char variable, *Read* reads one character from the file and assigns that character to the variable. If *Eof(f)* was True before *Read* was executed, the value *Chr(26)* (a *Ctrl-Z* character) is assigned to the variable. If *Eoln(f)* was True, the value *Chr(13)* (a carriage-return character) is assigned to the variable. The next *Read* will start with the next character in the file.

With a type integer variable, *Read* expects a sequence of characters that form a signed number, according to the syntax shown in the section "Numbers" in Chapter 1, "Tokens and Constants." Any blanks, tabs, or end-of-line markers preceding the numeric string are skipped. Reading ceases at the first blank, tab, or end-of-line marker following the numeric string or if *Eof(f)* becomes True. If the numeric string does not conform to the expected format, an I/O error occurs; otherwise, the value is assigned to the variable. If *Eof(f)* was True before *Read* was executed or if *Eof(f)* becomes True while skipping initial blanks, tabs, and end-of-line markers, the value 0 is assigned to the variable. The next *Read* will start with the blank, tab, or end-of-line marker that terminated the numeric string.

With a type real variable, *Read* expects a sequence of characters that form a signed whole number, according to the syntax shown in the section "Numbers" in Chapter 1, "Tokens and Constants" (except that hexadecimal notation is not allowed). Any blanks, tabs, or end-of-line markers preceding the numeric string are skipped. Reading ceases at the first blank, tab, or end-of-line marker following the numeric string or if *Eof(f)* becomes True. If the numeric string does not conform to the expected format, an I/O error occurs; otherwise, the value is assigned to the variable. If *Eof(f)* was True before *Read* was executed, or if *Eof(f)* becomes True while skipping initial blanks, tabs, and end-of-line markers, the value 0 is assigned to the variable. The next *Read* will start with the blank, tab, or end-of-line marker that terminated the numeric string.

With a type string variable, *Read* reads all characters up to, but not including, the next end-of-line marker or until *Eof(f)* becomes True. The resulting character string is assigned to the variable. If the resulting string is longer than the maximum length of the string variable, it

Read procedure (text files)

is truncated. The next *Read* will start with the end-of-line marker that terminated the string.

With {$I-}, *IOResult* will return a 0 if the operation was successful; otherwise, it will return a nonzero error code.

Restrictions *Read* with a type string variable does not skip to the next line after reading. For this reason, you cannot use successive *Read* calls to read a sequence of strings, since you will never get past the first line; after the first *Read*, each subsequent *Read* will see the end-of-line marker and return a zero-length string. Instead, use multiple *Readln* calls to read successive string values.

Differences See Appendix A in the *User's Guide*, "Differences between Turbo Pascal 3.0, 4.0, and 5.0."

See also *Readln, ReadKey, Write, Writeln*

Read procedure (typed files)

Function Reads a file component into a variable.

Declaration `Read(f , v1 [, v2,...,vn ] )`

Remarks *f* is a file variable of any type except text, and each *v* is a variable of the same type as the component type of *f*. For each variable read, the current file position is advanced to the next component. It's an error to attempt to read from a file when the current file position is at the end of the file, that is, when *Eof(f)* is True.

With {$I-}, *IOResult* will return a 0 if the operation was successful; otherwise, it will return a nonzero error code.

Restrictions File must be open.

See also *Write*

ReadKey function   Crt

Function Reads a character from the keyboard.

Declaration `ReadKey`

Result type char

Chapter 16, Turbo Pascal Reference Lookup 337

ReadKey function

Remarks The character read is not echoed to the screen. If *KeyPressed* was True before the call to *ReadKey*, the character is returned immediately. Otherwise, *ReadKey* waits for a key to be typed.

The special keys on the PC keyboard generate extended scan codes. (The extended scan codes are summarized in Appendix C.) Special keys are the function keys, the cursor control keys, *Alt* keys, and so on. When a special key is pressed, *ReadKey* first returns a null character (#0), and then returns the extended scan code. Null characters cannot be generated in any other way, so you are guaranteed the next character will be an extended scan code.

The following program fragment reads a character or an extended scan code into a variable called *Ch* and sets a Boolean variable called *FuncKey* to True if the character is a special key:

```
Ch := ReadKey;
if Ch <> #0 then FuncKey := False else
begin
  FuncKey := True;
  Ch := ReadKey;
end;
```

The *CheckBreak* variable controls whether *Ctrl-Break* should abort the program or be returned like any other key. When *CheckBreak* is False, *ReadKey* returns a *Ctrl-C* (#3) for *Ctrl-Break*.

See also *KeyPressed*

Readln procedure

Function Executes the *Read* procedure then skips to the next line of the file.

Declaration Readln([**var** f: text;] v1 [, v2,...,vn])

Remarks *Readln* is an extension to *Read*, as it is defined on text files. After executing the *Read*, *Readln* skips to the beginning of the next line of the file.

Readln(f) with no parameters causes the current file position to advance to the beginning of the next line (if there is one; otherwise, it goes to the end of the file). *Readln* with no parameter list altogether corresponds to *Readln(Input)*.

With {$I-}, *IOResult* will return a 0 if the operation was successful; otherwise, it will return a nonzero error code.

Restrictions Works only on text files, including standard input. File must be open for input.

See also *Read*

Rectangle procedure   Graph

Function Draws a rectangle using the current line style and color.

Declaration `Rectangle(x1, y1, x2, y2: integer)`

Remarks *(x1, y1)* define the upper left corner of the rectangle, and *(x2, y2)* define the lower right corner (0 <= x1 < x2 <= *GetMaxX*, and 0 <= y1 < y2 <= *GetMaxY*).

The rectangle will be drawn in the current line style and color, as set by *SetLineStyle* and *SetColor*. Use *SetWriteMode* to determine whether the rectangle is copied or XOR'd to the screen.

A similar routine exists in Turbo C 2.0.

Restrictions Must be in graphics mode.

See also *Bar, Bar3D, GetViewSettings, InitGraph, SetColor, SetLineStyle, SetViewPort, SetWriteMode*

Example
```
uses Crt, Graph;
var
  GraphDriver, GraphMode: integer;
  x1, y1, x2, y2: integer;
begin
  GraphDriver := Detect;
  InitGraph(GraphDriver,GraphMode,'');
  if GraphResult<> grOk then
    Halt(1);
  Randomize;
  repeat
    x1 := Random(GetMaxX);
    y1 := Random(GetMaxY);
    x2 := Random(GetMaxX-x1) + x1;
    y2 := Random(GetMaxY-y1) + y1;
```

Chapter 16, Turbo Pascal Reference Lookup

Rectangle procedure

```
        Rectangle(x1, y1, x2, y2);
    until KeyPressed;
    CloseGraph;
end.
```

RegisterBGIdriver function   Graph

Function   Registers a user-loaded or linked-in BGI driver with the graphics system.

Declaration   `RegisterBGIdriver(driver: pointer) : integer;`

Remarks   If an error occurs, the return value is less than 0; otherwise, the internal driver number is returned. This routine enables a user to load a driver file and "register" the driver by passing its memory location to *RegisterBGIdriver*. When that driver is used by *InitGraph*, the registered driver will be used (instead of being loaded from disk by the *Graph* unit). A user-registered driver can be loaded from disk onto the heap, or converted to an .OBJ file (using BINOBJ.EXE) and linked into the .EXE.

grInvalidDriver is a possible error return, where the error code equals –4 and the driver header is not recognized.

The following program loads the CGA driver onto the heap, registers it with the graphics system, and calls *InitGraph*:

```
program LoadDriv;
uses Graph;
var
  Driver, Mode: integer;
  DriverF: file;
  DriverP: pointer;
begin
  { Open driver file, read into memory, register it }
  Assign(DriverF, 'CGA.BGI');
  Reset(DriverF, 1);
  GetMem(DriverP, FileSize(DriverF));
  BlockRead(DriverF, DriverP^, FileSIze(DriverF));
  if RegisterBGIdriver(DriverP) < 0 then
  begin
    Writeln('Error registering driver: ',
            GraphErrorMsg(GraphResult));
    Halt(1);
```

RegisterBGIdriver function

```
  end;
  { Init graphics }
  Driver := CGA;
  Mode := CGAHi;
  InitGraph(Driver, Mode, '');
  if GraphResult < 0 then
    Halt(1);
  OutText('Driver loaded by user program');
  Readln;
  CloseGraph;
end.
```

The program begins by loading the CGA driver file from disk and registering it with the *Graph* unit. Then a call is made to *InitGraph* to initialize the graphics system. You may wish to incorporate one or more driver files directly into your .EXE file. In this way, the graphics drivers that your program needs will be built-in and only the .EXE will be needed in order to run. The process for incorporating a driver file into your .EXE is straightforward:

1. Run BINOBJ on the driver file(s).
2. Link the resulting .OBJ file(s) into your program.
3. Register the linked-in driver file(s) before calling *InitGraph*.

For a detailed explanation and example of the preceding, refer to the comments at the top of the GRLINK.PAS example program on the distribution disks. For information on the BINOBJ utility, refer to Appendix C of the *User's Guide*, "Turbo Pascal Utilities."

It is also possible to register font files; refer to the description of *RegisterBGIfont*.

A similar routine exists in Turbo C 2.0.

Restrictions Note that the driver must be registered *before* the call to *InitGraph*. If a call is made to *RegisterBGIdriver* once graphics have been activated, a value of –11 (*grError*) will be returned.

See also *InitGraph, InstallUserDriver, RegisterBGIfont*

Chapter 16, Turbo Pascal Reference Lookup 341

RegisterBGIfont function   Graph

Function   Registers a user-loaded or linked-in BGI font with the graphics system.

Declaration   `RegisterBGIfont(font: pointer) : integer;`

Remarks   The return value is less than 0 if an error occurs; otherwise, the internal font number is returned. This routine enables a user to load a font file and "register" the font by passing its memory location to *RegisterBGIfont*. When that font is selected with a call to *SetTextStyle*, the registered font will be used (instead of being loaded from disk by the *Graph* unit). A user-registered font can be loaded from disk onto the heap, or converted to an .OBJ file (using BINOBJ.EXE) and linked into the .EXE.

Here are some possible error returns:

Error Code	Error Identifier	Comments
–11	grError	There is no room in the font table to register another font. (The font table holds up to 10 fonts, and only 4 are provided, so this error should not occur.)
–13	grInvalidFont	The font header is not recognized.
–14	grInvalidFontNum	The font number in the font header is not recognized.

The following program loads the triplex font onto the heap, registers it with the graphics system, and then alternates between using triplex and another stroked font that *Graph* loads from disk (*SansSerifFont*):

```
program LoadFont;
uses Graph;
var
  Driver, Mode: integer;
  FontF: file;
  FontP: pointer;
begin
```

RegisterBGIfont function

```pascal
{ Open font file, read into memory, register it }
Assign(FontF, 'TRIP.CHR');
Reset(FontF, 1);
GetMem(FontP, FileSize(FontF));
BlockRead(FontF, FontP^, FileSize(FontF));
if RegisterBGIfont(FontP) < 0 then
begin
  Writeln('Error registering font: ',
          GraphErrorMsg(GraphResult));
  Halt(1);
end;
{ Init graphics }
Driver := Detect;
InitGraph(Driver, Mode, '..\');
if GraphResult < 0 then
  Halt(1);
Readln;
{ Select registered font }
SetTextStyle(TriplexFont, HorizDir, 4);
OutText('Triplex loaded by user program');
MoveTo(0, TextHeight('a'));
Readln;
{ Select font that must be loaded from disk }
SetTextStyle(SansSerifFont, HorizDir, 4);
OutText('Your disk should be spinning...');
MoveTo(0, GetY + TextHeight('a'));
Readln;
{ Re-select registered font (already in memory) }
SetTextStyle(TriplexFont, HorizDir, 4);
OutText('Back to Triplex');
Readln;
CloseGraph;
end.
```

The program begins by loading the triplex font file from disk and registering it with the *Graph* unit. Then a call to *InitGraph* is made to initialize the graphics system. Watch the disk drive indicator and press *Enter*. Because the triplex font is already loaded into memory and registered, *Graph* does not have to load it from disk (and therefore your disk drive should not spin). Next, the program will activate the sans serif font by loading it from disk (it is unregistered). Press *Enter* again and watch the drive spin. Finally, the triplex font is selected again. Since it is in memory and already registered, the drive will not spin when you press *Enter*.

There are several reasons to load and register font files. First, *Graph* only keeps one stroked font in memory at a

RegisterBGIfont function

time. If you have a program that needs to quickly alternate between stroked fonts, you may want to load and register the fonts yourself at the beginning of your program. Then *Graph* will not load and unload the fonts each time a call to *SetTextStyle* is made.

Second, you may wish to incorporate the font files directly into your .EXE file. This way, the font files that your program needs will be built-in, and only the .EXE and driver files will be needed in order to run. The process for incorporating a font file into your .EXE is straightforward:

1. Run BINOBJ on the font file(s).
2. Link the resulting .OBJ file(s) into your program.
3. Register the linked-in font file(s) before calling *InitGraph*.

For a detailed explanation and example of the preceding, refer to the comments at the top of the GRLINK.PAS example program on the distribution disks. Documentation on the BINOBJ utility is available in Appendix C of the *User's Guide*.

Note that the default (8×8 bit-mapped) font is built into GRAPH.TPU, and thus is always in memory. Once a stroked font has been loaded, your program can alternate between the default font and the stroked font without having to reload either one of them.

It is also possible to register driver files; refer to the description of *RegisterBGIdriver*.

A similar routine exists in Turbo C 2.0.

See also   *InitGraph, InstallUserDriver, InstallUserFont, RegisterBGIfont, SetTextStyle*

Release procedure

Function   Returns the heap to a given state.

Declaration   `Release(var p: pointer)`

Remarks   *p* is a pointer variable of any pointer type that was previously assigned by the *Mark* procedure. *Release* disposes all dynamic variables that were allocated by *New* or *GetMem* since *p* was assigned by *Mark*.

Restrictions *Mark* and *Release* cannot be used interchangeably with *Dispose* and *FreeMem* unless certain rules are observed. For a complete discussion of this topic, refer to the section "The Heap Manager" on page 181.

See also *Dispose, FreeMem, GetMem, Mark, New*

Rename procedure

Function Renames an external file.

Declaration Rename(**var** f; newname: **string**)

Remarks *f* is a file variable of any file type. *newname* is a string-type expression. The external file associated with *f* is renamed to *newname*. Further operations on *f* will operate on the external file with the new name.

With {$I-}, *IOResult* will return 0 if the operation was successful; otherwise, it will return a nonzero error code.

Restrictions *Rename* must never be used on an open file.

See also *Erase*

Reset procedure

Function Opens an existing file.

Declaration Reset(**var** f [: **file**; recsize: word])

Remarks *f* is a file variable of any file type, which must have been associated with an external file using *Assign*. *recsize* is an optional expression of type word, which can only be specified if *f* is an untyped file.

Reset opens the existing external file with the name assigned to *f*. It's an error if no existing external file of the given name exists. If *f* was already open, it is first closed and then re-opened. The current file position is set to the beginning of the file.

Chapter 16, Turbo Pascal Reference Lookup

Reset procedure

If *f* was assigned an empty name, such as *Assign(f,'')*, then after the call to *Reset*, *f* will refer to the standard input file (standard handle number 0).

If *f* is a text file, *f* becomes read-only. After a call to *Reset*, *Eof(f)* is True if the file is empty; otherwise, *Eof(f)* is False.

If *f* is an untyped file, *recsize* specifies the record size to be used in data transfers. If *recsize* is omitted, a default record size of 128 bytes is assumed.

With {$I-}, *IOResult* will return a 0 if the operation was successful; otherwise, it will return a nonzero error code.

Differences　　In 3.0, an empty file name was invalid.

See also　　*Append, Assign, Close, Rewrite, Truncate*

Example
```
function FileExists(FileName: string): boolean;
{ Boolean function that returns True if the file exists;
  otherwise, it returns False. Closes the file if it exists. }
var
  f: file;
begin
  {$I-}
  Assign(f, FileName);
  Reset(f);
  Close(f);
  {$I+}
  FileExists := (IOResult = 0) and (FileName <> '');
end; { FileExists }

begin
  if FileExists(ParamStr(1)) then { Get file name from command
                                                           line }
    Writeln('File exists')
  else
    Writeln('File not found');
end.
```

RestoreCrtMode procedure　　　　　　　Graph

Function　　Restores the screen mode to its original state before graphics was initialized.

Declaration　　RestoreCrtMode

RestoreCrtMode procedure

Remarks Restores the original video mode detected by *InitGraph*. Can be used in conjunction with *SetGraphMode* to switch back and forth between text and graphics modes.

Restrictions Must be in graphics mode.

A similar routine exists in Turbo C 2.0.

See also *CloseGraph, DetectGraph, GetGraphMode, InitGraph, SetGraphMode*

Example
```
uses Graph;
var
  Gd, Gm: integer;
  Mode  : integer;
begin
  Gd := Detect;
  InitGraph(Gd, Gm, '');
  if GraphResult <> grOk then
    Halt(1);
  OutText('<ENTER> to leave graphics:');
  Readln;
  RestoreCRTMode;
  Writeln('Now in text mode');
  Write('<ENTER> to enter graphics mode:');
  Readln;
  SetGraphMode(GetGraphMode);
  OutTextXY(0, 0, 'Back in graphics mode');
  OutTextXY(0, TextHeight('H'), '<ENTER> to quit:');
  Readln;
  CloseGraph;
end.
```

Rewrite procedure

Function Creates and opens a new file.

Declaration Rewrite(**var** f [: **file**; recsize: word])

Remarks *f* is a file variable of any file type, which must have been associated with an external file using *Assign*. *recsize* is an optional expression of type word, which can only be specified if *f* is an untyped file.

Rewrite creates a new external file with the name assigned to *f*. If an external file with the same name already exists, it is deleted and a new empty file is

Rewrite procedure

created in its place. If *f* was already open, *Rewrite* closes and recreates it. The current file position is set to the beginning of the empty file.

If *f* was assigned an empty name, such as *Assign(f,'')*, then after the call to *Rewrite*, *f* will refer to the standard output file (standard handle number 1).

If *f* is a text file, *f* becomes write-only. After a call to *Rewrite*, *Eof(f)* is always True.

If *f* is an untyped file, *recsize* specifies the record size to be used in data transfers. If *recsize* is omitted, a default record size of 128 bytes is assumed.

With {$I-}, *IOResult* will return a 0 if the operation was successful; otherwise, it will return a nonzero error code.

Differences In 3.0, an empty file name was invalid.

See also *Append, Assign, Reset, Truncate*

Example
```
var f: text;
begin
  Assign(f, 'NEWFILE.$$$');
  Rewrite(f);
  Writeln(f,'Just created file with this text in it...');
  Close(f);
end.
```

RmDir procedure

Function Removes an empty subdirectory.

Declaration RmDir(s: **string**)

Remarks *s* is a string-type expression. The subdirectory with the path specified by *s* is removed. If the path does not exist, is non-empty, or is the currently logged directory, an I/O error will occur.

With {$I-}, *IOResult* will return a 0 if the operation was successful; otherwise, it will return a nonzero error code.

See also *MkDir, ChDir, GetDir*

Example
```
begin
  {$I-}
  RmDir(ParamStr(1)); { Get directory name from command line }
```

```
if IOResult <> 0 then
  Writeln('Cannot remove directory')
else
  Writeln('directory removed');
end.
```

Round function

Function	Rounds a real-type value to an integer-type value.
Declaration	`Round(x: real)`
Result type	longint
Remarks	*x* is a real-type expression. *Round* returns a longint value that is the value of *x* rounded to the nearest whole number. If *x* is exactly halfway between two whole numbers, the result is the number with the greatest absolute magnitude. A run-time error occurs if the rounded value of *x* is not within the longint range.
Differences	In 3.0, *Round* returned an integer value.
See also	*Int, Trunc*

RunError procedure

Function	Stops program execution and generates a run-time error.
Declaration	`RunError [ ( ErrorCode : word ) ]`
Remarks	The *RunError* procedure corresponds to the *Halt* procedure except that in addition to stopping the program, it generates a run-time error at the current statement. *ErrorCode* is the run-time error number (0 if omitted). If the current module is compiled with Debug Information set to On and you're running the program from the IDE, Turbo Pascal automatically takes you to the *RunError* call, just as if an ordinary run-time error had occurred.
See also	*Exit, Halt*

Sector procedure

Example

```
{$IFDEF Debug}
  if P = nil then RunError(204);
{$ENDIF}
```

Sector procedure   Graph

Function   Draws and fills an elliptical sector.

Declaration   Sector(x, y: integer; StAngle, EndAngle,
                        XRadius, YRadius: word)

Remarks   Using (*X,Y*) as the center point, *XRadius* and *YRadius* specify the horizontal and vertical radii, respectively; *Sector* draws from *StAngle* to *EndAngle*. The sector is outlined using the current color, and filled using the pattern and color defined by *SetFillStyle* or *SetFillPattern*.

A start angle of 0 and an end angle of 360 will draw and fill a complete ellipse. The angles for *Arc*, *Ellipse*, *FillEllipse*, *PieSlice*, and *Sector* are counterclockwise with 0 degrees at 3 o'clock, 90 degrees at 12 o'clock, and so on.

If an error occurs while filling the sector, *GraphResult* will return a value of –6 (*grNoScanMem*).

A similar routine exists in Turbo C 2.0.

Restrictions Must be in graphics mode.

See also   *Arc, Circle, Ellipse, FillEllipse, GetArcCoords, GetAspectRatio, PieSlice, SetFillStyle, SetFillPattern, SetGraphBufSize*

Example
```
uses
  Graph;
const
  R = 50;
var
  Driver, Mode : integer;
  Xasp, Yasp : word;
begin
  Driver := Detect;                       { Put in graphics mode }
  InitGraph(Driver, Mode, '');
  if GraphResult < 0 then
    Halt(1);
  Sector(GetMaxX div 2, GetMaxY div 2, 0, 45, R, R);
  GetAspectRatio(Xasp, Yasp);             { Draw circular sector }
```

```
            Sector(GetMaxX div 2, GetMaxY div 2,      { Center point }
                  180, 135,                      { Mirror angle above }
                  R, R * LongInt(Xasp) div Yasp);         { Circular }
    Readln;
    Closegraph;
end.
```

Seek procedure

Function	Moves the current position of a file to a specified component.
Declaration	Seek(**var** f; n: longint)
Remarks	*f* is any file variable type except text, and *n* is an expression of type longint. The current file position of *f* is moved to component number *n*. The number of the first component of a file is 0. In order to expand a file, it is possible to seek one component beyond the last component; that is, the statement *Seek(f,FileSize(f))* moves the current file position to the end of the file.
	With {$I-}, *IOResult* will return a 0 if the operation was successful; otherwise, it will return a nonzero error code.
Restrictions	Cannot be used on text files. File must be open.
Differences	In 3.0, *n* was an integer; *LongSeek* took a real number value for *n*.
See also	*FilePos*

SeekEof function

Function	Returns the end-of-file status of a file.
Declaration	SeekEof [(**var** f: text)]
Result type	boolean
Remarks	*SeekEof* corresponds to *Eof* except that it skips all blanks, tabs, and end-of-line markers before returning the end-of-file status. This is useful when reading numeric values from a text file.

SeekEof function

	With {$I-}, *IOResult* will return a 0 if the operation was successful; otherwise, it will return a nonzero error code.
Restrictions	Can only be used on text files. File must be open.
See also	*Eof, SeekEoln*

SeekEoln function

Function	Returns the end-of-line status of a file.
Declaration	SeekEoln [(**var** f: text)]
Result type	boolean
Remarks	*SeekEoln* corresponds to *Eoln* except that it skips all blanks and tabs before returning the end-of-line status. This is useful when reading numeric values from a text file.
	With {$I-}, *IOResult* will return a 0 if the operation was successful; otherwise, it will return a nonzero error code.
Restrictions	Can only be used on text files. File must be open.
See also	*Eoln, SeekEof*

Seg function

Function	Returns the segment of a specified object.
Declaration	Seg(x)
Result type	word
Remarks	*x* is any variable, or a procedure or function identifier. The result, of type word, is the segment part of the address of *x*.
See also	*Addr, Ofs*

SetActivePage procedure — Graph

Function Set the active page for graphics output.

Declaration `SetActivePage(Page: word)`

Remarks Makes *Page* the active graphics page. All graphics output will now be directed to *Page*.

Multiple pages are only supported by the EGA (256K), VGA, and Hercules graphics cards. With multiple graphics pages, a program can direct graphics output to an off-screen page, then quickly display the off-screen image by changing the visual page with the *SetVisualPage* procedure. This technique is especially useful for animation.

A similar routine exists in Turbo C 2.0.

Restrictions Must be in graphics mode.

See also *SetVisualPage*

Example
```
uses Graph;
var
  Gd, Gm: integer;
begin
  Gd := Detect;
  InitGraph(Gd, Gm, '');
  if GraphResult <> grOk then
    Halt(1);
  if (Gd=HercMono) or (Gd=EGA) or
     (Gd=EGA64) or (Gd=VGA) then
    begin
      SetVisualPage(0);
      SetActivePage(1);
      Rectangle(10, 20, 30, 40);
      SetVisualPage(1);
    end
  else
    OutText('No paging supported.');
  Readln;
  CloseGraph;
end.
```

SetAllPalette procedure   Graph

Function   Changes all palette colors as specified.

Declaration   SetAllPalette(**var** Palette)

Remarks   *Palette* is an untyped parameter. The first byte is the length of the palette. The next *n* bytes will replace the current palette colors. Each color may range from –1 to 15. A value of –1 will not change the previous entry's value.

Note that valid colors depend on the current graphics driver and current graphics mode.

If invalid input is passed to *SetAllPalette*, *GraphResult* will return a value of –11 (*grError*), and no changes to the palette settings will occur.

Changes made to the palette are seen immediately on the screen. In the example listed here, several lines are drawn on the screen, then the palette is changed. Each time a palette color is changed, all occurrences of that color on the screen will be changed to the new color value.

The following types and constants are defined:

```
const
  Black         = 0;
  Blue          = 1;
  Green         = 2;
  Cyan          = 3;
  Red           = 4;
  Magenta       = 5;
  Brown         = 6;
  LightGray     = 7;
  DarkGray      = 8;
  LightBlue     = 9;
  LightGreen    = 10;
  LightCyan     = 11;
  LightRed      = 12;
  LightMagenta  = 13;
  Yellow        = 14;
  White         = 15;
  MaxColors     = 15;
```

SetAllPalette procedure

```
type
  PaletteType = record
                  Size: byte;
                  Colors: array[0...MaxColors] of shortint;
                end;
```

A similar routine exists in Turbo C 2.0.

Restrictions Must be in graphics mode, and can only be used with EGA, EGA 64, or VGA (not the IBM 8514 or the VGA in 256-color mode).

See also *GetBkColor, GetColor, GetPalette, GraphResult, SetBkColor, SetColor, SetPalette, SetRGBPalette*

Example
```
uses Graph;
var
  Gd, Gm : integer;
  Palette: PaletteType;
begin
  Gd := Detect;
  InitGraph(Gd, Gm, '');
  if GraphResult <> grOk then
    Halt(1);
  Line(0, 0, GetMaxX, GetMaxY);
  with Palette do
  begin
    Size      := 4;
    Colors[0] := 5;
    Colors[1] := 3;
    Colors[2] := 1;
    Colors[3] := 2;
    SetAllPalette(Palette);
  end;
  Readln;
  CloseGraph;
end.
```

SetAspectRatio procedure   Graph

Function Changes the default aspect-ratio correction factor.

Declaration `SetAspectRatio(Xasp, Yasp : word)`

Result type word

Remarks *SetAspectRatio* is used to change the default aspect ratio of the current graphics mode. The aspect ratio is used to

SetAspectRatio procedure

draw round circles. If circles appear elliptical, the monitor is not aligned properly. This can be corrected in the hardware by realigning the monitor, or can be corrected in the software by changing the aspect ratio using *SetAspectRatio*. To read the current aspect ratio from the system, use *GetAspectRatio*.

A similar routine exists in Turbo C 2.0.

Restrictions Must be in graphics mode.

See also *GetAspectRatio*

Example
```
uses
  Crt, Graph;
const
  R = 50;
var
  Driver, Mode : integer;
  Xasp, Yasp : word;
begin
  DirectVideo := false;
  Driver := Detect;                    { Put in graphics mode }
  InitGraph(Driver, Mode, '');
  if GraphResult < 0 then
    Halt(1);
  GetAspectRatio(Xasp, Yasp);          { Get default aspect ratio }
  { Adjust for VGA and 8514. They have 1:1 aspect }
  if Xasp = Yasp then
    Yasp := 5 * Xasp;
  { Keep modifying aspect ratio until 1:1 or key is pressed }
  while (Xasp < Yasp) and not KeyPressed do
  begin
    SetAspectRatio(Xasp, Yasp);
    Circle(GetMaxX div 2, GetMaxY div 2, R);
    Inc(Xasp, 20);
  end;
  SetTextJustify(CenterText, CenterText);
  OutTextXY(GetMaxX div 2, GetMaxY div 2, 'Done!');
  Readln;
  Closegraph;
end.
```

SetBkColor procedure   Graph

Function Sets the current background color using the palette.

Declaration SetBkColor(ColorNum: word)

SetBkColor procedure

Remarks Background colors may range from 0 to 15, depending on the current graphics driver and current graphics mode. On a CGA, *SetBkColor* sets the flood overscan color.

SetBkColor(N) makes the *N*th color in the palette the new background color. The only exception is *SetBkColor(0)*, which always sets the background color to black.

A similar routine exists in Turbo C 2.0.

Restrictions Must be in graphics mode.

See also *GetBkColor, GetColor, GetPalette, SetAllPalette, SetColor, SetPalette, SetRGBPalette*

Example
```
uses Crt, Graph;
var
  GraphDriver, GraphMode: integer;
  Palette: PaletteType;
begin
  GraphDriver := Detect;
  InitGraph(GraphDriver,GraphMode,'');
  Randomize;
  if GraphResult <> grOk then
    Halt(1);
  GetPalette(Palette);
  repeat
    if Palette.Size <> 1 then
      SetBkColor(Random(Palette.Size));
    LineTo(Random(GetMaxX),Random(GetMaxY));
  until KeyPressed;
  CloseGraph;
end.
```

SetCBreak procedure   Dos

Function Sets the state of *Ctrl-Break* checking in DOS.

Declaration `SetCBreak(Break: boolean)`

Remarks *SetCBreak* sets the state of *Ctrl-Break* checking in DOS. When off (False), DOS only checks for *Ctrl-Break* during I/O to console, printer, or communication devices. When on (True), checks are made at every system call.

See also *GetCBreak*

SetColor procedure — Graph

Function Sets the current drawing color using the palette.

Declaration SetColor(Color: word)

Remarks *SetColor(5)* makes the fifth color in the palette the current drawing color. Drawing colors may range from 0 to 15, depending on the current graphics driver and current graphics mode.

GetMaxColor returns the highest valid color for the current driver and mode.

A similar routine exists in Turbo C 2.0.

Restrictions Must be in graphics mode.

See also *DrawPoly, GetBkColor, GetColor, GetMaxColor, GetPalette, GraphResult, SetAllPalette, SetBkColor, SetPalette, SetRGBPalette*

Example
```
uses Crt, Graph;
var
  GraphDriver, GraphMode: integer;
begin
  GraphDriver := Detect;
  InitGraph(GraphDriver, GraphMode, '');
  if GraphResult <> grOk then
    Halt(1);
  Randomize;
  repeat
    SetColor(Random(GetMaxColor)+1);
    LineTo(Random(GetMaxX),Random(GetMaxY));
  until KeyPressed;
end.
```

SetDate procedure — Dos

Function Sets the current date in the operating system.

Declaration SetDate(Year, Month, Day : word)

Remarks Valid parameter ranges are *Year* 1980..2099, *Month* 1..12, and *Day* 1..31. If the date is invalid, the request is ignored.

SetFAttr procedure   Dos

Function   Sets the attributes of a file.

Declaration   SetFAttr(**var** f; Attr: word)

Remarks   *f* must be a file variable (typed, untyped, or text file) that has been assigned but not opened. The attribute value is formed by adding the appropriate attribute masks defined as constants in the *Dos* unit.

```
const
  ReadOnly  = $01;
  Hidden    = $02;
  SysFile   = $04;
  VolumeID  = $08;
  Directory = $10;
  Archive   = $20;
```

Errors are reported in *DosError*; possible error codes are 3 (Invalid Path) and 5 (File Access Denied).

Restrictions   *f* cannot be open.

See also   *GetFAttr, GetFTime, SetFTime*

Example
```
uses Dos;
var
  f: file;
begin
  Assign(f, 'C:\AUTOEXEC.BAT');
  SetFAttr(f, Hidden);                    {Uh-oh}
  Readln;
  SetFAttr(f, Archive);                   { Whew!}
end.
```

SetFillPattern procedure   Graph

Function   Selects a user-defined fill pattern.

Declaration   SetFillPattern(Pattern: FillPatternType; Color: word)

SetFillPattern procedure

Remarks Sets the pattern and color for all filling done by *FillPoly, FloodFill, Bar, Bar3D,* and *PieSlice* to the bit pattern specified in *Pattern* and the color specified by *Color*. If invalid input is passed to *SetFillPattern, GraphResult* will return a value of −11 (*grError*), and the current fill settings will be unchanged. *FillPatternType* is predefined as follows:

```
type
  FillPatternType = array[1..8] of byte;
```

The fill pattern is based on the underlying byte values contained in the *Pattern* array. The pattern array is 8 bytes long with each byte corresponding to 8 pixels in the pattern. Whenever a bit in a pattern byte is valued at 1, a pixel will be plotted. For example, the following pattern represents a checkerboard (50 % gray scale):

Binary		Hex	
10101010	=	$AA	(1st byte)
01010101	=	$55	(2nd byte)
10101010	=	$AA	(3rd byte)
01010101	=	$55	(4th byte)
10101010	=	$AA	(5th byte)
01010101	=	$55	(6th byte)
10101010	=	$AA	(7th byte)
01010101	=	$55	(8th byte)

User-defined fill patterns enable you to create patterns different from the predefined fill patterns that can be selected with the *SetFillStyle* procedure. Whenever you select a new fill pattern with *SetFillPattern* or *SetFillStyle*, all fill operations will use that fill pattern. Calling *SetFillStyle (UserField, SomeColor)* will always select the user-defined pattern. This lets you define and use a new pattern using *SetFillPattern*, then switch between your pattern and the built-ins by making calls to *SetTextStyle*.

A similar routine exists in Turbo C 2.0.

Restrictions Must be in graphics mode.

See also *Bar, Bar3D, FillPoly, GetFillPattern, GetFillSettings, GraphResult, PieSlice*

SetFillStyle procedure

Example

```
uses Graph;
const
  Gray50: FillPatternType = ($AA,$55,$AA,$55,
                             $AA,$55,$AA,$55);
var
  Gd, Gm: integer;
begin
  Gd := Detect;
  InitGraph(Gd, Gm, '');
  if GraphResult <> grOk then
    Halt(1);
  SetFillPattern(Gray50, White);
  Bar(0, 0, 100, 100);      { Draw a bar in a 50% gray scale }
  Readln;
  CloseGraph;
end.
```

SetFillStyle procedure   Graph

Function   Sets the fill pattern and color.

Declaration   SetFillStyle(Pattern: word; Color: word)

Remarks   Sets the pattern and color for all filling done by *FillPoly*, *Bar*, *Bar3D*, and *PieSlice*. A variety of fill patterns are available. The default pattern is solid, and the default color is the maximum color in the palette. If invalid input is passed to *SetFillStyle*, *GraphResult* will return a value of –11 (*grError*), and the current fill settings will be unchanged. The following constants are defined:

```
const
  { Fill patterns for Get/SetFillStyle: }
  EmptyFill      = 0;       { Fills area in background color }
  SolidFill      = 1;       { Fills area in solid fill color }
  LineFill       = 2;                           { --- fill }
  LtSlashFill    = 3;                           { /// fill }
  SlashFill      = 4;          { /// fill with thick lines }
  BkSlashFill    = 5;          { \\\ fill with thick lines }
  LtBkSlashFill  = 6;                           { \\\ fill }
  HatchFill      = 7;                    { Light hatch fill }
  XHatchFill     = 8;              { Heavy cross hatch fill }
  InterleaveFill = 9;              { Interleaving line fill }
  WideDotFill    = 10;            { Widely spaced dot fill }
  CloseDotFill   = 11;            { Closely spaced dot fill }
  UserFill       = 12;                  { User-defined fill }
```

SetFillStyle procedure

If *Pattern* equals *UserFill*, the user-defined pattern (set by a call to *SetFillPattern*) becomes the active pattern.

A similar routine exists in Turbo C 2.0.

Restrictions Must be in graphics mode.

See also *Bar, Bar3D, FillPoly, GetFillSettings, PieSlice, GetMaxColor, GraphResult*

Example
```
uses Graph;
var
  Gm, Gd : integer;
begin
  Gd := Detect;
  InitGraph(Gd, Gm, '');
  SetFillStyle(SolidFill,0);
  Bar(0, 0, 50, 50);
  SetFillStyle(XHatchFill,1);
  Bar(60, 0, 110, 50);
  Readln;
  CloseGraph;
end.
```

SetFTime procedure   Dos

Function Sets the date and time a file was last written.

Declaration `SetFTime(var f; Time: longint)`

Remarks *f* must be a file variable (typed, untyped, or text file) that has been assigned and opened. The *Time* parameter can be created through a call to *PackTime*. Errors are reported in *DosError*; the only possible error code is 6 (Invalid File Handle).

Restrictions *f* must be open.

See also *GetFTime, PackTime, SetFAttr, UnpackTime*

SetGraphBufSize procedure   Graph

Function Allows you to change the size of the buffer used for scan and flood fills.

Declaration `SetGraphBufSize(BufSize: word);`

SetGraphBufSize procedure

Remarks	The internal buffer size is set to *BufSize*, and a buffer is allocated on the heap when a call is made to *InitGraph*.

The default buffer size is 4K, which is large enough to fill a polygon with about 650 vertices. Under rare circumstances, enlarging the buffer may be necessary in order to avoid a buffer overflow.

A similar routine exists in Turbo C 2.0. |
| **Restrictions** | Note that once a call to *InitGraph* has been made, calls to *SetGraphBufSize* are ignored. |
| **See also** | *FloodFill, FillPoly, InitGraph* |

SetGraphMode procedure — Graph

Function	Sets the system to graphics mode and clears the screen.
Declaration	`SetGraphMode(Mode: integer)`
Remarks	*Mode* must be a valid mode for the current device driver. *SetGraphMode* is used to select a graphics mode different than the default one set by *InitGraph*.

SetGraphMode can also be used in conjunction with *RestoreCrtMode* to switch back and forth between text and graphics modes.

SetGraphMode resets all graphics settings to their defaults (current pointer, palette, color, viewport, and so forth).

GetModeRange returns the lowest and highest valid modes for the current driver.

If an attempt is made to select an invalid mode for the current device driver, *GraphResult* will return a value of –10 (*grInvalidMode*). |

Chapter 16, Turbo Pascal Reference Lookup   363

SetGraphMode procedure

The following constants are defined:

Graphics Driver	Graphics Modes	Value	Column x Row	Palette	Pages
CGA	CGAC0	0	320x200	C0	1
	CGAC1	1	320x200	C1	1
	CGAC2	2	320x200	C2	1
	CGAC3	3	320x200	C3	1
	CGAHi	4	640x200	2 color	1
MCGA	MCGAC0	0	320x200	C0	1
	MCGAC1	1	320x200	C1	1
	MCGAC2	2	320x200	C2	1
	MCGAC3	3	320x200	C3	1
	MCGAMed	4	640x200	2 color	1
	MCGAHi	5	640x480	2 color	1
EGA	EGALo	0	640x200	16 color	4
	EGAHi	1	640x350	16 color	2
EGA64	EGA64Lo	0	640x200	16 color	1
	EGA64Hi	1	640x350	4 color	1
EGA-MONO	EGAMonoHi	3	640x350	2 color	1*
MONO	EGAMonoHi	3	640x350	2 color	2**
HERC	HercMonoHi	0	720x348	2 color	2
ATT400	ATT400C0	0	320x200	C0	1
	ATT400C1	1	320x200	C1	1
	ATT400C2	2	320x200	C2	1
	ATT400C3	3	320x200	C3	1
	ATT400Med	4	640x200	2 color	1
	ATT400Hi	5	640x400	2 color	1
VGA	VGALo	0	640x200	16 color	2
	VGAMed	1	640x350	16 color	2
	VGAHi	2	640x480	16 color	1
PC3270	PC3270Hi	0	720x350	2 color	1
8514	IBM8514Lo	0	640x480	256 color	1
8514	IBM8514Hi	0	1024x768	256 color	1

* 64K on EGAMono card
** 256K on EGAMono card

A similar routine exists in Turbo C 2.0.

Restrictions   A successful call to *InitGraph* must have been made before calling this routine.

See also ClearDevice, CloseGraph, DetectGraph, GetGraphMode, InitGraph, RestoreCrtMode, GraphResult, GetModeRange

Example
```
uses Graph;
var
  GraphDriver: integer;
  GraphMode   : integer;
  LowMode     : integer;
  HighMode    : integer;
begin
  GraphDriver := Detect;
  InitGraph(GraphDriver, GraphMode, '');
  if GraphResult <> grOk then
    Halt(1);
  GetModeRange(GraphDriver, LowMode, HighMode);
  SetGraphMode(LowMode);         { Select low-resolution mode }
  Line(0, 0, GetMaxX, GetMaxY);
  Readln;
  CloseGraph;
end.
```

SetIntVec procedure   Dos

Function Sets a specified interrupt vector to a specified address.

Declaration SetIntVec(IntNo: byte; Vector: pointer)

Remarks *IntNo* specifies the interrupt vector number (0..255), and *Vector* specifies the address. *Vector* is often constructed with the @ operator to produce the address of an interrupt procedure. Assuming *Int1BSave* is a variable of type pointer, and *Int1BHandler* is an interrupt procedure identifier, the following statement sequence installs a new interrupt $1B handler and later restores the original handler:

```
GetIntVec($1B,Int1BSave);
SetIntVec($1B,@Int1BHandler);
 :
 :
SetIntVec($1B,Int1BSave);
```

See also *GetIntVec*

SetLineStyle procedure — Graph

Function Sets the current line width and style.

Declaration `SetLineStyle(LineStyle: word; Pattern: word; Thickness: word)`

Remarks Affects all lines drawn by *Line*, *LineTo*, *Rectangle*, *DrawPoly*, *Arc*, and so on. Lines can be drawn solid, dotted, centerline, or dashed. If invalid input is passed to *SetLineStyle*, *GraphResult* will return a value of −11 (*grError*), and the current line settings will be unchanged. The following constants are declared:

```
const
  SolidLn    = 0;
  DottedLn   = 1;
  CenterLn   = 2;
  DashedLn   = 3;
  UserBitLn  = 4;          { User-defined line style }
  NormWidth  = 1;
  ThickWidth = 3;
```

LineStyle is a value from *SolidLn* to *UserBitLn*(0..4), *Pattern* is ignored unless *LineStyle* equals *UserBitLn*, and *Thickness* is *NormWidth* or *ThickWidth*. When *LineStyle* equals *UserBitLn*, the line is output using the 16-bit pattern defined by the *Pattern* parameter. For example, if *Pattern* = $AAAA, then the 16-bit pattern looks like this:

```
1010101010101010                                    { NormWidth }

1010101010101010                                    { ThickWidth }
1010101010101010
1010101010101010
```

A similar routine exists in Turbo C 2.0.

Restrictions Must be in graphics mode.

See also *DrawPoly, GetLineSettings, Line, LineRel, LineTo, GraphResult, SetWriteMode*

Example
```
uses Graph;
var
  Gd, Gm: integer;
  x1, y1, x2, y2: integer;
begin
  Gd := Detect;
  InitGraph(Gd, Gm, '');
  if GraphResult <> grOk then
    Halt(1);
```

```
        x1 := 10;
        y1 := 10;
        x2 := 200;
        y2 := 150;
        SetLineStyle(DottedLn, 0, NormWidth);
        Rectangle(x1, y1, x2, y2);
        SetLineStyle(UserBitLn, $C3, ThickWidth);
        Rectangle(Pred(x1), Pred(y1), Succ(x2), Succ(y2));
        Readln;
        CloseGraph;
    end.
```

SetPalette procedure   Graph

Function   Changes one palette color as specified by *ColorNum* and *Color*.

Declaration   `SetPalette(ColorNum: word; Color: shortint)`

Remarks   Changes the *ColorNum* entry in the palette to *Color*. *SetPalette(0,LightCyan)* makes the first color in the palette light cyan. *ColorNum* may range from 0 to 15, depending on the current graphics driver and current graphics mode. If invalid input is passed to *SetPalette*, *GraphResult* will return a value of –11 (*grError*), and the palette will be unchanged.

Changes made to the palette are seen immediately on the screen. In the example here, several lines are drawn on the screen, then the palette is changed randomly. Each time a palette color is changed, all occurrences of that color on the screen will be changed to the new color value.

The following constants are defined:

```
const
    Black     = 0;
    Blue      = 1;
    Green     = 2;
    Cyan      = 3;
    Red       = 4;
    Magenta   = 5;
    Brown     = 6;
    LightGray = 7;
    DarkGray  = 8;
    LightBlue = 9;
```

SetPalette procedure

```
         LightGreen   = 10;
         LightCyan    = 11;
         LightRed     = 12;
         LightMagenta = 13;
         Yellow       = 14;
         White        = 15;
```

A similar routine exists in Turbo C 2.0.

Restrictions Must be in graphics mode, and can only be used with EGA, EGA 64, or VGA (not the IBM 8514 or the VGA in 256-color mode).

See also *GetBkColor, GetColor, GetPalette, GraphResult, SetAllPalette, SetBkColor, SetColor, SetRGBPalette*

Example

```pascal
uses Crt, Graph;
var
  GraphDriver, GraphMode: integer;
  Color: word;
  Palette: PaletteType;
begin
  GraphDriver := Detect;
  InitGraph(GraphDriver, GraphMode, '');
  if GraphResult <> grOk then
    Halt(1);
  GetPalette(Palette);
  if Palette.Size <> 1 then
    begin
      for Color := 0 to Pred(Palette.Size) do
        begin
          SetColor(Color);
          Line(0, Color*5, 100, Color*5);
        end;
      Randomize;
      repeat
        SetPalette(Random(Palette.Size),Random(Palette.Size));
      until KeyPressed;
    end
  else
    Line(0, 0, 100, 0);
  Readln;
  CloseGraph;
end.
```

SetRGBPalette procedure — Graph

Function Modifies palette entries for the IBM 8514 and VGA drivers.

Declaration SetRGBPalette(ColorNum, RedValue,
                      GreenValue, BlueValue: integer)

Remarks *ColorNum* defines the palette entry to be loaded, while *RedValue*, *GreenValue*, and *BlueValue* define the component colors of the palette entry.

For the IBM 8514 display, *ColorNum* is in the range 0..255. For the VGA in 256K color mode, *ColorNum* is the range 0..15. Only the lower byte of *RedValue*, *GreenValue* or *BlueValue* is used, and out of this byte, only the 6 most-significant bits are loaded in the palette.

Note: For compatibility with other IBM graphics adapters, the BGI driver defines the first 16 palette entries of the IBM 8514 to the default colors of the EGA/VGA. These values can be used as is, or they can be changed by using *SetRGBPalette*.

A similar routine exists in Turbo C 2.0.

Restrictions *SetRGBPalette* can only be used with the IBM 8514 driver and the VGA.

See also *GetBkColor, GetColor, GetPalette, GraphResult, SetAllPalette, SetBkColor, SetColor, SetPalette*

Example
```
uses
  Graph;
type
  RGBRec = record
    RedVal, GreenVal, BlueVal : integer;
  end;
const
  EGAColors : array[0..MaxColors] of RGBRec =
    (                                             {NAME      COLOR}
    (RedVal:$00;GreenVal:$00;BlueVal:$00),{Black    EGA  0}
    (RedVal:$00;GreenVal:$00;BlueVal:$FC),{Blue     EGA  1}
    (RedVal:$24;GreenVal:$fc;BlueVal:$24),{Green    EGA  2}
    (RedVal:$00;GreenVal:$fc;BlueVal:$FC),{Cyan     EGA  3}
    (RedVal:$FC;GreenVal:$14;BlueVal:$14),{Red      EGA  4}
    (RedVal:$B0;GreenVal:$00;BlueVal:$FC),{Magenta  EGA  5}
    (RedVal:$70;GreenVal:$48;BlueVal:$00),{Brown    EGA 20}
    (RedVal:$C4;GreenVal:$C4;BlueVal:$C4),{White    EGA  7}
    (RedVal:$34;GreenVal:$34;BlueVal:$34),{Gray     EGA 56}
```

SetRGBPalette procedure

```
                   (RedVal:$00;GreenVal:$00;BlueVal:$70),(Lt Blue     EGA 57)
                   (RedVal:$00;GreenVal:$70;BlueVal:$00),(Lt Green    EGA 58)
                   (RedVal:$00;GreenVal:$70;BlueVal:$70),(Lt Cyan     EGA 59)
                   (RedVal:$70;GreenVal:$00;BlueVal:$00),(Lt Red      EGA 60)
                   (RedVal:$70;GreenVal:$00;BlueVal:$70),(Lt Magenta EGA 61)
                   (RedVal:$FC;GreenVal:$fc;BlueVal:$24),(Yellow      EGA 62)
                   (RedVal:$FC;GreenVal:$fc;BlueVal:$FC) (Br. White  EGA 63)
                   );
               var
                 Driver, Mode,
                 i : integer;
               begin
                 Driver := IBM8514;                    { Override detection }
                 Mode := IBM8514Hi;
                 InitGraph(Driver, Mode, '');          { Put in graphics mode }
                 if GraphResult < 0 then
                   Halt(1);
                 { Zero palette, make all graphics output invisible }
                 for i := 0 to MaxColors do
                   with EGAColors[i] do
                     SetRGBPalette(i, 0, 0, 0);
                 { Display something }
                 { Change 1st 16 8514 palette entries }
                 for i := 1 to MaxColors do
                 begin
                   SetColor(i);
                   OutTextXY(10, i * 10, ' ..Press any key.. ');
                 end;
                 { Restore default EGA colors to 8514 palette }
                 for i := 0 to MaxColors do
                   with EGAColors[i] do
                     SetRGBPalette(i, RedVal, GreenVal, BlueVal);
                 Readln;
                 Closegraph;
               end.
```

SetTextBuf procedure

Function   Assigns an I/O buffer to a text file.

Declaration   `SetTextBuf(var f: text; var buf [ ; size: word ] )`

Remarks   *f* is a text-file variable, *buf* is any variable, and *Size* is an optional expression of type word.

Each text-file variable has an internal 128-byte buffer that, by default, is used to buffer *Read* and *Write*

SetTextBuf procedure

operations. This buffer is adequate for most applications. However, heavily I/O-bound programs, such as applications that copy or convert text files, will benefit from a larger buffer, because it reduces disk head movement and file system overhead.

SetTextBuf changes the text file *f* to use the buffer specified by *buf* instead of *f*'s internal buffer. *Size* specifies the size of the buffer in bytes. If *Size* is omitted, *SizeOf(buf)* is assumed; that is, by default, the entire memory region occupied by *buf* is used as a buffer. The new buffer remains in effect until *f* is next passed to *Assign*.

Restrictions *SetTextBuf* should never be applied to an open file, although it can be called immediately after *Reset*, *Rewrite*, and *Append*. Calling *SetTextBuf* on an open file once I/O operations has taken place can cause loss of data because of the change of buffer.

Turbo Pascal doesn't ensure that the buffer exists for the entire duration of I/O operations on the file. In particular, a common error is to install a local variable as a buffer, and then use the file outside the procedure that declared the buffer.

Differences Alternative to 3.0's syntax: **var** `f:text[2048]`.

Example
```
var
  f  : text;
  ch : char;
  buf: array[1..10240] of char;           { 10K buffer }
begin
  { Get file to read from command line }
  Assign(f, ParamStr(1));
  { Bigger buffer for faster reads }
  SetTextBuf(f, buf);
  Reset(f);
  { Dump text file onto screen }
  while not Eof(f) do
  begin
    Read(f, ch);
    Write(ch);
  end;
end.
```

Chapter 16, Turbo Pascal Reference Lookup

SetTextJustify procedure · Graph

Function Sets text justification values used by *OutText* and *OutTextXY*.

Declaration `SetTextJustify(Horiz, Vert: word)`

Remarks Text output after a *SetTextJustify* will be justified around the current pointer in the manner specified. Given the following:

```
SetTextJustify(CenterText, CenterText);
OutTextXY(100, 100, 'ABC');
```

The point(100,100) will appear in the middle of the letter B. The default justification settings can be restored by *SetTextJustify(LeftText, TopText)*. If invalid input is passed to *SetTextJustify*, *GraphResult* will return a value of –11 (*grError*), and the current text justification settings will be unchanged.

The following constants are defined:

```
const
  { Horizontal justification }
  LeftText   = 0;
  CenterText = 1;
  RightText  = 2;
  { Vertical justification }
  BottomText = 0;
  CenterText = 1;                    { Not declared twice }
  TopText    = 2;
```

A similar routine exists in Turbo C 2.0.

Restrictions Must be in graphics mode.

See also *GetTextSettings, GraphResult, OutText, OutTextXY, SetLineStyle, SetUserCharSize, TextHeight, TextWidth*

Example
```
uses Graph;
var
  Gd, Gm: integer;
begin
  Gd := Detect;
  InitGraph(Gd, Gm, '');
  if GraphResult <> grOk then
    Halt(1);
  { Center text onscreen }
  SetTextJustify(CenterText, CenterText);
```

```
      OutTextXY(Succ(GetMaxX)
        div 2, Succ(GetMaxY)
        div 2, 'Easily Centered');
      Readln;
      CloseGraph;
    end.
```

SetTextStyle procedure   Graph

Function   Sets the current text font, style, and character magnification factor.

Declaration   `SetTextStyle(Font: word; Direction: word; CharSize: word)`

Remarks   Affects all text output by *OutText* and *OutTextXY*. One 8×8 bit-mapped font and several "stroked" fonts are available. Font directions supported are normal (left to right) and vertical (90 degrees to normal text, starts at the bottom and goes up). The size of each character can be magnified using the *CharSize* factor. A *CharSize* value of one will display the 8×8 bit-mapped font in an 8×8 pixel rectangle on the screen, a *CharSize* value equal to 2 will display the 8×8 bit-mapped font in a 16×16 pixel rectangle and so on (up to a limit of 10 times the normal size). Always use *TextHeight* and *TextWidth* to determine the actual dimensions of the text.

The normal size values for text are 1 for the default font and 4 for a stroked font. These are the values that should be passed as the *CharSize* parameter to *SetTextStyle*. *SetUserCharSize* can be used to customize the dimensions of stroked font text.

Normally, stroked fonts are loaded from disk onto the heap when a call is made to *SetTextStyle*. However, you can load the fonts yourself or link them directly to your .EXE file. In either case, use *RegisterBGIfont* to register the font with the *Graph* unit.

When "stroked" fonts are loaded from disk, errors can occur when trying to load them. If an error occurs, *GraphResult* will return one of the following values:

  –8   Font file not found
  –9   Not enough memory to load the font selected
  –11 Graphics error

SetTextStyle procedure

```
        -12     Graphics I/O error
        -13     Invalid font file
        -14     Invalid font number
```

The following type and constants are declared:

```
const
  DefaultFont    = 0;                     { 8x8 bit mapped font }
  TriplexFont    = 1;                           { "Stroked" fonts }
  SmallFont      = 2;
  SansSerifFont  = 3;
  GothicFont     = 4;

  HorizDir       = 0;                               { Left to right }
  VertDir        = 1;                               { Bottom to top }
```

A similar routine exists in Turbo C 2.0.

Restrictions Must be in graphics mode.

See also *GetTextSettings, GraphResult, OutText, OutTextXY, RegisterBGIfont, SetTextJustify, SetUserCharSize, TextHeight, TextWidth*

Example
```
uses Graph;
var
  Gd, Gm : integer;
  Y, Size: integer;
begin
  Gd := Detect;
  InitGraph(Gd, Gm, '');
  if GraphResult <> grOk then
    Halt(1);
  Y := 0;
  for Size := 1 to 4 do
  begin
    SetTextStyle(DefaultFont, HorizDir, Size);
    OutTextXY(0, Y, 'Size = ' + Chr(Size+48));
    Inc(Y, TextHeight('H') + 1);
  end;
  Readln;
  CloseGraph;
end.
```

SetTime procedure   Dos

Function Sets the current time in the operating system.

Declaration `SetTime(Hour, Minute, Second, Sec100: word)`

Remarks	Valid parameter ranges are *Hour* 0..23, *Minute* 0..59, *Second* 0..59, and *Sec*100 (hundredths of seconds) 0-99. If the time is not valid, the request is ignored.
See also	*GetDate, GetTime, PackTime, SetDate, UnpackTime*

SetUserCharSize procedure — Graph

Function	Allows the user to vary the character width and height for stroked fonts.
Declaration	`SetUserCharSize(MultX, DivX, MultY, DivY: word)`
Remarks	*MultX:DivX* is the ratio multiplied by the normal width for the active font; *MultY:DivY* is the ratio multiplied by the normal height for the active font. In order to make text twice as wide, for example, use a *MultX* value of 2, and set *DivX* equal to 1 (2 **div** 1 = 2).
	You don't have to call *SetTextStyle* immediately after calling *SetUserCharSize* to make that character size take effect. Calling *SetUserCharSize* sets the current character size to the values given.
	A similar routine exists in Turbo C 2.0.
Restrictions	Must be in graphics mode.
See also	*SetTextStyle, OutText, OutTextXY, TextHeight, TextWidth*
Example	The following program shows how to change the height and width of text:

```
uses Graph;
var
  Driver, Mode : integer;
begin
  Driver := Detect;
  InitGraph(Driver, Mode, '');
  if GraphResult <> grOK then
    Halt(1);
  { Showoff }
  SetTextStyle(TriplexFont, Horizdir, 4);
  OutText('Norm');
  SetUserCharSize(1, 3, 1, 1);
    OutText('Short ');
  SetUserCharSize(3, 1, 1, 1);
  OutText('Wide');
```

```
         Readln;
         CloseGraph;
     end.
```

SetVerify procedure   Dos

Function   Sets the state of the verify flag in DOS.

Declaration   `SetVerify(Verify: boolean)`

Remarks   *SetVerify* sets the state of the verify flag in DOS. When off (False), disk writes are not verified. When on (True), all disk writes are verified to ensure proper writing.

See also   *GetVerify*

SetViewPort procedure   Graph

Function   Sets the current output viewport or window for graphics output.

Declaration   `SetViewPort(x1, y1, x2, y2: integer; Clip: boolean)`

Remarks   *(x1, y1)* define the upper left corner of the viewport, and *(x2, y2)* define the lower right corner (0 <= x1 < x2 and 0 <= y1 < y2). The upper left corner of a viewport is (0,0).

The Boolean variable *Clip* determines whether drawings are clipped at the current viewport boundaries. *SetViewPort(0, 0, GetMaxX, GetMaxY, True)* always sets the viewport to the entire graphics screen. If invalid input is parsed to *SetViewPort*, *GraphResult* will return –11 *(grError)*, and the current view settings will be unchanged. The following constants are defined:

```
const
   ClipOn  = True;
   ClipOff = False;
```

All graphics commands (for example, *GetX*, *OutText*, *Rectangle*, *MoveTo*, and so on) are viewport-relative. In the example, note that *MoveTo* moves the current pointer to (5,5) *inside* the viewport (the absolute coordinates would be (15,25)).

SetViewPort procedure

```
(0,0)                    (GetMaxX,0)




              ┌───┐
              │ · │
              └───┘



(0,Get MaxY)            (GetMaxX, GetMaxY)
```

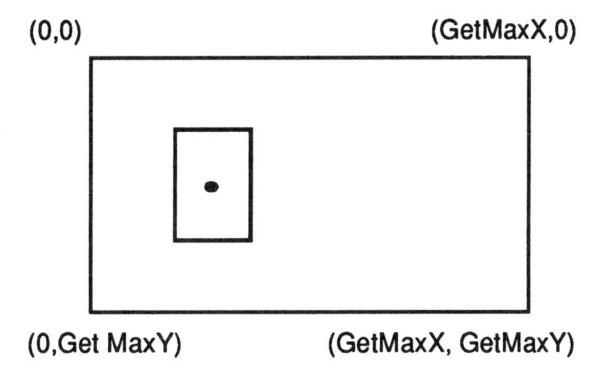

If the Boolean variable *Clip* is set to True when a call to *SetViewPort* is made, all drawings will be clipped to the current viewport. Note that the "current pointer" is never clipped. The following will not draw the complete line requested because the line will be clipped to the current viewport:

```
SetViewPort(10, 10, 20, 20, ClipOn);
Line(0, 5, 15, 5);
```

The line would start at absolute coordinates (10,15) and terminate at absolute coordinates (25,15) if no clipping was performed. But since clipping was performed, the actual line that would be drawn would start at absolute coordinates (10,15) and terminate at coordinates (20,15).

InitGraph, GraphDefaults, and *SetGraphMode* all reset the viewport to the entire graphics screen. The current viewport settings are available by calling the procedure *GetViewSettings,* which accepts a parameter of the following global type:

```
type
  ViewPortType = record
                   x1, y1, x2, y2: integer;
                   Clip: boolean;
                 end;
```

SetViewPort moves the current pointer to (0,0).

A similar routine exists in Turbo C 2.0.

Restrictions   Must be in graphics mode.

See also   *ClearViewPort, GetViewSettings, GraphResult*

Chapter 16, Turbo Pascal Reference Lookup   377

SetViewPort procedure

Example
```
uses Graph;
var
  Gd, Gm: integer;
begin
  Gd := Detect;
  InitGraph(Gd, Gm, '');
  if GraphResult <> grOk then
    Halt(1);
  if (Gd = HercMono)
    or (Gd = EGA) or (Gd = EGA64) or (Gd = VGA) then
    begin
      SetVisualPage(0);
      SetActivePage(1);
      Rectangle(10, 20, 30, 40);
      SetVisualPage(1);
    end
  else
    OutText('No paging supported.');
  Readln;
  CloseGraph;
end.
```

SetVisualPage procedure Graph

Function Sets the visual graphics page number.

Declaration SetVisualPage(Page: word)

Remarks Makes *Page* the visual graphics page.

Multiple pages are only supported by the EGA (256K), VGA, and Hercules graphics cards. With multiple graphics pages, a program can direct graphics output to an off-screen page, then quickly display the off-screen image by changing the visual page with the *SetVisualPage* procedure. This technique is especially useful for animation.

A similar routine exists in Turbo C 2.0.

Restrictions Must be in graphics mode.

See also *SetActivePage*

Example
```
uses Graph;
var
  Gd, Gm: integer;
begin
  Gd := Detect;
```

```
      InitGraph(Gd, Gm, '');
      if GraphResult <> grOk then
        Halt(1);
      if (Gd = HercMono)
        or (Gd = EGA) or (Gd = EGA64) or (Gd = VGA) then
      begin
        SetVisualPage(0);
        SetActivePage(1);
        Rectangle(10, 20, 30, 40);
        SetVisualPage(1);
      end
      else
        OutText('No paging supported.');
      Readln;
      CloseGraph;
    end.
```

SetWriteMode procedure   Graph

Function   Sets the writing mode for line drawing.

Declaration   SetWriteMode(WriteMode : integer)

Remarks   The following constants are defined:

```
const
  CopyPut = 0;     { MOV }
  XORPut  = 1;     { XOR }
```

Each constant corresponds to a binary operation between each byte in the line and the corresponding bytes on the screen. *CopyPut* uses the assembly language **MOV** instruction, overwriting with the line whatever is on the screen. *XORPut* uses the **XOR** command to combine the line with the screen. Two successive **XOR** commands will erase the line and restore the screen to its original appearance.

Note: *SetWriteMode* only affects calls to the following routines: *DrawPoly, Line, LineRel, LineTo,* and *Rectangle* .

A similar routine exists in Turbo C 2.0.

See also   *Line, LineTo, PutImage, SetLineStyle*

Example
```
uses
  Crt, Graph;
var
  Driver, Mode,
```

SetWriteMode procedure

```
            i : integer;
            x1, y1, dx, dy : integer;
            FillInfo : FillSettingsType;
          begin
            DirectVideo := false;              { Turn off screen write }
            Randomize;
            Driver := Detect;                  { Put in graphics mode }
            InitGraph(Driver, Mode, '');
            if GraphResult < 0 then
              Halt(1);
            { Fill screen with background pattern }
            GetFillSettings(FillInfo);         { Get current settings }
            SetFillStyle(WideDotFill, FillInfo.Color);
            Bar(0, 0, GetMaxX, GetMaxY);
            dx := GetMaxX div 4;      { Determine rectangle's dimensions }
            dy := GetMaxY div 4;
            SetLineStyle(SolidLn, 0, ThickWidth);
            SetWriteMode(XORput);              { XOR mode for rectangle }
            repeat                        { Draw until a key is pressed }
              x1 := Random(GetMaxX - dx);
              y1 := Random(GetMaxY - dy);
              Rectangle(x1, y1, x1 + dx, y1 + dy);           { Draw it }
              Delay(10);                               { Pause briefly }
              Rectangle(x1, y1, x1 + dx, y1 + dy);          { Erase it }
            until KeyPressed;
            Readln;
            Closegraph;
          end.
```

Sin function

Function	Returns the sine of the argument.
Declaration	Sin(x: real)
Result type	real
Remarks	x is a real-type expression. The result is the sine of x. x is assumed to represent an angle in radians.
See also	*ArcTan, Cos*
Example	```var
r: real;
begin
r := Sin(Pi);
end.```

SizeOf function

Function	Returns the number of bytes occupied by the argument.
Declaration	SizeOf(x)
Result type	word
Remarks	*x* is either a variable reference or a type identifier. *SizeOf* returns the number of bytes of memory occupied by *x*.

SizeOf should always be used when passing values to *FillChar, Move, GetMem,* and so on:

```
FillChar(s, SizeOf(s), 0);
GetMem(p, SizeOf(RecordType));
```

Example

```
type
  CustRec = record
              Name  : string[30];
              Phone : string[14];
            end;
var
  p: ^CustRec;
begin
  GetMem(p, SizeOf(CustRec));
end.
```

Sound procedure   Crt

Function	Starts the internal speaker.
Declaration	Sound(Hz: word)
Remarks	*Hz* specifies the frequency of the emitted sound in hertz. The speaker continues until explicitly turned off by a call to *NoSound*.
See also	*NoSound*

Example

```
uses Crt;
begin
  Sound(220);                              { Beep }
  Delay(200);                              { Pause }
  NoSound;                                 { Relief! }
end.
```

SPtr function

Function	Returns the current value of the SP register.
Declaration	SPtr
Result type	word
Remarks	The result, of type word, is the offset of the stack pointer within the stack segment.
See also	SSeg

Sqr function

Function	Returns the square of the argument.
Declaration	Sqr(x)
Result type	Same type as parameter.
Remarks	x is an integer-type or real-type expression. The result, of the same type as x, is the square of x, or $x * x$.

Sqrt function

Function	Returns the square root of the argument.
Declaration	Sqrt(x: real)
Result type	real
Remarks	x is a real-type expression. The result is the square root of x.

SSeg function

Function	Returns the current value of the SS register.
Declaration	SSeg
Result type	word

Str procedure

Function	Converts a numeric value to its string representation.
Declaration	Str(x [: width [: decimals]]; **var** s: **string**)
Remarks	*x* is an integer-type or real-type expression. *width* and *decimals* are integer-type expressions. *s* is a string-type variable. *Str* converts *x* to its string representation, according to the *width* and *decimals* formatting parameters. The effect is exactly the same as a call to the *Write* standard procedure with the same parameters, except that the resulting string is stored in *s* instead of being written to a text file.
See also	*Val, Write*
| **Example** | ```
function IntToStr(i: longint): string;
{ Convert any integer type to a string }
var
  s: string[11];
begin
  Str(i, s);
  IntToStr := s;
end;

begin
  Writeln(IntToStr(-5322));
end.
``` |

Succ function

Function	Returns the successor of the argument.
Declaration	Succ(x)
Result type	Same type as parameter.
Remarks	*x* is an ordinal-type expression. The result, of the same type as *x*, is the successor of *x*.
```

Swap function

Function	Swaps the high- and low-order bytes of the argument.
Declaration	Swap(x)
Result type	Same type as parameter.
Remarks	*x* is an expression of type integer or word.
See also	*Hi, Lo*
Example	

```
var
  x: word;
begin
  x := Swap($1234);   { $3412 }
end.
```

SwapVectors procedure   Dos

Function	Swaps interrupt vectors.
Declaration	SwapVectors
Remarks	Swaps the contents of the *SaveIntXX* pointers in the *System* unit with the current contents of the interrupt vectors. *SwapVectors* is typically called just before and just after a call to *Exec*. This ensures that the *Exec*'d process does not use any interrupt handlers installed by the current process and vice versa.
See also	*Exec*
Example	

```
{$M 8192,0,0}
uses Dos;
var
  Command: string[79];
begin
  Write('Enter DOS command: ');
  ReadLn(Command);
```

```
if Command <> '' then
  Command := '/C ' + Command;
SwapVectors;
Exec(GetEnv('COMSPEC'), Command);
SwapVectors;
if DosError <> 0 then
  Writeln('Could not execute COMMAND.COM');
end.
```

TextBackground procedure   Crt

Function	Selects the background color.
Declaration	`TextBackground(Color: byte);`
Remarks	*Color* is an integer expression in the range 0..7, corresponding to one of the first eight color constants:

```
const
  Black     = 0;
  Blue      = 1;
  Green     = 2;
  Cyan      = 3;
  Red       = 4;
  Magenta   = 5;
  Brown     = 6;
  LightGray = 7;
```

There is a byte variable in *Crt—TextAttr—*that is used to hold the current video attribute. *TextBackground* sets bits 4-6 of *TextAttr* to *Color*.

The background of all characters subsequently written will be in the specified color.

See also   *TextColor, HighVideo, NormVideo, LowVideo*

TextColor procedure   Crt

Function	Selects the foreground character color.
Declaration	`TextColor(Color: byte)`
Remarks	*Color* is an integer expression in the range 0..15, corresponding to one of the color constants defined in *Crt*:

TextColor procedure

```
const
  Black        = 0;
  Blue         = 1;
  Green        = 2;
  Cyan         = 3;
  Red          = 4;
  Magenta      = 5;
  Brown        = 6;
  LightGray    = 7;
  DarkGray     = 8;
  LightBlue    = 9;
  LightGreen   = 10;
  LightCyan    = 11;
  LightRed     = 12;
  LightMagenta = 13;
  Yellow       = 14;
  White        = 15;
```

There is a byte variable in *Crt*—*TextAttr*—that is used to hold the current video attribute. *TextColor* sets bits 0-3 to *Color*. If *Color* is greater than 15, the blink bit (bit 7) is also set; otherwise, it is cleared.

You can make characters blink by adding 128 to the color value. The *Blink* constant is defined for that purpose; in fact, for compatibility with Turbo Pascal 3.0, any *Color* value above 15 causes the characters to blink. The foregound of all characters subsequently written will be in the specified color.

Differences In 3.0, *Blink* was equal to 16.

See also *TextBackground, HighVideo, NormVideo, LowVideo*

Example
```
TextColor(Green);                    { green characters }
TextColor(LightRed+Blink);   { blinking light-red characters }
TextColor(14);                       { yellow characters }
```

TextHeight function   Graph

Function   Returns the height of a string in pixels.

Declaration TextHeight(TextString: **string**)

Result type word

Remarks   Takes the current font size and multiplication factor, and determines the height of *TextString* in pixels. This is

TextHeight function

useful for adjusting the spacing between lines, computing viewport heights, sizing a title to make it fit on a graph or in a box, and more.

For example, with the 8×8 bit-mapped font and a multiplication factor of 1 (set by *SetTextStyle*), the string *Turbo* is 8 pixels high.

It is important to use *TextHeight* to compute the height of strings, instead of doing the computation manually. In that way, no source code modifications have to be made when different fonts are selected.

A similar routine exists in Turbo C 2.0.

Restrictions   Must be in graphics mode.

See also   *OutText, OutTextXY, SetTextStyle, TextWidth, SetUserCharSize*

Example
```
uses Graph;
var
  Gd, Gm : integer;
  Y, Size: integer;
begin
  Gd := Detect;
  InitGraph(Gd, Gm, '');
  if GraphResult <> grOk then
    Halt(1);
  Y := 0;
  for Size := 1 to 5 do
  begin
    SetTextStyle(DefaultFont, HorizDir, Size);
    OutTextXY(0, Y, 'Turbo Graphics');
    Inc(Y, TextHeight('Turbo Graphics'));
  end;
  Readln;
  CloseGraph;
end.
```

TextMode procedure   Crt

Function   Selects a specific text mode.

Declaration   `TextMode(Mode: word)`

Remarks   The following constants are defined:

TextMode procedure

```
const
  BW40    = 0;        { 40x25 B/W on color adapter }
  BW80    = 2;        { 80x25 B/W on color adapter }
  Mono    = 7;        { 80x25 B/W on monochrome adapter }
  CO40    = 1;        { 40x25 color on color adapter }
  CO80    = 3;        { 80x25 color on color adapter }
  Font8x8 = 256;      { For EGA/VGA 43 and 50 line }
  C40 = CO40;         { For 3.0 compatibility }
  C80 = CO80;         { For 3.0 compatibility }
```

Other values cause *TextMode* to assume C80.

When *TextMode* is called, the current window is reset to the entire screen, *DirectVideo* is set to True, *CheckSnow* is set to True if a color mode was selected, the current text attribute is reset to normal corresponding to a call to *NormVideo*, and the current video is stored in *LastMode*. In addition, *LastMode* is initialized at program startup to the then-active video mode.

Specifying *TextMode(LastMode)* causes the last active text mode to be re-selected. This is useful when you want to return to text mode after using a graphics package, such as *Graph* or *Graph3*.

The following call to *TextMode*:

```
TextMode(c80 + Font8x8)
```

will reset the display into 43 lines and 80 columns on an EGA, or 50 lines and 80 columns on a VGA with a color monitor. *TextMode(Lo(LastMode))* always turns off 43- or 50-line mode and resets the display (although it leaves the video mode unchanged); while

TextMode(Lo(LastMode) + Font8×8)

will keep the video mode the same, but reset the display into 43 or 50 lines.

If your system is in 43- or 50-line mode when you load a Turbo Pascal program, the mode will be preserved by the *Crt* startup code, and the window variable that keeps track of the maximum number of lines on the screen (*WindMax*) will be initialized correctly.

Here's how to write a "well-behaved" program that will restore the video mode to its original state:

```
program Video;
uses Crt;
```

TextMode procedure

```
var
  OrigMode: integer;
begin
  OrigMode := LastMode;        { Remember original mode }
  ...
  TextMode(OrigMode);
end.
```

Note that *TextMode* does not support graphics modes, and therefore *TextMode(OrigMode)* will only restore those modes supported by *TextMode*.

Differences In 3.0, a call to *TextMode* with no parameters is now done by calling *TextMode(LastMode)*.

See also *RestoreCrtMode*

TextWidth function   Graph

Function Returns the width of a string in pixels.

Declaration `TextWidth(TextString: string)`

Result type word

Remarks Takes the string length, current font size, and multiplication factor, and determines the width of *TextString* in pixels. This is useful for computing viewport widths, sizing a title to make it fit on a graph or in a box, and so on.

For example, with the 8×8 bit-mapped font and a multiplication factor of 1 (set by *SetTextStyle*), the string *Turbo* is 40 pixels wide.

It is important to use *TextWidth* to compute the width of strings, instead of doing the computation manually. In that way, no source code modifications have to be made when different fonts are selected.

A similar routine exists in Turbo C 2.0.

Restrictions Must be in graphics mode.

See also *OutText, OutTextXY, SetTextStyle, TextHeight, SetUserCharSize*

Example
```
uses Graph;
var
  Gd, Gm: integer;
```

TextWidth function

```
          Row   : integer;
          Title : string;
          Size  : integer;
        begin
          Gd := Detect;
          InitGraph(Gd, Gm, '');
          if GraphResult <> grOk then
            Halt(1);
          Row := 0;
          Title := 'Turbo Graphics';
          Size := 1;
          while TextWidth(Title) < GetMaxX do
          begin
            OutTextXY(0, Row, Title);
            Inc(Row, TextHeight('M'));
            Inc(Size);
            SetTextStyle(DefaultFont, HorizDir, Size);
          end;
          Readln;
          CloseGraph;
        end.
```

Trunc function

Function	Truncates a real-type value to an integer-type value.
Declaration	Trunc(x: real)
Result type	longint
Remarks	*x* is a real-type expression. *Trunc* returns a longint value that is the value of *x* rounded toward zero.
Restrictions	A run-time error occurs if the truncated value of *x* is not within the longint range.
Differences	In 3.0, the result type was an integer.
See also	*Round, Int*

Truncate procedure

Function	Truncates the file size at the current file position.
Declaration	`Truncate(var f)`
Remarks	*f* is a file variable of any type. All records past *f* are deleted and the current file position also becomes end-of-file (*Eof(f)* is True).
	If I/O-checking is off, the *IOResult* function will return a nonzero value if an error occurs.
Restrictions	*f* must be open. *Truncate* does not work on text files.
See also	*Seek, Reset, Rewrite*

UnpackTime procedure   Dos

Function	Converts a 4-byte, packed date-and-time longint returned by *GetFTime*, *FindFirst*, or *FindNext* into an unpacked *DateTime* record.
Declaration	`UnpackTime(Time: longint; var DT: DateTime)`
Remarks	*DateTime* is a record declared in the *Dos* unit:

```
DateTime = record
             Year, Month, Day, Hour,
             Min, Sec: word
           end;
```

The fields of the *Time* record are not range-checked.

See also *PackTime, GetFTime, SetFTime, GetTime, SetTime*

UpCase function

Function	Converts a character to uppercase.
Declaration	`UpCase(ch: char)`
Result type	char

Val procedure

Remarks *ch* is an expression of type char. The result of type char is *ch* converted to uppercase. Character values not in the range *a..z* are unaffected.

Val procedure

Function Converts the string value to its numeric representation.

Declaration Val(s: **string**; **var** v; **var** code: integer)

Remarks *s* is a string-type expression. *v* is an integer-type or real-type variable. *code* is a variable of type integer. *s* must be a sequence of characters that form a signed whole number according to the syntax shown in the section "Numbers" in Chapter 1. *Val* converts *s* to its numeric representation and stores the result in *v*. If the string is somehow invalid, the index of the offending character is stored in *code*; otherwise, *code* is set to zero.

Val performs range-checking differently depending on the state of {$R} and the type of the parameter *v*.

With range-checking on, {$R+}, an out-of-range value always generates a run-time error. With range-checking off, {$R-}, the values for an out-of-range value vary depending upon the data type of *v*. If *v* is a real or longint type, the value of *v* is undefined and *code* returns a nonzero value. For any other numeric type, *code* returns a value of zero, and *v* will contain the results of an overflow calculation (assuming the string value is within the long integer range).

Therefore, you should pass *Val* a longint variable and perform range-checking before making an assignment of the returned value:

```
{$R-}
Val('65536', LongIntVar, Code)
if (Code <> 0) or
   (LongIntVar < 0) or (LongIntVar > 65535) then
    ...                                         { Error }
else
    WordVar := LongIntVar;
```

In this example, *LongIntVar* would be set to 65536, and *Code* would equal 0. Because 65536 is out of range for a word variable, an error would be reported.

392 *Turbo Pascal Reference Guide*

Val procedure

Restrictions	Trailing spaces must be deleted.
See also	*Str*
| **Example** | ```
var i, code: integer;
begin
  { Get text from command line }
  Val(ParamStr(1), i, code);
  { Error during conversion to integer? }
  if code <> 0 then
    Writeln('Error at position: ', code)
  else
    Writeln('Value = ', i);
end.
``` |

WhereX function   Crt

Function	Returns the X-coordinate of the current cursor position, relative to the current window.
Declaration	WhereX
Result type	byte
See also	*WhereY, GotoXY, Window*

WhereY function   Crt

Function	Returns the Y-coordinate of the current cursor position, relative to the current window.
Declaration	WhereY
Result type	byte
See also	*WhereX, GotoXY, Window*
```

Window procedure   Crt

Function   Defines a text window on the screen.

Declaration   `Window(X1, Y1, X2, Y2: byte)`

Remarks   X1 and Y1 are the coordinates of the upper left corner of the window, and X2 and Y2 are the coordinates of the lower right corner. The upper left corner of the screen corresponds to (1,1). The minimum size of a text window is one column by one line. If the coordinates are in any way invalid, the call to *Window* is ignored.

The default window is (1,1,80,25) in 25-line mode, and (1,1,80,43) in 43-line mode, corresponding to the entire screen.

All screen coordinates (except the window coordinates themselves) are relative to the current window. For instance, *GotoXY*(1,1) will always position the cursor in the upper left corner of the current window.

Many *Crt* procedures and functions are window-relative, including *ClrEol, ClrScr, DelLine, GotoXY, Insline, WhereX, WhereY, Read, Readln, Write, Writeln*.

WindMin and *WindMax* store the current window definition (refer to the "WindMin and WindMax" section on page 131).

A call to the *Window* procedure always moves the cursor to (1,1).

See also   *ClrEol, ClrScr, DelLine, GotoXY, WhereX, WhereY*

Example
```
uses Crt;
var
  x, y: byte;
begin
  TextBackground(Black);                        { Clear screen }
  ClrScr;
  repeat
    x := Succ(Random(80));                { Draw random windows }
    y := Succ(Random(25));
    Window(x, y, x + Random(10), y + Random(8));
    TextBackground(Random(16));              { In random colors }
    ClrScr;
  until KeyPressed;
end.
```

Write procedure (text files)

Function Writes one or more values to a text file.

Declaration `Write( [ var f: text; ] v1 [, v2,...,vn ] )`

Remarks *f*, if specified, is a text-file variable. If *f* is omitted, the standard file variable *Output* is assumed. Each *p* is a write parameter. Each write parameter includes an output expression whose value is to be written to the file. A write parameter can also contain the specifications of a field width and a number of decimal places. Each output expression must be of a type char, integer, real, string, packed string, or boolean.

A write parameter has the form

```
OutExpr [ : MinWidth [ : DecPlaces ] ]
```

where *OutExpr* is an output expression. *MinWidth* and *DecPlaces* are type integer expressions.

MinWidth specifies the minimum field width, which must be greater than 0. Exactly *MinWidth* characters are written (using leading blanks if necessary) except when *OutExpr* has a value that must be represented in more than *MinWidth* characters. In that case, enough characters are written to represent the value of *OutExpr*. Likewise, if *MinWidth* is omitted, then the necessary number of characters are written to represent the value of *OutExpr*.

DecPlaces specifies the number of decimal places in a fixed-point representation of a type real value. It can be specified only if *OutExpr* is of type real, and if *MinWidth* is also specified. When *MinWidth* is specified, it must be greater than or equal to 0.

Write with a type char value: If *MinWidth* is omitted, the character value of *OutExpr* is written to the file. Otherwise, *MinWidth* −1 blanks followed by the character value of *OutExpr* is written.

Write with a type integer value: If *MinWidth* is omitted, the decimal representation of *OutExpr* is written to the file with no preceding blanks. If *MinWidth* is specified and its value is larger than the length of the decimal string, enough blanks are written before the decimal string to make the field width *MinWidth*.

Write procedure (text files)

Write with a type real value: If *OutExpr* has a type real value, its decimal representation is written to the file. The format of the representation depends on the presence or absence of *DecPlaces*.

If *DecPlaces* is omitted (or if it is present, but has a negative value), a floating-point decimal string is written. If *MinWidth* is also omitted, a default *MinWidth* of 17 is assumed; otherwise, if *MinWidth* is less than 8, it is assumed to be 8. The format of the floating-point string is

```
[ | - ] <digit> . <decimals> E [ + | - ] <exponent>
```

The components of the output string are shown in Table 16.1:

Table 16.1: Components of the Output String

[| –]	" " or "-", according to the sign of *OutExpr*
<digit>	Single digit, "0" only if *OutExpr* is 0
<decimals>	Digit string of *MinWidth*-7 (but at most 10) digits
E	Uppercase [E] character
[+ | –]	According to sign of exponent
<exponent>	Two-digit decimal exponent

If *DecPlaces* is present, a fixed-point decimal string is written. If *DecPlaces* is larger than 11, it is assumed to be 11. The format of the fixed-point string follows:

```
[ <blanks> ] [ - ] <digits> [ . <decimals> ]
```

The components of the fixed-point string are shown in Table 16.2:

Table 16.2: Components of the Fixed-Point String

[<blanks>]	Blanks to satisfy *MinWidth*
[–]	If *OutExpr* is negative
<digits>	At least one digit, but no leading zeros
[. <decimals>]	Decimals if *DecPlaces* > 0

Write with a string-type value: If *MinWidth* is omitted, the string value of *OutExpr* is written to the file with no leading blanks. If *MinWidth* is specified, and its value is larger than the length of *OutExpr*, enough blanks are written before the decimal string to make the field width *MinWidth*.

Write with a packed string type value: If *OutExpr* is of packed string type, the effect is the same as writing a string whose length is the number of elements in the packed string type.

Write with a Boolean value: If *OutExpr* is of type boolean, the effect is the same as writing the strings True or False, depending on the value of *OutExpr*.

With {$I-}, *IOResult* will return a 0 if the operation was successful; otherwise, it will return a nonzero error code.

Restrictions   File must be open for output.

Differences   See Appendix A in the *User's Guide*, "Differences Between Turbo Pascal 3.0, 4.0, and 5.0."

See also   *Read, Readln, Writeln*

Write procedure (typed files)

Function   Writes a variable into a file component.

Declaration   `Write(f, v1 [, v2,...,vn ] )`

Remarks   *f* is a file variable, and each *v* is a variable of the same type as the component type of *f*. For each variable written, the current file position is advanced to the next component. If the current file position is at the end of the file—that is, if *Eof(f)* is True—the file is expanded.

With {$I-}, *IOResult* will return a 0 if the operation was successful; otherwise, it will return a nonzero error code.

See also   *Writeln*

Writeln procedure

Function   Executes the *Write* procedure, then outputs an end-of-line marker to the file.

Declaration   `Writeln( [ var f: text; ] v1 [, v2,...,vn ] )`

Writeln procedure

Remarks	*Writeln* procedure is an extension to the *Write* procedure, as it is defined for text files. After executing the Write, *Writeln* writes an end-of-line marker (carriage-return/line-feed) to the file.
	Writeln(f) with no parameters writes an end-of-line marker to the file. (*Writeln* with no parameter list altogether corresponds to *Writeln(Output)*.)
Restrictions	File must be open for output.
Differences	See Appendix A in the *User's Guide*, "Differences Between Turbo Pascal 3.0, 4.0, and 5.0."
See also	*Write*

PART 2

Appendices

APPENDIX A

Comparing Turbo Pascal 5.0 with ANSI Pascal

This appendix compares Turbo Pascal to ANSI Pascal as defined by ANSI/IEEE770X3.97-1983 in the book *American National Standard Pascal Computer Programming Language* (ISBN 0-471-88944-X), published by The Institute of Electrical and Electronics Engineers in New York).

Exceptions to ANSI Pascal Requirements

Turbo Pascal complies with the requirements of ANSI/IEEE770X3.97-1983 with the following exceptions:

- In ANSI Pascal, an identifier can be of any length and all characters are significant. In Turbo Pascal, an identifier can be of any length, but only the first 63 characters are significant.
- In ANSI Pascal, the @ symbol is an alternative for the ^ symbol. In Turbo Pascal, the @ symbol is an operator, which is never treated identically with the ^ symbol.
- In ANSI Pascal, a comment can begin with { and end with *), or begin with (* and end with }. In Turbo Pascal, comments must begin and end with the same set of symbols.
- In ANSI Pascal, each possible value of the tag type in a variant part must appear once. In Turbo Pascal, this requirement is not enforced.
- In ANSI Pascal, the component type of a file type cannot be a structured type having a component of a file type. In Turbo Pascal, this requirement is not enforced.

- In ANSI Pascal, a file variable has an associated buffer variable, which is referenced by writing the ^ symbol after the file variable. In Turbo Pascal, a file variable does not have an associated buffer variable, and writing the ^ symbol after a file variable is an error.
- In ANSI Pascal, the statement part of a function must contain at least one assignment to the function identifier. In Turbo Pascal, this requirement is not enforced.
- In ANSI Pascal, a field that is the selector of a variant part cannot be an actual variable parameter. In Turbo Pascal, this requirement is not enforced.
- In ANSI Pascal, a component of a variable of a packed type cannot be an actual variable parameter. In Turbo Pascal, this requirement is not enforced.
- In ANSI Pascal, a procedural or functional parameter is declared by writing a procedure or function heading in the formal parameter list. In Turbo Pascal, the declaration of a procedural or functional parameter is achieved through a procedural or functional type, and uses the same syntax as the declaration of other types of parameters.
- In ANSI Pascal, the standard procedures *Reset* and *Rewrite* do not require pre-initialization of file variables. In Turbo Pascal, file variables must be assigned the name of an external file using the *Assign* procedure before they are passed to *Reset* or *Rewrite*.
- ANSI Pascal defines the standard procedures *Get* and *Put*, which are used to read from and write to files. These procedures are not defined in Turbo Pascal.
- In ANSI Pascal, the syntax *New(p,c1,...,cn)* creates a dynamic variable with a specific active variant. In Turbo Pascal, this syntax is not allowed.
- In ANSI Pascal, the syntax *Dispose(q,k1,...,km)* removes a dynamic variable with a specific active variant. In Turbo Pascal, this syntax is not allowed.
- ANSI Pascal defines the standard procedures *Pack* and *Unpack*, which are used to "pack" and "unpack" packed variables. These procedures are not defined in Turbo Pascal.
- In ANSI Pascal, the term i **mod** j always computes a positive value, and it is an error if j is zero or negative. In Turbo Pascal, i **mod** j is computed as $i - (i$ **div** $j) * j$, and it is not an error if j is negative.
- In ANSI Pascal, a **goto** statement within a block can refer to a label in an enclosing block. In Turbo Pascal, this is an error.
- In ANSI Pascal, it is an error if the value of the selector in a **case** statement is not equal to any of the case constants. In Turbo Pascal, this is not an error; instead, the **case** statement is ignored unless it contains an **else** clause.

- In ANSI Pascal, statements that *threaten* the control variable of a **for** statement are not allowed. In Turbo Pascal, this requirement is not enforced.
- In ANSI Pascal, a *Read* from a text file with a char-type variable assigns a blank to the variable if *Eoln* was True before the *Read*. In Turbo Pascal, a carriage return character (ASCII 13) is assigned to the variable in this situation.
- In ANSI Pascal, a *Read* from a text file with an integer-type or real-type variable ceases as soon as the next character in the file is not part of a signed integer or a signed number. In Turbo Pascal, reading ceases when the next character in the file is a blank or a control character (including the end-of-line marker).
- In ANSI Pascal, a *Write* to a text file with a packed string-type value causes the string to be truncated if the specified field width is less than the length of the string. In Turbo Pascal, the string is always written in full, even if it is longer than the specified field width.
- ANSI Pascal defines the standard procedure *Page*, which causes all subsequent output to a specific text file to be written on a new page. This procedure is not defined in Turbo Pascal. However, the typical equivalent of *Page(F)* is *Write(F,Chr(12))*.

Note: Turbo Pascal is unable to detect whether a program violates any of the exceptions listed here.

Extensions to ANSI Pascal

The following Turbo Pascal features are extensions to Pascal as specified by ANSI/IEEE770X3.97-1983.

- The following are reserved words in Turbo Pascal:

absolute	**interface**	**string**
external	**interrupt**	**unit**
implementation	**shl**	**uses**
inline	**shr**	**xor**

- An identifier can contain underscore characters (_).
- Integer constants can be written in hexadecimal notation; such constants are prefixed by a $.
- Identifiers can serve as labels.
- String constants are compatible with the Turbo Pascal string types, and can contain control characters and other nonprintable characters.
- Label, constant, type, variable, procedure, and function declarations can occur any number of times in any order in a block.

- Wherever the syntax of ANSI Pascal requires a simple constant, Turbo Pascal allows the use of a constant expression (also known as a computed constant).
- Turbo Pascal implements the additional integer types shortint, longint, byte, and word, and the additional real types single, double, extended, and comp.
- Turbo Pascal implements string types, which differ from the packed string types defined by ANSI Pascal in that they include a dynamic-length attribute that can vary during execution.
- Turbo Pascal implements procedural and functional types. In addition to procedural and functional parameters, these types make possible the declaration and use of procedural and functional variables.
- The type compatibility rules are extended to make char types and packed string types compatible with string types.
- Variables can be declared at absolute memory addresses using an **absolute** clause.
- A variable reference can contain a call to a pointer-type function, the result of which is then dereferenced to denote a dynamic variable.
- String-type variables can be indexed as arrays to access individual characters in a string.
- The type of a variable reference can be changed to another type through a variable typecast.
- Turbo Pascal implements typed constants, which can be used to declare initialized variables of all types except file types.
- Turbo Pascal implements three new logical operators: **xor, shl**, and **shr**.
- The **not, and, or**, and **xor** operators can be used with integer-type operands to perform bitwise logical operations.
- The + operator can be used to concatenate strings.
- The relational operators can be used to compare strings.
- Turbo Pascal implements the @ operator, which is used to obtain the address of a variable or a procedure or function.
- The type of an expression can be changed to another type through a value typecast.
- The **case** statement allows constant ranges in **case** label lists, and provides an optional **else** part.
- Procedures and functions can be declared with **external, inline,** and **interrupt** directives to support assembly language subroutines, inline machine code, and interrupt procedures.
- A variable parameter can be untyped (typeless), in which case any variable reference can serve as the actual parameter.

- Turbo Pascal implements units to facilitate modular programming and separate compilation.
- Turbo Pascal implements the following file-handling procedures and functions, which are not available in ANSI Pascal:

Append	*Close*	*Flush*	*RmDir*
BlockRead	*Erase*	*GetDir*	*Seek*
BlockWrite	*FilePos*	*MkDir*	*SeekEof*
ChDir	*FileSize*	*Rename*	*SeekEoln*

- String-type values can be input and output with the *Read*, *Readln*, *Write*, and *Writeln* standard procedures.
- Turbo Pascal implements the following standard procedures and functions, which are not found in ANSI Pascal:

Addr	*GetMem*	*MemAvail*	*Release*
Concat	*Halt*	*Move*	*RunError*
Copy	*Hi*	*Ofs*	*SPtr*
CSeg	*Inc*	*ParamCount*	*Seg*
DSeg	*Insert*	*ParamStr*	*SizeOf*
Dec	*Int*	*Pi*	*SSeg*
Delete	*Length*	*Pos*	*Str*
Exit	*Lo*	*Ptr*	*Swap*
FillChar	*Mark*	*Random*	*UpCase*
Frac	*MaxAvail*	*Randomize*	*Val*
FreeMem			

- Turbo Pascal implements further standard constants, types, variables, procedures, and functions through standard units.

Note: Turbo Pascal is unable to detect whether a program uses any of the extensions listed here.

Implementation-Dependent Features

The effect of using an implementation-dependent feature of Pascal, as defined by ANSI/IEEE770X3.97-1983, is unspecified. Programs should not depend on any specific path being taken in cases where an implementation-dependent feature is being used. Implementation-dependent features include:

- the order of evaluation of index expressions in a variable reference
- the order of evaluation of expressions in a set constructor
- the order of evaluation of operands of a binary operator
- the order of evaluation of actual parameters in a function call
- the order of evaluation of the left and right sides of an assignment

- the order of evaluation of actual parameters in a procedure statement
- the effect of reading a text file to which the procedure *Page* was applied during its creation
- the binding of variables denoted by the program parameters to entities external to the program

Treatment of Errors

This section lists those errors from Appendix D of the ANSI Pascal Standard that are not automatically detected by Turbo Pascal. The numbers referred to here are the numbers used in the ANSI Pascal Standard. Errors 6, 19-22, and 25-31 are not detected because they are not applicable to Turbo Pascal.

2. If t is a tag field in a variant part and f is a field within the active variant of that variant part, it is an error to alter the value of t while a reference to f exists. This error is not detected.

3. If p is a pointer variable, it is an error to reference $p\char`\^$ if p is **nil**. This error is not detected.

4. If p is a pointer variable, it is an error to reference $p\char`\^$ if p is undefined. This error is not detected.

5. If p is a pointer variable, it is an error to alter the value of p while a reference to $p\char`\^$ exists. This error is not detected.

42. The function call *Eoln(f)* is an error if *Eof(f)* is True. In Turbo Pascal this is not an error, and *Eoln(f)* is True when *Eof(f)* is True.

43. It is an error to reference a variable in an expression if the value of that variable is undefined. This error is not detected.

46. A term of the form i **mod** j is an error if j is zero or negative. In Turbo Pascal, it is not an error if j is negative.

48. It is an error if a function does not assign a result value to the function identifier. This error is not detected.

51. It is an error if the value of the selector in a **case** statement is not equal to any of the case constants. In Turbo Pascal, this is not an error; instead, the **case** statement is ignored unless it contains an **else** clause.

APPENDIX B

Compiler Directives

Some of the Turbo Pascal compiler's features are controlled through *compiler directives*. A compiler directive is a comment with a special syntax. Turbo Pascal allows compiler directives wherever comments are allowed.

A compiler directive starts with a $ as the first character after the opening comment delimiter, and is immediately followed by a name (one or more letters) that designates the particular directive. There are three types of directives:

- **Switch directives.** These directives turn particular compiler features on or off by specifying + or – immediately after the directive name.
- **Parameter directives.** These directives specify parameters that affect the compilation, such as file names and memory sizes.
- **Conditional directives.** These directives control conditional compilation of parts of the source text, based on user-definable conditional symbols.

All directives, except switch directives, must have at least one blank between the directive name and the parameters. Here are some examples of compiler directives:

```
{$B+}
{$R- Turn off range-checking}
{$I TYPES.INC}
{$O EdFormat}
{$M 65520,8192,655360}
{$DEFINE Debug}
{$IFDEF Debug}
{$ENDIF}
```

You can put compiler directives directly into your source code. You can also change the default directives for both the command-line compiler

(TPC.EXE) and the IDE (TURBO.EXE). The **Options/Compiler** menu contains all the compiler directives; any changes you make to the settings there will affect all subsequent compilations (see Chapter 7 of the *User's Guide* for details). When using the command-line compiler, you can specify compiler directives on the command line (for example, `TPC /$R+ MYPROG`), or you can place directives in a configuration file (TPC.CFG—refer to Chapter 8 of the *User's Guide* for information). Compiler directives in the source code always override the default values in both the command-line compiler and the IDE.

Switch Directives

Switch directives are either *global* or *local*. Global directives affect the entire compilation, whereas local directives affect only the part of the compilation that extends from the directive until the next occurrence of the same directive.

Global directives must appear before the declaration part of the program or the unit being compiled, that is, before the first **uses, label, const, type, procedure, function,** or **begin** keyword. Local directives, on the other hand, can appear anywhere in the program or unit.

Multiple switch directives can be grouped in a single compiler directive comment by separating them with commas; for example,

```
{$B+,R-,S-}
```

There can be no spaces between the directives in this case.

Align Data

Syntax: {$A+} or {$A-}

Default: {$A+}

Type: Global

Menu equivalent: Options/Compiler/Align Data

This directive switches between byte and word alignment of variables and typed constants. Word alignment has no effect on the 8088 CPU. However, on all 80x86 CPUs, word alignment means faster execution, since word-sized items on even addresses are accessed in one memory cycle, in comparison to two memory cycles for words on odd addresses.

In the {$A+} state, all variables and typed constants larger than one byte are aligned on a machine-word boundary (an even-numbered address). If required, unused bytes are inserted between variables to achieve word alignment. The {$A+} directive does not affect byte-sized variables; neither does it affect fields of record structures and elements of arrays. A field in a record will align on word boundary only if the total size of all fields before it is even. Likewise, for every element of an array to align on a word boundary, the size of the elements must be even.

In the {$A-} state, no alignment measures are taken. Variables and typed constants are simply placed at the next available address, regardless of their size. If you are recompiling programs using the Turbo Pascal Editor Toolbox, make sure to compile all programs that use the toolbox with {$A-}.

Note: Regardless of the state of the $A directive, each global **var** and **const** declaration section always starts at a word boundary. Likewise, the compiler always attempts to keep the stack pointer (SP) word aligned, by allocating an extra unused byte in a procedure's stack frame if required.

Also note: The $A compiler directive is equivalent to the Options/Compiler/Align Data command in the integrated environment; the command-line compiler equivalent is the /$A option.

Boolean Evaluation

Syntax: {$B+} or {$B-}

Default: {$B-}

Type: Local

Menu equivalent: Options/Compiler/Boolean Evaluation

Boolean Evaluation switches between the two different models of code generation for the **and** and **or** Boolean operators.

In the {$B+} state, the compiler generates code for complete Boolean expression evaluation. This means that every operand of a Boolean expression, built from the **and** and **or** operators, is guaranteed to be evaluated, even when the result of the entire expression is already known.

In the {$B-} state, the compiler generates code for short-circuit Boolean expression evaluation, which means that evaluation stops as soon as the result of the entire expression becomes evident.

For further details, refer to the section "Boolean Operators" in Chapter 6, "Expressions."

Debug Information

Syntax: {$D+} or {$D-}

Default: {$D+}

Type: Global

Menu equivalent: Options/Compiler/Debug Information

Debug Information enables or disables the generation of debug information. This information consists of a line-number table for each procedure, which maps object code addresses into source text line numbers.

When Debug Information is turned on for a given program or unit, Turbo Pascal's integrated debugger allows you to single-step and set breakpoints in that module. Furthermore, when a run-time error occurs in a program or unit compiled with {$D+}, Turbo Pascal can automatically take you to the statement that caused the error with Compile/Find Error.

The Debug/Stand-alone Debugging and Options/Linker/Map File switches produce complete information for a given module only if you've compiled that module in the {$D+} state.

For units, the debug information is recorded in the .TPU file along with the unit's object code. Debug information increases the size of .TPU files, and takes up additional room when compiling programs that use the unit, but it does not affect the size or speed of the executable program.

The debug information switch is usually used in conjunction with the Local Symbols switch, which enables and disables the generation of local symbol information for debugging.

Note: If you want to use the Turbo Debugger to debug your program, set Compile/Destination to Disk and Debug/Stand-alone Debugging to On.

Emulation

Syntax: {$E+} or {$E-}

Default: {$E+}

Type: Global

Menu equivalent: Options/Compiler/Emulation

Emulation enables or disables linking with a run-time library that will emulate the 8087 numeric coprocessor if it is not present.

When you compile a program in the {$N+,E+} state, Turbo Pascal links with the full 8087 emulator. The resulting .EXE file can be used on any machine, regardless of whether an 8087 is present. If one is found, Turbo Pascal will use it; otherwise, the run-time library emulates it.

In the {$N+,E-} state, Turbo Pascal links with a substantially smaller floating-point library, which can only be used if an 8087 is present.

The 8087 emulation switch has no effect if used in a unit; it applies only to the compilation of a program. Furthermore, if the program is compiled in the {$N-} state, and if all the units used by the program were compiled with {$N-}, then an 8087 run-time library is not required, and the 8087 emulation switch is ignored.

Force FAR Calls

Syntax: {$F+} or {$F-}

Default: {$F-}

Type: Local

Menu equivalent: Options/Compiler/Force Far Calls

Force Far Calls controls which call model to use for subsequently compiled procedures and functions. Procedures and functions compiled in the {$F+} state always use the FAR call model. In the {$F-} state, Turbo Pascal automatically selects the appropriate model: FAR if the procedure or function is declared in the **interface** section of a unit; NEAR otherwise.

The NEAR and FAR call models are described in full in Chapter 15, "Inside Turbo Pascal."

Note: For programs that use overlays, we suggest that you place a {$F+} directive at the beginning of the program and each unit, in order to satisfy the FAR call requirement. For more discussion, refer to Chapter 13, "Overlays." For programs that use procedural variables, all such procedures must use the FAR code model. For more discussion, refer to "Procedural Variables" on page 85.

Input/Output-Checking

Syntax: {$I+} or {$I-}

Default: {$I+}

Type: Local

Menu equivalent: Options/Compiler/I/O-Checking

I/O-checking enables or disables the automatic code generation that checks the result of a call to an I/O procedure. I/O procedures are described in Chapter 10, "Input and Output." If an I/O procedure returns a nonzero I/O result when this switch is on, the program terminates, displaying a run-time error message. When this switch is off, you must check for I/O errors by using the *IOResult* function.

Local Symbol Information

Syntax: {$L+} or {$L-}

Default: {$L+}

Type: Global

Menu equivalent: Options/Compiler/Local Symbols

Local Symbols enables or disables the generation of local symbol information. Local symbol information consists of the names and types of all local variables and constants in a module, that is, the symbols in the module's implementation part, and the symbols within the module's procedures and functions.

When local symbols are on for a given program or unit, Turbo Pascal's integrated debugger allows you to examine and modify the module's local variables. Furthermore, calls to the module's procedures and functions can be examined via the Debug/Call Stack menu.

The Options/Linker/Map File and Debug/Stand-alone Debugging switches produce local symbol information for a given module only if that module was compiled in the {$L+} state.

For units, the local symbol information is recorded in the .TPU file along with the unit's object code. Local symbol information increases the size of .TPU files, and takes up additional room when compiling programs that use the unit, but it does not affect the size or speed of the executable program.

The Local Symbol information switch is usually used in conjunction with the Debug Information switch, which enables and disables the generation of line-number tables for debugging. Note that the $L directive is ignored if Debug Information is set to Off {$D-}.

Numeric Processing

Syntax: {$N+} or {$N-}

Default: {$N-}

Type: Global

Menu equivalent: Options/Compiler/Numeric Processing

Numeric Processing switches between the two different models of floating-point code generation supported by Turbo Pascal. In the {$N-} state, code is generated to perform all real-type calculations in software by calling run-time library routines. In the {$N+} state, code is generated to perform all real-type calculations using the 8087 numeric coprocessor.

Note that you can also use the {$E+} directive to emulate the 8087. This gives you access to the IEEE floating-point types without requiring that you install an 8087 chip.

Overlay Code Generation

Syntax: {$O+} or {$O-}

Default: {$O-})

Type: Global

Menu equivalent: Options/Compiler/Overlays Allowed

The $O directive enables or disables overlay code generation. Turbo Pascal allows a unit to be overlaid only if it was compiled with {$O+}. In this state, the code generator takes special precautions when passing string and set constant parameters from one overlaid procedure or function to another.

The use of {$O+} in a unit does not force you to overlay that unit. It just instructs Turbo Pascal to ensure that the unit can be overlaid, if so desired. If you develop units that you plan to use in overlaid as well as non-overlaid applications, then compiling them with {$O+} ensures that you can indeed do both with just one version of the unit.

Note: A {$O+} compiler directive is almost always used in conjunction with a {$F+} directive to satisfy the overlay manager's FAR call requirement.

For further details on overlay code generation, refer to Chapter 13, "Overlays."

Range-Checking

Syntax: {$R+} or {$R-}

Default: {$R-}

Type: Local

Menu equivalent: Options/Compiler/Range-Checking

Range-Checking enables or disables the generation of range-checking code. In the {$R+} state, all array and string-indexing expressions are verified as being within the defined bounds, and all assignments to scalar and subrange variables are checked to be within range. If a range check fails, the program terminates and displays a run-time error message. Enabling range-checking slows down your program and makes it larger. Use this option when debugging, then turn it off once the program is bug-free.

Stack-Overflow Checking

Syntax: {$S+} or {$S-}

Default: {$S+}

Type: Local

Menu equivalent: Options/Compiler/Stack-Checking

Stack-Checking enables or disables the generation of stack-overflow checking code. In the {$S+} state, the compiler generates code at the beginning of each procedure or function that checks whether there is sufficient stack space for the local variables and other temporary storage. When there is not enough stack space, a call to a procedure or function compiled with {$S+} causes the program to terminate and display a run-time error message. In the {$S-} state, such a call is most likely to cause a system crash.

Var-String Checking

Syntax: {$V+} or {$V-}

Default: {$V+}

Type: Local

Menu equivalent: Options/Compiler/Var-String Checking

Var-String Checking controls type-checking on strings passed as variable parameters. In the {$V+} state, strict type-checking is performed, requiring the formal and actual parameters to be of *identical* string types. In the {$V-} state, any string type variable is allowed as an actual parameter, even if the declared maximum length is not the same as that of the formal parameter.

Parameter Directives

Include File

Syntax: `{$I filename}`

Type: Local

Menu equivalent: Options/Directories/Include Directories

Include Directories instructs the compiler to include the named file in the compilation. In effect, the file is inserted in the compiled text right after the {$I *filename*} directive. The default extension for *filename* is .PAS. If *filename* does not specify a directory, then, in addition to searching for the file in the current directory, Turbo Pascal searches in the directories specified in the Options/Directories/Include directories menu (or in the directories specified in the */I* option on the TPC command line).

You can nest Include files up to 15 levels deep.

There is one restriction to the use of Include files: An Include file cannot be specified in the middle of a statement part. In fact, all statements between the **begin** and **end** of a statement part must reside in the same source file.

Link Object File

Syntax: `{$L filename}`

Type: Local

Menu equivalent: Options/Directories/Object Directories

Object Directories instructs the compiler to link the named file with the program or unit being compiled. The $L directive is used to link with code written in assembly language for subprograms declared to be **external**. The named file must be an Intel relocatable object file (.OBJ file). The default extension for *filename* is .OBJ. If *filename* does not specify a directory, then, in addition to searching for the file in the current directory, Turbo Pascal searches in the directories specified in the Options/Directories/Object Directories menu (or in the directories specified in the */O* option on the TPC command line).

For further details about linking with assembly language, refer to Chapter 15, "Inside Turbo Pascal."

Memory Allocation Sizes

Syntax: {$M stacksize,heapmin,heapmax}

Default: {$M 16384,0,655360}

Type: Global

Menu equivalent: Options/Compiler/Memory Sizes

Memory Sizes specifies a program's memory allocation parameters. *stacksize* must be an integer number in the range 1024 to 65520, which specifies the size of the stack segment. *heapmin* must be in the range 0 to 655360, and *heapmax* must be in the range *heapmin* to 655360. *heapmin* and *heapmax* specify the minimum and maximum sizes of the heap, respectively.

The stack segment and the heap are further discussed in Chapter 4, "Variables," and Chapter 15, "Inside Turbo Pascal."

Note: The $M directive has no effect when used in a unit.

Overlay Unit Name

Syntax: {$O unitname}

Type: Local

Menu equivalent: none

Overlay Unit Name turns a unit into an overlay.

The {$O *unitname*} directive has no effect if used in a unit; when compiling a program, it specifies which of the units used by the program should be placed in an .OVR file instead of in the .EXE file.

{$O *unitname*} directives must be placed after the program's **uses** clause. Turbo Pascal reports an error if you attempt to overlay a unit that wasn't compiled in the {$O+} state. Any unit named in a {$O *unitname*} directive must have been compiled with Overlays Allowed set to On in the IDE (the equivalent of the {$O+} compiler directive).

For further details on overlays, refer to Chapter 13, "Overlays."

Conditional Compilation

Turbo Pascal's conditional compilation directives allow you to produce different code from the same source text, based on conditional symbols.

There are two basic conditional compilation constructs, which closely resemble Pascal's **if** statement. The first construct

    {$IFxxx} ... {$ENDIF}

causes the source text between {$IF*xxx*} and {$ENDIF} to be compiled only if the condition specified in {$IF*xxx*} is True; if the condition is False, the source text between the two directives is ignored.

The second conditional compilation construct

    {$IFxxx} ... {$ELSE} ... {$ENDIF}

causes either the source text between {$IF*xxx*} and {$ELSE} or the source text between {$ELSE} and {$ENDIF} to be compiled, based on the condition specified by the {$IF*xxx*}.

Here are some examples of conditional compilation constructs:

```
{$IFDEF Debug}
  Writeln('X = ',X);
{$ENDIF}

{$IFDEF CPU87}
  {$N+}
  type
    real = double;
{$ELSE}
  {$N-}
  type
    single = real;
    double = real;
    extended = real;
    comp = real;
{$ENDIF}
```

You can nest conditional compilation constructs up 16 levels deep. For every {$IF*xxx*}, the corresponding {$ENDIF} must be found within the same source file—which means there must be an equal number of {$IF*xxx*}'s and {$ENDIF}'s in every source file.

Conditional Symbols

Conditional compilation is based on the evaluation of conditional symbols. Conditional symbols are defined and undefined (forgotten) using the directives

    {$DEFINE name}
    {$UNDEF name}

You can also use the /D switch in the command-line compiler (or the menu command **O/C**/Conditional Defines from within the integrated environment).

Conditional symbols are best compared to Boolean variables: They are either True (defined) or False (undefined). The {$DEFINE} directive sets a given symbol to True, and the {$UNDEF} directive sets it to False.

Conditional symbols follow the exact same rules as Pascal identifiers: They must start with a letter, followed by any combination of letters, digits, and underscores. They can be of any length, but only the first 63 characters are significant.

Note: Conditional symbols and Pascal identifiers have no correlation whatsoever. Conditional symbols cannot be referenced in the actual program, and the program's identifiers cannot be referenced in conditional directives. For example, the construct

```
const
  Debug = True;
begin
  {$IFDEF Debug}
    Writeln('Debug is on');
  {$ENDIF}
end;
```

will *not* compile the *Writeln* statement. Likewise, the construct

```
{$DEFINE Debug}
begin
  if Debug then
    Writeln('Debug is on');
end;
```

will result in an unknown identifier error in the **if** statement.

Turbo Pascal defines the following standard conditional symbols:

VER50 Always defined, indicating that this is version 5.0 of Turbo Pascal. Other versions (starting with 4.0) define their corresponding version symbol; for instance, VER40 for version 4.0, and so on.

MSDOS Always defined, indicating that the operating system is MS-DOS or PC-DOS. Versions of Turbo Pascal for other operating systems will instead define a symbolic name for that particular operating system.

CPU86 Always defined, indicating that the CPU belongs to the 80x86 family of processors. Versions of Turbo Pascal for other CPUs will instead define a symbolic name for that particular CPU.

CPU87   Defined if an 8087 numeric coprocessor is present at compile time. If the construct

```
{$IFDEF CPU87} {$N+} {$ELSE} {$N-} {$ENDIF}
```

appears at the beginning of a compilation, Turbo Pascal automatically selects the appropriate model of floating-point code generation for that particular computer.

Other conditional symbols can be defined before a compilation using the O/C/Conditional Defines menu, or the /D command-line option if you are using TPC.

The DEFINE Directive

Syntax: `{$DEFINE name}`

Defines a conditional symbol of *name*. The symbol is recognized for the remainder of the compilation of the current module in which the symbol is declared, or until it appears in an {$UNDEF *name*} directive. The {$DEFINE *name*} directive has no effect if *name* is already defined.

The UNDEF Directive

Syntax: `{$UNDEF name}`

Undefines a previously defined conditional symbol. The symbol is forgotten for the remainder of the compilation or until it reappears in a {$DEFINE *name*} directive. The {$UNDEF *name*} directive has no effect if *name* is already undefined.

The IFDEF Directive

Syntax: `{$IFDEF name}`

Compiles the source text that follows it if *name* is defined.

The IFNDEF Directive

Syntax: `{$IFNDEF name}`

Compiles the source text that follows it if *name* is not defined.

The IFOPT Directive

Syntax: {$IFOPT switch}

Compiles the source text that follows it if *switch* is currently in the specified state. *switch* consists of the name of a switch option, followed by a + or a – symbol. For example, the construct

```
{$IFOPT N+}
  type real = extended;
{$ENDIF}
```

will compile the type declaration if the *$N* option is currently active.

The ELSE Directive

Syntax: {$ELSE}

Switches between compiling and ignoring the source text delimited by the last {$IF*xxx*} and the next {$ENDIF}.

The ENDIF Directive

Syntax: {$ENDIF}

Ends the conditional compilation initiated by the last {$IF*xxx*} directive.

APPENDIX C

Reference Materials

This chapter is devoted to certain reference materials, including an ASCII table, keyboard scan codes, and extended codes.

ASCII Codes

The **American Standard Code for Information Interchange (ASCII)** is a code that translates alphabetic and numeric characters and symbols and control instructions into 7-bit binary code. Table C.1 shows both printable characters and control characters.

Table C.1: ASCII Table

DEC	HEX	CHAR	DEC	HEX	CHAR	DEC	HEX	CHAR	DEC	HEX	CHAR
0	0		32	20		64	40	@	96	60	`
1	1	☺	33	21	!	65	41	A	97	61	a
2	2	☻	34	22	"	66	42	B	98	62	b
3	3	♥	35	23	#	67	43	C	99	63	c
4	4	♦	36	24	$	68	44	D	100	64	d
5	5	♣	37	25	%	69	45	E	101	65	e
6	6	♠	38	26	&	70	46	F	102	66	f
7	7	•	39	27	'	71	47	G	103	67	g
8	8	◘	40	28	(	72	48	H	104	68	h
9	9	○	41	29	)	73	49	I	105	69	i
10	A	◉	42	2A	*	74	4A	J	106	6A	j
11	B	♂	43	2B	+	75	4B	K	107	6B	k
12	C	♀	44	2C	,	76	4C	L	108	6C	l
13	D	♪	45	2D	-	77	4D	M	109	6D	m
14	E	♫	46	2E	.	78	4E	N	110	6E	n
15	F	¤	47	2F	/	79	4F	O	111	6F	o
16	10	►	48	30	0	80	50	P	112	70	p
17	11	◄	49	31	1	81	51	Q	113	71	q
18	12	↕	50	32	2	82	52	R	114	72	r
19	13	‼	51	33	3	83	53	S	115	73	s
20	14	¶	52	34	4	84	54	T	116	74	t
21	15	§	53	35	5	85	55	U	117	75	u
22	16	■	54	36	6	86	56	V	118	76	v
23	17	↨	55	37	7	87	57	W	119	77	w
24	18	↑	56	38	8	88	58	X	120	78	x
25	19	↓	57	39	9	89	59	Y	121	79	y
26	1A	→	58	3A	:	90	5A	Z	122	7A	z
27	1B	←	59	3B	;	91	5B	[	123	7B	{
28	1C	∟	60	3C	<	92	5C	\	124	7C		
29	1D	↔	61	3D	=	93	5D	]	125	7D	}
30	1E	▲	62	3E	>	94	5E	^	126	7E	~
31	1F	▼	63	3F	?	95	5F	_	127	7F	⌂

Table C.1: ASCII Table (continued)

DEC	HEX	CHAR	DEC	HEX	CHAR	DEC	HEX	CHAR	DEC	HEX	CHAR
128	80	Ç	160	A0	á	192	C0	└	224	E0	α
129	81	ü	161	A1	í	193	C1	┴	225	E1	β
130	82	é	162	A2	ó	194	C2	┬	226	E2	Γ
131	83	â	163	A3	ú	195	C3	├	227	E3	π
132	84	ä	164	A4	ñ	196	C4	─	228	E4	Σ
133	85	à	165	A5	Ñ	197	C5	┼	229	E5	σ
134	86	å	166	A6	ª	198	C6	╞	230	E6	μ
135	87	ç	167	A7	º	199	C7	╟	231	E7	τ
136	88	ê	168	A8	¿	200	C8	╚	232	E8	Φ
137	89	ë	169	A9	⌐	201	C9	╔	233	E9	θ
138	8A	è	170	AA	¬	202	CA	╩	234	EA	Ω
139	8B	ï	171	AB	½	203	CB	╦	235	EB	δ
140	8C	î	172	AC	¼	204	CC	╠	236	EC	∞
141	8D	ì	173	AD	¡	205	CD	═	237	ED	ø
142	8E	Ä	174	AE	«	206	CE	╬	238	EE	∈
143	8F	Å	175	AF	»	207	CF	╧	239	EF	∩
144	90	É	176	B0	░	208	D0	╨	240	F0	≡
145	91	æ	177	B1	▓	209	D1	╤	241	F1	±
146	92	Æ	178	B2	█	210	D2	╥	242	F2	≥
147	93	ô	179	B3	│	211	D3	╙	243	F3	≤
148	94	ö	180	B4	┤	212	D4	╘	244	F4	⌠
149	95	ò	181	B5	╡	213	D5	╒	245	F5	⌡
150	96	û	182	B6	╢	214	D6	╓	246	F6	÷
151	97	ù	183	B7	╖	215	D7	╫	247	F7	≈
152	98	ÿ	184	B8	╕	216	D8	╪	248	F8	°
153	99	Ö	185	B9	╣	217	D9	┘	249	F9	∙
154	9A	Ü	186	BA	║	218	DA	┌	250	FA	·
155	9B	¢	187	BB	╗	219	DB	█	251	FB	√
156	9C	£	188	BC	╝	220	DC	▄	252	FC	ⁿ
157	9D	¥	189	BD	╜	221	DD	▌	253	FD	²
158	9E	₧	190	BE	╛	222	DE	▐	254	FE	■
159	9F	ƒ	191	BF	┐	223	DF	▀	255	FF	

Appendix C, Reference Materials

Extended Key Codes

Extended key codes are returned by those keys or key combinations that cannot be represented by the standard ASCII codes listed in Table C.1. (See *ReadKey* in Chapter 16 for a description about how to determine if an extended key has been pressed.)

Table C.2 shows the second code and what it means.

Table C.2: Extended Key Codes

Second Code	Meaning
3	*NUL* (null character)
15	*Shift Tab (—<vv)*
16-25	*Alt-Q/W/E/R/T/Y/U/I/O/P*
30-38	*Alt-A/S/D/F/G/H/J/K/L*
44-50	*Alt-Z/X/C/V/B/N/M*
59-68	Keys *F1-F10* (disabled as softkeys)
71	Home
72	Up arrow
73	PgUp
75	Left arrow
77	Right arrow
79	End
80	Down arrow
81	PgDn
82	Ins
83	Del
84-93	*F11-F20 (Shift-F1 to Shift-F10)*
94-103	*F21-F30 (Ctrl-F1 through F10)*
104-113	*F31-F40 (Alt-F1 through F10)*
114	*Ctrl-PrtSc*
115	*Ctrl-Left arrow*
116	*Ctrl-Right arrow*
117	*Ctrl-End*
118	*Ctrl-PgDn*
119	*Ctrl-Home*
120-131	*Alt-1/2/3/4/5/6/7/8/9/0/−/=*
132	*Ctrl-PgUp*
133	*F11*
134	*F12*
135	*Shift-F11*
136	*Shift-F12*
137	*Ctrl-F11*
138	*Ctrl-F12*
139	*Alt-F11*
140	*Alt-F12*

Keyboard Scan Codes

Keyboard scan codes are the codes returned from the keys on the IBM PC keyboard, as they are seen by Turbo Pascal. These keys are useful when you're working at the assembly language level. Note that the keyboard scan codes displayed in Table C.3 on page 426 are in hexadecimal values.

Table C.3: Keyboard Scan Codes

Key	Scan Code in Hex	Key	Scan Code in Hex
Esc	01	Left/Right arrow	0F
! 1	02	Q	10
@ 2	03	W	11
# 3	04	E	12
$ 4	05	R	13
% 5	06	T	14
^ 6	07	Y	15
& 7	08	U	16
* 8	09	I	17
(9	0A	O	18
) 0	0B	P	19
_ -	0C	{ [	1A
+ =	0D	}]	1B
Backspace	0E	Return	1C
Ctrl	1D	| \	2B
A	1E	Z	2C
S	1F	X	2D
D	20	C	2E
F	21	V	2F
G	22	B	30
H	23	N	31
J	24	M	32
K	25	< ,	33
L	26	> .	34
: ;	27	? /	35
" '	28	RightShift	36
~ `	29	PrtSc *	37
LeftShift	2A	Alt	38
SpaceBar	39	7 Home	47
Caps Lock	3A	8 Up arrow	48
F1	3B	9 PgUp	49
F2	3C	Minus sign	4A
F3	3D	4 Left arrow	4B
F4	3E	5	4C
F5	3F	6 Right arrow	4D
F6	40	+	4E
F7	41	1 End	4F
F8	42	2 Down arrow	50
F9	43	3 PgDn	51
F10	44	0 Ins	52
F11	D9	Del	53
F12	DA	Num Lock	45
Scroll Lock	46		

APPENDIX D

Error Messages and Codes

Compiler Error Messages

The following lists the possible error messages you can get from the compiler during program development. Whenever possible, the compiler will display additional diagnostic information in the form of an identifier or a file name, for example:

```
Error 15: File not found (WINDOW.TPU).
```

When an error is detected, Turbo Pascal (in the integrated environment) automatically loads the source file and places the cursor at the error. The command-line compiler displays the error message and number and the source line, and uses a caret (^) to indicate where the error occurred. Note, however, that some errors are not detected until a little later in the source text. For example, a type mismatch in an assignment statement cannot be detected until the entire expression after the := has been evaluated. In such cases, look for the error to the left of or above the cursor.

1 Out of memory.

This error occurs when the compiler has run out of memory. There are a number of possible solutions to this problem:

- If Compile/Destination is set to Memory, set it to Disk in the integrated environment.
- If Options/Linker/Link Buffer in the integrated environment is set to Memory, set it to Disk. Use the /L option to link to disk in the command-line compiler.
- If you are using any memory-resident utilities, such as SideKick and SuperKey, remove them from memory.

- If you are using TURBO.EXE, try using TPC.EXE instead—it takes up less memory.

If none of these suggestions help, your program or unit may simply be too large to compile in the amount of memory available, and you may have to break it into two or more smaller units.

2 Identifier expected.

An identifier was expected at this point. You may be trying to redeclare a reserved word.

3 Unknown identifier.

This identifier has not been declared, or may not be visible within the current scope.

4 Duplicate identifier.

The identifier has already been used within the current block.

5 Syntax error.

An illegal character was found in the source text. You may have forgotten the quotes around a string constant.

6 Error in real constant.

The syntax of real-type constants is defined in Chapter 1, "Tokens and Constants."

7 Error in integer constant.

The syntax of integer-type constants is defined in Chapter 1, "Tokens and Constants." Note that whole real numbers outside the maximum integer range must be followed by a decimal point and a zero; for example, 12345678912.0.

8 String constant exceeds line.

You have most likely forgotten the ending quote in a string constant.

9 Too many nested files.

The compiler allows no more than 15 nested source files. Most likely you have more than four nested Include files.

10 Unexpected end of file.

You might have gotten this error message because of one of the following:

- Your source file ends before the final **end** of the main statement part. Most likely, your **begins** and **ends** are unbalanced.
- An Include file ends in the middle of a statement part. Every statement part must be entirely contained in one file.
- You didn't close a comment.

11 Line too long.

The maximum line length is 126 characters.

12 Type identifier expected.

The identifier does not denote a type as it should.

13 Too many open files.

If this error occurs, your CONFIG.SYS file does not include a FILES=xx entry or the entry specifies too few files. Increase the number to some suitable value, for instance, 20.

14 Invalid file name.

The file name is invalid or specifies a nonexistent path.

15 File not found.

The file could not be found in the current directory or in any of the search directories that apply to this type of file.

16 Disk full.

Delete some files or use a new disk.

17 Invalid compiler directive.

The compiler directive letter is unknown, one of the compiler directive parameters is invalid, or you are using a global compiler directive when compilation of the body of the program has begun.

18 Too many files.

There are too many files involved in the compilation of the program or unit. Try not to use that many files, for instance, by merging Include files or making the file names shorter.

19 Undefined type in pointer definition.

The type was referenced in a pointer-type declaration previously, but it was never declared.

20 Variable identifier expected.

The identifier does not denote a variable as it should.

21 Error in type.

This symbol cannot start a type definition.

22 Structure too large.

The maximum allowable size of a structured type is 65520 bytes.

23 Set base type out of range.

The base type of a set must be a subrange with bounds in the range 0..255 or an enumerated type with no more than 256 possible values.

24 File components may not be files.

file of file constructs are not allowed.

25 Invalid string length.

The declared maximum length of a string must be in the range 1..255.

26 Type mismatch.

This is due to one of the following:

- incompatible types of the variable and the expression in an assignment statement
- incompatible types of the actual and formal parameter in a call to a procedure or function
- an expression type that is incompatible with index type in array indexing
- incompatible types of operands in an expression

27 Invalid subrange base type.

All ordinal types are valid base types.

28 Lower bound greater than upper bound.

The declaration of a subrange type specifies a lower bound greater than the upper bound.

29 Ordinal type expected.

Real types, string types, structured types, and pointer types are not allowed here.

30 Integer constant expected.

31 Constant expected.

32 Integer or real constant expected.

33 Type identifier expected.

The identifier does not denote a type as it should.

34 Invalid function result type.

Valid function result types are all simple types, string types, and pointer types.

35 Label identifier expected.

The identifier does not denote a label as it should.

36 BEGIN expected.

A **begin** is expected here, or there is an error in the block structure of the unit or program.

37 END expected.

An **end** is expected here, or there is an error in the block structure of the unit or program.

38 Integer expression expected.

The preceding expression must be of an integer type.

39 Ordinal expression expected.

The preceding expression must be of an ordinal type.

40 Boolean expression expected.

The preceding expression must be of type boolean.

41 Operand types do not match operator.

The operator cannot be applied to operands of this type, for example, 'A' div '2'.

42 Error in expression.

This symbol cannot participate in an expression in the way it does. You may have forgotten to write an operator between two operands.

43 Illegal assignment.

- Files and untyped variables cannot be assigned values.
- A function identifier can only be assigned values within the statement part of the function.

44 Field identifier expected.

The identifier does not denote a field in the preceding record variable.

45 Object file too large.

Turbo Pascal cannot link in .OBJ files larger than 64K.

46 Undefined external.

The **external** procedure or function did not have a matching PUBLIC definition in an object file. Make sure you have specified all object files in {$L *filename*} directives, and check the spelling of the procedure or function identifier in the .ASM file.

47 Invalid object file record.

The .OBJ file contains an invalid object record; make sure the file is in fact an .OBJ file.

48 Code segment too large.

The maximum size of the code of a program or unit is 65520 bytes. If you are compiling a program, move some procedures or functions into a unit. If you are compiling a unit, break it into two or more units.

49 Data segment too large.

The maximum size of a program's data segment is 65520 bytes, including data declared by the used units. If you need more global data than this, declare the larger structures as pointers, and allocate them dynamically using the *New* procedure.

50 DO expected.

The reserved word **do** does not appear where it should.

51 Invalid PUBLIC definition.

- The identifier was made public through a PUBLIC directive in assembly language, but is has no matching **external** declaration in the Pascal program or unit.
- Two or more PUBLIC directives in assembly language define the same identifier.
- The .OBJ file defines PUBLIC symbols that do not reside in the CODE segment.

52 Invalid EXTRN definition.

- The identifier was referred to through an EXTRN directive in assembly language, but it is not declared in the Pascal program or unit, nor in the interface part of any of the used units.
- The identifier denotes an **absolute** variable.
- The identifier denotes an **inline** procedure or function.

53 Too many EXTRN definitions.

Turbo Pascal cannot handle .OBJ files with more than 256 EXTRN definitions.

54 OF expected.

The reserved word **of** does not appear where it should.

55 INTERFACE expected.

The reserved word **interface** does not appear where it should.

56 Invalid relocatable reference.

- The .OBJ file contains data and relocatable references in segments other than CODE. For example, you are attempting to declare initialized variables in the DATA segment.
- The .OBJ file contains byte-sized references to relocatable symbols. This error occurs if you use the HIGH and LOW operators with relocatable symbols or if you refer to relocatable symbols in DB directives.
- An operand refers to a relocatable symbol that was not defined in the CODE segment or in the DATA segment.
- An operand refers to an EXTRN procedure or function with an offset, for example, *CALL SortProc+8*.

57 THEN expected.

The reserved word **then** does not appear where it should.

58 TO or DOWNTO expected.

The reserved word **to** or **downto** does not appear where it should.

59 Undefined forward.

- The procedure or function was declared in the **interface** part of a unit, but its definition never occurred in the **implementation** part.
- The procedure or function was declared with **forward**, but its definition was never found.

60 Too many procedures.

Turbo Pascal does not allow more than 512 procedures or functions per module. If you are compiling a program, move some procedures or functions into a unit. If you are compiling a unit, break it into two or more units.

61 Invalid typecast.

- The sizes of the variable reference and the destination type differ in a variable typecast.
- You are attempting to typecast an expression where only a variable reference is allowed.

62 Division by zero.

The preceding operand attempts to divide by zero.

63 Invalid file type.

The file type is not supported by the file-handling procedure; for example, *Readln* with a typed file or *Seek* with a text file.

64 Cannot Read or Write variables of this type.

- *Read* and *Readln* can input variables of char, integer, real, and string types.
- *Write* and *Writeln* can output variables of char, integer, real, string, and boolean types.

65 Pointer variable expected.

The preceding variable must be of a pointer type.

66 String variable expected.

The preceding variable must be of a string type.

67 String expression expected.

The preceding expression must be of a string type.

68 Circular unit reference.

Two units are not allowed to use each other:

```
unit U1;        unit U2;
uses U2;        uses U1;
...             ...
```

In this example, doing a Make on either unit will generate error 68.

69 Unit name mismatch.

The name of the unit found in the .TPU file does not match the name specified in the **uses** clause.

70 Unit version mismatch.

One or more of the units used by this unit have been changed since the unit was compiled. Use Compile/Make or Compile/Build in the integrated environment and /M or /B options in the command-line compiler to automatically compile units that need recompilation.

71 Duplicate unit name.

You have already named this unit in the **uses** clause.

72 Unit file format error.

The .TPU file is somehow invalid; make sure it is in fact a .TPU file.

73 IMPLEMENTATION expected.

The reserved word **implementation** does not appear where it should.

74 Constant and case types do not match.

The type of the **case** constant is incompatible with the **case** statement's selector expression.

75 Record variable expected.

The preceding variable must be of a record type.

76 Constant out of range.

You are trying to:
- index an array with an out-of-range constant
- assign an out-of-range constant to a variable
- pass an out-of-range constant as a parameter to a procedure or function

77 File variable expected.

The preceding variable must be of a file type.

78 Pointer expression expected.

The preceding expression must be of a pointer type.

79 Integer or real expression expected.

The preceding expression must be of an integer or a real type.

80 Label not within current block.

A **goto** statement cannot reference a label outside the current block.

81 Label already defined.

The label already marks a statement.

82 Undefined label in preceding statement part.

The label was declared and referenced in the preceding statement part, but it was never defined.

83 Invalid @ argument.

Valid arguments are variable references and procedure or function identifiers.

84 UNIT expected.

The reserved word **unit** does not appear where it should.

85 ";" expected.

A semicolon does not appear where it should.

86 ":" expected.

A colon does not appear where it should.

87 "," expected.

A comma does not appear where it should.

88 "(" expected.

An opening parenthesis does not appear where it should.

89 ")" expected.

A closing parenthesis does not appear where it should.

90 "=" expected.

An equal sign does not appear where it should.

91 ":=" expected.

An assignment operator does not appear where it should.

92 "[" or "(." expected.

A left bracket does not appear where it should.

93 "]" or ".)" expected.

A right bracket does not appear where it should.

94 "." expected.

A period does not appear where it should.

95 ".." expected.

A subrange does not appear where it should.

96 Too many variables.

- The total size of the global variables declared within a program or unit cannot exceed 64K.
- The total size of the local variables declared within a procedure or function cannot exceed 64K.

97 Invalid FOR control variable.

The **for** statement control variable must be a simple variable defined in the declaration part of the current subprogram.

98 Integer variable expected.

The preceding variable must be of an integer type.

99 Files are not allowed here.

A typed constant cannot be of a file type.

100 String length mismatch.

The length of the string constant does not match the number of components in the character array.

101 Invalid ordering of fields.

The fields of a record-type constant must be written in the order of declaration.

102 String constant expected.

A string constant does not appear where it should.

103 Integer or real variable expected.

The preceding variable must be of an integer or real type.

104 Ordinal variable expected.

The preceding variable must be of an ordinal type.

105 INLINE error.

The < operator is not allowed in conjunction with relocatable references to variables—such references are always word-sized.

106 Character expression expected.

The preceding expression must be of a char type.

107 Too many relocation items.

The size of the relocation table part of the .EXE file exceeds 64K, which is Turbo Pascal's upper limit. If you encounter this error, your program is simply too big for Turbo Pascal's linker to handle. It is probably also too big for DOS to execute. You will have to split the program into a "main" part that executes two or more "subprogram" parts using the *Exec* procedure in the *Dos* unit.

112 CASE constant out of range.

For integer type **case** statements, the constants must be within the range –32768..32767.

113 Error in statement.

This symbol cannot start a statement.

114 Cannot call an interrupt procedure.

You cannot directly call an interrupt procedure.

116 Must be in 8087 mode to compile this.

This construct can only be compiled in the {$N+} state. Operations on the 8087 real types, single, double, extended, and comp, are not allowed in the {$N-} state.

117 Target address not found.

The Compile/Find error command in the integrated environment or the /F option in the command-line version could not locate a statement that corresponds to the specified address.

118 Include files are not allowed here.

Every statement part must be entirely contained in one file.

120 NIL expected.

Typed constants of pointer types may only be initialized to the value **nil**.

121 Invalid qualifier.

You are trying to do one of the following:

- index a variable that is not an array
- specify fields in a variable that is not a record
- dereference a variable that is not a pointer

122 Invalid variable reference.

The preceding construct follows the syntax of a variable reference, but it does not denote a memory location. Most likely, you are calling a pointer function, but forgetting to dereference the result.

123 Too many symbols.

The program or unit declares more than 64K of symbols. If you are compiling with {$D+}, try turning it off—note, however, that this will prevent you from finding run-time errors in that module. Otherwise, you could try moving some declarations into a separate unit.

124 Statement part too large.

Turbo Pascal limits the size of a statement part to about 24K. If you encounter this error, move sections of the statement part into one or more procedures. In any case, with a statement part of that size, it's worth the effort to clarify the structure of your program.

126 Files must be var parameters.

You are attempting to declare a file type value parameter. File type parameters must be **var** parameters.

127 Too many conditional symbols.

There is not enough room to define further conditional symbols. Try to eliminate some symbols, or shorten some of the symbolic names.

128 Misplaced conditional directive.

The compiler encountered an {$ELSE} or {$ENDIF} directive without a matching {$IFDEF}, {$IFNDEF}, or {$IFOPT} directive.

129 ENDIF directive missing.

The source file ended within a conditional compilation construct. There must be an equal number of {$IF*xxx*}s and {$ENDIF}s in a source file.

130 Error in initial conditional defines.

The initial conditional symbols specified in Options/Compiler/Conditional Defines (with the IDE) or in a /D directive (with the command-line compiler) are invalid. Turbo Pascal expects zero or more identifiers separated by blanks, commas, or semicolons.

131 Header does not match previous definition.

The procedure or function header specified in the **interface** part or **forward** declaration does not match this header.

132 Critical disk error.

A critical error occurred during compilation (for example, drive not ready error).

133 Cannot evaluate this expression.

You are attempting to use a non-supported feature in a constant expression or in a debug expression. For example, you are attempting to use the *Sin* function in a **const** declaration, or you are attempting to call a user-defined function in a debug expression. For a description of the allowed syntax of constant expressions, please refer to Chapter 1, "Tokens and Constants." For a description of the allowed syntax of debug expressions, please refer to Chapter 6 in the *User's Guide*, "Debugging Your Turbo Pascal Programs."

134 Expression incorrectly terminated.

Turbo Pascal expects either an operator or the end of the expression at this point, but neither was found.

135 Invalid format specifier.

You are using an invalid format specifier, or the numeric argument of a format specifier is out of range. For a list of valid format specifiers, refer to Chapter 6 in the *User's Guide*, "Debugging Your Turbo Pascal Programs"

136 Invalid indirect reference.

The statement attempts to make an invalid indirect reference. For example, you are using an **absolute** variable whose base variable is not known in the current module, or you are using an **inline** routine that references a variable not known in the current module.

137 Structured variables are not allowed here.

You are attempting to perform a non-supported operation on a structured variable. For example, you are trying to multiply two records.

138 Cannot evaluate without System unit.

Your TURBO.TPL library must contain the *System* unit for the debugger to be able to evaluate expressions.

139 Cannot access this symbol.

A program's entire set of symbols is available as soon as you have compiled the program. However, certain symbols, such as variables, cannot be accessed until you actually run the program.

140 Invalid floating-point operation.

An operation on two real type values produced an overflow or a division by zero.

141 Cannot compile overlays to memory.

A program that uses overlays must be compiled to disk.

142 Procedural or function variable expected.

In this context, the address operator (@) can only be used with a procedural or function variable.

143 Invalid procedure or function reference.

- You are attempting to call a procedure in an expression.
- If you are going to assign a procedure or function to a procedural variable, it must be compiled in the {$F+} state and cannot be declared with **inline** or **interrupt**.

144 Cannot overlay this unit

You are attempting to overlay a unit that wasn't compiled in the {$O+} state.

145 Too many nested scopes.

Your program has too many nested scopes. Each project can have no more than 512 nested scopes with no more than 128 nested scopes in each module. Each unit in a **uses** clause, each nested record type declaration, and each nested **with** context count toward the total number of nested scopes.

Run-time Errors

Certain errors at run time cause the program to display an error message and terminate:

```
Run-time error nnn at xxxx:yyyy
```

where *nnn* is the run-time error number, and *xxxx:yyyy* is the run-time error address (segment and offset).

The run-time errors are divided into four categories: DOS errors 1-99; I/O errors, 100-149; critical errors, 150-199; and fatal errors, 200-255.

DOS Errors

1 Invalid function number.

You made a call to a nonexistent DOS function.

2 File not found.

Reported by *Reset*, *Append*, *Rename*, or *Erase* if the name assigned to the file variable does not specify an existing file.

3 Path not found.

- Reported by *Reset*, *Rewrite*, *Append*, *Rename*, or *Erase* if the name assigned to the file variable is invalid or specifies a nonexistent subdirectory.
- Reported by *ChDir*, *MkDir*, or *RmDir* if the path is invalid or specifies a nonexistent subdirectory.

4 Too many open files.

Reported by *Reset*, *Rewrite*, or *Append* if the program has too many open files. DOS never allows more than 15 open files per process. If you get this error with less than 15 open files, it may indicate that the CONFIG.SYS file does not include a FILES=*xx* entry or that the entry specifies too few files. Increase the number to some suitable value, for instance, 20.

5 File access denied.

- Reported by *Reset* or *Append* if *FileMode* allows writing and the name assigned to the file variable specifies a directory or a read-only file.
- Reported by *Rewrite* if the directory is full or if the name assigned to the file variable specifies a directory or an existing read-only file.
- Reported by *Rename* if the name assigned to the file variable specifies a directory or if the new name specifies an existing file.
- Reported by *Erase* if the name assigned to the file variable specifies a directory or a read-only file.
- Reported by *MkDir* if a file with the same name exists in the parent directory, if there is no room in the parent directory, or if the path specifies a device.
- Reported by *RmDir* if the directory isn't empty, if the path doesn't specify a directory, or if the path specifies the root directory.
- Reported by *Read* or *BlockRead* on a typed or untyped file if the file is not open for reading.
- Reported by *Write* or *BlockWrite* on a typed or untyped file if the file is not open for writing.

6 Invalid file handle.

This error is reported if an invalid file handle is passed to a DOS system call. It should never occur; if it does, it is an indication that the file variable is somehow trashed.

12 Invalid file access code.

Reported by *Reset* or *Append* on a typed or untyped file if the value of *FileMode* is invalid.

15 Invalid drive number.

Reported by *GetDir* or *ChDir* if the drive number is invalid.

16 Cannot remove current directory.

Reported by *RmDir* if the path specifies the current directory.

17 Cannot rename across drives.

Reported by *Rename* if both names are not on the same drive.

I/O Errors

These errors cause termination if the particular statement was compiled in the {$I+} state. In the {$I-} state, the program continues to execute, and the error is reported by the *IOResult* function.

100 Disk read error.

Reported by *Read* on a typed file if you attempt to read past the end of the file.

101 Disk write error.

Reported by *Close, Write, Writeln, Flush,* or *Page* if the disk becomes full.

102 File not assigned.

Reported by *Reset, Rewrite, Append, Rename,* and *Erase* if the file variable has not been assigned a name through a call to *Assign*.

103 File not open.

Reported by *Close, Read, Write, Seek, Eof, FilePos, FileSize, Flush, BlockRead,* or *BlockWrite* if the file is not open.

104 File not open for input.

Reported by *Read, Readln, Eof, Eoln, SeekEof,* or *SeekEoln* on a text file if the file is not open for input.

105 File not open for output.

Reported by *Write* and *Writeln* on a text file if the file is not open for output.

106 Invalid numeric format.

Reported by *Read* or *Readln* if a numeric value read from a text file does not conform to the proper numeric format.

Critical Errors

150 Disk is write-protected.

151 Unknown unit.

152 Drive not ready.

153 Unknown command.

154 CRC error in data.

155 Bad drive request structure length.

156 Disk seek error.

157 Unknown media type.

158 Sector not found.

159 Printer out of paper.

160 Device write fault.

161 Device read fault.

162 Hardware failure.

Refer to your DOS programmer's reference manual for more information about critical errors.

Fatal Errors

These errors always immediately terminate the program.

200 Division by zero.

The program attempted to divide a number by zero during a /, **mod**, or **div** operation.

201 Range check error.

This error is reported by statements compiled in the {$R+} state when one of the following situations arises:

- The index expression of an array qualifier was out of range.
- You attempted to assign an out-of-range value to a variable.
- You attempted to assign an out-of-range value as a parameter to a procedure or function.

202 Stack overflow error.

This error is reported on entry to a procedure or function compiled in the {$S+} state when there is not enough stack space to allocate the subprogram's local variables. Increase the size of the stack by using the $M compiler directive.

This error may also be caused by infinite recursion, or by an assembly language procedure that does not maintain the stack project.

203 Heap overflow error.

This error is reported by *New* or *GetMem* when there is not enough free space in the heap to allocate a block of the requested size.

For a complete discussion of the heap manager, refer to Chapter 15, "Inside Turbo Pascal."

204 Invalid pointer operation.

This error is reported by *Dispose* or *FreeMem* if the pointer is **nil** or points to a location outside the heap, or if the free list cannot be expanded due to a full free list or to *HeapPtr* being too close to the bottom of the free list.

205 Floating point overflow.

A floating-point operation produced a number too large for Turbo Pascal or the numeric coprocessor (if any) to handle.

206 Floating point underflow

A floating-point operation produced an underflow. This error is only reported if you are using the 8087 numeric coprocessor with a control word that unmasks underflow exceptions. By default, an underflow causes a result of zero to be returned.

207 Invalid floating point operation

- The real value passed to *Trunc* or *Round* could not be converted to an integer within the longint range (-2147483648 to 2147483647).
- The argument passed to the *Sqrt* function was negative.
- The argument passed to the *Ln* function was zero or negative.
- An 8087 stack overflow occurred. For further details on correctly programming the 8087, refer to Chapter 14, "Using the 8087."

208 Overlay manager not installed

Your program is calling an overlaid procedure or function, but the overlay manager is not installed. Most likely, you are not calling *OvrInit*, or the call to *OvrInit* failed. Note that, if you have initialization code in any of your overlaid units, you must create an additional non-overlaid unit which calls *OvrInit*, and use that unit before any of the overlaid units. For a complete description of the overlay manager, refer to Chapter 13, "Overlays."

209 Overlay file read error

A read error occurred when the overlay manager tried to read an overlay from the overlay file.

Index

$ *See* compiler, directives
8087/80287/80387 coprocessor *See*
   numeric coprocessor
256-color mode 134
@ (address-of) operator *See* address-of (@) operator
^ (pointer) symbol 32, 42
# (pound) character 14

A

$A compiler directive 219, 408
Abs function 111, 218, 224
absolute clause 39
actual parameters 62, 66
Addr function 112, 224
address-of (@) operator 32, 42, 61, 90
   double 90
   versus ^ (pointer) symbol 401
   versus Addr 224
Align Data command 408
aligning data 408
and operator 56, 137
AndPut constant 332
ANSI Pascal 401
   errors in 406
Append procedure 101, 104, 225
.ARC files 2
Arc procedure 147, 148, 155, 226
ArcTan function 111, 226
arithmetic
   functions 110
   operators 54
array-type constants 47
arrays 28, 41, 47
   types 28, 193
   variables 41
ASCII codes 421
.ASM files 178
aspect ratio 265
   correction factor, changing 355
assembly language 199, 415
   8087 emulation and 178
   examples 201
   inline
      directives 207
      statements 205
   interfacing program routines with 200

routines, overlays and 169
Assign procedure 101, 102, 211, 227
AssignCrt procedure 132, 211, 228
assignment statements 66
automatic
   call model selection, overriding 197
   word alignment 219
Aux (version 3.0) 212
AUXINOUT.PAS 212
AX register 196, 207

B

$B compiler directive 409
Back procedure 155
Bar3D procedure 133, 145, 148, 229
Bar procedure 148, 229
BGI, Zenith Z-449 and 299
.BGI files 133
BINOBJ 3, 340, 342
BIOS 126, 130
bit images 137, 276
bit-mapped fonts 136
bit-oriented routines 133
BitBlt
   operations 137, 332
   operators 146
bitwise operators 56
BlockRead procedure 105, 230
blocks, program 17
BlockWrite procedure 105, 232
Boolean
   evaluation, compiler switch 409
   operators 56
   type 24, 189
   values 24
Boolean Evaluation command 409
BP register 169, 199, 206, 209
brackets, in expressions 63
buffers, flushing 261
BX register 196, 209
byte data type 23

C

calling conventions 195
case statements 69
CBreak variable 154

CGA 128, 133
  CheckSnow and 130
char data type 24, 189
characters
  special 127
  strings 14
ChDir procedure 102, 233
CheckBreak variable 129
CheckEOF variable 130
CheckSnow variable 130
.CHR files 133
Chr function 110, 218, 233
Circle procedure 133, 148, 155, 234
circular unit references 97
ClearDevice procedure 148, 234
clearing the overlay buffer 323
ClearScreen procedure 155
ClearViewPort procedure 148, 235
clipping parameters 287
Close function 212
Close procedure 102, 210, 236
CloseGraph procedure 133, 148, 236
ClrEol procedure 132, 237
ClrScr procedure 132, 237
CODE 199
colors 272, 273
  background 266
  drawing 267
ColorTable procedure 155
COM devices 107, 212
command-line compiler 3
command-line parameters 113, 328
comments, program 16
common type 23
communications, serial 212
comp floating-point type 173, 191
comparing values of real types 174
compilation, conditional 416
compiler
  command-line 3
  directives 16, 407-420
    $A 219, 408
    $B 409
    Boolean evaluation 409
    conditional 407, 416-420
    $D 410
    $DEFINE 417, 419
    $E 172, 410
    $ELSE 420

$ENDIF 420
$F 86, 165, 197, 411
$I 102, 119, 306, 411, 415
$IFDEF 419
$IFNDEF 419
$IFOPT 420
$L 199, 412, 415
local symbol 412
$M 38, 181, 307, 313, 314, 327, 416
$N 26, 171, 223, 412
$O 164, 413, 416
  non-overlay units and 168
  parameter 407, 415-416
$R 413
$S 38, 414
switch 407, 408-414
$UNDEF 417, 419
$V 414
error messages 427
integrated environment 1
compound statements 67
CON device 107
Concat function 112, 238
concatenation 58
conditional
  compilation 416
  statements 68
  symbols 417
CONFIG.SYS 326
constant expressions 15
  restrictions 15
  type definition 26
constants 120
  array-type 47
  Crt mode 128
  declaration part 18
  declarations 15
  defined by Overlay unit 161
  file attribute 121
  folding 218
  Graph3 unit 155
  Graph unit 142
  merging 218
  pointer-type 49
  record-type 48
  set-type 48
  simple 15
  simple-type 46

Index 451

string-type 46
structured-type 46
text color 128
typed 45
control characters 14, 421
Copy function 112, 239
Cos function 111, 239
CPU symbols 418, 419
critical errors
　messages 446
　trapping 118
Crt unit 103, 108, 115, 116, 126, 153
　AssignCrt procedure 228
　ClrEol procedure 237
　ClrScr procedure 237
　constants 128
　Delay procedure 240
　DelLine procedure 241
　functions 132
　GotoXY procedure 290
　HighVideo procedure 295
　InsLine procedure 300
　KeyPressed function 307
　line input 127
　LowVideo procedure 312
　mode constants 128
　NormVideo procedure 319
　NoSound procedure 319
　procedures 132
　ReadKey function 337
　Sound procedure 381
　special characters 127
　text color 128
　TextBackground procedure 385
　TextColor procedure 385
　TextMode procedure 387
　variables 129
　WhereX function 393
　WhereY function 393
　Window procedure 394
CS register 209, 240
CSEG 199, 200
CSeg function 112, 199, 200, 240
current pointer 135
cursor position
　reading 393
　setting 290
customizing Turbo Pascal 3
CX register 209

D

$D compiler directive 410
DATA 199
data
　alignment 408
　encryption 118
　ports 208
　segment 38
　types *See* types
date and time procedures 124
　GetDate 268
　GetFTime 274
　GetTime 287
　SetDate 358
　SetFTime 362
　SetTime 374
DateTime type 122
dead code removal 220
Debug Information command 410
debugging
　information switch 410
　overlays 169
　range-checking switch 413
　run-time error messages 443
　stack overflow switch 414
Dec procedure 111, 240
decimal notation 13
declaration part, block 17
$DEFINE compiler directive 417, 419
Delay procedure 132, 240
Delete procedure 112, 241
DelLine procedure 132, 241
DetectGraph procedure 143, 148, 242
devices 106, 234
　drivers 210
　　installing 301
　handlers 153, 209, 210
DI register 209
direct memory 208
directives *See* compiler, directives
directories 269
　changing 233
　procedures 348
　scan procedures for 122
　searching 258, 262
DirectVideo variable 130
DiskFree function 124, 243
disks
　distribution 1

space 243
status functions 124
DiskSize function 124, 243
Dispose procedure 110, 182, 183, 185, 244
distribution disks 1
div operator 55
DOS
  device handling 210
  devices 106
  environment 179
  error level 217
  exit code 216
  operating system routines 119
  Pascal functions for 318
  registers and 122
  verify flag 287
    setting 376
Dos unit 115, 119
  constants 120
  date and time procedures 124
  disk status functions 124
  DiskFree function 243
  DiskSize function 243
  DosError in 123
  DosExitCode function 245
  DosVersion function 245
  EnvCount function 248
  environment-handling functions 125
  EnvStr function 248
  Exec procedure 251
  FExpand function 254
  file-handling procedures and functions 124
  FindFirst procedure 258
  FindNext procedure 259
  FSearch function 262
  FSplit procedure 263
  GetCBreak procedure 267
  GetDate procedure 268
  GetEnv function 270
  GetFAttr procedure 271
  GetFTime procedure 274
  GetIntVec procedure 277
  GetTime procedure 287
  GetVerify procedure 287
  interrupt support procedures 123
  Intr procedure 305
  Keep procedure 307
  miscellaneous procedures and functions 125
  MsDos procedure 318
  PackTime procedure 328
  process-handling procedures and functions 125
  SetCBreak procedure 357
  SetFTime procedure 362
  SetIntVec procedure 365
  SetTime procedure 374
  SetVerify 376
  SwapVectors procedure 384
  types 120
  UnpackTime procedure 391
DosError variable 123, 251, 258, 259, 271, 274, 359, 362
DosExitCode function 125, 245
DosVersion function 126, 245
double floating-point type 172, 190
Draw procedure 156
DrawPoly procedure 133, 148, 246
drivers
  active, returning
    maximum mode number 279
    name 270
  graphics 133
DS register 199, 206, 209, 247
DSEG 199, 200
DSeg function 112, 199, 200, 247
DX register 196, 209
dynamic
  memory allocation 116
    functions 109
  variables 32, 38, 42, 181

E

$E compiler directive 172, 410
East constant 155
EGA, CheckSnow and 130
ellipse, drawing 256
Ellipse procedure 147, 148, 247
elliptical sector, drawing and filling 350
$ELSE compiler directive 420
empty set 31
EMS memory, overlay files and 159, 165

emulating numeric coprocessor
    (8087) 27
  compiler switch 410
Emulation command 410
end of file
  error messages 429
  status 249
$ENDIF compiler directive 420
entry code, procedures and functions
    198
enumerated type 24, 189
EnvCount function 125, 248
EnvStr function 125, 248
Eof function 103, 249
Eoln function 104, 250
Erase procedure 102, 250
ErrorAddr variable 118, 217
errors
  ANSI Pascal 406
  codes for graphics operations 291, 292
  critical 446
  fatal, in OvrInit 167
  handling 137
  messages 291, 427
    critical 446
    fatal 447
  range 413
  reporting 216
  run-time *See* run-time, errors
ES register 209
.EXE files 159
  building 220
Exec procedure 125, 251
exit
  codes 245
  functions 198
  procedures 198, 216, 253
    implementing 118
Exit procedure 109
ExitCode variable 118, 217
exiting a program 216
ExitProc variable 118, 216
Exp function 111, 253
Expanded Memory Specification *See*
    EMS memory
exponents 189
expressions 51
  constant 15

examples 54
extended
  floating-point type 173
  key codes 126, 424
  memory support *See* EMS
  memory
  range arithmetic 173
extended floating-point type 191
extensions, ANSI Pascal 403
external
  declarations 79, 199, 415
  procedure errors 432
ExternProc 169
EXTRN definition errors 199, 200, 433

F

$F compiler directive 86, 165, 197, 411
factor (syntax) 52
FAR calls 197
  model 164
    forcing use of 216, 411
  requirement 160
fatal run-time errors 447
FExpand function 125, 254
Fibonacci numbers 175
field
  designators 41
  list (of records) 29
file-handling procedures 124, 405
  Rename 345
  Reset 345
  Rewrite 347
  routines 119
  Seek 351
  SetFAttr 359
  Truncate 391
FileMode variable 105, 118
FilePos function 105, 254
FileRec 120, 193
files
  access, read-only 105
  access-denied error 444
  .ASM 178
  Assign procedure 227
  attributes 271
    constants 121
  .BGI 133
  buffer 194

.CHR 133
closing 236
erasing 250
.EXE 159
  building 220
handles 193, 194
I/O 116, 126
modes 193, 194
  constants 120
.OBJ 199
  linking with 415
.OVR 159
record types 120
text 103
typed 118, 193
types 31, 193
untyped 105, 118, 193
  variable 230, 232
FileSize function 105, 255
fill patterns 272
FillChar procedure 112, 255
FillEllipse procedure 148, 256
filling areas 259
FillPattern procedure 156
FillPoly procedure 137, 148, 257
FillScreen procedure 156
FillShape procedure 156
FindFirst procedure 121, 124, 258
  SearchRec and 122
FindNext procedure 121, 124, 259
  SearchRec and 122
fixed part (of records) 29
flags constants 120
floating-point
  calculations, type real and 173
  code generation, switching 171
  errors 447
  numbers 171
  numeric coprocessor (8087) 27
  parameters 196
  routines 116
  software 26
  types *See* types, floating-point
FloodFill procedure 134, 137, 149, 259
Flush function 212
Flush procedure 104, 261
Font8x8 variable 128, 387, 388
fonts
  files 141

installing 304
stroked 375
for statements, syntax 72
Force Far Calls command 86, 165, 411
force FAR calls compiler switch 411
formal parameters 66, 82
forward declarations 78
Forwd procedure 156
Frac function 111, 261
fractions, returning 261
free list 185
  overflow 187
FreeMem procedure 110, 182, 183, 185, 187, 261
FreeMin variable 118, 186
FreePtr variable 118, 185
FSearch function 125, 262
FSplit procedure 124, 254, 263
functions 77
  address 112
  arithmetic 110
  body 80
  calls 62, 195
  Crt unit 132
  declarations 80
  disk status 124
  dynamic allocation 109
  file-handling 124
  Graph unit 151
  headings 80
  nested 86
  non-ANSI 405
  ordinal 111
  pointer 112
  results 196
  standard 109
  string 112
  transfer 110
  Turbo3 unit 154

G

GetArcCoords procedure 147, 149, 264
GetAspectRatio procedure 149, 265
GetBkColor function 151, 266
GetCBreak procedure 125, 267
GetColor function 151, 267
GetDate procedure 124, 268

GetDefaultPalette function 146, 151, 268
GetDir procedure 102, 269
GetDotColor procedure 156
GetDriverName function 151, 270
GetEnv function 125, 270
GetFAttr procedure 121, 125, 271
GetFillPattern procedure 147, 149, 272
GetFillSettings procedure 145, 147, 149, 273
GetFTime procedure 124, 274
GetGraphMode function 151, 274
GetImage procedure 133, 149, 276
GetIntVec procedure 123, 277
GetLineSettings procedure 145, 146, 149, 277
GetMaxColor function 151, 278
GetMaxMode function 151, 279
GetMaxX function 151, 280
GetMaxY function 151, 281
GetMem procedure 110, 186, 187, 188, 281
GetModeName function 151, 282
GetModeRange procedure 143, 149, 283
GetPalette procedure 146, 149, 283
  IBM 8514 and 284
GetPaletteSize function 151, 284
GetPic procedure 156
GetPixel function 137, 151, 285
GetTextSettings procedure 136, 145, 147, 149, 285
GetTime procedure 124, 287
GetVerify procedure 126, 287
GetViewSettings procedure 147, 149, 287
GetX function 151, 288
GetY function 151, 289
goto statements 67
GotoXY procedure 132, 290
GRAPH3.TPU 3
Graph3 unit 115, 116, 155
  constants 155
  procedures 155
GRAPH.BIN 155
GRAPH.P 155
GRAPH.TPU 2, 134
Graph unit 115, 133, 166

Arc procedure 226
Bar3D procedure 229
Bar procedure 229
bit images in 137
Circle procedure 234
ClearDevice procedure 234
ClearViewPort procedure 235
CloseGraph procedure 236
colors 137
constants 142
DetectGraph procedure 242
DrawPoly procedure 246
Ellipse procedure 247
error-handling 137
figures and styles in 136
FillEllipse procedure 256
FillPoly procedure 257
FloodFill procedure 259
functions 151
GetArcCoords procedure 264
GetAspectRatio procedure 265
GetBkColor function 266
GetColor function 267
GetDefaultPalette function 268
GetDriverName function 270
GetFillPattern procedure 272
GetFillSettings procedure 273
GetGraphMode function 274
GetImage procedure 276
GetLineSettings procedure 277
GetMaxColor function 278
GetMaxMode function 279
GetMaxX function 280
GetMaxY function 281
GetModeName function 282
GetModeRange procedure 283
GetPalette procedure 283
GetPaletteSize function 284
GetPixel function 285
GetTextSettings procedure 285
GetViewSettings procedure 287
GetX function 288
GetY function 289
GraphDefaults procedure 291
GraphErrorMsg function 291
GraphResult function 292
heap management routines 140
ImageSize function 296
InitGraph procedure 297

InstallUserDriver function 301
InstallUserFont function 304
Line procedure 308
LineRel procedure 309
LineTo procedure 310
MoveRel procedure 316
MoveTo procedure 317
OutText procedure 320
OutTextXY procedure 322
paging 137
PieSlice procedure 329
procedures 148
PutImage procedure 331
PutPixel procedure 334
Rectangle procedure 339
RegisterBGIdriver function 340
RegisterBGIfont function 342
RestoreCrtMode procedure 346
sample program 138, 139
Sector procedure 350
SetActivePage procedure 353
SetAllPalette procedure 354
SetAspectRatio procedure 355
SetBkColor procedure 356
SetColor procedure 358
SetFillPattern procedure 359
SetFillStyle procedure 361
SetGraphBufSize procedure 362
SetGraphMode procedure 363
SetLineStyle procedure 366
SetPalette procedure 367
SetRGBPalette procedure 369
SetTextJustify procedure 372
SetTextStyle procedure 373
SetUserCharSize procedure 375
SetViewPort procedure 376
SetVisualPage procedure 378
SetWriteMode 379
text in 136
TextHeight function 386
TextWidth function 389
types 146
variables 148
viewports in 137
GraphBackground procedure 156
GraphColorMode procedure 156
GraphDefaults procedure 149, 291
GraphDriver variable
  IBM 8514 and 134, 299
GraphErrorMsg function 151, 291
GraphFreeMem procedure 140
GraphFreeMemPtr variable 148
GraphGetMem procedure 140
GraphGetMemPtr variable 148
graphics
  bit-image operations 331
  cards 242, 298
  CloseGraph 133
  current pointer in 135
  drawing operations 308, 309, 310, 329, 339, 366
  drivers 133, 297
  figures and styles 136
  fill operations 359, 361
  InitGraph in 133
  mode 274, 297, 309, 310, 311
  page operations 353, 378
  palette operations 354, 356, 358, 367
  plotting operations 334
  pointer operations 317
  polygons, drawing 246
  resolution 265
  sample program 138, 139
  system operations 363
  text operations 320, 322, 372, 386
  turtlegraphics 155
  video mode operations 346
  viewport operations 376
GraphMode procedure 156, 297
GraphResult function 137, 138, 142, 151, 292
  error codes 292
GraphWindow procedure 156
GREP.COM 3
grError 293
grInvalidFont 293
grInvalidFontNum 293
grIOerror 293
GROUP directives 199

H

Halt procedure 109, 216, 294
handles
  DOS 227
  file 193, 194
hardware, interrupts 209

Index   457

Heading procedure 156
heap management 179, 181
   allocating 181, 182, 185, 187
   deallocating 182
   dynamic memory allocation 118
   fragmenting 181
   free list 185
   granularity 186
   map 179
   pointers 180
   procedures 344
   routines 140
   sizes 416
HeapError variable 118, 187
HeapOrg variable 118, 181, 183
HeapPtr variable 118, 181, 186
HELPME!.DOC 1
hexadecimal constants 13
Hi function 113, 218, 295
HideTurtle procedure 156
high
   intensity characters 295
   order bytes 295
   resolution graphics 134
HighVideo procedure 132, 154, 295
HiRes procedure 156
HiResColor procedure 156
Home procedure 156
host type 25

I

$I compiler directive 102, 119, 306, 411, 415
I/O 101
   checking 306
   devices 211
   DOS standard 227
   error-checking 102, 411
   errors 445
   files 116, 126
      standard 118
   redirection 126
   variables 101
I/O-Checking command 411
IBM 8514 133
   driver support 134-134
   GetPalette procedure and 284
   GraphDriver variable and 134, 299

   InitGraph procedure and 134, 299
   palette entries, modifying 369
   SetAllPalette procedure and 355
   SetPalette procedure and 368
   SetRGBPalette and 134
IBM8514.BGI 134
IBM8514HI mode 134
IBM8514LO mode 134
identifiers 11
if statements 68
$IFDEF compiler directive 419
$IFNDEF compiler directive 419
$IFOPT compiler directive 420
ImageSize function 151, 296
implementation
   dependent features, Pascal 405
   part (program) 95, 197
   sections 99
in operator 58, 60
Inc procedure 111, 297
Include Directories command 415
include directories command-line
   option 415
Include files 415
   nesting 415
index expressions 41
indirect unit references 96
InitGraph procedure 133, 143, 149, 297
   SetGraphMode and 363
initialization part (program) 96
initialized variables 45
inline
   declarations 80
   directives 207
   machine code 205
   statements 205
InOut function 212
InOutRes variable 118
input
   DOS standard 227
   files 101, 118
Input standard file 118
Insert procedure 112, 300
inserting
   lines 300
   strings 300
InsLine procedure 132, 300
INSTALL.EXE 2, 4

INSTALL utility 2
installation, Turbo Pascal 2, 4
InstallUserDriver function 152, 301
InstallUserFont function 152, 304
INT 24 handler 118
Int function 111, 305
integer data type 23, 188
integrated environment, using 1
interface section (program) 95, 100, 152, 197, 199
interfacing Turbo Pascal with Turbo Assembler 200
internal data formats 179, 188
interrupt
   directives 78
   handlers 209
      units and 169
   handling routines 118, 209
   procedures 365
   service routines (ISRs) 209
   support procedures 123
   vectors 118, 119, 277
      swapping 384
Intr procedure 123, 305
   registers and 122
invalid typecasting errors 434
IOResult function 103, 118, 154, 306
IP flag 209
ISRs (interrupt service routines) 209

J

justification, font 285

K

Kbd 153
Keep procedure 125, 307
key codes 424
keyboard
   operations 307, 337
   scan codes 425
   status 128
KeyPressed function 128, 132, 307

L

$L compiler directive 199, 412, 415
labels 12
   declaration part 17

LastMode variable 131
Length function 112, 218, 308
line
   drawing, setting writing mode for 379
   input, Crt 127
   settings 277
Line procedure 149, 308
LineRel procedure 149, 309
LineTo procedure 149, 310
linking
   assembly language 199
   object files 415
   smart 220
Ln function 111, 311
Lo function 113, 218, 312
local symbol information switch 412
Local Symbols command 412
logical operators 56
LongFilePos function 154
LongFileSize function 154
longint data type 23
LongSeek procedure 154
LowVideo procedure 132, 154, 312
LPT devices 107, 119
Lst variable 119

M

$M compiler directive 38, 181, 307, 313, 314, 327, 416
machine code 205
macros, inline 207
MAKE utility 3
Mark procedure 110, 182, 313
math coprocessor *See* numeric coprocessor
MaxAvail function 110, 155, 186, 313
Mem array 208
MemAvail function 110, 152, 155, 186, 314
MemL array 208
memory 261, 281
   allocation 166
      compiler directive 416
   DirectVideo and 130
   error messages 427
   map 179
   size 416

Memory Sizes command 416
MemW array 208
MicroCalc 2
MkDir procedure 102, 314
mod operator 55
.MODEL directive
   setting up calling conventions with 200
modular programming 94
monochrome adapters, CheckSnow and 130
Move procedure 113, 315
MoveRel procedure 149, 316
MoveTo procedure 149, 317
MsDos procedure 124, 318
MSDOS symbol 418

N

$N compiler directive 26, 171, 223, 412
NEAR calls 197
nested scopes 443
nesting
   files 415
   procedures and functions 197
network file access, read-only 105
New procedure 32, 110, 181, 186, 188, 318
nil 32, 42
NormalPut constant 332
NormVideo procedure 132, 154, 319
North constant 155
NoSound procedure 132, 319
not operator 56, 137
NotPut constant 332
NoWrap procedure 156
NUL device 107
null strings 14, 27
numbers, counting 13, 188
numeric coprocessor
   compiler switch 412
   detecting 176
   emulating 27, 116, 172
      assembly language and 178
   evaluation stack 175
   floating-point 27
   mode 440
   numeric processing option 27

   using 171-178
Numeric Processing command 172, 413

O

$O compiler directive 164, 413, 416
   non-overlay units and 168
.OBJ files 199
   linking with 415
object
   directories, compiler directive 415
   files 199
      linking with 415
Object Directories command 415
Odd function 111, 218, 319
Ofs function 112, 320
op code 205
Open function 211
operands 51
operators 10, 51, 54
   @ (address-of) 32, 42
      versus ^ (pointer) symbol 401
   address-of (@) 90
   and 56, 137
   arithmetic 54
   BitBlt 146
   bitwise 56
   Boolean 56
   div 55
   logical 56
   mod 55
   not 56, 137
   or 56, 137
   precedence of 51, 55
   relational 58
   set 58
   shl 56
   shr 56
   string 57
   xor 56, 137
optimization of code 217
or operator 56, 137
Ord function 22, 25, 110, 218, 320
order of evaluation 219
ordinal
   functions 111
   procedures 111
   types 22

OrPut constant 332
out-of-memory errors 427
output
   DOS standard 227
   files 101, 118
Output standard file 118
OutText procedure 136, 149, 320
OutTextXY procedure 136, 150, 322
overlaid
   code, storing 181
   initialization code 167
   programs
     designing 164
     writing 160
   routines, calling via procedure pointers 169
Overlay unit 115, 117, 160
   name option 416
   OvrClearBuf procedure 163, 323
   OvrGetBuf function 163, 324
   OvrInit procedure 162, 325
   OvrInitEMS procedure 162, 325
   OvrResult variable 161
   OvrSetBuf procedure 163, 327
overlays 159, 159-170
   assembly language routines and 169
   BP register and 169
   buffers
     clearing 163, 323
     size
       default 181
       increasing 118
         with OvrSetBuf 181
       returning 163, 324
       setting 163, 327
   cautions 168
   code generation, compiler switch 413
   debugging 169
   files
     loading into EMS 165, 325
     opening 325
   loading
     into EMS 162
     into memory 159
   manager 116
     implementing 117
     initializing 162, 165, 167, 325

Overlays Allowed command 413
.OVR files 159
OvrClearBuf procedure 163, 323
OvrCodeList variable 117
OvrDebugPtr variable 117
OvrDosHandle variable 117
OvrEmsHandle variable 117
OvrGetBuf function 163, 324
OvrHeapEnd variable 117
OvrHeapOrg variable 117
OvrHeapPtr variable 117
OvrHeapSize variable 117
OvrInit procedure 162, 325
OvrInitEMS procedure 162, 166, 325
OvrLoadList variable 117
OvrResult variable 161
OvrSetBuf procedure 118, 163, 166, 327
OvrSetBuf routine, increasing size of overlay buffer with 181

P

Pack procedure 110
packed (reserved word) 28
PackTime procedure 124, 328
   DateTime and 122
palette
   color lookup table, returning size 284
   definition record 268
   manipulation routines 134
Palette procedure 156
ParamCount function 113, 328
parameter directives *See* compiler, directives, parameter
parameters
   actual 66
   command-line 113, 328
   floating-point 196
   formal 66, 82
   passing 66, 195
   procedural type 87
   value 82, 195
   variable 83
     untyped 83
ParamStr function 113, 328
.PAS files 2
Pattern procedure 156

PenDown procedure 156
PenUp procedure 157
Pi function 111, 329
PieSlice procedure 150, 329
pixel values 285
Plot procedure 157
pointer (^) symbol 32, 42
pointer and address functions 112
pointer-type constants 49
pointers
   comparing 60
   types 32, 192
   values 42
   variables 42, 61
polygons, drawing 246
port access 208
Port array 208
PortW array 208
Pos function 112, 330
pound (#) character 14
precedence of operators 51, 55
Pred function 22, 111, 218, 331
PreFixSeg variable 179
PrefixSeg variable 118
printer devices 107
Printer unit 115, 119
PRN 107
PROC directive, defining parameters with 200
procedural
   types 33, 84, 84-91
      declarations 84
      in expressions 89
      in statements 89
      variable declaration 85
      variable typecasts and 90
   values, assigning 85
   variables 85
      restrictions 86
      using standard procedures and functions with 86
procedural type parameters 87
procedure and function declaration part (program) 18
procedures 77
   body 77
   declarations 77
   dynamic allocation 109
   Exit 109

file-handling 124
Graph3 unit 155
Graph unit 148
Halt 109
headings 78
nesting 86, 197
non-ANSI 405
ordinal 111
pointers, calling overlaid routines 169
standard 109
statements 66
string 112
Turbo3 unit 154
process-handling routines 125, 307
Program Segment Prefix (PSP) 118, 179
programs
   execution, stopping 349
   halting 294
   headings 93
   lines 16
   parameters 93
   syntax 93
   termination 216
Ptr function 32, 112, 218, 331
PUBLIC 199
   definition errors 433
PutImage procedure 133, 137, 146, 150, 331
PutPic procedure 157
PutPixel procedure 137, 150, 334

Q

qualified identifiers 11, 19

R

$R compiler directive 413
Random function 113, 118, 334
random number generator 118
Randomize procedure 113, 335
RandSeed function 118
range-checking
   compile time 219
   compiler switch 413
   Val and 392
Range-Checking command 413
read-only file access 105

Read procedure
  text files 102, 104, 335
  typed files 337
reading records 230
ReadKey function 128, 132, 153, 337
Readln procedure 104, 338
README 1
README.COM 3
real
  numbers 26, 171, 189
  types 26
record-type constants 48
records 29, 41, 48, 193
Rectangle procedure 150, 339
redeclaration 19, 37
redirection 126
reentrant code 209, 210
referencing errors 440
register-saving conventions 199
RegisterBGIdriver function 133, 141, 152, 169, 340
RegisterBGIfont function 141, 152, 169, 342
registers
  AX 196, 207
  BP 199, 206, 209
    overlays and 169
  BX 196, 209
  CS 209, 240
  CX 209
  DI 209
  DS 199, 206, 209
  DX 196, 209
  ES 209
  SI 209
  SP 118, 199
  SS 199
  using 196, 199, 206, 209
Registers type 122
relational operators 58
relaxed string parameter-checking 414
Release procedure 110, 182, 344
relocatable reference errors 434
Rename procedure 102, 345
repeat statements 70
repetitive statements 70
reserved words 10, 403
Reset procedure 101, 103, 118, 345

resolution, graphics 265
RestoreCrtMode procedure 133, 150, 346
result codes 161
Rewrite procedure 101, 103, 347
RmDir procedure 103, 348
Round function 110, 218, 349
round-off errors, minimizing 174
routines, operating system 125
rules, scope 19
run-time
  errors 216, 443
    fatal 447
    generating 349
  support routines 116
RunError procedure 349

S

$S compiler directive 38, 414
SaveInitXX variables 118
SaveInt24 119
scale factor 13
scan codes, keyboard 425
scope (of declaration) 19
scopes, nested 443
screen
  mode control 126
  output operations 126
search utility 3
searching directories 258
SearchRec type 122
Sector procedure 150, 350
Seek procedure 102, 105, 351
SeekEof function 104, 351
SeekEoln function 104, 352
Seg function 352
Seq function 112
serial communications port 212
set-type constants 48
set types 31, 192
SetActivePage procedure 150, 353
SetAllPalette procedure 144, 146, 150, 354
  IBM 8514 and 355
SetAspectRatio procedure 150, 355
SetBkColor procedure 150, 356
SetCBreak procedure 126, 357
SetColor procedure 150, 358

SetDate procedure 124, 358
SetFAttr procedure 121, 125, 359
SetFillPattern procedure 137, 145,
    147, 150, 359
SetFillStyle procedure 137, 145, 150,
    361
SetFTime procedure 124, 362
SetGraphBufSize procedure 141, 150,
    362
SetGraphMode procedure 133, 150,
    363
SetHeading procedure 157
SetIntVec procedure 124, 365
SetLineStyle procedure 137, 145, 150,
    366
SetPalette procedure 144, 150, 367
    IBM 8514 and 368
SetPenColor procedure 157
SetPosition procedure 157
SetRGBPalette procedure 144, 150,
    369
    IBM 8514 and 134
SetRGBPalette routine 134
sets
    comparing 60
    constructors 52, 63
    membership 60
    operators 58
SetTextBuf procedure 104, 370
SetTextJustify procedure 136, 145,
    150, 372
SetTextStyle procedure 136, 145, 150,
    373
    OutText and 320
    OutTextXY and 323
SetTime procedure 124, 374
SetUserCharSize procedure 136, 150,
    375
SetVerify procedure 126, 376
SetViewPort procedure 133, 145, 150,
    376
SetVisualPage procedure 151, 378
SetWriteMode procedure 146, 151,
    379
shl operator 56
short-circuit Boolean evaluation 218,
    409
shortint data type 23
ShowTurtle procedure 157

shr operator 56
SI register 209
signed number (syntax) 14
significand 189
simple
    statements 65
    types 22
simple-type constants 46
Sin function 111, 380
single floating-point type 172, 190
SizeOf function 113, 256, 381
smart linking 220
snow-checking 130
software
    floating-point 26
    interrupts 209, 305
    numeric processing *See* numeric
        coprocessor, emulating
sound operations
    NoSound 132, 319
    Sound 132, 381
Sound procedure 132, 381
source debugging compiler switch
    410
South constant 155
SP register 118, 199, 206
space characters 9
SPtr function 112, 382
Sqr function 111, 382
Sqrt function 111, 382
SS register 199, 206
SSeg function 112, 382
stack
    8087 175
    checking switch directive 414
    overflow 38
        switch directive 414
    segment 38
    size 416
Stack-Checking command 414
StackLimit variable 118
standard
    functions, constant expressions and
        16
    Pascal 401
    units *See* units, standard
statement part (program) 18
statements 65
    assignment 66

case 69
compound 67
conditional 68
for 72
goto 67
if 68
procedure 66
repeat 70
repetitive 70
simple 65
structured 67
uses 93
while 71
with 74
storing overlaid code 181
Str procedure 112, 383
string-type constants 46
strings 46
  character 14
  comparing 59, 60
  concatenation 58, 238
  construction 238
  deletion 241
  functions 112
  handling 116
  initializing 255
  length byte 192, 255
  maximum length 192
  null 27
  operators 57
  procedures 112, 300, 383, 392
  relaxed parameter-checking 414
  types 27, 192
  variables 41
stroked fonts 133, 136, 375
structured
  statements 67
  types 28
    declaring 87
structured-type constants 46
subrange type 25
substrings
  copying 239
  deleting 241
  inserting 300
  position 330
Succ function 22, 111, 218, 383
Swap function 113, 218, 384
SwapVectors procedure 119, 125, 384

switch compiler directives 407, 408-414
symbols 9
  conditional 417
  CPU 418
  local information 412
syntax diagrams, reading 9
System unit 94, 115, 116, 223
  floating-point routines 172
  interrupt vectors and 118
  trapping critical errors 118
  variables in 116-119

T

tag field (of records) 30
technical support 5
terminating a program 216, 253
terms (syntax) 53
Test8087 variable 118
text 136
  attributes 285
  color constants 128
  files 103, 249
    devices 108
      drivers 210
    records 194
TextAttr variable 131
  ClrEol and 237
  ClrScr and 237
  HighVideo and 295
  LowVideo and 312
  NormVideo and 319
  TextBackground and 385
  TextColor and 386
TextBackground procedure 128, 132, 385
TextColor procedure 128, 132, 385
TextHeight function 152, 386
TextMode procedure 128, 132, 387
TextRec records 120, 193, 210
TextWidth function 152, 389
THELP.COM 2
THELP utility 2
time procedures
  GetFTime 274
  GetTime 287
  SetFTime 362
  SetTime 374

TINST 2
TINSTXFR.EXE 3
TINSTXFR utility 3
tokens 9
TOUCH 3
TPC.EXE 2
TPCONFIG.EXE 3
TPUMOVER.EXE 2, 116
transfer functions 110
trapping
   critical errors 118
   critical errors, System unit and 118
   I/O errors 411
   interrupts 209
Trunc function 110, 218, 390
Truncate procedure 105, 391
TURBO3.TPU 3
Turbo3 unit 115, 116, 152
   CBreak 154
   functions 154
   interface section 152
   Kbd in 153
   procedures 154
Turbo Assembler 199, 200
   8087 emulation and 178
   example program 204
TURBO.EXE 1
TURBO.HLP 2
Turbo Pascal 3.0 3
   compatibility with 5.0 115
   conversion
      ANSI compatibility 401
      chaining 392
   versus 5.0 306, 307, 313, 314
Turbo Pascal, installing 2
Turbo Pascal Editor Toolbox 409
TURBO.TPL 1, 116
TurnLeft procedure 157
TurnRight procedure 157
TurtleDelay procedure 157
turtlegraphics 155
TurtleThere procedure 157
TurtleWindow procedure 157
type-checking, strings and 414
typecasting, invalid 434
typed
   constants 45
   files 118, 193
types 21

array 28, 193
boolean 24, 189
byte 23
char 24, 189
common 23
compatibility 34
declaration 21
   part 18, 35
definition, constant expressions and 26
enumerated 24, 189
file 31
floating-point 172, 189
   comp 26, 173, 191
   comparing values of 174
   double 26, 172, 190
   extended 26, 173, 191
   single 26, 172, 190
Graph unit 146
host 25
identity 33
integer 23, 188
longint 23
mismatches, error messages 430
ordinal 22
pointer 32, 192
procedural 33, 84, 89
real 26
real numbers 189
record 29, 193
set 31, 192
shortint 23
simple 22
string 27, 192
structured 28
subrange 25
word 23

U

$UNDEF compiler directive 417, 419
units 1
   8087 coprocessor and 176
   circular references 97
   dependencies 116
   heading 95
   identifiers 11
   indirect references 96
   initialization code 167

non-overlay 168
scope of 19
standard 115
   Crt 103, 108, 126
   Dos 119
   Graph 133
   Graph3 155
   Overlay 160
   overlays and 161
   Printer 119
   System 116
   system 94
   Turbo3 152
syntax 94
version
   mismatch errors 435
   number 97
Unpack procedure 110
UnpackTime procedure 124, 391
   DateTime and 122
unsigned
   constant 52
   integer 13
   number 13
   real 13
untyped
   files 105, 118, 193
      variable 230, 232
   var parameters 83
UpCase function 113, 391
UPGRADE.DTA 3
UPGRADE.EXE 3
uses statement 93, 116
utilites
   INSTALL 2
utilities
   GREP 3
   MAKE 3
   THELP 2
   TINST 3
   TINSTXFR 3
   TOUCH 3
   TPC 2
   TPCONFIG 3
   TPUMOVER 2
   UPGRADE 3

V

$V compiler directive 414
Val procedure 112, 392
value
   parameters 82, 195
   typecasts 64
var
   declaration section 221
   parameters 83, 195
      untyped 83
   string checking, compiler switch 414
Var-String Checking command 414
variables 37
   absolute 39
   arrays 41
   CBreak 154
   CheckBreak 129
   CheckEOF 130
   CheckSnow 130
   Crt 129
   declaration part 18
   declarations 37
   defined by Overlay unit 161
   DirectVideo 130
   disposing of 244, 261
   DosError 123, 251, 258, 259, 271, 274, 359, 362
   dynamic 32, 42, 181
   FileMode 105
   global 38
   Graph unit 148
   I/O 101
   increasing 297
   initializing 45
   LastMode 131
   local 38
   Lst 119
   parameters 195
   pointer 42, 61
   procedural 85
      restrictions 86
   record 41
   references 39
   strings 41
   TextAttr 131
   typecasts 42, 90
   WindMax 131

WindMin 131
variant part (syntax) 30
VER50 symbol 418
VGA
  driver, modifying palette entries for 369
  modes 242, 275, 364
    emulated 134, 299
VGAHi 275, 364
VGALo 275, 364
VGAMed 275, 364
video
  memory 126
  operations
    AssignCrt 228
    ClrEol 237
    ClrScr 237
    DelLine procedure 241
    GotoXY 290
    HighVideo 295
    InsLine 300
    LowVideo 312
    NormVideo 319
    RestoreCrtMode 346
    TextBackground 385
    TextColor 385
    WhereX 393
    WhereY 393
    Window 394
    Write (text) 395
    Write (typed) 397
    Writeln 397
viewports 137, 235
  parameter 287

W

West constant 155
WhereX function 132, 393
WhereY function 132, 393

while statements (syntax) 71
WindMax variable 131
WindMin variable 131
Window procedure 126, 132, 394
  current coordinates 131
windows 126
with statements 74
word
  alignment 200
    automatic 219
  data type 23
Wrap procedure 157
write
  procedures 101
  statements
    8087 coprocessor and 176
    AUX devices and 212
    BIOS 130
    DirectVideo and 130
    DOS 227
Write procedure 104
  text files 395
  typed files 397
Writeln procedure 104, 397
  8087 coprocessor and 176
  DirectVideo and 130
writing records 232

X

XCor procedure 157
xor operator 56, 137
XORPut constant 332

Y

YCor procedure 157

Z

Zenith Z-449, BGI and 299